World Poverty

Global Inequality and the Modern World System

Harold R. Kerbo

California Polytechnic State University

Boston   Burr Ridge, IL   Dubuque, IA   Madison, WI   New York
San Francisco   St. Louis   Bangkok   Bogotá   Caracas   Kuala Lumpur
Lisbon   London   Madrid   Mexico City   Milan   Montreal   New Delhi
Santiago   Seoul   Singapore   Sydney   Taipei   Toronto

Higher Education

WORLD POVERTY: GLOBAL INEQUALITY AND THE MODERN WORLD SYSTEM

This book is printed on acid-free paper.

1 2 3 4 5 6 7 8 9 0 DOC/DOC 0 9 8 7 6 5

ISBN   0-07-304295-1

Editor in Chief: *Emily Barrosse*
Publisher: *Phillip A. Butcher*
Sponsoring Editor: *Sherith H. Pankratz*
Development Editor: *Kate Scheinman*
Senior Marketing Manager: *Daniel M. Loch*
Managing Editor: *Jean Dal Porto*
Project Manager: *Emily Hatteberg*
Art Director: *Jeanne Schreiber*
Designer: *Srdjan Savanovic*
Art Editor: *Katherine McNab*
Photo Research Coordinator: *Nora Agbayani*
Cover Credit: *Jon Resh*
Senior Production Supervisor: *Carol A. Bielski*
Composition: *10/12 Times, by International Typesetting and Composition*
Printing: *45 # New Era Matte Plus, R.R. Donnelley/Crawfordsville, IN.*

Credits: All photos courtesy of Harold J. Kerbo except for the following: p. 16 © F. Damm/Zefa/Corbis; p. 20 left © Daniel Zheng/Corbis; p. 20 right © Sean Sprague/The Image Works; p. 31 © Peter Turnley/ Corbis; p. 97 © Joel Simon/Getty Images; p. 150 © Bettman/Corbis; p. 154 © Gideon Mendel/Corbis; p. 194 © Stephanie Maze/Corbis.

Library of Congress Cataloging-in-Publication Data

Kerbo, Harold R.
    World poverty: global inequality and the modern world system/Harold R. Kerbo.
       p. cm.
    Includes bibliographical references and index.
    ISBN 0-07-304295-1 (alk. paper)
      1. Poverty. 2. Poverty—Case studies. I. Title.
HC79.P6K46 2006
339.4'6—dc22   2005052211

www.mhhe.com

For Nina
1925–2005

Perhaps as much as anything,
she taught compassion and concern for others

Preface

I began notes for this book soon after the Seattle World Trade Organization protests in the fall of 1999. Living in Britain at the time, as I sat watching the events unfold on the BBC, I seemed to be in a time warp—back in the 1960s, when people showed more concern about issues such as world poverty. I changed channels to find the same events were happening on CNN—my fellow Americans were also paying attention. As the days progressed, I became both excited and troubled; excited because it seemed the world was waking up to the *unprecedented* levels of world poverty and inequality, and troubled because of the dangerous and inaccurate explanations of human misery given by protest leaders.

Some of their *solutions* to world poverty would clearly make matters worse. In particular, I felt I knew something about Asia after a couple of years teaching and conducting research in Japan, then 2 more years in Southeast Asia. I had seen the sweatshops and the desperately poor in huge urban slums throughout Southeast Asia. But from direct experience I knew the charge that multinational corporations *always* bring lower wages and more poverty was wrong. After studying older research suggesting multinational corporate investment has sometimes made conditions worse in developing countries, I knew that more recent sociological research indicated such outside investment could *sometimes* help reduce poverty. The research was not yet clear on why some countries are helped while others are harmed by this outside investment, but I believed I had some explanations from my work in Asia.

I began my focus on Southeast Asia in Thailand with the help of a Fulbright grant in 1990. Returning to Southeast Asia almost every year since that time, I had learned more about the preconditions for economic development and poverty reduction in the area. From the mid to late 1990s I spent much of my time conducting research on conditions in American and Japanese corporations in Thailand, with additional observations of these conditions in Laos and Vietnam. Yes, there were sweatshops, but I was surprised to see excellent working conditions for Southeast Asian employees in most of the well-known American and Japanese corporations where I conducted interviews. In fact, the 1,000 plus Thai employees of American and Japanese corporations who responded to the questionnaire portion of our research overwhelmingly told us they preferred working for American or Japanese corporations over Thai corporations. Conditions of work in large American and Japanese factories (in contrast to the small sweatshops where other American corporations subcontract for production) were obviously above standard, and Thai employees told us their pay and benefits were better than in Thai corporations.

There is certainly a lot of poverty to be seen in Thailand. I have interviewed many people in depressing slums, such as one where as many as 100,000 *homeless* people are crammed into a few city blocks on the fringes of Bangkok. I have seen even worse poverty in Burma, Laos, Cambodia, and Vietnam. But with visits throughout these countries again and again since 1990, I have also seen considerable change for the better—though almost exclusively in Thailand and Vietnam. I became increasingly aware that the literature and research suggesting the world's poor are often harmed by multinational corporate investment was especially misleading in some countries of Southeast Asia. Multinational corporations from the United States, Europe, and Japan are seen all over Thailand. Every trip back to Vietnam between 1995 and 2005, I also found more and more of these corporations setting up operations. As an American who had lived through the Vietnam War experience, a sign that first appeared not far from the Hanoi airport in 1998 was rather amazing: "Ford Welcomes You." On another research trip I saw some of those new Fords built in Vietnam displayed at a trade fair in Saigon.

After my focus on poverty and economic development in East and Southeast Asia, I turned my attention to Africa and Latin America. The contrasts between Asia and Africa, as I demonstrate in this book, could not be greater. In the case of most Latin American countries, their overall GNP per capita is similar to many of the developing Southeast Asian countries. But the big differences are (1) while most Southeast Asian countries are continuing to develop, many in Latin America have fallen into stagnation, and (2) Asian countries have been developing *with* poverty reduction while Latin American countries are less likely to do so. My previous writings, to say the least, have not exactly been in praise of American-style capitalism and its impact on people in the United States and elsewhere in the world. But recent years in Southeast Asia have led me to understand that *under certain conditions* increasing globalization *can* benefit the world's poor. I attempt to spell out some of these conditions in this book.

In the pages that follow, I first provide a general summary of world poverty at the beginning of the 21st century, then an introduction to modern world system theory and its attempts to explain world poverty and inequality. Remaining chapters offer explanations for why some countries in the world (mostly in Asia) have become richer and reduced the ranks of their poor through ties with the global economy while others have not. I provide extensive evidence for why the *nature of the state* in developing countries is the most important factor in stagnation or economic development with poverty reduction. But, in contrast to previous research and new statements by the World Bank, I have created a model attempting to explain *why and how* some countries have *good governance* and others do not.

With unprecedented levels of inequality between the rich and poor of this world becoming a focal point for conflict as we begin the new century, I hope that *World Poverty: Global Inequality and the Modern World System* can make at least a small contribution to our understanding of why this has occurred and what might be done to reduce world poverty.

❧ Acknowledgments

Several old friends have helped me understand the developing countries of Southeast Asia. Bob Slagter has been especially important; we have learned a lot together as we have traveled the region since 1990. Patrick Ziltener of the University of Zurich has also learned with me as we have traveled the region together in recent years. Uthai Dulaykasem,

Thai activist and professor, has probably taught me more about the poor of Southeast Asia than anyone over the years. Dr. Pramote in the Isan region of Thailand, and many faculty members at Silpakorn, Chiang Mai, and Prince of Songkla Universities have taught me a lot about the region. Others at Hanoi National University and the University of Da Nang, especially President Bui Van Ga, have helped me considerably in their country. Nantakan Songsuman and Hoyhuan Boonchoo, among others living in village Thailand, have helped me learn about the lives of their people. Wil Scott at Oklahoma University helped enlighten me about Vietnam as we traveled much of the country together; Susan Bass at Oklahoma University helped me better understand Africa. Volker Bornschier, Hans-Peter Muller, and Mark Herkenrath, at the University of Zurich, listened to and responded to my papers and lectures to give me a better understanding of the modern world system. Chris Chase-Dunn, now at UC Riverside, has done much the same. Faculty and students at University of Vienna, Helmut Kramer in particular, have helped me understand the state of the modern world system today. Several of these students have followed me to Southeast Asia for a few months to learn more together.

In addition, McGraw-Hill and I would like to thank the following reviewers for their helpful comments during the development and writing of *World Poverty: Global Inequality and the Modern World System:*

Vilna F. Bashi, Rutgers University; Loretta E. Bass, University of Oklahoma; Claudia Buchmann, Duke University; James W. Coleman, California Polytechnic State University, San Luis Obispo; Karen Coen Flynn, University of Akron; Thomas D. Hall, DePauw University & Colgate University; Robert Hanneman, University of California, Riverside; Fayyaz Hussain, Michigan State University; Carmen R. Lugo-Lugo, Washington State University; Susan R. Pitchford, University of Washington; Marvin Prosono, Southwest Missouri State University; Stephen C. Zehr, University of Southern Indiana.

Finally, I thank my wife and daughters who have put up with my wanderings around the world, sometimes joining me, but not as often as I would have liked.

Harold R. Kerbo

Contents

About the Author

Harold Kerbo is professor of sociology and chair of the Social Sciences Department at California Polytechnic State University, San Luis Obispo. He has been a Fulbright professor or visiting professor in Great Britain, Germany, Switzerland, Austria, Japan, Thailand, and at the University of Oklahoma. He has served as resident director of Cal Poly's Thailand Study Program several times since 1995. He is the author of the leading textbook on social stratification (*Social Stratification and Inequality*, 6th edition published by McGraw-Hill and recently translated into Spanish). Along with John A. McKinstry, he is also the author of *Who Rules Japan?: The Inner Circles of Economic and Political Power* (Greenwood/Praeger, 1995). Professor Kerbo is creator and general editor of the McGraw-Hill *Comparative Societies Series* which includes books on 11 countries. The first volume, *Modern Japan* (by Harold Kerbo and John McKinstry) was published in 1998. He has also coauthored the volumes *Modern Germany*, with Hermann Strasser, and *Modern Thailand*, with Robert Slagter, both of which were published in 2000. His current research involves comparative poverty reduction programs in Thailand and Vietnam.

A World Divided: Rich Corporations and the Poor of This Earth

Toward the end of the twentieth century the world had far more people living in extreme poverty than in any other time in world history. The gap between the world's rich and poor had grown to unprecedented levels (Korzeniewicz & Moran, 1997). The World Bank noted that "As late as 1820, annual per capita (average per person) incomes were quite similar around the world—and very low, ranging from around $500 in China and South Asia to $1,000–1,500 in the richest countries of Europe."[1] As the twenty-first century began, the annual per capita income of people in rich countries like the United States was $30,600, compared to $500 in many poor countries such as Sierra Leone, Tanzania, and Ethiopia.[2] Some 20 percent of the world's population (approximately 1.2 billion people) live on less than $1 a day. This is *not* what one American dollar would buy in a poor country. It is what $1 would buy in the United States—perhaps a cheap sandwich and nothing more for the rest of the day![3] Some 2.8 billion people live on less than $2 per day, almost *half of the world's population.* As shown in Figure 1.1, the World Bank figures that the number of people existing on less than $1 a day has increased directly with globalization in the last two centuries (United Nations [U.N.], World Bank, International Monetary Fund [IMF], & Organization for Economic Cooperation and Development [OECD], 2000; United Nations Development Program [UNDP], 2000b). There is disagreement about the World Bank's estimate of extreme poverty dropping from about 1.4 billion people to 1.2 billion people during the last few years, but we do know that any drop is mainly due to much better conditions in the world's most populous nation, China.

As for the extreme gap between the rich and poor, one estimate is that the top 20 percent of people in the world held 85 percent of the world's wealth, whereas the bottom 20 percent held only 2 percent by the end of the 1990s. Another estimate found that the top 20 percent of the world's population received 150 times the income of the bottom 20 percent. Just 30 years before, this income gap had been 60 to 1. In 1999 the three richest people in the world (not nations, people) had $135 billion in assets, more wealth than all of the combined national incomes of the 43 least developed nations in the world. In 2004 the world's three richest men (Bill Gates[4] and Warren Buffett of the United States, and Karl Albrecht of Germany) held $103 billion after the drop in high-tech stock prices, but still more wealth than the combined incomes of the bottom 600 million people in the world (*Forbes,* 2004).

As one would expect, today's unprecedented level of world poverty has life and death consequences. For example, while people in rich nations today can expect to live into their late 70s, the life expectancy in many of the least developed nations is 40 years or less (Population Reference Bureau, 2000). Five years ago the United Nations Food and Agriculture Organization estimated that 800 million people in the world were chronically

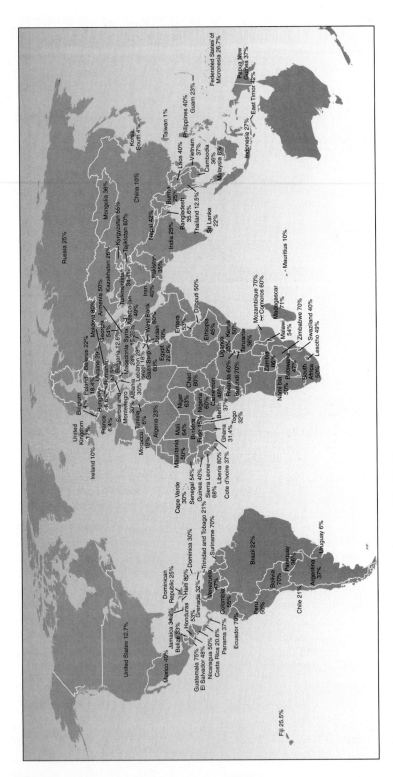

MAP 1.1 *Poverty Estimates in Countries Around the World.*

NOTE: Figures represent country estimates with differing definitions of poverty. These estimates, while not exactly comparable, do give us a rough idea of different levels of poverty around the globe.

SOURCE: World Bank, *World Development Report*, 2000/2001 (2000).

TABLE 1.1

Leading Conditions Producing Death in Poor versus Rich Countries

Less Developed Countries with High Death Rates	Rich Countries
1. Lack of food	1. Tobacco
2. Unsafe sex	2. High blood pressure
3. Unsafe water, lack of sanitation	3. Alcohol
4. Indoor smoke from solid fuels	4. High cholesterol
5. Zinc deficiency	5. Overweight
6. Iron deficiency	6. Low fruit and vegetable intake
7. Vitamin A deficiency	7. Physical inactivity
8. High blood pressure	8. Illicit drugs
9. Tobacco	9. Unsafe sex
10. High cholesterol	10. Iron deficiency

Source: WHO, 2002: 83.

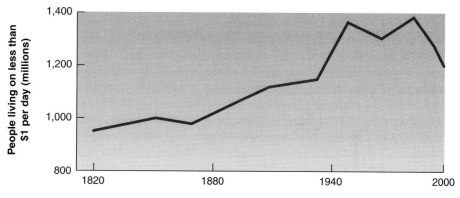

FIGURE 1.1 *People Living on Less than $1 per Day since 1820*

NOTE: This estimate uses "real dollars" which means that in 1820 $1 also bought only a cheap sandwich in the United States as it does today.

SOURCE: World Bank, 2002b:8.

undernourished, with another 2 billion people experiencing crucial deficiencies in nutrients. In 2003 this same agency reported that the number of chronically undernourished people in the world has not improved, and in fact may have increased (United Nations Food and Agriculture Organization, 2003). The United Nations Children's Fund (UNICEF) reported that malnutrition is a factor in about 55 percent of the 12 million preventable deaths among children younger than five every year. "To find a disease that killed children on a comparable scale, researchers had to reach back to the Middle Ages and the bubonic plague, termed the Black Death" (*Los Angeles Times,* December 16, 1997). In 2002 the World Health Organization for the first time estimated the ultimate cause of death among people in less developed countries. As shown in Table 1.1, lack of food was the number one killer, not AIDS or any other terrible disease. For people in rich countries, too much food was the fifth leading cause of death (World Health Organization [WHO], 2002:83). Most of the other top ten killers for the world's poor also involve the lack of something we take for granted. While the world can easily produce enough food to feed the current population, hundreds of millions of people face possible starvation today.

Not surprisingly, when the world's poor can, they move from areas of hunger and hopelessness to richer nations. The World Resources Institute estimates 30 million refugees and displaced persons in the world.[5] Many of the world's poor, however, do not make such moves voluntarily or understand where they will end up. Worldwide it is estimated that every year from 700,000 to 2 million women and children from poor countries are sent to other countries against their will and forced to work as prostitutes. In 2001, UNICEF estimated that approximately 1 million children from poor countries are forced into prostitution every year (*International Herald Tribune,* December 24, 2001). In a detailed analysis published in the spring of 2000 titled *International Trafficking in Women to the United States: A Contemporary Manifestation of Slavery,* the CIA reported that every year as many as 50,000 women and children from Asia, Latin America, and Eastern Europe are brought to the United States under false pretenses, with many held as sex slaves (*International Herald Tribune,* January 12, 1998, April 3, 2000; U.S. Central Intelligence Agency [CIA], 2001).

In this book I will present some of the best social science explanations of this appalling level of poverty and world inequality. While several explanations will be examined, I believe a type of conflict theory as represented in dependency theory or modern world system theory explains much more than others. There are many reasons a particular country might be poor, but one historical situation is most associated with the unprecedented global inequality of today: Expansion of the world economy, a key aspect of globalization, has allowed wealthy nations to disrupt weaker nations and take advantage of the people in poorer nations. What we think of as "globalization" today started centuries ago, but became much more important in the age of colonization, reaching its high point in the 1800s when most of the world's territory was controlled by European colonizers. Since then a subtler form of colonialism, or *neocolonialism,* has taken its place. It is this economic dominance of poor countries by rich nations and their multinational corporations that most epitomizes the outcomes of globalization today.

After consideration of theory and research on the subject of world poverty and the modern world system, I will examine the situations of countries from each world region with high levels of poverty. At times I will rely heavily upon my own observations and research in Southeast Asian nations because it is this world region, along with China, that today has the best record of economic development with poverty reduction. We need to know why many countries in Southeast Asia are doing better, and what makes them different from countries in other world regions unable to significantly reduce poverty.

Before taking up these subjects, we have some "ground work" to do. In the remainder of this chapter I will touch upon some key issues, frame key questions, and attempt to put a more human face on the subject of world poverty. I will also try to give you a sense of what is going on in Southeast Asia today by describing what I have seen in this part of the world. In the next chapter we will cover in more detail the conditions of poverty in all world regions before moving on to attempted explanations in the remaining chapters. At the end of this book I hope you will have a far better understanding of this critical issue of the twenty-first century, as well as what we can and cannot do to relieve this human suffering.

CASE IN POINT

A Walk through Klong Toey

It is useful to consider some actual cases of people living in poverty around the world so that we can put a human face on this condition. Estimates of the extent of poverty and how it might be changing are vital for our subject. But so is a simple understanding of the human condition that actual cases can bring us.

In the south of Bangkok, within a seaport area along the Chao Parya River, is a neighborhood called Klong Toey. Perhaps "neighborhood" is not the best description because Klong Toey is one of the largest slum areas in Thailand. When I last visited Klong Toey in April of 2002, some 100,000 poor squatters lived in the 3- to 4-square-mile section of the Port Authority land that has been left undeveloped. Walking through the narrow pathways among the shacks one sees families of four, five, or more living in makeshift huts of cardboard, plywood, and tin measuring no more than 10 to 15 feet in each direction. Each hut is built with the common walls and roofs of the neighboring shack, one after the other throughout this poor squatters' settlement of 100,000 people. Inside the huts there is barely enough room for all family members to lie down at the same time. Usually a few food items are on shelves, and charcoal burners are there to cook meals. Located on a low-lying river bank, the area is usually pocketed with large, stagnant pools of green, slimy, highly pungent water—water usually filled with all sorts of trash and a dead animal here and there. Amid all of this, thousands of children play, quite happy to see *farang* (westerners) and follow them around the area, smiling and curious, with no plans for begging like the poor children in the cities of Vietnam. These children generally look healthy, though thinning hair and bad teeth sometimes suggest malnutrition at least one time in their young lives.

Across Bangkok from Klong Toey, in another slum area along train tracks, I have been invited to dinner a couple of times by some of the residents. I had earlier met some of their relatives when I spent time in a small village about an hour and a half's drive from Bangkok. The shacks along the train tracks in Bangkok are quite similar to those in Klong Toey, though the slimy water doesn't seem to surround everything. The crude construction pattern seems the same in poor countries all over the world; people always find the same kind of discarded cardboard, scrap wood, and tin. My dinner hosts in this slum live in a much smaller slum area when compared to Klong Toey, but again it was on unused land so close to the train tracks I could have reached out to touch a train going by as we ate dinner on a makeshift table of wood. Most of the people in shacks around us were unskilled laborers seeking work in Bangkok, or street vendors who get up at 2:30 a.m. to visit the night markets for fruits and vegetables they can sell on street corners in Bangkok during the morning rush hour. It is easy to see that life is often quite hard for these people, but they are working hard to make it.

When walking through squatters' slums such as those in Bangkok, people from rich countries usually find it almost impossible to believe other humans could live in such a way. The residents of Klong Toey and my dinner hosts are comparatively lucky. As third world slums go, *it can get much worse*. Thousands of homeless people in Manila live in massive garbage dumps, scavenging to stay alive. Many die when mountains of garbage explode or collapse to bury them. In India, for example, the Bombay–Dharavi slum is claimed to be the biggest in the world, with people far more desperate than most people in slums like Klong Toey. It is estimated that 58 percent of the 6.7 million residents of Bombay, India, live in slums such as Dharavi, which itself has perhaps as many as 1 million people. Another example is the famous Kibera slum in Nairobi, Africa, where all world leaders seem to be taken to show them how bad things can become. Although it is hard to imagine while walking through the Klong

(Continued)

Pictured here is the fringe of Klong Toey, the biggest slum area in Bangkok. Some 100,000 people are crammed into an area of less than two square miles. However, unlike most urban slums in Africa and Latin America, most of these people have village homes to which they can return after looking for temporary work in Bangkok.

Toey slum in Thailand, those like Kibera and Dharavi are worse, with people who have much less hope, fewer options in life, and almost no aid from the national government where they live (*International Herald Tribune,* October 1, 2001, December 12, 2001, February 12, 2002). For these people, Klong Toey would be a definite step up in the world.

The people of Klong Toey are also fortunate because of a young middle-class Thai girl many years ago who started teaching their children after her own school let out in the afternoons. Over the years, she got more people involved and finally started receiving money from government grants. All of this led to a highly respected organization, the Duang Prateep Foundation, that helps run schools and clinics for the people of Klong Toey. In 2000, the woman who started it all as a teenage girl was elected to the Thai Senate by people in the area.

Compared to the poor of most other developing countries, the 100,000 or so people crammed into Klong Toey are lucky in other ways as well. Even when an economic crisis hits, as it did in 1997, most can move back with family in the countryside when things become hopeless in the city. In other regions of the world, the slum area homeless have nowhere else to go because the vast majority of land is in the hands of just a few wealthy people. As we will see, these people of Klong Toey are also lucky because they live in a country that has been making admirable progress toward reducing poverty and providing jobs for its people. In recent decades the poorest countries in other world regions have at best had steady levels of poverty, and very often accelerating poverty. One of the key goals of this book is to understand *why some less developed countries are moving their people out of poverty while people in other countries are getting poorer.*

The Affluent of This Earth

With communism no longer a viable threat, during the early 1990s the "winners of the Cold War" believed that the road ahead led only to the "expansion and perfection of the capitalist system." One nation after another, it was proclaimed, especially from American shores, would realize the superiority of the free market as the final perfection of human organization. It seemed difficult to fault the world's free-market leader when America achieved its longest period of sustained economic growth in history as the twenty-first century began. Megamergers were creating the biggest corporate conglomerates the world had ever seen, with $3 trillion in merger deals in 1999 alone. The stock market had risen 14-fold during the last 18 years of the twentieth century, making the 60 percent of Americans who own stock quite happy, and happier still the 1 percent of Americans who own a majority of that privately held corporate stock (Kerbo, 2000:29–32; Mishel, Bernstein, & Schmitt, 1999:260). In large part because of this sustained stock-market boom, the average wealth of Americans more than doubled in just 10 years. But this unprecedented American economic expansion has a dark side in today's global economy, both at home and abroad.

Wealth and Poverty in America

While the stock market was booming and luxury cars were breaking sales records, most Americans ignored the fact that income inequality in the United States had been growing for more than 20 years. By 2003 the level of income inequality in the United States was at an all-time high, and much higher than in any other industrial nation (Gottschalk & Smeeding, 1997; U.S. Bureau of the Census, 2004). Another historic record was "achieved" in 2001: The top 20 percent of Americans finally got more than 50 percent of the total national income in that year. The poorest 20 percent of Americans got only 3.5 percent of the total income for 2001 (U.S. Bureau of the Census, 2000:Table A2). As we will see toward the end of Chapter 3, no other industrial nation is even close to that level of inequality. Poverty in the United States also remained much higher than in the industrial nations of Europe, except for Great Britain, the country most accepting of America's free-market preaching. At around 11 to 13 percent of the American population, poverty dropped imperceptibly during the longest economic expansion in U.S. history, despite the fact that only some 4 to 5 percent of Americans were unemployed at the end of the twentieth century. Again, this was completely unprecedented in the industrialized world. Think about this situation for a minute; only 4 percent of Americans were out of work, but throughout the longest economic boom in American history, 11 percent to 13 percent of Americans were living on less than what government experts estimate they need to buy basic necessities! Almost half of all these American poor were living in families where someone was working full time, over 40 hours per week, more than 50 weeks a year, and they still could not get out of poverty (U.S. Bureau of the Census, 2001a:Table C).

Not until the last 2 years of the 1990s could the U.S. government boast that *finally*, after many years of economic growth and rising inequality, there was a *slight* increase in the incomes of the poorest Americans. Despite this slight increase, incomes of the poorest Americans continued to fall behind those of the top half of the American people

WHY WE SHOULD CARE

People in richer countries usually find it difficult to understand the reality of life for the world's poor. We have a "mental map" of human behavior based upon the realities and options presented to us in affluent societies. That people have to react to a whole different set of options and opportunities that are far more restricted than ours is seldom recognized. In addition, we are often too caught up in our own lives and daily routines to pay much attention to starving children in countries far away. We should, of course, be more concerned about the world's poor for simple humanitarian reasons: Millions of people on this earth are dying needlessly. But as the world becomes more and more interconnected we had better learn to care and understand because the well-being of the world's rich will increasingly become threatened by the global gap of wealth and poverty. Throughout this book we will often pause to consider why the rich of this world should be concerned about world poverty for reasons that affect all of us. We can now begin with some preliminary considerations.

When confronted with facts—such as there are 800 million hungry people in the world; more than 50 percent of the 14 million young children who die each year die because of malnutrition; and 1.3 billion people in the world live on less than $1 per day— the magnitude of the problem can render people pessimistic, even fatalistic about it all. We continue to hear "we will always have the poor with us," or "there will always be people at the bottom." Well, yes; but that explains nothing. How many poor will we have? How poor will they be? How far below the average standard of living will they be? These are much more meaningful and realistic questions. It is also important to remember that the level of inequality and poverty presently existing in the world is unique. Yes, we will always have the poor with us; but it is easy to see their situation is worsening and there are more of them than in any other time in world history. To begin explaining "why we should care" it is important to recognize that *world poverty rates are not fixed;* they have been lower, and for simple humanitarian reasons, we should care about fellow human beings.

Related to this almost fatalistic view that nothing can be done is the common myth, especially in the United States, that governments can do nothing to help—only "market forces" can reduce poverty. In fact, the American view is often that not only can government do nothing about poverty (domestic or international), but that if it tries to do something the situation will only get worse. In reality, we will see in coming chapters that, left to themselves, *world market forces can make people in some countries poorer than they otherwise would be.* A free world market where multinational corporations can come and go at will, without controls on their behavior in poor nations, can and has actually increased poverty and inequality in many nations. It is also clear that governments can have an impact on reducing poverty in their own countries and in the world. Thailand and Vietnam, as we will see, are good examples, but there are others.

(Continued)

Besides humanitarian calls for reducing world poverty, one must also point out "what is in it for us." The affluent of this world need to know how world poverty negatively affects them. For example, as we will see in more detail in Chapter 3, this mass of world poverty is now clearly bringing down the wages and standards of living for the bottom 50 percent of Americans. For another example, the World Health Organization tells us people weakened by lack of food and living in unhealthy conditions are the breeding grounds for many deadly infectious diseases that eventually spread to wealthier nations. AIDS is only one that needs mention. Severe acute respiratory syndrome (SARS) and avian influenza or "bird flu" are more recent examples (WHO, 1999).

But there are also positive effects for us in reducing world poverty; one positive can be noted in one word—consumers. Multinational corporations in North America, Europe, and Japan are thrilled over prospects of a 1 billion-plus consumer market in China. Almost half of the world's population, nearly 3 billion people, live on less than $2 per day and would love to be consumers if they could get out of their desperate conditions of poverty. There is another positive in this for many Americans: If the world's poor had higher wages and standards of living there would be far fewer people in the world willing to work in "sweatshops." This in turn would keep the world's poor from dragging down the incomes of low-wage Americans. With no one willing to work in those sweatshops big corporations would have to pay better wages to Americans as well. And with more consumers in the world, these big corporations could afford to pay higher wages.

Other reasons that we should care about world poverty and global inequalities are related to war, political violence, and international terrorism. Rich nations of the world united to fight terrorism after the horror of the World Trade Center collapse in September of 2001. As horrible as it was, in recent decades there have been too many other cases where even more innocent people were massacred far from American shores.

World poverty and inequality by themselves do not create political violence and terrorism, but they are prime breeding grounds. World Bank figures show that between 1990 and 1995 about 90 percent of all cases of "civil war and strife" occurred in poor nations (World Bank, 2000:50). A recent study by the National Defense Council found 59 cases of "serious conflict" in 193 countries around the world in 2001, compared to 35 just over 10 years ago. "Major conflicts" involving 1,000 or more deaths in 1 year were found in 38 of these 193 countries, again a big increase compared to the decade earlier (Associated Press, December 24, 2001). Research by sociologists has also shown the importance of world inequality for sparking political violence. Measuring the gap between the rich and poor in countries and cities all over the world, several studies have shown a significant correlation between inequality and levels of political violence (Blau & Blau, 1982; Messner, 1982; Muller, 1985; Williams, 1984). All of this suggests that any war against terrorism by rich countries cannot stop with arresting or killing famous leaders supporting terrorism. Other Osama bin Ladens will emerge as long as extreme poverty and social disruption remain breeding grounds for their supporters.

(Kerbo, 2000; Mishel et al., 1999). Then, as the unprecedented economic boom of the 1990s slid into recession during the second half of 2001, with the dismantling of the American welfare system in 1996, homelessness and hunger shot up quickly. With economic recovery slowly returning from 2002, America achieved another record: By 2004 the United States had experienced two years of economic recovery but the unemployment rate was still going up, not down! Most Europeans point to this when European elites say their nations should copy America.

None of this, of course, was supposed to happen during a time of long economic expansion, or economic recovery. It is clear that the U.S. economy has moved into uncharted waters of coexisting prosperity and poverty. As we will see in Chapter 3, these unprecedented figures of simultaneous growth of wealth and high levels of poverty in the United States can be understood only with reference to changes in the global economy during the last decades of the twentieth century. The bottom half of the world's population living on less than $2 per day have started to drag the bottom half of Americans down to more poverty as well.

To the Barricades, Again: Protesting Globalization

Fewer and fewer people around the world agree with the American gospel of "free markets for all." Since the protest movements of the 1960s in rich nations, not many of the world's affluent had given much thought to the world's poor, except perhaps for a few moments when scenes of terrible famine flash across their TV screens. But to the surprise of almost everyone, world poverty again became a serious concern among many people in rich nations when massive protest stopped much of the activities of the World Trade Organization's[6] international meeting in Seattle during November 1999. Protestors were again raising their voices against the "exploitation of the world's poor by rich multinational corporations," a theme often heard during the protests of the 1960s. The protests have been sustained into the new century with more protests held at each additional meeting of the World Trade Organization since 1999, along with all other meetings of international organizations, including the U.N.-sponsored World Summit on Sustainable Development that ended in September 2002 with more meaningless pledges by rich nations to cut world poverty. Despite questionable evidence, leaders of rich nations continue to tell the world's poor that the free market will take care of them if they are patient and allow more free trade (Stiglitz, 2004). From the protestors we hear countercalls to halt all investments from multinational corporations going to poor countries where wages are often $1 a day or less and where child labor is not uncommon. There is the widespread belief that when rich corporations from the outside move into a poor country these corporations enrich only the elites of poor nations, leaving the masses of people worse off than before. Profits made from the labor of the poor in sweatshops are sent home to corporate headquarters to enrich managers and stockholders; multinational corporations work with governments in poor countries to suppress wages of the poor, prevent labor unions, and evade international laws protecting the environment, all keeping multinational corporations and the wealthy in the poor nations happy.

In contrast to these charges by antiglobalization protestors, leaders of rich nations call for more open markets and free trade, along with more investments from multinational corporations, as part of the remedy for the world's poor. This so-called

Washington consensus about fighting world poverty was agreed upon by rich countries a few years ago. International economic organizations dominated by the rich nations, especially the International Monetary Fund (IMF) and World Bank,[7] have been most vocal in preaching open markets and free trade. The IMF usually calls for (and at times forces) basic economic and political reforms in poor nations, reforms creating more free markets, which they believe can make these poor nations more like the United States. But the charge from people of the poor nations, as well as a growing number of social scientists, is that international organizations such as the IMF and World Bank are tools of the capitalist rich nations, and the activities of these organizations primarily further the exclusive interests of multinational corporations.

As we will see in Chapters 3 and 4, for decades debates among social scientists have reflected the two sides of the debate described above. Toward the middle of the twentieth century the dominant perspective was "modernization" theory. The idea was that help from rich nations in the form of outside investments and aid would lead these poor nations to go through a process of development and modernization just as the rich nations did one to two centuries ago. More recently, "dependency" theories and "modern world system" theory have shown the situation is much more complicated. Indeed, outside investment can at times make a country poorer and less likely to achieve economic development. We will examine these theories and their research especially in Chapter 4. In this introductory chapter, however, it is most important to recognize that the situation is much more complex than either free-market preachers or antiglobalization protestors realize. More precisely, coming chapters will explain how and why some countries can have economic growth and reduce poverty when multinational corporations bring in new factories, while other poor nations cannot. It will be helpful to turn to some preliminary observations on this subject now.

Exploiting the World's Poor—Some Exceptions

When asked about conditions for workers in less developed countries, most people who have cared enough to notice will likely cite the infamous case of Nike. The controversy over Nike's labor practices surfaced when soaring profits, along with soaring prices of Nike athletic shoes, created a vivid contrast with conditions for their laborers in poor countries. There have been numerous reports of abuse of poor workers and wages below what it takes to buy basic necessities.[8] In March of 1998 Nike reported that its workers in one country received a 15 percent raise, to $11.75 *per month,* during a time when basic food prices were tripling in that country. Another study estimated a daily cost of living at $3 in Vietnam while Nike workers there were paid about $1.48 per day. An investigation of one small factory for Nike in Vietnam claimed 12 of 35 workers interviewed in detail were making below the official Vietnamese government minimum wage of approximately $35 per month. Still another study of Nike workers in Vietnam claimed workers were paid $1.60 per day while the daily cost of food was $2.10. After first trying to claim these reports were incorrect, Nike finally admitted their accuracy after funding its own study and finding much the same thing in some of its Indonesian sweatshops (*International Herald Tribune,* February 23, 2001). Soon afterward, The Gap admitted much the same about some of its sweatshops in El Salvador (*International Herald Tribune,* April 26, 2001). But are these conditions typical of circumstances for workers in plants owned by rich multinational corporations around the world?

We must pause to consider what is meant by the exploitation of people in poor countries by multinational corporations from rich countries. A situation of exploitation defies simple definition, but the following questions can help:

1. Are the wages and benefits provided by outside multinationals on average with or better than such wages and benefits provided by companies owned and operated by citizens of the poorer country? Are these wages and benefits at least enough for the employees of multinational corporations to buy basic necessities and maintain long-term health?
2. Are opportunities being created for employees of multinational corporations in poor nations that would otherwise not exist?
3. Are the lives of people in poor countries likely to be better off in the future because of outside multinational corporate investments? Put another way, will these people be able to save money obtained from their multinational corporate labor, and will they perhaps be able to help their relatives move out of poverty?
4. In the longer term, will the overall living conditions of the poor be improved due to multinational corporate investments? Will the economy improve, providing more jobs at better pay in the future? Further, will poverty rates go down?
5. Related to the above, are the foreign multinational corporations paying their fair share of taxes in poor nations where they set up factories or extract raw materials? Are high percentages of the profits gained by multinational corporations from their business in the poorer country being reinvested in the poor country or taken home to the rich countries? In other words, are the profits made by these multinational corporations providing money for infrastructure development in the poorer country, with the building of schools, electric power, hospitals, roads, and so on?
6. Finally, in the process of doing business in the poorer nation, are the rich multinationals protecting the environment of the poor country so that current business activity will not be paid for by future generations because of depleted resources and an unhealthy environment?

We will address these questions in several places throughout this book, but in raising these issues a contrast to charges of exploitation by Nike must now be considered. At least in East and Southeast Asia, the Nike example is not so typical.

American and Japanese Corporations in Thailand

During the second half of the 1990s a research colleague and I spent considerable time conducting interviews in 24 large factories in Thailand owned by famous American and Japanese corporations.[9] In each of these corporations we had detailed personal interviews with top managers (American, Japanese, and Thai), as well as employees down the corporate hierarchy to the factory floor. Many people will likely be surprised to know that our information showed that the vast majority of employees in these American and Japanese corporations in Thailand make more than the average wage in Thailand, and substantially more than the $4.40 a day minimum wage in Thailand at the time (or about $8.50 to $9 daily minimum wage estimated in Purchasing Power

Parity).[10] Our analysis of over 1,000 detailed questionnaires returned by Thai employees from several of these factories indicates these employees rate their income and benefits to be significantly above average when compared to Thai-owned factories.

To assess the typical image of a sweatshop, more than wages must be considered. We found working conditions in all 24 companies in our sample to be far from conditions described in reports about Nike in Southeast Asia. For example, conditions at a large American computer chip factory just north of Bangkok are above average, but not considerably different from the other American and Japanese corporations around Bangkok. The factory is quite new, clean, and certainly rates very well when put up against American factories. Employees buy their meals at below the already low cost for the typical Thai meal at a large cafeteria. A well-supplied library provides books, videos, and music tapes for checkout during lunch hours and breaks. Employees may use a gym indoors and an impressive athletic court outdoors before and after working hours, as well as during breaks. There is a well-staffed, free clinic always open for employees, with nurses constantly on duty and a physician visiting three times a week. As our questionnaire data indicate, as with other U.S. corporations in our Thai sample, worker satisfaction is comparatively high.

Several miles farther north of Bangkok, not far from the picturesque ruins of one of Thailand's ancient capitals, we visited a large factory managed by two middle-aged Japanese men only three months into their new positions, and recently transferred to Thailand from Japan. We were given an extensive tour of the factory, which made mostly cameras, by both Japanese managers and the top-ranking Thai manager of the factory. Again, the factory was newly built, clean and modern, with excellent facilities for employees. We were treated to a good Thai lunch midway through the factory tour, dining in a section of the large cafeteria where all of the employees were eating the same food, again subsidized by the company. Questionnaire data showed a high level of work satisfaction among the employees of this Japanese factory, and they rated their pay and benefits as above the typical Thai-owned factory.

Other factories we visited in our sample of Japanese and American corporations in Thailand indicated these two were among the best. Other facilities were often older, not as clean, and lacked the impressive employee facilities of the American computer chip factory or Japanese camera factory. But none of the Japanese or American factories in our random sample could be described as anything close to the sweatshops reported in the studies of Nike subcontractors in Vietnam, Indonesia, or Central American factories. This is not to say there were no problems in these Japanese and American factories in the Bangkok area. Especially in the case of Japanese factories, there were complaints that managers were too distant and promotions to the higher positions were all but nonexistent. Japanese managers tended to be almost fearful at times of labor organizing in their plants.

So what causes the discrepancies between the American and Japanese corporations we visited in Thailand and the conditions described for workers making Nike shoes around the world? One answer is that companies such as Wal-Mart, Nike, or The Gap *subcontract* with small local factories for clothing to be made. These small companies and subcontractors remain more invisible, and more easily bribe local officials to maintain sweatshop conditions. When large foreign corporations set up business in countries like Thailand, Malaysia, Taiwan, and more recently even Vietnam, their visibility makes it unlikely they will employ workers with wages and conditions *below the standards of the country*. But the second answer is far more important, and a central point of coming chapters.

In countries such as Thailand, Malaysia, Taiwan, South Korea, and increasingly Vietnam, the governments are able and willing to *protect their people from the negative consequences of foreign corporate exploitation*. They have strong governments and leaders who can confront multinational corporations and demand that they operate to protect the interests of their people. They have the will and authority to create and maintain domestic policies that will lead to long-term economic development that helps all their citizens, not just the rich. Foreign multinationals are regulated so that they follow reasonable standards for pay and labor conditions. These foreign corporations must pay reasonable taxes to help develop the country, and must keep some of the profits in the country, reinvesting them to provide further economic development for the country. This is certainly not to say these foreign multinationals always adhere to these standards, but their visibility makes them easy targets for violations. In many other developing countries around the world, local governments are either too weak to stop the outside exploitation or don't care, with corrupt leaders preferring to enrich themselves at the expense of their own citizens.

The contrast between relatively strong states willing and able to protect national interests and carry out rational development policies, and those who cannot or will not, is found even within Southeast Asia. This contrast is worth considering before we turn toward explaining the reasons *why* some states can protect national interests and others cannot in later chapters.

Preliminary Lessons from Asia: The Richer and Poorer Nations of East and Southeast Asia

As most businesspeople in rich capitalist nations around the world know, some of the best prospects for economic growth in the last several decades have been found in East and Southeast Asia. Countries like Thailand have grown at double-digit rates most years since the early 1980s. Since 2001 China has been the world leader in economic growth, sucking in much of the investment from rich multinational corporations in North America, Europe, and Japan. One estimate is that it took England about 58 years to double its economy when the Industrial Revolution began at the end of the eighteenth century. During the American economic takeoff in the late nineteenth century it took the United States 47 years to double its economy. Several rapidly growing East and Southeast Asian countries today have been doubling their economies *every 10 years* (Kristof & WuDunn, 2000:51).

Equally important, it is not just that the rich are getting richer (which they certainly are), but *the poor are becoming less poor* in most of these Asian nations. As we will see in much more detail, in countries such as Thailand, inequality has at times increased with economic development, but at the same time, poverty has dropped dramatically. Reports in the 1960s showed 60 percent of the Thai population below a poverty level estimated with costs of basic necessities. By 2004 similar estimates suggest poverty in Thailand was down to around 13 to 15 percent of the population. Some World Bank figures show that Thailand has had the best record for reducing poverty per increase in gross national product (GNP) of any country in the world (Nabi &

Shivakumar, 2001; UNDP, 1999; World Bank, 2000:48). Vietnam is now reducing poverty at an even more rapid rate.[11]

A key question to be examined in coming chapters, therefore, is "what are the differences among many East and Southeast Asian nations compared to more of the nations in Latin America and especially Africa?" Certainly not all African, Middle Eastern, or Latin American countries have stagnant economies or increasing poverty. Some countries in these other world regions *are* able to achieve economic development with poverty reduction. *Also,* some countries in Southeast Asia have not been able to achieve economic development or poverty reduction. A brief "tour" of these contrasting Southeast Asian countries will help us establish some of the key issues to be followed throughout the following chapters.

A Brief Tour of Economic Development in Southeast Asia

Observations of Thai cities and rural areas in the past 10 years support these figures on economic growth and reduced poverty. The growth in Bangkok over the years has been nothing less than dramatic; skyscrapers have gradually covered much of the skyline, and the streets are so full of cars that traffic is perhaps worse in Bangkok than anywhere else in the world. While several new elevated highways through Bangkok and the new sky train that opened at the end of 1999 have helped, Bangkok is still almost choking in too much growth, too quickly. In the countryside, while conditions still lag behind those in the urban areas, signs of improved standards of living also suggest the statistics showing reduced poverty are accurate. Farmers are building new homes or improving old ones, and new "iron buffalos" (small tractors for plowing rice paddies) and Japanese pickup trucks are common sights. The classic view of poor peasants in rice fields with only water buffalos to help with their labor is rare these days. Statistics on improved levels of education and health also go along with the scenes of improved living standards in the countryside.

To be sure, pockets of miserable poverty exist in Thailand, such as in the northeast of the country where climate has always made farming more difficult, and in hill tribe areas in the north where people (in many ways like earlier American Indians) have been struggling to adjust to a developing economy cutting into their traditional living patterns. In the southern parts of Thailand as well, where predominantly Muslim people have been shut out of growing economic opportunities, there is more poverty and less development. But this has been changing most rapidly since the early 1990s as the Thai government, along with encouragement by the king, has put more resources into southern Thailand. Driving down to the Malaysian border from the city of Hat Yai it seems there are new ponds for shrimp farming almost everywhere, along with new orchards and more activity in the rubber plantations. In recent years foreign multinationals have begun setting up more factories in the south where the negatives of crowded Bangkok are fewer.

Malaysia has a higher standard of living than Thailand, and Taiwan and South Korea are far ahead of Thailand. Walking through the streets of major cities in Taiwan and South Korea today, one finds a level of development hard to imagine 40 years ago—a level of development that makes these major cities look much like the affluent cities of Japan. And of course there are Hong Kong and Singapore, different from the other Asian nations we are considering because of their small city-state status (and the

Shenzhen, China, is one of the original industrial zones inland from Hong Kong established for Chinese economic development. When I first visited Shenzhen over 15 years ago it was nothing but a small town with no high rise buildings.

continued special enterprise zone status of Hong Kong after China regained posses-sion), also bustling with affluence and growth along with the massive presence of for-eign multinationals.

There is an economic hierarchy among nations in East and Southeast Asia. Flying from Singapore or Taiwan, into Thailand, Thailand looks less developed, with many more old, dilapidated buildings and slums along the train tracks, waterways, and rural roads lead-ing into Bangkok. But when one flies to the Philippines from Bangkok, Thailand looks much wealthier. Flying back to the mainland, into Vietnam, the Philippines doesn't look so poor, though one can see Vietnam is moving ahead fast while the Philippines seems to be going nowhere. Then again, when visiting Laos, Cambodia, or Burma (Myanmar)[12] after being in Vietnam, it is Vietnam that suddenly seems a richer nation. One indicator of such a hierarchy of the wealth of nations anywhere, of course, is the flow of immigrants, legal or otherwise; in Southeast Asia, Thailand and Malaysia receive the vast majority of immigrants.

Vietnam is one of the most interesting and important countries in the region when considering economic development. During my first trip to Vietnam in 1995, I walked through Ho Chi Minh City (Saigon) and Hanoi days before the American secretary of state arrived to sign a treaty of new relations between Vietnam and the United States. My friend and research colleague who is a veteran of the American part of the Vietnamese

War was with me. We had been invited by Hanoi National Pedagogic University to discuss cooperative research and exchange programs now that our two countries were moving toward better relations. My friend had returned to Vietnam previously since the war, in 1990 when economic reforms had not yet taken effect. As we walked through the largest park in central Saigon our first night in the city, my friend was amazed: A few years ago, he told me, when he walked these same streets the park was full of homeless people. Small lights from the hundreds of homemade lanterns of these homeless people made an eerie sight. In daylight the next day we walked through the streets and he again stopped me many times in amazement. In contrast to a few years before, the streets were full of people hawking a rich variety of food. Inside the food stores the shelves were full, again in vast contrast to just a few years before.

A few days later we arrived in Hanoi with more signs of growth. Although there were fewer high-rise apartments, office buildings, and hotels, and the center of the city remained older and less affluent, the growth was still striking. Everywhere there were little shops with no space for their crates of new TVs, VCRs, and all kinds of other consumer goods piled out on the sidewalks with customers carrying them away almost as soon as they were restocked. On subsequent trips to Vietnam, almost every year since 1995, I continue to see evidence of growing prosperity. By 2002 the massive bicycle traffic in Hanoi's narrow streets had been replaced by massive motorcycle traffic—most seemed to be shinny new Honda Dreams. In the next few years I am sure the massive motorcycle traffic will be replaced by auto traffic worse than Bangkok. In 2004 I went down to the southern part of Vietnam for the first time in two years; I had trouble finding my favorite little hotel in Saigon. It was encircled by huge new hotels blocking out the sky. The automobile traffic is already picking up down there.

By the late 1990s I saw other sights common throughout the other developing nations of Southeast Asia. One sight came suddenly in 1998 after leaving the international airport in Hanoi: There to my right was a large, new billboard proclaiming, "Ford Welcomes You to Hanoi." Soon after reaching the center of Hanoi I saw evidence of other American auto companies setting up business. Among the Japanese office buildings I had seen for several years in Hanoi there were many other offices telling visitors that American corporations are now open for business in Vietnam. On one of the tallest buildings in Ho Chi Minh City (Saigon) the sign now reads "Citibank." In June of 2000, I might add, we drove by that Ford factory: A nice new building ready to pour out its products and employ hundreds of Vietnamese. Again in the summer of 2001 I looked in on a mainly American trade fair in Ho Chi Minh City; one section of the grounds was covered with nice new Ford sport utility vehicles and pickups recently made in Vietnam.

As in Thailand, it is important to recognize that economic development in Vietnam is *not just an urban phenomenon*. In many developing nations, especially in Latin America and Africa, what little economic development there is can be found mostly in the major cities, producing huge disparities between the rural and urban areas of the country (International Fund for Agricultural Development [IFAD], 2001). The economic reforms from 1988 called *Doi Moi* in Vietnam also targeted the countryside. The disastrous collective farms[13] the Vietnamese communist government copied from the old Soviet Union were eliminated with *Doi Moi* economic reforms and farmers were given individual plots with the freedom to sell their produce in a relatively free market (Boothroyd & Nam, 2000). More than anything this explains the big increase in the amount of food sold in Vietnamese cities by the early 1990s. Also in June of 2000 I took a long trip by car from Ho Chi Minh City (Saigon) up to the Central Highlands of Vietnam with two American friends who are veterans of the Vietnam War. As we drove around the rural areas outside of cities such as Pleiku and Kontum where much of the worst fighting took place in the late 1960s, my friends were amazed at the changes and how little evidence of the war remained. Now, 30 years after the war ended, the hills are covered with coffee plantations, fruit orchards, and of course rice paddies. New rubber tree plantations were producing alongside the remnants of the old plantations held by the French colonialists many years ago. For many years Thailand has been the leading exporter of rice in Asia; as of 2000, however, Vietnam had almost reached Thailand's level of rice exports to become the world's second largest exporter of rice. During 2001 Vietnam became the world's second largest exporter of coffee behind Brazil.

Things are certainly not perfect in rural Vietnam, with plenty of poverty and a lower standard of living than in Hanoi and Ho Chi Minh City (Gwatkin, Johnson, Wagstaff, Rutstein, & Pande, 2000). In a few places there are signs of deforestation where young trees are starting to grow again, and we have seen homes for disabled people born since the war who have deformities, no doubt caused by the Agent Orange chemicals sprayed through the Central Highlands by the U.S. military. (About half a million Vietnamese have died or become ill because of Agent Orange chemicals, and there are estimated to be some 70,000 "Agent Orange babies" in Vietnam today.)[14] But despite these lingering effects of the war, the overall picture of rural central Vietnam today is one of agrarian economic expansion, though many more water buffalo continue to do the work than the mechanical variety found throughout the Thai countryside these days.

There are certainly problems in the Vietnamese economy, and as in China, the communist rulers are still divided over how much and how quickly the economy should be freed from their controls. There is still too much corruption. But change is moving along in the right direction for more economic growth and poverty reduction.

Burma, Cambodia, and Laos, however, offer quite different stories. During several trips to Laos since 1998, I spent many days in Vientiane, the capital of Laos, just across the Mekong River from one of the poorest sections of Thailand. Still, even the poor northeastern part of Thailand presents the image of a much richer nation. Despite being the capital city, Vientiane seems deserted compared to most other cities in the region, especially Singapore, Saigon, Bangkok, or Manila. Very few cars were on the dusty streets in 1998. There are even few bicycles or motor bikes compared to cities in Vietnam. Sitting on a street corner in the center of Vientiane in 1998, cooling ourselves with a cold beer, a friend and I noticed something else about the scarcity of traffic: Of the few cars passing, a large percentage of them had the markings of some international aid agency on the door or window. We brought the subject to a European friend who had lived in Vientiane for some time and were told that a large percentage of the visitors booking hotel rooms in Vientiane were from these international aid agencies.

As in other places in Southeast Asia, in Laos I rented a bicycle to explore the city, its temples, and some of the nearby countryside. Driving around the city one finds little construction going on, in the city or surrounding area, and certainly no large buildings in progress. There has been major construction going on at the city's airport, and a drainage system was being dug in some of the central streets. But that was all the proof one could see of any growth occurring in the capital of Laos. When I visited Laos in 2003, the new airport was finished and the plaza in the city center where most foreign restaurants are located had a new "facelift." By 2005 there was a little more development to be seen, a new Honda motorcycle factory, for example. The cars seemed a little more numerous, and in fact the World Bank economic data did show some small improvement. Still, compared to Thailand or Vietnam, Laos is a sleepy little country with much less economic advancement or poverty reduction.

Since early 2000, Vientiane (the capital city of Laos) has been hit by a series of bombings, at first wounding dozens and killing one person. By 2004 the low-grade bombing campaign had killed a few more people and moved to some other cities in Laos (*Bangkok Post,* May 13, 2004). Poor hill tribe people have been officially blamed for the bombings. A few journalists in the area, however, are convinced that the bombings are the work of one faction of the Laotian Communist Party frustrated because of the lack of action to improve their country compared to Vietnam next door.[15] Ironically, while global protestors are attacking symbols of corporate America to publicize their demands that rich corporations leave the world's poor alone, some of the world's poor are attacking their inept governments for *not* attracting these same rich corporations into their country.

Traveling across Thailand to the west, one again goes from what seems a comparatively rich nation into serious poverty. Very little evidence of economic growth can be seen in Burma, and most people live with the bare minimum of material possessions. A difference when reflecting upon the contrast with Laos is that one can see Burma was once a thriving place with many old buildings and better infrastructure development. But since the political strife after its independence from British rule soon after World War II, and a harsh military dictatorship during most of this postcolonial period, the economy has fallen into ruin. There is no question that General Ne Win's "Burmese way to socialism" was the Burmese way to economic ruin.[16] During 2000 and 2001 there were small indications that the military government would achieve some compromise with Suu Kyi, whose coalition of parties in 1990 won a huge victory in fair elections that were immediately thrown out by the military government.[17] Since this time almost nothing has changed as the Burmese economy, along with the Burmese people, fall further into despair. Perhaps most depressing about Burma is that after World War II, Burma was judged by some to be the country most likely to prosper after colonialism in Southeast Asia (Smith 1999; Turnbull, 1999).

Back across Thailand, now to the southeast, there is the most tragic case of Cambodia. As I sat in the Choeung Ek Killing Fields one afternoon, I wondered what could have become of Cambodia had the French not reentered Indochina after World War II to set the stage for the bloody war in the region that lasted until 1975, and then the Khmer Rouge takeover for 4 more years that killed 1.7 million people, 25 percent of the population. The 9,000 or so skulls that looked out at me from the monument pagoda in the killing fields that day, and the other almost 9,000 still in the ground below my feet, represented a good deal of the best and brightest in Cambodia at the time. Most had been targeted for death by the Khmer Rouge because they were educated, and thus a threat to the radical communist government. Back in Phnom Penh, in striking contrast to the capital of Laos, one sees the remnants of a once relatively prosperous city, now in serious decline. Cambodia's poverty today, however, cannot be blamed only on French colonialism or the American part of the Indochina War.[18] These factors, as we will see, certainly pushed Cambodia further into ruin. But in contrast to several other countries in the region, particularly its Thai neighbors, Cambodia had been in decline long before colonialism (Chandler, 1996, 1999). After U.N.-sponsored elections and the capture of remaining Khmer Rouge forces in the 1990s, there is more hope in Cambodia than there has been in many decades. A walk through the capital city as well as the countryside, however, suggests that Cambodia has a long way to go.

Pictured here is one of the famous "killing fields," Choeung Ek, close to the capital city of Cambodia. About 17,000 of the estimated 1.7 million Cambodians killed by the Khmer Rouge between 1975 and 1978 were found in mass graves at this site. The pagoda is a memorial to these people, which contains some 9,000 skulls shown in the picture.

This sketch of countries in Southeast Asia will be expanded in coming chapters. For now, though, the introductory points are these: Despite, and in fact partly because of, a heavy dose of direct investment by rich multinational corporations in several countries of East and Southeast Asia, we find extensive economic development in recent decades. And in a direct contrast to countries in Sub-Saharan Africa and even most in Latin America, economic development in East and Southeast Asia has brought poverty reduction as well. The common pattern in Latin America has been economic development at times, but with the rich getting richer and the poor no better off, if not poorer. The more common pattern in Sub-Saharan Africa has been no economic development or poverty reduction at all. Research using data from developing countries all over the world has indicated that extensive direct investment from rich multinationals is related to stunted economic development. These findings support critics of the global economy who charge that rich multinational corporations most often exploit poor countries, making their people worse off in the process. With East and Southeast Asia, though, we find the situation is far more complex. In fact, countries where multinational corporations *have been most absent* (such as Laos, Burma, and Cambodia) are the countries with the most poverty and fewest prospects of economic development. Further, we must recognize that prospects for economic development are not simply related to whether a country in the region calls itself capitalist or communist. There is extensive economic development and poverty reduction going on in Vietnam, and even more economic development (though with less successful poverty reduction) going on in China.

DATA FILE

An Introduction to Data on World Poverty
by Harold Kerbo and Patrick Ziltener

As social scientists concerned about human conditions such as health, economic develop-ment, and poverty, we have a wealth of data sources to choose from. Throughout this book there will be many tables using specific data related to poverty in developing countries. I will often rely upon "qualitative historical data" for key countries of Latin America, Africa, and Asia. Qualitative historical data refers to detailed information about the his-tory of a country, its culture, and the many other aspects that cannot easily or reliably give a numerical score. The social scientist attempting to understand one or more countries using qualitative historical methods must herself or himself weigh all of the relevant fac-tors and use judgment about what is happening. On the other hand, social scientists can use "quantitative methods" which utilize numerically scored data from many cases in an attempt to uncover relationships between variables that suggest the causes or solutions to poverty. Unfortunately, much of the quantitative data sources are of poor quality and we lack data from some of the poorest countries.

In coming pages we will use both types of data. With the qualitative data the com-parisons will usually be restricted to just a few countries. However, from time to time, espe-cially in these special sections called "Data Files," some figures called scatter plots will be presented for the interesting ideas they suggest about world poverty. A scatter plot refers to a simple graph that locates each country or case on two variables, such as level of democracy and level of poverty. The data used will come from various sources such as the World Bank and United Nations. But we will often use a new and unique data set recently constructed by sociologists and anthropologists at the University of Zurich.[19] Unfortunately, most of this rich data set pertains only to countries in Africa, the Middle East, and Asia, excluding Latin American countries. Much of the data set focuses upon ancient values, culture, and social organization of countries, and how these things influ-ence economic development and poverty today. In the case of Latin America these ancient features have been almost completely erased by European colonists. But this Zurich data set remains highly useful and in this book has been combined with World Bank and United Nations data from Latin American countries when possible. Especially useful for our task, this data set has been made available on the Web for use by faculty and students wanting to develop classroom presentations or student projects.

In this first chapter we begin with an example of how these scatter plots using quantita-tive data can be useful. Figure 1.2 is a scatter plot ranking countries on two key vari-ables: first, their general level of economic development as indicated by the average income for people in the country; and second, the percent of their population living in extreme poverty as indicated by living on less than $1 per day.

The first thing we notice from this scatter plot is that when the average income (GNP per capita) in a country goes up, the level of extreme poverty goes down. This is the usual argument made by rich countries and the World Bank to focus their efforts on economic development with "open world markets." However, we find many cases in the scatter plot which show that much more is happening. The average income for India and Indonesia, for example, is about the same but extreme poverty is much higher in India

(Continued)

(Continued)

than it is in Indonesia. Vietnam and the Philippines are also contrasting cases. Vietnam has a lower average income than does the Philippines, but the Philippines has a much higher rate of extreme poverty. Mexico and Brazil are also interesting cases of countries that are wealthier than many others but still have high levels of extreme poverty. These cases tells us that in the coming pages we need to find out why such countries as India, the Philippines, Mexico, and Brazil have higher poverty rates "than they should." What makes them different from other countries like Indonesia, Vietnam, and Tanzania which have lower standards of living for the average person but have been more successful in reducing poverty?

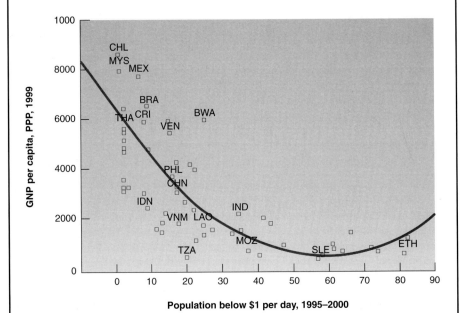

FIGURE 1.2 *Relation between per Capita National Income and Extreme Poverty*

NOTE: THA = Thailand, MYS = Malaysia, PHL = Philippines, CHN = China, IND = India, IDN = Indonesia, VNM = Vietnam, LAO = Laos, TZA = Tanzania, MOZ = Mozambique, SLE = Sierra Leone, ETH = Ethopia, BWA = Botswana, CHL = Chile, BRA = Brazil, CRI = Caribbean, VEN = Venezuela.

The Important Questions: A Preview

Soon after the historic protest at the 1999 World Trade Organization meeting in Seattle a new report from the Asian Development Bank noted that East and Southeast Asia have been one of the world's brighter spots in recent decades (*International Harold Tribune*, January 7, 2000). The report, covering all of the rich and poor nations in the region, claims that absolute poverty is now one-third of the total population in this region compared to approximately one-half of the population in 1970. The average life expectancy

TABLE 1.2

Population Living on $1 a Day or Less

	1987 (%)	1990 (%)	1993 (%)	1996 (%)	1998 (%)	Projected Change 1998–2015* (%)
East Asia and Pacific	26.6%	27.6%	25.2%	14.9%	15.3%	−61%
(excluding China)	23.9	18.5	15.9	10.0	11.3	−63
Latin America and Caribbean	15.3	16.8	15.3	15.6	15.6	−5
South Asia	44.9	44.0	42.2	42.3	40.0	−21
Sub-Saharan Africa	46.6	47.7	49.7	48.5	46.3	+30

*Projected figures are the least optimistic projections for East Asia and the Pacific of several calculated by the World Bank.

Sources: Adapted from the World Bank, 2000:23; World Bank, 2001b, *World View:4.*

is now 65 years compared to only 48 years in 1970. Some 70 percent of adults are literate compared to only 40 percent in 1970. As shown in Table 1.2, further projections by the World Bank suggest that between 1998 and 2015 the number of people living on $1 a day or less will be cut by more than 60 percent in East and Southeast Asia, but cut only by 5 percent in Latin America. The poverty level is expected to increase by about 30 percent in Sub-Saharan Africa (World Bank, 2001b, *World View:4*).

World Bank estimates show that in general East and Southeast Asia have a far better record of poverty reduction per each percentage increase in GNP (World Bank, 2000:Figure 3.4). Figures such as these, of course, lump together countries within each region that have varied success in GNP growth and poverty reduction. In East Asia and the Pacific we have countries lumped together that have been among the most successful in the world in promoting economic growth and poverty reduction (such as Taiwan, South Korea, Singapore, Thailand, and Malaysia) with countries that are among the least successful in the world (such as Laos, Burma, and Cambodia). We will consider these countries in Southeast Asia separately later in this book when I attempt to develop a general explanation for both the successful and failed economies of Southeast Asia.

The key point is worth restating: For most of the countries in East and Southeast Asia, some factor has made their *prospects of economic development, and economic development with more poverty reduction, greater than for poorer nations in other parts of the world.* International development agencies are learning new techniques that seem to create better prospects for sustained development all over the world, techniques that help the poor and not just the rich as many large development projects of the past were more likely to do. But questions remain: Why are some poor nations, and especially elites in these nations, more willing and motivated to use these new methods of promoting *sustained and more evenly distributed economic development?*[20] Why are more of the poorer nations that are motivated and able to use many methods for sustained and more evenly distributed economic development located in East and Southeast Asia? Finally, why is there so much contrast among countries within Southeast Asia with respect to economic development? We find that neighboring countries who share common cultures have very different prospects for economic development and poverty reduction today.

These questions call for a comparative examination of Asian political and economic systems, along with their relation to richer countries and multinational corporations of the world. All of this must then be considered in relation to poorer countries in other parts of the world. We need to know, and the world's poor need to know, what it is about East and Southeast Asia that has made their prospects for achieving economic development and reducing poverty generally much better. In coming chapters we will consider the characteristics of Asian nations shaped by their past civilizations, and the very important legacy of Western colonialism throughout East and Southeast Asia. We will then contrast these characteristics to countries in Latin America, Africa, and the Middle East.

Before considering these national characteristics and legacies, we must first get a better idea of differences in the level of poverty across world regions. We will do this in the next chapter. Then we must examine important aspects of research and theory of the modern world system. We will start with the characteristics and history of the modern world system in Chapter 3. With more global competition from a mass of poor people willing to work for very low wages, this chapter will help us understand why there is more inequality, lower wages, reduced worker benefits, and longer working hours for American workers. In recent decades U.S. government policies have helped U.S. corporations better compete in the global economy by reducing standards of living for the bottom half of Americans. But we will see that European governments, in contrast, have adopted economic policies allowing European corporations to compete without as much harm to their employees.

In Chapter 4 we begin consideration of how modern world system theory explains persistent underdevelopment and poverty in less developed nations. We will examine research illustrating why extensive outside foreign investment can be detrimental to long-term economic development and poverty reduction around the world. Remaining chapters will focus on the differing characteristics of countries in Asia, Latin America, Africa, and the Middle East that influence why some countries remain so poor while others have been able to achieve economic development with significant poverty reduction.

Notes

1. World Bank, *World Development Report 2000/2001* (New York: Oxford University Press, 2000), 45; World Bank, *World Development Report 2004* (New York: Oxford University Press, 2004); United Nations Development Program, *Human Development Report 2004* (New York: Oxford University Press, 2004). I will more often refer to the World Bank 2000/2001 report because this report was specifically devoted to the topic of world poverty. Very few countries have had significant change in poverty since data included in the 2000/2001 report, but the 2004 report has included data for a few additional nations that will be used throughout this book. The United Nations includes the same poverty data in its *Human Development Report* every year, but with much more data on the human condition, such as health, education, and so forth. Both will be used extensively.

2. World Bank, *World Development Report 2000/2001,* 274–275. Note that these figures are calculated in the new Purchasing Power Parity Index which more accurately takes into account lower prices for basic necessities in poor countries compared to rich countries in North America, Europe, as well as Japan. Using the standard measures of per capita income there are dozens of countries listed as having annual per capita incomes of $200 and $300.

3. The World Bank and other agencies estimate this new $1 per person per day measure using *Purchasing Power Parity* (PPP). The PPP estimate begins with what goods $1 per day would buy in the United States, then estimates the cost of the same goods in the actual currency of each country. It might be clearer to use what a friend of mine came up with—the "sandwich index." Given that $1 in the United States could buy a sandwich (well, a cheap one anyway), we can say that the World Bank estimates that 1.2 billion people in the world do not have enough money to buy one sandwich per day. There are of course many factors, making this $1 per day only a rough estimate, as the World Bank admits. For example, while in one country the one sandwich per day means the person must go without a place to sleep because all of his or her daily wage has gone for the one sandwich, another country has a tradition of families taking other family members under their roof. Thus, in this country the person has a sandwich *and* a place to sleep. It seems, nonetheless, that this $1 per day rough indicator of economic means for people in the world gives us a reasonable idea of comparative levels of poverty. For more details see the World Bank, 2000, Technical Notes:p.320.

4. With mention of Bill Gates, founder of Microsoft, we should note that he has given more to charitable causes than any person in history, already several billion dollars. Unlike other wealthy donors in history, most of his contributions go to people in poor countries. His donations to anti-AIDS programs and his 2005 contribution of $750 million for child immunizations in poor countries have saved the lives of an estimated 670,000 children already. See the *Los Angeles Times,* January 27, 2005.

5. See the World Resources Institute Web site, http://www.wri.org.

6. The World Trade Organization is like a debating society among the world's nations who are involved in international trade. All rich nations are members, as are most less developed nations. As we will see in more detail in later chapters, there are agreements designed to produce more "fair trade" in the world and something like a world economic court to enforce these agreements. But while less developed nations are often members of the World Trade Organization, rich nations are usually able to dominate.

7. We will see in more detail in coming chapters that the IMF and World Bank were created by rich nations, led by the United States, after World War II. The stated intent in forming these organizations was to bring more stability in the world economy. However, there is no doubt that the IMF and World Bank are undemocratic and dominated by rich nations, especially the United States.

8. A summary of several reports involving Nike subcontractors in Asia can be found in the *International Herald Tribune,* June 26, 1998.

9. These corporations were from a larger list of 50 corporations drawn in a stratified random sample of corporations listed in the Japanese and American Chamber of Commerce booklets. Surprisingly, we were denied access in the case of only one

corporation. The study was eventually held to 24 corporations because of time restraints conducting research in the Bangkok area over a 2-year period. In addition to interviews with top and middle managers who were Thai employees, Japanese and American nationals, we obtain slightly more than 1,000 detailed questionnaires (11 pages each) from lower level Thai employees in these corporations. While much of our research findings are still forthcoming, summaries can be found in Harold Kerbo and Robert Slagter, "The Asian Economic Crisis and the Decline of Japanese Leadership in Asia," in *The Asian Economic Crisis,* ed. Frank-Jürgen Richter (New York: Quorum Press, 2000); Robert Slagter and Harold Kerbo, "The Foreign Boss: Employee Commitment and Management Styles in Japanese and American Corporations in Thailand." Paper presented at the annual meeting of the National Association of Social Sciences, New Orleans, October 1998; and Robert Slagter and Harold Kerbo, *Modern Thailand: A Volume in the Comparative Societies Series* (New York: McGraw-Hill, 2000).

10. Figures indicating a minimum wage of $4.40 per day (162 baht as of April 2000) often appear shocking to North Americans and Europeans, but we must caution that such figures be understood in their proper context of societies with extremely low costs of living. It should be stressed that prices quoted below are dollar estimates after the Asian economic crisis sent the dollar much higher than previously (e.g., in 1997, before the crisis the exchange rate was $1 (U.S.) to 24 baht, while it was holding at about $1 (U.S.) to 38 baht during 2000). At the older, more consistent exchange rate of 24 baht to the dollar the minimum wage would be $6.75 in April of 2000. Some examples of the costs of basic necessities in Bangkok are also necessary to understand what a minimum wage of $6.75 or $4.40 means to people. But also note, these quotes are for the capital city of Bangkok where prices are significantly higher than in smaller cities or the countryside where a larger percentage of people would be closer to the minimum wage of $4 per day.

Food: A dinner in a typical street-side Thai restaurant frequented mostly by Thai people could cost less than $1 (not including beer of course). However, most Thais would be making food at home or buying prepared foods from a street vender to consume at home and therefore pay much less than $1 per meal per person.

Medical care: For anyone living around the minimum wage in Thailand, medical care is primarily free, including long-term hospital stays. Since 2001 there has been a new 30 baht national health insurance system in place which requires people to pay 30 baht (less than $1) for all doctor's visits and medications. However, the more affluent can go to private hospitals which are less crowded and provide patients more service. For 24 hours in such a hospital, including private room, drugs, lab tests, and three doctor's visits, a typical bill is around $150 at the best hospital.

Housing: A typical lower-middle-class to working-class apartment in Bangkok with kitchen, living room, bathroom, and one to two bedrooms is about $50 per month.

Transportation: A water taxi ride of 30 minutes to an hour along the main river in Bangkok costs $0.25, as does the public bus. Private taxis are more expensive, with the meter beginning at just under $1.

11. See World Bank, *Poverty: Vietnam Economic Development Report 2004* (2004) at http://www.worldbank.org. Only recently has research on multinational corporate investment and economic growth carefully considered differing effects in different world regions; Jalilian and Weiss have shown that outside corporate investment is much more likely to lead to future economic development in East and Southeast Asia than in Latin America and Africa. Jalilian and Weiss (2003:247) offer *no explanation for why* outside corporate investment produces more economic development is Southeast Asia but note that the question is of critical importance and needs further research. See also K. S. Jomo, "Globalisation, Liberalisation, Poverty and Income Inequality in Southeast Asis." Technical Paper No. 185, Organization for Economic Cooperation and Development, Paris, December 2001.

12. A few years ago the military dictators of Burma declared that the new official name of the country is Myanmar. At first the dictators threatened to kick out journalists who continued to use the name Burma. After they forced all of the journalists to leave the country anyway in the late 1990s everyone seemed to go back to the name Burma, as will be done in this book.

13. During the early years of the old Soviet Union in Russia, in the 1920s and 1930s, the communist leaders took land from all private land owners to make collective farms where agricultural laborers worked collectively in the fields like in a large factory. Other countries becoming communist later, including Vietnam, adopted the practice of collective farms. All were disasters, with falling food production and increasing hunger in the nation.

14. For reports of the continuing effects of Agent Orange in Vietnam today see the *Los Angeles Times,* September 26, 1998.

15. Based on personal interviews in Laos and northeastern Thailand, and several issues of the *Bangkok Post* and *International Herald Tribune,* July 21, 2000. More recently the same conclusions were drawn by journalist (then student intern) Brett Dakin after 2 years of living in Vientiane; see *Another Quiet American: Stories of Life in Laos* (Bangkok: Asia Books, 2003).

16. General Ne Win's Burmese way to socialism meant it would not be communist or ally itself with a powerful communist country like China, but would close off the country from outside corporate investment and development with central government ownership and control.

17. After major riots in 1988 the military dictatorship in Burma decided to try democratic elections. Suu Kyi's party won over 80 percent of the vote in these elections and the military dictators quickly placed Suu Kyi under arrest and nullified the elections. Except for a brief release in the spring of 2002, Suu Kyi remains under house arrest as of 2004. She won the Nobel Peace Prize soon after she was placed under house arrest more than 14 years ago.

18. The French had fully taken Vietnam as a colony by the late 1800s. Japan took control of Vietnam during most of World War II, then the French come back in to reclaim their old colony as the Japanese were defeated. Communist and nationalist Vietnamese fighters lead by Ho Chi Minh defeated the French in 1953 and were able to take control of the northern part of the country. The United States slowly stepped in to take over when the French were kicked out of the country. Full warfare between North Vietnamese and American forces began in 1964 until the American forces finally pulled out from 1972, much like the French had done.

Through this period of U.S. military intervention, Laos and Cambodia were also pulled into the disruption of war. Considering the size of its population, Laos had more bombs dropped upon it than any other country in history, including the bombing in Europe and Japan during World War II. By 1975 all of Vietnam was under the control of the North Vietnamese communist government.

19. The data set includes over 400 coded variables from the World Bank, United Nations, and other international organizations, all of which can be accessed on the Web. The unique part of the data set are indicators of the state and social complexity of precolonial societies. These indicators were constructed for several sources to indicate the level of social, political, and cultural diversity before the impact of European colonialism took over much of the world. This data set includes the hundreds of ethnic groups in the *Ethnographic Atlas* between 1940 and 1980 (George Peter Murdock, "Ethnographic Atlas," *World Cultures* 2, no. 4, 1986). These data have been transformed into population-weighted variables on national level. The original data are published in the *Atlas of Pre-colonial Societies: Cultural Heritage and Social Structures of African, Asian and Melanesian Countries* (Hans-Peter Müller et al. *Atlas of Precolonial Societies,* Berlin:Reimer, 1999. hereinafter referred to as ATLAS).

In the ATLAS, 22 ethnological variables are coded, not counting the larger number of index constructions. Ten of these 22 variables are regarded as indicators for structural or political and social complexity. Two main factors of structural complexity have to be distinguished: sociopolitical differentiation *hierarchy* and traditional level of technology, in agriculture and beyond *technology. Technology* is composed of the following four variables for traditional level of agricultural technology: *plow cultivation, predominant type of animal husbandry, major crop type,* and *intensity of cultivation.* In addition, two theoretically important variables are included, namely *weaving* and *metal working.*

Regarding the concept of hierarchy, the index includes four indicators: political integration which consists of a 5-point scale. It measures the number of levels of precolonial jurisdictional hierarchy beyond the local community from its lowest value, ranging from no jurisdictional hierarchy beyond the local community, to its highest value, which signifies complex states. Class stratification consists of a 4-point scale measuring vertical social differentiation. Its lowest value denotes an absence of significant class distinctions among freemen (differences of status between age groups or sexes do not count as class differentiation). Its highest value indicates complex stratification into social classes. Slavery and caste structures are coded as separate variables. Size of local communities consists of an 8-point scale indicating the size of local groups. In societies with settlements of over 5,000 inhabitants the biggest settlement size is used as a basis for the graded value. The lowest value denotes an average size of communities smaller than 50 people, while the highest value signifies a city with no less than 50,000 inhabitants. The variable *writing system* records the literacy of a society. Behind the 3-point grade scale there is an almost dichotomous coding: 71 percent of all ethnic groups are without script, 23 percent with script, 5 percent with ideas and knot script, and 1 percent is not known. Here again we have to consider the difference between number of ethnic groups and the number of people involved: Though 77 percent of all ethnic groups had no writing system, the overwhelming majority of people (84 percent) lived in societies with a writing system.

20. By "sustained economic development" we mean economic development that can continue over a longer period of time, even if the multinational corporate investment leaves the country. By "evenly distributed economic development" we mean economic growth that benefits almost all people in the country, rural and urban people, as well as people who were better off before and the poor.

World Poverty at the Twenty-first Century: Regional Comparisons

U ntil somewhat recently the inhabitants of this planet were not so divided by levels of wealth, sickness, and hunger. As we saw in the first chapter, the standard of living for common people all over the world was not very high. Most of our grandparents or great-grandparents lived on farms with no running water or electricity, had rather meager diets, and seldom lived much beyond their 50s. Life expectancy did not go above 50 for Americans until the beginning of the twentieth century, about the time just over half of our ancestors already in America lived in cities for the first time. As late as 1940 about 45 percent of American households continued to lack complete plumbing, usually meaning no indoor toilets (U.S. Bureau of the Census, 1999:874, 878). Before the twentieth century conditions for the common people in large American cities were usually appalling. European cities, however, were worse. Waterways through European cities were often polluted, and rarely did people make distinctions between sewers and water mains. In England during the 1800s "ditches in cities were everywhere used as latrines. Dead animals were left to rot where they lay. The decomposing bodies of the poor in common graves stank" (Thomas, 1979:417). Visiting Venice in the 1800s the German literary giant, Goethe, complained that rubbish and human excrement were simply pushed into piles in the street to be carried away, but carried away infrequently. With rapid growth, cities had a most serious problem with sewage. In 1850, London dealt with the problem by collecting human waste in "privy buckets" to be dumped in one of 250,000 open cesspools around the city, which of course created further problems, owing to the city's dependence upon well water (Thomas, 1979).

Elites in nations all over the world had become richer and richer for centuries. The average people in North America and Europe finally saw slow improvements in their standards of living beginning in the nineteenth century (Lenski, 1966). Since that time, however, the world's population of extremely poor people (living on less than $1 per day) has soared. But the number has soared in some parts of the world to a much greater extent than in others.

World Inequalities by Region

Almost half of today's poor live in cities where it is impossible to grow their own food. Very soon the vast majority of the world's poor will live in huge slums in megacities in Latin America, Africa, and Asia. Unlike our great-grandparents living in nations going through rapid economic development, a large percentage of today's poor see no prospects for improving their lives. When hope for some of these people finally materialized a few decades ago (as shown in Table 1.2 at the end of the previous chapter), that hope was spread unevenly around the world and concentrated almost exclusively in East and Southeast Asia.

August 1992, Wajid, Somalia—Small orphan boy sitting with others as they wait for aid to arrive in their famine-stricken village of Wajid. In the 1980s a civil war began when warlord factions joined together to overthrow then president Siad Barre, who finally lost power in 1991. Since then, power struggles between warlords have ravaged the country with famine. These orphans are starving from hunger due to famine brought on by the civil war.

Using the new Purchasing Power Parity measure to make comparisons of world currencies more realistic, the poorest world region is certainly Sub-Saharan Africa. Table 2.1 shows that while per capita income is considerably higher in South and Central America than in East and Southeast Asia, the percentage of people living

TABLE 2.1

Standards of Living by World Regions

	2002 Per Capita Income (PPP measure)* ($)	Population Living on Less than $1 per Day (%)
South and Central America	$6,750	15.6%
Eastern Europe and Central Asia	6,690	5.1
Middle East and North Africa	5,410	1.9
East and Southeast Asia	4,160	15.3
South Asia	2,390	40.0
Sub-Saharan Africa	1,620	46.3

*This is the average income per person in these regions using the new Purchasing Power Parity measure for comparing the currencies of different countries to make them similar in what the money will actually buy.

Sources: World Bank, 2004d:Table 1; World Bank, 2000:23.

TABLE 2.2

Cross-National Comparison of Income Inequality within Nations—Mid to Late 1990s

Country	% of Total Household Income		Gini Index
	Poorest 20%	**Top 20%**	
Asian Countries			
Bangladesh	8.7	42.8	0.336
India	8.1	46.1	0.376
Indonesia	6.0	44.9	0.365
Philippines	5.4	52.3	0.462
Thailand	6.4	48.4	0.414
China	5.9	46.6	0.403
Malaysia	4.5	53.8	0.485
Vietnam	8.0	44.5	0.361
South Korea	7.5	39.3	0.316
African Countries			
Ethiopia	7.1	47.7	0.400
Egypt	9.8	39.0	0.289
Kenya	5.0	50.2	0.445
Zambia	4.2	54.8	0.498
Mozambique	6.5	46.5	0.396
Sierra Leone	1.1	63.4	0.629
Latin American Countries			
Guatemala	2.1	63.0	0.596
El Salvador	3.4	56.5	0.523
Peru	4.4	51.2	0.462
Costa Rica	4.0	51.8	0.470
Brazil	2.5	63.8	0.600
Panama	3.6	52.8	0.485
Mexico	3.6	58.2	0.537
Chile	3.5	60.1	0.565
Venezuela	3.7	53.1	0.488

Source: Adapted from World Bank, 2001:282–283.

on less than $1 per day is about the same. And as we saw in concluding Chapter 1, the future prospect for reducing poverty is far greater in East and Southeast Asia, and even in South Asia, compared to Central and South America. Table 2.2 indicates one important reason for the Latin American and Asian contrast. When we examine income inequality within countries by region we find marked differences. It is important to remember that two countries can have the same per capita income (a kind of average income for the country), but one country can have a much larger gap between the rich and poor. The gap between the percentage of national income going

TABLE 2.3

Land Inequality in the Developing World, Gini Index

Country	Gini Land Concentration Index	Year of Estimate*
Southeast Asia		
Thailand	0.36	1981–1990
Burma	0.44	1991–2000
Indonesia	0.56	1971–1980
Malaysia	0.58	1971–1980
Philippines	0.51	1971–1980
Africa		
Ethiopia	0.47	1981–1990
Guyana	0.68	1981–1990
Ivory Coast	0.73	1981–1990
Kenya	0.77	1981–1990
Liberia	0.73	1971–1980
Latin America		
Argentina	0.86	1981–1990
Brazil	0.85	1971–1980
Columbia	0.77	1981–1990
Costa Rica	0.81	1981–1990
Ecuador	0.82	1981–1990
El Salvador	0.81	1981–1990
Mexico	0.74	1971–1980
Paraguay	0.78	1991–2000
Peru	0.91	1971–1980

*Data were not available for every country; the most recent data available are presented here.
Source: Data from IFAD, 2001:Annex 3.1.

to the poorest 20 percent of people compared to the richest 20 percent of people is significantly lower in Asia than in Latin America. The Gini index, which gives us a summary score of inequality, is shown in the far right column of Table 2.2. (The Gini index ranges from 0.0 which would indicate complete equality in a nation, to 1.0 which would indicate one person or family in the country had all the income.) Except for the small African country of Sierra Leone, this Gini index shows that Brazil has the highest income inequality in the world and that all Latin American countries have more inequality than Asian countries.

The Gini index of land inequality shown in Table 2.3 is often even more important than income inequality. A slight majority of people in less developed countries are still rural people working the land. Having no land, therefore, means a person is at the mercy of landowners for their jobs and food. Again we find much higher levels of land inequality in Latin America compared to Southeast Asia, with African countries usually closer to the level of land inequality in Latin American than Asia. In some Latin

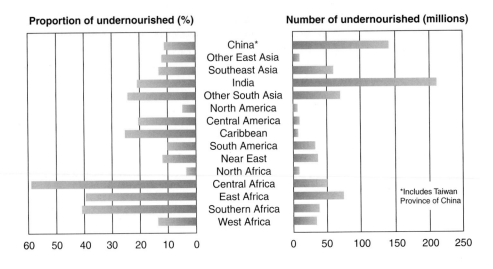

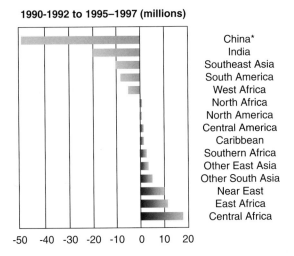

FIGURE 2.1 *Number and Proportion of Population Undernourished by Region, and Percent Reduction in 1990s*

SOURCE: UNDP, 2003:7.

American countries 10 percent of the people own about 90 percent of all the land. As we will see in coming chapters, it is this contrasting level of inequality that we must understand if we are to better comprehend differences in life chances around the world as well as world poverty.

With the above inequality and world poverty data in mind, huge regional disparities in rates of malnutrition and hunger are not surprising. The United Nations tells us that more of the total number of people undernourished in this world are located in India and secondly in China. However, we have already seen the evidence of improving conditions in those two countries, and, in contrast to Africa, few people are actually starving to death in China or India today. As Figure 2.1 clearly shows, rates of malnutrition are far greater in Sub-Saharan Africa. In Central Africa almost 60 percent of the population is malnourished, with rates of about 40 percent of the population in eastern and southern Africa. The bottom part of Figure 2.1 indicates another dimension of the situation: China and India are making great strides in reducing hunger while the situation is getting worse in much of Africa.

Democracy and Good Government

One of the conditions most dear to the hearts of people in the United States is democratic political institutions. In contrast to world poverty, the global trend of increasing democratic institutions has been more encouraging. Twenty or 30 years ago a "democracy map" would have looked quite different. All of Eastern Europe and Russia would have been shaded for dictatorship, as would much of Latin America. Democracy also would have shown up less in Southeast Asia. As it stands now mostly Africa and parts of the Middle East are dominated by dictatorship. Not only does Africa have the most dictatorial political regimes but it also has much higher levels of political instability, revolution, and mass murder today. One of Africa's, and the world's, most difficult problems will be to overcome this political instability and political violence. Until these situations are remedied there is little chance for more lasting solutions to poverty and hunger in many African countries.

Despite this global trend toward more democracy, however, we must not let our ideological preference for democratic institutions cloud our understanding of solutions to poverty, hunger, and disease. There is no simple relationship between democracy and economic development, and especially evenly spread economic development that helps all in a society. In fact, less developed countries that have what can be called "hard states," or development states, have better records of economic development and poverty reduction than do many less developed countries with high levels of democracy (Chibber, 2002; Evans & Rauch, 1999; Jomo, 2001; Weder, 1999). As we will see in coming chapters, economic development with poverty reductions usually requires a state that is able to enforce policies for long-term economic development against the wishes of some of its citizens, especially the wealthy. There *is* evidence that long-term economic development leads to more democracy, but not that democracy necessarily leads to more poverty reduction. When people become more affluent and better educated in a society they begin to demand more democracy (Jackman, 1974, 1975). But in the transition between less developed nation status to a wealthy country, a high level of democracy seldom prevails or is even always most helpful. We can cite a few simple examples by noting the strong movement toward economic development and poverty reduction in China and Vietnam compared to Russia. China and Vietnam have communist governments that are making great strides toward economic development and poverty reduction compared to Russia which moved to political democracy first, then tried to improve its economy and reduce poverty. Russia is only now returning to economic growth, and much more slowly, but with a serious increase in poverty.

The data in Table 2.4 indicate there is often a contrast between democracy and government efficiency. In the first column we have what is called the "Weberianness" Scale which was constructed to indicate how well a nation's government bureaucracy works in an efficient, rational, and less corrupt manner as described by the classic

TABLE 2.4

State Bureaucratic Efficiency and Level of Democracy, National Rankings of Less Developed Countries, Late 1990s

Country/Region	Score on Weberianness Scale*	Democracy Score**
East and Southeast Asia		
Singapore	13.5	—
South Korea	13.0	8.0
Taiwan	12.0	—
Hong Kong	11.0	–7.0***
Malaysia	10.5	4.0
Thailand	8.0	9.0
Philippines	6.0	7.0
South Asia		
Pakistan	11.0	–6.0
India	10.0	9.0
Sri Lanka	8.0	6.0
North Africa and Middle East		
Tunisia	9.0	–3.0
Egypt	7.8	–6.0
Morocco	7.0	—
Turkey	7.0	7.0
Syria	3.8	–9.0
Latin America		
Costa Rica	9.0	10.0
Mexico	8.5	6.0
Colombia	8.5	8.0
Brazil	7.6	8.0
Argentina	3.8	7.0
Chile	5.0	7.0
Peru	5.0	3.0
Uruguay	4.5	9.0
Haiti	4.0	6.0
Ecuador	4.0	8.0
Guatemala	3.0	—
Dominican Republic	2.0	8.0
Sub-Saharan Africa		
Côte d'Ivoire (Ivory Coast)	8.0	–6.0
Zaire	4.0	—
Nigeria	3.0	4.0
Kenya	1.0	–2.0

*The Weberianness scale is constructed from 10 items rating things such as merit-based recruitment and promotion of government bureaucrats, efficience in policy formation, and level of corruption. Higher numbers mean higher scores on the Weberianness scale.

**Democracy scale is taken from Polity IV Project, University of Maryland, at http://www.bsos.umd.edu/cidcm/inscr/index.htm#polity via ciesin.org. Scores range from –10 (autocracy) to +10 (full democracy).

***Taken from the overall democracy score for China.

Note: Em dashes (—) indicate data are unavailable or inapplicable.

Source: Constructed from Evans and Raugh, 1999:763.

DATA FILE

Poverty Reduction, Economic Development, and Democracy

by Patrick Ziltener

Listening to statements from political leaders in Western countries, especially from the United States, one gets the idea that democracy cures all social problems. Among these standard assumptions is that democracy is essential for economic development. Democracy is certainly a condition that should be valued simply for its own sake. But we must be realistic: Democracy does not always promote economic development or poverty reduction. The scatter plot in Figure 2.2 lines up countries with respect to their average level of democracy over a period from 1980 to 1995 and the percent of their population living on less than $1 per day. The scatter plot shows absolutely no relationship. For example, there is India with a high ranking on democracy but with high levels of poverty, compared to China with no democracy but good poverty reduction. Thailand and Vietnam are also interesting examples: Thailand has a high level of democracy while Vietnam is communist, but both countries have a good record of poverty reduction.

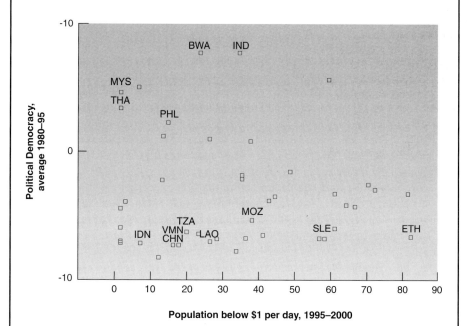

FIGURE 2.2 *Level of Democracy and Poverty Reduction*

NOTE: THA = Thailand, MYS = Malaysia, PHL = Philippines, CHN = China, IND = India, IDN = Indonesia, VNM = Vietnam, LAO = Laos, TZA = Tanzania, MOZ = Mozambique, SLE = Sierra Leone, ETH = Ethiopia, BWA = Botswana.

sociologist Max Weber. In the second column countries are ranked in one of the traditional scales for democratic institutions. As can be seen, the two rankings do not always correspond. A high score on the Weberianness Scale has been shown rather strongly related to economic development and poverty reduction whereas the democratic institutions scale has not. The East and Southeast Asian countries that have the better records of economic development and poverty reduction in recent decades rank highest on this Weberianness scale. The few African nations that were ranked in the study of government efficiency have very low scores, with Latin American countries in a middle but mixed position in Table 2.4.

The World Bank and United Nations have recently picked up on this idea of efficient government as a central solution to poverty, hunger, and disease, calling the condition "good governance." But these world institutions promoting economic development and poverty reduction have given no clue as to where this good governance comes from or how a nation actually gets it. We can tell countries they need more efficient government and less corruption, but how is it achieved? Why are some countries able to achieve good governance while others, especially in Africa, are not? These are questions we will attempt to answer, at least partially, in coming chapters.

Health Disparities

We should not be surprised to find that health conditions are related to inefficient government, poverty, inequality, and hunger in this world. As discussed in Chapter 1, one of the most telling indicators of this was shown for the first time by the World Health Organization in 2002. In this unique study the WHO calculated death rates for the ultimate cause of the death rather than the immediate cause (such as heart attack, cancer, and so on). Lack of food is the number one killer in poor countries. Most of the top 10 killers in poor countries are due to a lack of such things as safe drinking water, sanitation, or vitamins. AIDS, of course, makes unsafe sex the second leading cause of death in poor countries, especially in Africa.

As we would expect, Table 2.5 shows that life expectancy is lower and infant mortality is higher in regions with more poverty, and again, especially so for Sub-Saharan Africa. Most striking is the death rate for children under 5 which varies from 7 in 1,000 births in rich countries to 171 in 1,000 births in Sub-Saharan Africa. Also shown in Table 2.5 is the widely used Human Development Index created by the United Nations. This Human Development Index is calculated from the combined scores on life expectancy, literacy, and per capita GNP in the country using PPP (Purchasing Power Parity).

Finally on the subject of poverty and health, we must consider two of the world's most severe problems, HIV and AIDS. HIV is human immunodeficiency virus which causes AIDS, or acquired immune deficiency syndrome. This disease was unknown to the world before 1980 and has since killed millions of people. As shown in Table 2.6, again it is Sub-Saharan Africa that is in crisis. Not only are HIV and AIDS infection rates highest in Sub-Saharan Africa, but they are rising rapidly. Already it is estimated that each day more than 5,000 people die of AIDS-related illnesses in some of these African countries. Some 13,000 people die of AIDS *each day* in this part of Africa. Life expectancy is already dropping dramatically: In the next

TABLE 2.5

Mortality and Human Development Index by Region, 2002

	Life Expectancy at Birth (years)	Under 5 Mortality Rate per 1,000 Births*	Human Development Index Score*
High-income countries	78.3	7	0.93
South and Central America	70.5	34	0.77
Middle East and North Africa	66.3	54	0.65
East and Southeast Asia	69.8	44	0.73
South Asia	63.2	99	0.57
Sub-Saharan Africa	46.3	171	0.47

*The United Nations Human Development Index is calculated from combined scores on life expectancy, literacy rate, and PPP per capita GNP.
Sources: UNDP, 2004b:142; World Bank, 2004d:Table 2.

TABLE 2.6

Rates of HIV and AIDS Infection by Region, 2001

Region	Population Infected (%)
East and Southeast Asia	0.20%
Latin America	0.61
South Asia	0.55
Sub-Saharan Africa	9.00
High Human Development*	0.31
Medium Human Development	0.61
Low Human Development	3.75
All Countries	1.20

*Score on the U.N. Human Development Index.
Source: UNDP, 2002:173.

few years the average age at death will be around 29 in Botswana, 30 in Swaziland, and 33 in Namibia and Zimbabwe. As of December 1999, the infection rates, meaning the percent of the total population infected, for the following countries have been estimated:

Botswana	35.8%	Swaziland	25.3%
Zimbabwe	25.1%	Lesotho	23.6%
Zambia	20.0%	South Africa	19.9%
Namibia	19.5%	Malawi	16.0%
Kenya	14.0%		

WHY WE SHOULD CARE
New Plagues of the Twenty-first Century

Germs have always traveled well. We know that far more American Indians were killed by diseases brought by Europeans after 1492 than were killed in the wars against American Indians. The Black Death (bubonic plague) killed about one-quarter of Europe's population as it spread from one country to the next between 1346 and 1352. Some crowded cities had death tolls of up to 70 percent. The most deadly epidemic of its time was an influenza outbreak that killed about 21 million people soon after World War I in 1918. With something like 72 million people in the world currently infected with HIV, the death rate from AIDS far surpasses the 1918 record.

The World Health Organization tells us people weakened by lack of food and living in unhealthy conditions are the breeding grounds for many deadly infectious diseases. These new diseases eventually spread to wealthier nations. With some 1.3 billion people living on less than $1 per day in the world, and almost half the world's population living on less than $2 per day, the danger has never been greater. And never before in history have so many people been moving so quickly all over the world. We know that AIDS developed in African monkeys before it was passed on to African people and then the rest of the world. It is suspected that the influenza that killed 21 million people after World War I developed from pigs or foul in China. The case of SARS (severe acute respiratory syndrome) that panicked the world in 2003, and is likely to return, also developed in poor regions of southern China from a catlike animal eaten by people in the area. During 2004, the avian influenza spread through almost all of East and Southeast Asia, killing millions of chickens, but luckily only a few humans so far. Again, we know that the avian flu evolved somewhere in poverty regions of Asia. If this particular type of bird influenza ever mutates to be passed from human to human, we are in for the biggest plague in world history.

For the sake of themselves, as well as all of the world's humanity, rich countries must put more money into quickly detecting and stopping these plagues before they spread their death around the world. The situation for AIDS was certainly not helped when the American government, with pressure from the U.S. pharmaceutical industry, was *the only country* in the world that temporarily blocked the World Trade Organization deal to provide low-cost drugs successful in fighting AIDS to poor countries. But as the World Health Organization points out, dramatically reducing the number of people living on less than $1 per day would be one of the best preventive measures.

Sources: Diamond, 1999; *International Herald Tribune,* March 15–16, 2003; WHO, 1999, 2002.

These figures, for example, compare with an infection rate of 0.61 percent for the United States, 0.70 percent for India, 2.15 percent for Thailand, and 0.57 for Brazil.

There are many other negative outcomes of the AIDS epidemic throughout societies with such high rates of infections as in Sub-Saharan Africa. There are now some 13.2 million orphans in these countries because of the AIDS deaths of their parents, with the figure expected to be 42 million orphans in about 10 years. Not counting all the human suffering of these people and their families, in countries such as South

Africa, Zimbabwe, and Kenya it is estimated that the economic costs of AIDS (such as for hospitalization and drug treatments) and the loss of workers will cut 20 percent off the gross national product in the next 4 years. This is a 20 percent cut in economies where large percentages of people live in extreme poverty already and perhaps on the edge of starvation. More specifically, a United Nations report estimates that in families where an adult has AIDS, food production normally drops by 50 percent or more. Rates of malnutrition are about 38 percent in Sub-Saharan African countries having more than a 5 percent HIV infection rate compared to 25 percent in Sub-Saharan African countries with less than a 5 percent infection rate (U.N., 2003:10–11). Another fact puts the AIDS epidemic in perspective: In 10 years the number of AIDS-related deaths in Africa will exceed all of those killed in both World War I and World War II, and many times more than the 20 million people that were killed by the infamous bubonic plague that devastated Europe in the fourteenth century.[1]

Population Problems

One of the most basic problems for the world, and especially for less developed countries, is population growth. For the future, one question is whether we have enough resources for the rapidly growing world population. It was only some 200 years ago that world population shot above 1 billion people. For at least 2,000 years the number of people in the world had remained fairly steady and low. By the end of the twentieth century we had surpassed the 6 billion mark.[2] One of the biggest concerns, of course, is food. As we have already seen, at 6 billion people, or even 9 billion people, the problem is not how much food the world is able to produce, but its unequal distribution. At 15 billion people, 18 billion people, or over 20 billion people in the world, however, all bets are off. Even at 9 billion people there are questions about adequate food production because of global warming and water shortages in many world regions.

There is some good news for the world on this subject, but not for developing countries. The good news is that population growth rates have generally slowed. Only 15 years ago, population growth rates at the time suggested there would be at least 12 billion people by 2050. Currently, though, the estimate for 2050 is 9 billion people—3 billion people less than we expected in 50 years. As shown in Table 2.7, in less developed countries and in world regions with most poverty, population rates will continue to go up.

One simple reason that current population growth rates are a problem for less developed countries is that it means more mouths to feed. If the population is growing by 3 percent per year, for example, the economy must also grow by 3 percent a year to simply keep the same standard of living. A GNP growth rate of 3 percent is seldom achieved in less developed countries, meaning that with a population growth rate of 3 percent or more they are getting behind—their average standard of living is dropping. Another problem with rapid population growth is the unnatural age distribution it creates. Countries with high birth rates tend to have lower life expectancy rates as well. A rapid population growth rate means more unproductive people under the age of 5 or 10 compared to adults who are producing most of the food. And when they become adults, if those young people reproduce themselves at the same rate as their parents did, the problem is compounded again and again into the future: There are more and more

TABLE 2.7

Population Growth by Level of Economic Development and Region, 2000–2050

	In Billions of People	
	2000	**2050**
World population	6.06	9.04
Developed countries	1.18	1.23
Less developed countries	4.88	7.81

	In Millions of People	
Population by region	**2000**	**2050**
North Africa	173	306
Western Africa	234	567
Eastern Africa	246	583
Middle Africa	96	302
Southern Africa	49	43
Central America	136	232
Caribbean	36	49
South America	344	539
Middle East	188	395
South and Central Asia	1,475	2,450
India alone	(1,002)	(1,628)
Southeast Asia	527	836
East Asia	1,492	1,668
China alone	(1,264)	(1,369)

Source: Created from Population Reference Bureau, 2000.

TABLE 2.8

Total Fertility Rates by Region, 2000–2005

	Total Fertility Rate
High-income countries	1.7
South and Central America	2.5
Middle East and North Africa	3.8
East and Southeast Asia	2.0
South Asia	3.3
Sub-Saharan Africa	5.4

Source: UNDP, 2004b:155.

Population Pyramid Summary for United States

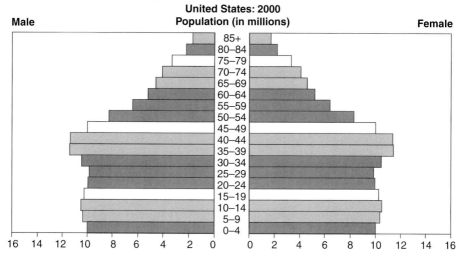

Population Pyramid Summary for Angola

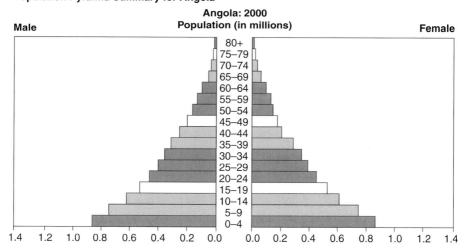

FIGURE 2.3 *Population Pyramids for Rich versus Less Developed Countries*

SOURCE: Population Reference Bureau (http://www.prb.org).

young unproductive mouths to feel all the time. This problem is usually indicated with "population pyramids" as shown in Figure 2.3. The top of this figure depicts the usual population pyramid for rich countries, whereas the bottom shows the pyramid for poorer countries.

Another side of this population problem is shown in Table 2.8 which lists the total fertility rates for regions of the world. The *total fertility rate* simply indicates the average number of children born to females in the country. Thus, of course, just over two children born per female keeps the population rate at about zero population growth. The

further a country is above this total fertility rate, the more rapidly its population is growing. Without an equally rapid growth in the economy, the people are getting poorer.

With the exception of the United States, rich countries will soon experience population declines because the total fertility rates are down to as low as 1.3 and 1.4 compared to 2.1 for the United States. East and Southeast Asian countries have good
projections because their rapid economic growth (in some cases up to 10 percent) is
well above their average 2.1 total fertility rate. All other world regions, however, have
total fertility rates well above 2.1. Total fertility rates are highest in Sub-Saharan Africa
where economic growth is generally lowest in the world. As we saw earlier, however,
some of these Sub-Sahara African countries, especially in southern Africa, will soon
experience population decline because of the impact of AIDS on their death rates. In
this case, population growth will not be as rapid as it might otherwise be because of the
AIDS death rate among adults. But the problem is compounded because more and more
of these children born in the region will have no parents to take care of them and produce food. South and Central American total fertility rates have gone down in recent
decades though economic problems have not always kept their economic improvement
above population growth. While there have been some improvements in South Asia, the
Middle East, and North Africa, they still have a long way to go in reducing population
growth to a rate where most people will have higher standards of living in the future.

Demographic Transition

A process called the *demographic transition* describes the patterns of population changes
currently rich countries have experienced throughout their history. (Figure 2.4). There
are four stages in this demographic transition. In the first stage, birth rates are high, but

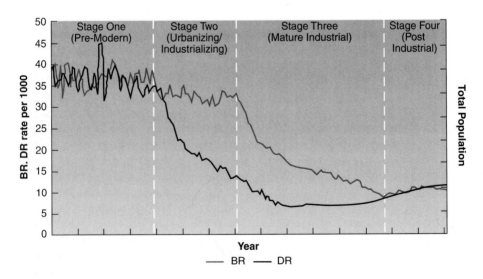

FIGURE 2.4 *Demographic Transition Model*

*BR = birth rates, DR = death rates

SOURCE: Montgomery, n.d.

so are death rates, so they roughly balance each other. This is why for at least 2,000 years the world's population remained relatively stable even in the face of high birth rates. In traditional agricultural societies, it in fact made good sense to have many children. On one hand, more children often meant more laborers in the fields to ensure a good food supply. On the other hand, because the infant mortality rate was high, and because there were no social security or pension systems, parents wanted to have many children so at least some would be alive when the parents are too old and ill to take care of themselves.

The second stage of demographic transition is one of rapid population growth. Because of better health care, sanitation, and nutrition, death rates drop rapidly. People begin living much longer and more infants survive. However, the birth rate has not gone down. Because of what can be called "cultural lag," people's beliefs, values, and religious ideologies change, if at all, more slowly than technological changes (such as better health care and sanitation and more economic production). Thus, people are living longer and babies are surviving, but there is a continued high birth rate, making population grow rapidly.

In the third stage of this demographic transition, beliefs and values usually change, bringing down the birth rate. Thus, the birth rate and death rate are again in adjustment, producing stable populations. In fact, in the fourth stage, all other advanced countries except the United States are experiencing total fertility rates at below sustainable levels leading to future population declines for them. As people become more affluent, as life provides many more opportunities beyond having children, and as it becomes much more expensive to raise each child from birth through university years, many people are deciding not to have children at all.

The demographic transition experienced by rich nations might give hope for the world's poor. However, we cannot assume less developed countries will always follow the earlier pattern of rich nations. These less developed countries, in fact, may get stuck in the transition phase of this demographic transition—one of the worst places to get stuck. Many of the less developed countries today have experienced some economic growth and improved health and sanitation, but then it seems to stop. The economic and health improvements do not seem to be enough or sustainable, or evenly spread around the nation, to have an impact on people's values and beliefs about the worth of having large families. There is, in fact, some research evidence for this. As we will see in Chapter 4, in many less developed nations around the world, more outside corporate investment from rich countries can end up producing less long-term economic development. In other words, because of the sometimes harmful intervention from rich countries in the global economy, the earlier economic development for some poor countries stagnates (something that did not happen to the already rich countries 200 or 300 years ago because there were no "already rich" countries interfering with domestic economic development). Such stagnation in the early economic progress brings down death rates but does not bring down birth rates (see, for example, Bornschier & Ballmer-Cao, 1979; Bornschier & Chase-Dunn, 1985; Chase-Dunn, 1975; Herkenrath & Bornschier, 2003; Wimberly & Bello, 1992). As will be seen again in coming pages of this book, less developed countries desperately need sustained economic growth, but to help this along it is also important to introduce population control programs to help reduce poverty.

CASE IN POINT

Fighting Population Growth and AIDS in Thailand

One evening in the early 1990s a research associate and I were leaving a restaurant in Bangkok and walking toward our campus apartment. A short way from the restaurant, down a long side street near the center of Bangkok, we heard what sounded like cheers from a large crowd. Being curious sociologists, we walked toward the noise. After walking about two blocks we found ourselves in the middle of a bar district (Soi Cowboy) and an amazing Miss Anti-AIDS Beauty Contest. A stage had been set up in the middle of a street lined with bars and strip places. On the stage "working girls" from the bars were being voted on for the title of Miss Anti-AIDS. While all of this was in progress, a young man dressed in a Superman suit walked through the crowd, then jumped on the stage, throwing out boxes of condoms and little cards describing how to protect oneself from HIV infection. Soon after the Miss Anti-AIDS contest, "Superman" with a few girls in tow went into each bar and danced on the stage, again throwing out condoms and literature about AIDS and HIV infection. We later learned that we had walked into one of the projects stimulated by the now famous Senator Mechai Viravaidya of Thailand.

With the realistic assumption that prostitution will never be completely eliminated, Mechai's approach is to find ways to educate people as quickly as possible about the AIDS epidemic and provide them with the means to protect themselves. In the 1970s, when Thailand, like most developing countries, was experiencing a dangerously rapid rate of population growth, Mechai first became involved in activities to educate people about the benefits of smaller families and helped provide the means for limiting family size. At that time he founded the Population and Community Development Association. This is when he also came up with innovative methods to achieve the organization's goals of reducing population growth. One such innovation was the health food restaurant still in operation in Bangkok called Cabbages and Condoms where one can get an excellent vegetarian meal and shop in the section of the store reported to have the biggest variety and supply of condoms anywhere in the world. An added feature: Male customers of the restaurant can take the dinner receipt to the clinic next door for a free vasectomy.

After 25 years, the rate of population growth in Thailand dropped from 3.3 percent to 0.9 percent. According to the United Nation's annual *Human Development Report* for 2004 Thailand currently has only 1.9 births per woman, a rate that is just below zero population growth. On top of this, Thailand is now one of the few developing countries in the world to reduce the growth of HIV infection and actually have the rate drop (WHO, 2004:12). One American university research team reported an 80 percent drop in all sexually transmitted diseases in Thailand since 1984. The number of new infections each year has dropped almost fourfold since 1990. One estimate is that over the coming decades perhaps 2 million lives have been saved in Thailand because of programs like Mechai's. AIDS and HIV infection is still a serious problem in Thailand, but rational and well-designed action has been taken with positive results. In its annual report for 2000 and 2004, the WHO singled out Thailand as one of the best examples of how to reduce the spread of HIV and recommended its model to the rest of the development world.

Mechai is now affectionately referred to in Thailand as "Mr. Condom" and condoms are sometimes referred to as "Mechais." During the 1990s Mechai received eight honorary degrees from Thai and Australian universities, the Ramon Magasaysay Award for public service (often called the Asian Nobel Prize), and was included among *Asia Week* magazine's 1995 list of the 20 greatest Asians.

Sources: Information compiled from UNDP, 2004b:98; and various issues of the *Bangkok Post* and the *International Herald Tribune*. See also Pasuk and Baker, 1998; Slagte and Kerbo, 2000.

Rapid Urbanization

Currently most of the world's people are rural, farming people (IFAD, 2001). But by 2025 the world's urban population is expected to reach 5 billion, surpassing the number of people living in rural farming areas.[3] About 90 percent of this urban increase will occur in the less developed countries. One reason for this shift in world population is intervention by the global economy. As we will see in Chapter 4, global agribusiness firms have gone to less developed countries seeking supplies of food for the global market. When this happens, rich land owners in poor nations are encouraged to put more land under cultivation and change to "capital-intensive" agricultural methods. Capital-intensive methods of farming are in contrast to the old labor-intensive methods using more people working the fields and less farming technology. This combines with the movement by rich land owners to take away land held by small peasant farmers, pushing more and more landless peasants into the cities in search of jobs to feed their families (Chase-Dunn, 1975, 1989; Kentor, 1981). The jobs are seldom there and people crowd into huge slum areas that have some of the world's worst rates of poverty, disease, and other social problems. One simple way to show the magnitude of the problem is to consider the world's largest cities by 2015. As shown in Table 2.9, Tokyo will remain the world's largest city in 2015, but almost all of the other largest cities in the world will be in less developed countries.

Empowered Women

Another condition related to the chances for economic growth and poverty reduction in less developed countries is the position of women in these societies, and the level of gender inequality in these countries. One of the new buzz words in the development literature, in fact, is "empowering women." Numerous studies and reports by the International Fund for Agricultural Development (IFAD), World Bank, and United Nations are showing evidence that improvements in women's rights help reduce poverty and speed economic development (IFAD, 2001; World Bank, 2000, 2001a). There seem to be several reasons for this: (1) better educated women contribute more to the economy; (2) when given the chance, rural women seem to manage family budgets and economic resources better than men and are even more likely to repay microloans; and (3) women who have more rights and education are more aware of the importance of population control for the family, with the influence to demand the use of birth control. The World Bank, for example, shows that when these conditions are improving for women the income level of less developed countries often improves and government corruption decreases (World Bank, 2001a:12,19).

One indication of the level of gender inequality and the position of women around the world is presented in Figure 2.5. A score of 1 (lowest) to 4 (highest position for women) is given to countries and world regions based on three indexes of gender equality: One index ranks countries on equality of political and legal rights, another on social and economic rights, and the third on rights in marriage and divorce proceedings. The OECD countries (the rich capitalist countries, all of whom belong to the Organization for Economic Cooperation and Development) and Eastern Europe and

TABLE 2.9

World's Largest Cities, 1995–2015

City/Country	Size in Millions	
	1995	2015
Tokyo, Japan	26.96	28.89
Mexico City, Mexico	16.56	19.18
São Paulo, Brazil	16.53	20.32
New York City, United States	16.33	17.60
Bombay, India*	15.14	26.22
Shanghai, China	13.58	17.97
Los Angeles, United States	12.41	14.22
Calcutta, India	11.92	17.31
Buenos Aires, Argentina	11.80	13.86
Seoul, Korea Republic	11.61	12.98
Beijing, China	11.30	15.57
Osaka, Japan	10.61	10.61
Lagos, Nigeria*	10.29	24.61
Rio de Janeiro, Brazil	10.18	11.86
Delhi, India*	9.95	16.86
Karachi, Pakistan*	9.73	19.38
Cairo, Egypt	9.69	14.42
Paris, France	9.52	9.69
Tianjin, China	9.42	13.53
Metro Manila, Philippines*	9.29	14.66
Moscow, Russian Federation	9.27	9.30
Jakarta, Indonesia*	8.62	13.92
Dhaka, Bangladesh	8.55	19.49

*Cities expected to grow by more than 50 percent by 2015.
Source: World Resources Institute (http://www.wri.org).

Central Asia rank highest. East and Southeast Asian nations rank slightly above Central and South American countries, with Middle Eastern, African, and South Asian countries ranking lowest. (South Asia, remember, is primarily dominated by India.) There is, of course, more complexity within each region, but levels of economic development generally correspond to these indexes.

The United Nations publishes a Gender Development Index that ranks countries on the positions of women in government, life expectancy, literacy, education level, and income compared to men. Table 2.10 ranks 144 nations based on U.N. data. We find the world's poorest countries ranked in the lowest positions in the world.

The position of women in Thailand provides a good example of gender empowerment and economic development. The situation for women in Thailand is rather complex these days because of a large population of people with Chinese

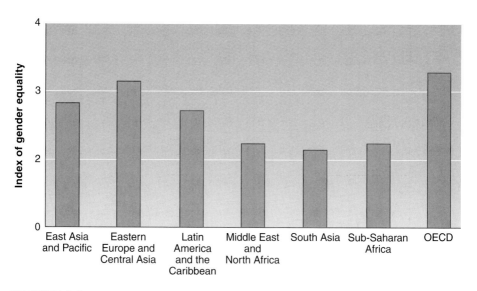

FIGURE 2.5   *Gender Inequalities in Basic Rights by Region*

*This basic rights index comes from a combination of three indexes measuring political and legal rights, social and economic rights, and rights in marriage and divorce proceedings.

NOTE: A value of 1 indicates low gender equality in rights; a value of 4 indicates high equality.

SOURCE: Adapted from World Bank, 2001a:4. Original research from Humana, 1992.

heritage that have intermarried with Thais of non-Chinese ancestors. Some of the Chinese traditions of male dominance have been transported to urban areas in Thailand. Also, the political position of Thai women is quite low, creating a relatively high "gender gap" score for Thailand on the United Nations Gender Development Index. However, the male–female income gap in Thailand is equal to most in rich nations, with more than half of professional and technical positions held by women in Thailand (UNDP, 2004b:222). Thai women are also represented in top positions in the business world in percentages higher than in many industrial nations (Kulick & Wilson, 1996:77–79; Pasuk & Baker, 1996:111–114; UNDP, 2000a; World Bank, 2000). Of the top 10 exporting corporations accounting for much of Thailand's rapid growth in the 1980s and early 1990s, 7 had a majority of women at the top. In medicine, universities, and in other professions, women account for a large percentage of the positions. Overall, female participation in the labor force is 70 percent, among the highest in the world. In a particularly striking contrast to other developing countries today, women account for approximately 50 percent of university students in Thailand. The strong influence of Thai women within the family is no doubt one reason for the success Thailand has had in reducing population growth (Kulick & Wilson, 1996:72; UNDP, 2000a).

Social scientists agree that one traditional practice has especially favored the status of Thai women—a *matrilocal* family system in most Thai peasant areas. A matrilocal family system refers to one in which daughters inherit the land while the men they marry move onto the daughters' family land. It is not difficult to realize how this

TABLE 2.10

United Nations Gender Development Index, 2004

GDI ranks for 144 countries			
1 Norway	49 Russian Federation	74 Peru	99 Egypt
2 Sweden	50 Mexico	75 Paraguay	100 Morocco
3 Australia	51 Belarus	76 Jordan	101 Namibia
4 Canada	52 Malaysia	77 Tunisia	102 Botswana
5 Netherlands	53 Panama	78 Dominican Republic	103 India
6 Iceland	54 Albania	79 Ecuador	104 Ghana
7 Belgium	55 Mauritius	80 Belize	105 Cambodia
8 United States	56 Romania	81 Guyana	106 Papua New Guinea
9 United Kingdom	57 Ukraine	82 Iran, Islamic Rep. of	107 Lao People's Dem. Rep.
10 Finland	58 Venezuela	83 Cape Verde	108 Comoros
11 Switzerland	59 Colombia	84 El Salvador	109 Swaziland
12 Japan	60 Brazil	85 Uzbekistan	110 Bangladesh
13 Denmark	61 Thailand	86 Equatorial Guinea	111 Cameroon
14 Ireland	62 Jamaica	87 Viet Nam	112 Congo
15 France	63 Kazakhstan	88 Syrian Arab Republic	113 Uganda
16 Luxembourg	64 Lebanon	89 Algeria	114 Kenya
17 Austria	65 Armenia	90 Indonesia	115 Sudan
18 New Zealand	66 Philippines	91 Moldova, Rep. of	116 Nepal
19 Germany	67 Turkmenistan	92 Bolivia	117 Lesotho
20 Spain	68 Oman	93 Tajikistan	118 Zimbabwe
21 Italy	69 Fiji	94 Mongolia	119 Togo
22 Israel	70 Turkey	95 Honduras	120 Pakistan
23 Hong Kong, China (SAR)	71 China	96 South Africa	121 Madagascar
24 Portugal	72 Saudi Arabia	97 Nicaragua	122 Nigeria
25 Greece	73 Sri Lanka	98 Guatemala	123 Haiti
26 Slovenia			124 Mauritania
27 Barbados			125 Gambia
28 Singapore			126 Yemen
29 Korea, Rep. of			127 Eritrea
30 Cyprus			128 Senegal
31 Malta			129 Rwanda
32 Czech Republic			130 Benin
33 Estonia			131 Tanzania, U. Rep. of
34 Poland			132 Cote d'Ivoire
35 Hungary			133 Zambia
36 Argentina			134 Malawi
37 Lithuania			135 Chad
38 Slovakia			136 Congo, Dem. Rep. of the
39 Bahrain			137 Ethiopia
40 Chile			138 Central African Republic
41 Uruguay			139 Mozambique
42 Kuwait			140 Burundi
43 Croatia			141 Guinea-Bissau
44 Costa Rica			142 Mali
45 Latvia			143 Burkina Faso
46 Bahamas			144 Niger
47 Trinidad and Tobago			
48 Bulgaria			

Note: The Gender Development Index is based upon a scale including the gender gap in life expectancy, literacy, educational attainment, and income inequality.
Source: UNDP, 2004b:220.

tradition has given women a distinct advantage with respect to influence in the family and economy (Girling, 1981:5).

Environment

We often hear charges that multinational corporations go to poor countries to escape environmental protection laws. But when rich countries like the United States try to lecture less developed countries about its environmental record, there is usually an embarrassing response. With some forms of environmental pollution the United States is by far the world's leader. For example, the United States is the world's biggest air polluter, annually pumping out over 20 tons of carbon dioxide *per person*, more than double any other country in the world. All of the other rich countries are far below this level (U.S. Bureau of the Census, 1999:839). But without improvement in environmental protection laws, when some of the world's less developed countries reach even half the level of economic development achieved by the world's rich countries today, the world's environment will be in crisis. For example, the United States now has about 75 motor vehicles per 100 people. China and India have less than 1 vehicle per 100 people. What happens when these two nations, accounting for over one-third of the total world's population, reach even half the U.S. level of car ownership? Where is the world to find all of the oil to power those additional automobiles in India and China?

Many sources of environmental destruction, though, are more often found in less developed countries. Thailand, for example, used to be a land abundant in beautiful hardwood trees such as teak. Traveling around the country today one sees few of these trees. Some 70 percent of Thailand's teak forests are gone because of overlogging. In neighboring Cambodia and Burma the same thing is occurring. Thailand now has a rather strong environmental movement with more laws enacted to protect the Thai environment. Cambodia and Burma do not, which means logging companies move into those much poorer countries. Today only 25 percent of the world's original forest cover remains in undisturbed forests. Over the past 150 years, deforestation has caused about 30 percent of the atmospheric buildup of CO_2 which is adding to global warming and the destruction of ecosystems around the world. The next environmental crisis on the horizon is water shortage. It is now estimated that about 30 percent of the world's population experiences water shortages. In 30 years that number is likely to be two-thirds of the world's population.[4] In the future, in other words, environmental pollution and depletion of resources will not only cause disease and death themselves, they will also slow economic development causing more hunger and diseases poverty produces. The world's poor will be hurt the most.

World Regions: A Historical and Contemporary Introduction

Before leaving our overview of world poverty it will be useful to consider each world region in more detail. When attempting to answer questions of why some countries are so poor while others are improving it is necessary to understand the commonalities as well as differences of nations in each world region. We can start with the cradle of humanity and the region now deep in crisis—Africa.

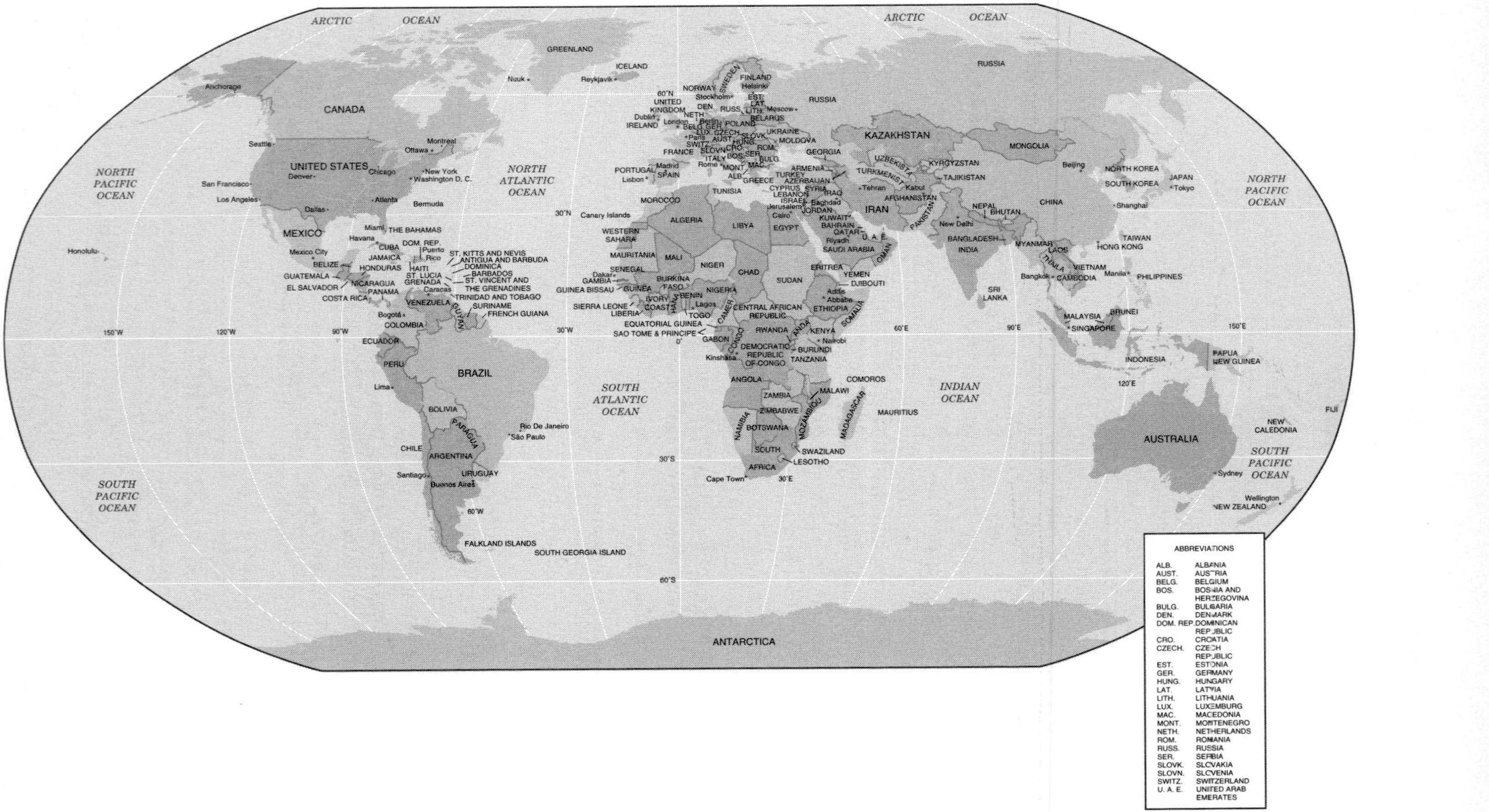

MAP 2.1

ABBREVIATIONS

ALB.	ALBANIA
AUST.	AUSTRIA
BELG.	BELGIUM
BOS.	BOSNIA AND HERTEGOVINA
BULG.	BULGARIA
DEN.	DENMARK
DOM. REP.	DOMINICAN REP JBLIC
CRO.	CROATIA
CZECH.	CZECH REP JBLIC
EST.	ESTONIA
GER.	GERMANY
HUNG.	HUNGARY
LAT.	LATVIA
LITH.	LITHUANIA
LUX.	LUXEMBURG
MAC.	MACEDONIA
MONT.	MONTENEGRO
NETH.	NETHERLANDS
ROM.	ROMANIA
RUSS.	RUSSIA
SER.	SERBIA
SLOVAK.	SLOVAKIA
SLOVN.	SLOVENIA
SWITZ.	SWITZERLAND
U. A. E	UNITED ARAB EMIRATES

Oceans: ARCTIC OCEAN, NORTH PACIFIC OCEAN, SOUTH PACIFIC OCEAN, NORTH ATLANTIC OCEAN, SOUTH ATLANTIC OCEAN, INDIAN OCEAN

Labeled regions and countries include: CANADA, UNITED STATES, MEXICO, GREENLAND, ICELAND, BRAZIL, ARGENTINA, CHILE, PERU, BOLIVIA, PARAGUAY, URUGUAY, COLOMBIA, ECUADOR, VENEZUELA, GUYANA, SURINAME, FRENCH GUIANA, RUSSIA, KAZAKHSTAN, CHINA, MONGOLIA, INDIA, IRAN, AUSTRALIA, NEW ZEALAND, PAPUA NEW GUINEA, INDONESIA, JAPAN, NORTH KOREA, SOUTH KOREA, TAIWAN, PHILIPPINES, ANTARCTICA

Africa: The Origins of Human Development and a Continent in Crisis

Regional groupings often include North Africa and the Middle East as distinct for Sub-Saharan Africa. In many ways the categorization makes sense. Most North African countries are predominantly Islamic, as are countries in the Middle East. Like many Middle Eastern countries, many North African countries also have substantial oil reserves. Algeria, for example, is the world's 17th largest oil producer and Libya is the world's 19th largest. Little Tunisia even produces over 72,000 barrels of oil per day (U.S. CIA, 2003). Like Middle Eastern countries, countries of North Africa are also more likely to be directly linked to ancient civilizations. None of the countries in North Africa are even close to the league of rich nations, but once one descends south through the Sahara Desert the picture changes dramatically.

Most Sub-Saharan countries are among the world's poorest. In fact, of the world's poorest countries in terms of per capita GNP, all but 8 of these poorest countries are in Sub-Saharan Africa (ranks 200 to the poorest country, ranked 231). However, not all Sub-Saharan countries are in crisis. Botswana's economy has experienced healthy growth for some years (in part because of new diamond mines), as has Mozambique after independence from Portugal and the end of civil war. South Africa is the richest nation in Sub-Saharan Africa with a per capita GNP (PPP) of over $10,000. But almost all the other countries in the region are found on the worst end of all world rankings, from percent of the country's people living on less than $1 per day, and infant mortality and life expectancy, to levels of political violence and political instability. Zambia and Nigeria, for example, have about 70 percent of their people living on less than $1 per day. Of the 25 countries with the highest infection rates of HIV and AIDS, only 1, Haiti at 24th, is not in Sub-Saharan Africa.[5] In contrast to all of these terrible rankings for Sub-Saharan Africa is the continent's wealth of natural resources. As asked by the African author Ali Mazrui, "if Africa is so rich, why are its people so poor?" (Mazrui, 1986).

Some of the obvious reasons for African poverty are unstable, inefficient, and corrupt governments. But that begs the question of why these governments are too often this way. Other obvious answers are related to European colonialism. This colonial experience was most brutal and disruptive compared to other world regions during the 1800s and early twentieth century. But again we need to probe further. Sub-Saharan Africa had a lower level of technology compared to many Asian nations before European colonizers took over the continent in the nineteenth century, and no national governments with the power to protect their people. After examination of the modern world system in coming chapters we will return to explore the roots of these African problems in more detail.

East and Southeast Asia: A Region on the Move

The vibrant countries of East and Southeast Asia present one of the most striking contrasts to African countries. With the major exception of North Korea (with a harsh communist dictatorship, and one of the world's poorest countries), as we move from China, South Korea, and Japan down to Taiwan, Thailand, Vietnam, Malaysia, and Indonesia, we encounter countries where economic development is proceeding at

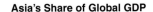
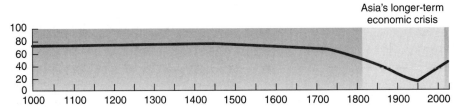

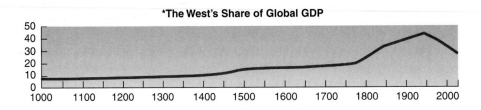

FIGURE 2.6   *Share of Global Economy, AD 1000 to 2000, Asia versus the West*

*The West includes Western Europe, the United States and Canada.

SOURCE: World Bank projections from Kristof and WuDunn, 2000:344.

high to moderate levels. There are striking exceptions: Cambodia, Laos, and Burma (Myanmar) are among the world's poorest countries with little prospects for economic development in the near future. But these are exceptions in a region of hot economic activity.

Many of the countries of East and Southeast Asia have ancient civilizations going back for thousands of years. Few Westerners realize that East, Southeast, and South Asia (primarily India) had the most economically dominant countries in the world a few centuries ago. To use a pop phrase, "they're back." Figure 2.6 indicates that for most of the last 1,000 years this region of the world accounted for far more of the world's economic activity and wealth than did Europe and North America. Most of this economic strength was in China and India, but there were trading empires scattered throughout Southeast Asia between the China and India trade routes. China was far ahead of the West in many areas of science and technology at about AD 1500. In the early 1400s China had the biggest navy the world has yet to see, with some 3,000 ships far bigger and more advanced than any others in the world (Kristof & WuDunn, 2000; Levathes, 1994; Menzies, 2002). We know that this huge fleet of ships sailed over much of the world, trading in Africa and the Middle East, as well as throughout Asia. There is even some evidence (though very little thus far) that a Chinese fleet sailed to the Americas long before Columbus in 1492. The West moved ahead of this broad Asian region only from the beginning of the 1800s. Already in the twenty-first century this region has pulled even with or ahead of Europe and North American in percent share of the world's GNP. One recent attempt to include all economic activity in every country, often not reported by government data or World Bank estimates, gives the United States the usual number one rating, but then lists China, Japan, and India as second, third, and fourth until we reach Germany at fifth (*International Herald Tribune,* May 23, 2001; U.S. CIA, 2003). The populations of China and India are each over 1 billion, of course, so the per capita GNP, or average standard of living, is lower in these two nations. But the fact remains that in overall economic size they are huge, and in the case of China, growing rapidly.

Other than their economic vibrance and ancient civilizations, however, there is less to unite the nations of East and Southeast Asia than most non-Asians recognize. There is a greater verity of cultures and languages in this part of the world than anywhere else. There are some common themes of the different sects of Buddhism found through most of the region, but there are other religious philosophies that divide them. During the 1400s, for example, when Islamic empires were still strong in the Middle East, a wave of Islam spread through Southeast Asia. About 60 and 90 percent of the populations of Malaysia and Indonesia and from 5 to 10 percent of Thailand and the Philippines are Muslim. Indonesia is the world's fourth most populous country and the largest Muslim country in the world. Christianity has not had much impact on most countries in East and Southeast Asia, but major exceptions are South Korea and the northern half of the Philippines, where almost half and 90 percent respectively are Christian. We have seen that governments in East and Southeast Asia range from the most democratic in the world to very undemocratic. North Korea is perhaps the most repressive country in the world today. China, Vietnam, and Laos are still communist countries, though the first two countries are perhaps better described as "state socialist market economies" with economic reforms making them behave like capitalist countries.

One commonality throughout East and Southeast Asia, though, was domination by European colonial powers. Every country in the region except Japan and Thailand was a colony of European powers until sometime in the twentieth century. China was cut up into spheres of control by several European powers, while the British, French, and Dutch were most dominant throughout Southeast Asia (though Spain ruled the Philippines until the United States took it in 1898). But we will see that these European powers affected the countries of East and Southeast Asia quite differently, setting the stage for the ease or difficulties these countries faced with economic development in the second half of the twentieth century.

South Asia: Stagnation and Poverty

The region called South Asia includes India, Pakistan to the northwest of India, Nepal and Bangladesh to the northeast, and the island country of Sri Lanka to the south of India. At one time in history all these areas were dominated by India, with India's influence extending through much of Southeast Asia as well. During the 1700s the British slowly began moving into India, taking more and more territory, until all of South Asia was a colony of the British by the mid-1800s. Soon after World War II, in 1947, British colonialists were pushed out by Gandhi's social movement. In one of the most tragic blows to India and Gandhi's hopes, however, independence brought civil war between the Hindus and Muslims. To settle the conflict Pakistan broke away from India, with the Hindus moving out of Pakistan into India and the Muslims moving into Pakistan. Later, civil war again broke out between the two divided parts of Pakistan because the much poorer eastern side of the country felt neglected and exploited. The result was an independent nation of Bangladesh in 1972.

With 1.1 billion people, India is often called the world's largest democracy because of its parliamentary system inherited from the British colonial period. But despite its relatively good score on the Weberianness scale noted earlier, most people describe India's inherited colonial administration as one of the most obstructive government bureaucracy's in the world (see Chibber, 2002). While India's middle class is larger than that of the United States in sheer numbers, and has more scientists and engineers than the United States, India continues to have one of the biggest concentrations of poverty in the world. India's average income was only $2,670 in 2002, but even worse is that 35 percent of Indians live on less than $1 per day, and 80 percent live on less than $2 per day (U.N., 2004b:148). There is finally some hope for economic development and poverty reduction in the future, with the number living on less than $1 per day expected to shrink by about 20 percent in the next 10 years. Still, India will remain one of the world's poorest countries, with other social problems like AIDS also advancing rapidly. All of this is in a country that 300 years ago formed an economic block with China that was the world's most powerful at the time. Why China is more rapidly pulling itself out of extreme poverty while India is having difficulty doing so will be a theme in coming pages of this book.

It is interesting that Pakistan has actually shown more economic growth and poverty reduction than India in recent years, with just over 13 percent of Pakistanis now living on less than $1 per day, though over 65 percent are under $2 per day. As was shown in Table 2.4, Pakistan is certainly not a democracy but has a government efficiency rating that is quite high. The future of Pakistan is in doubt, however, because of organized terrorist groups on its borders and many supporters of Osama bin Laden in the country.

Sri Lanka, on the other hand, has the lowest poverty rate of South Asia, with only 6 percent of its people living on less than $1 per day, though that number will no doubt increase dramatically after the terrible tsunami at the end of 2004. Sri Lanka is a Buddhist country and the country that helped spread Theravada Buddhism throughout Southeast Asia during the seventh century. Political and religious conflict has raged for the last several decades, with one faction allied with India. Only now this civil war has some hope of cooling, and with it, much better hope for further economic development and poverty reduction.

Finally, Bangladesh and Nepal are among the world's poorest countries, both having about 30 percent of their people living on less than $1 per day. Whereas India has a higher rate of extreme poverty, at least prospects for poverty reduction appear greater for India. In Bangladesh and Nepal per capita GNP increased to about $600 between 1990 and 2001. Bangladesh has at last achieved some political stability and prospects for improvement, while Nepal is in the midst of a revolution involving communist rebels.

Latin America: Economic Development without Poverty Reduction

As we all read in our high school history books, what is now South and Central America had some of the world's earliest agrarian empires. The best evidence suggests that what would later be called American Indians arrived in the American continent from Asia some 20,000 to 25,000 years ago. Long before Europeans arrived these settlers from Asia had already established the empires we know of as the Incas, Maya, and Aztecs.

Even though they practiced some advanced agriculture for their age and were able to create large cities, their civilization was not sustainable. By the time Europeans arrived some 500 years ago, these old civilizations had already been in decline for centuries. Military conquest and disease brought by Europeans finished them off. It is difficult to say how much of the native civilizational legacy remains in Central and South America. Colonization by Spain and Portugal was established much earlier than it was by Europeans in African and Asia, and soon settlers from Europe, along with European values and institutions, came to almost completely dominate the region.

Colonization also ended much earlier in Central and South America than in Africa or Asia. When the European powers began taking territory in Asia and Africa in the early 1800s most of Latin America was already independent from this colonial rule. Countries such as Chile, Argentina, and Brazil were already achieving some economic development in the late 1800s and early twentieth century, though it was highly dependent upon U.S. corporate dominance. For our focus on world poverty, however, it is the nature of these more developed economies that is most important. Latin American countries have become very unequal societies with extremes of poverty and wealth existing side-by-side. Brazil is the world's second most unequal society. It has a modern economy making all kinds of industrial goods, but with 17 percent of its people living on less than $2 per day. The poorest 20 percent of Brazilians receive only 2.5 percent of national income while the richest 20 percent of Brazilians receive about 64 percent of all income. Chile as well has a rather modern industrial society, but over 17 percent of its population live on less than $2 per day. Chile is only slightly less unequal, with the bottom 20 percent of people getting about 3.4 percent of income while the top 20 percent gets 61 percent of all income. Their northernmost Latin American neighbor, Mexico, has about 26 percent of its people living on less than $2 per day, and 10 percent living on less than $1 per day. Like Chile, Mexico is only slightly less unequal than Brazil. Other Latin American countries have even higher levels of extreme poverty: Ecuador has over 40 percent of its population living on less than $2 per day.

One of the most important things we need to explore later in this book is how more than a century of economic dominance from the United States has affected Latin American economies. Related to this, we need to consider how political and economic institutions in Latin America, which are more similar to those in the United States, have resulted in more poverty and unevenly distributed economic development when compared to political and economic institutions in East and Southeast Asian countries.

Eastern Europe and Central Asia: Overcoming Communism?

Unless one recognizes the Western bias in regional terminology, regional labels sometimes sounds rather odd today. I have always found the name of the most important university center for the study of Africa, the Middle East, and Asia—located in Great Britain—rather strange. The name is the School for Oriental and African Studies (SOAS), and it is attached to the University of London. Africa, of course, is Africa. But Oriental is everyone else east of Europe until you reach the Pacific Ocean. A rather wide and diverse group of peoples and countries to say the least. The old term "the Far East" is also rather unusual when you think about it. East of whom? How far is far? Where I live, New York is the Far East.

To be more precise and less biased, the region east of the Central and Western European countries all the way to East and South Asia is generally referred to as Eastern Europe and Central Asia. Even though a bit more precise, this geographical grouping contains nations that have very different civilizations and prospects for economic development in the twenty-first century. The countries of Eastern Europe used to be among the most advanced in Europe. One of the first European empires, the Habsburg Empire, held much of Eastern Europe by AD 1200. By the 1500s it contained what is now Austria, Hungary, Slovakia, the Czech Republic, Poland, and much of the old Yugoslavia. Traveling through this part of the world today one sees the old grandeur of cathedrals and castles of this earlier age. Eastern Europe's problems of the twentieth century were related to superpower politics. First they were in the middle of World Wars I and II, and then dominated by the Soviet Union until the beginning of the 1990s. The communist governments put in place by the Soviets crushed economic progress as well as human rights. Still, soon after the end of communism in this part of the world the poverty level in these countries was very low by African and even Latin American standards. Most of these countries have less than 1 or 2 percent of their people living on less than $1 per day. With the fall of communism, this part of the world has some of the best prospects for renewed economic development. In 2004, several of these East European countries formally joined the European Union. They are almost certain to get a strong economic boost with open markets throughout all of the European Union countries.

The prospects for Central Asia are more varied and less certain. Central Asia was once the middle of one the biggest empires in history. Some 1,500 years ago nomadic Asian tribes led by Attila the Hun and his descedents held territory from China and into much of what is Europe today. But this empire was not to last long, and it was dominance by Russia and then the Soviet Union that shaped prospects for people of this region in the nineteenth and twentieth centuries. At the beginning of the twenty-first century, countries such as Tajikistan, Kyrgyzstan, and Azerbaijan are among the poorest in the region, with well over half their population living in poverty. (The World Bank has yet to supply $1 per day figures for these newly independent Central Asian countries so we must rely on less comparable methods of defining poverty.) Tajikistan's 2002 per capita GNP was only $900, though it was more than $2,000 for other countries in the region, including some with a per capita GNP of over $4,000. Many of these Central Asian countries have oil resources, but most also have unstable and very corrupt governments. The mix of Asian and Islamic civilizations has also led to conflict and opposition movements that are likely to keep these countries from achieving much economic development and poverty reduction in the near future.

The Middle East: Ancient Civilizations in Conflict

We can conclude with a region of the world that Western countries hear much about but know so little about. The Middle East, as we know, is a region of ancient civilizations and the birth place of the most populous monotheistic religions—Christianity, Judaism, and Islam. These religions began some 1,500 to more than 2,000 years ago, and are all three interrelated, each sharing some of the prophets and religious leaders in their own religious history. The central source of their conflict today is their ancient status, all claiming the same region. Century upon century there were movements in and out of specific areas by these central religious groups, each group taking and losing territory to the other groups. The centuries' old claims and counterclaims are almost impossible to reconcile.

On a more global scale, Christianity and Islam have repeatedly clashed as one group spread its following only to decline and have the other reclaim the region. It was the Roman Empire that spread Christianity through much of what is Europe, Central Europe, and parts of the Middle East until the Roman Empire collapsed some 1,500 years ago. Mongol invaders from Central Asia stepped in to take up some of the power vacuum from the fall of the Roman Empire about the time Islam was born. An Islamic Empire quickly began its spread throughout the Middle East, North Africa, and into much of Europe. But as the Renaissance pulled Christian Europe out of its "Dark Ages," the centuries-long clash between Christian Europe and Islam in the Middle East began. One of world history's lowest points began just before AD 1100 as the Crusades began with European Christians marching to battle against Islam. There were a total of eight Crusades between AD 1097 and 1212, with many thousands of Muslims killed. An eyewitness account described the religious "frenzy": "The slaughter was terrible; the blood of the conquered ran down the streets, until men splashed in blood as they rode." (Wells, 1971:564).

After the Crusades, Islam began losing control in the western realms of its empire, but spread even more to its east, through Central Asia, South Asia, and Southeast Asia by the 1400s. The end of World War I in 1918, however, brought down the last of the Islamic Empire, the Ottoman Empire based in Turkey, which was allied with Germany. Before and after World War I, the nations and people of the Middle East were almost completely taken over by European colonial regimes. The new oil riches were exploited and countries in the region had new boundaries drawn to suit the needs of European powers without much regard to natural and historic boundaries. Middle Eastern leaders trying to throw off European dominance were disposed by European, and later American military or covert actions to keep cheap oil flowing (see, for example, Mosley, 1978; Roosevelt, 1979). Although the nations of the Middle East are now free of any formal colonial control from Western nations, Islamic countries in the Middle East today continue to have little trust of Western nations. But they are also without a central unifying nation able to focus this opposition to the West (see Huntington, 1996). The region is at conflict within itself as much as with Western nations and Israel. This is especially so after the Israeli revolution in 1948 took control of what was before that time the country of Palestine, sending hundreds of thousands of Palestinians from their homes and into refugee camps around the Middle East.

It is this state of conflict and disarray that has left much poverty in the Middle East, though not nearly as much poverty as many other places in the world. Not including the very small oil rich countries such as Kuwait and Qatar, and also not including Israel, Turkey and Iran have the highest per capita GNPs using the new Purchasing Power Parity estimate for 2002, both around $7,000. Lebanon and Jordan are next at around $5,000 and $4,000 per capita. Syria comes in at just over $3,000 and Iraq at $2,500 (before the war with the United States which began in 2003). Yemen and the Gaza Strip territory (full of Palestinians displaced by Israel) are by far the poorest with per capita GNPs at only $700. But while we have less complete data compared to other world regions, even the countries with higher GNPs per capita have high poverty rates by the old World Bank measure. (We do not have $1 per day figures for these countries.) Iran, for example, is listed as having more than 50 percent of its population living in poverty, with Jordan and Lebanon at about 30 percent of their people in poverty.

World Poverty: Conclusion and Next Questions

With this broad survey of poverty around the world we are ready to take up the next questions. We need to know why some countries and world regions have much more poverty than others. We need to know the prospects for reducing poverty in countries and regions around the world. In coming chapters we will pay most attention to Latin America, Africa, and Asia. We will focus on Latin America because it is a region with fairly good economic development, but mostly unevenly spread development and continuing high rates of poverty. We will focus on Africa because Sub-Saharan Africa has the world's highest and most persistent rates of poverty And we will focus on East and Southeast Asia because the region contains some of the world's most dynamic countries as we enter the twenty-first century. While some Southeast Asian countries remain among the world's poorest (such as Burma, Laos, and Cambodia), several other countries in East and Southeast Asia have had the best records of poverty reduction in the world. *We need to know how they have done it.* We need to know what lessons we can gain to help people in other world regions.

Before considering these questions, however, we must examine the history of the global economy and relations between rich and poor countries in this history. The perspective known as modern world system theory has been especially useful in understanding this history, as well as the impact of the global economy on both rich and poor nations today.

Notes

1. Information comes from the United Nations, World Health Organization, and other international health and aid agencies. Recently summarized reports from these agency reports can be found in the *International Herald Tribune,* October 5, 1999, December 13, 1999, and July 6, 2000, and the *Los Angeles Times,* July 11, 2000.
2. All figures in this section can be found in World Bank publications, like the annual *World Development Report,* and information on the Web from the World Resource Institute (http://www.wri.org) and Population Reference Bureau (http://www.prb.org), both in Washington, DC.
3. See several reports by the World Resource Institute (http://www.wri.org) and the World Resource Bureau (http://www.wrb.org).
4. World Resource Institute http://www.wri.org.
5. All data cited in this section come from the World Bank, United Nations, the CIA publication *World Factbook,* or university research data listed in the remarkable new Web service Nation Master (http://www.nationmaster.com).

The Modern World System: Explanations of Globalization and Conflict

The Jarawa tribes of hunter-gatherers inhabit a small island off the coast of Burma in the Andaman Sea. Today members of this tribe live much as they have for thousands of years. Their isolation was recently demonstrated when one young Jarawan boy was found injured by outsiders and taken to a hospital. This boy, named Enmay, had never seen electric lights, TV, and was even "frightened by the water tap, a strange metal object on the wall which when twisted magically produced water (BBC News, 2004a). At first thought, people of the modern world might consider these people "backward," even ignorant, but such is certainly not the case. They simply live in another type of world where their knowledge is much greater than ours. One example of this was demonstrated during the terrible tsunami that hit the region in December of 2004. Tribal people along the southern part of the island chain had survival skills the others lacked; ancient traditions told them that when the seas suddenly become almost empty, run for higher ground (*Los Angeles Times*, February 3, 2005). Today these people are safe. Tens of thousands of others stood and watched the exposed beaches in amazement, not realizing a huge tsunami was on its way to kill them.

Only some 250 of these people remain today, members of six different tribes on two of these islands. Not long ago there were 12 tribes. The Indian government that controls the islands has tried to keep the Jarawa people isolated in hopes they will not be wiped out by diseases, as happened when other tribal people in the area had contact with the outside world. There is also hope their old traditions will survive, especially their impressive knowledge of herbal medicines in their jungle habitat. But their days as hunter-gatherers are clearly numbered. The Jarawa may be among the last remaining people to be brought into the global economy. Settlers from other islands have been allowed to take parts of the island belonging to the Jarawa, and wild game is becoming scarce. Not only do they need wild game for their food, but central tribal rituals are also associated with this wild game. Jarawa boys, for example, cannot be considered a man, nor can they marry, until they have tracked and killed a wild boar.

When we think about it, the isolation of the Jarawa tribe is somewhat amazing in today's global economy and also in the face of more than 1,000 years of a Pan-Asian economy that dominated the region. India and China were at opposite ends of this Asian-wide economy that was far greater than other regional economies until the global dominance of European countries emerged only 200 to 300 years ago. Thousands of huge ships must have sailed not many miles from the shores of the Jarawa tribe's island on their way between India and China over the centuries.

Others living in the region of the Jarawa tribe today are much more typical of people caught in the global economy. The high-tech Silicon Valley industries of California, for example, have drawn thousands of people from cities not far from the Jarawa people. Some 30 percent of all engineers in California computer software companies are from India (*International Herald Tribune*, April 3, 2001). The current global economy, or what can be called the modern world system, has brought almost all of the world's nations into economic conflict, conflict usually won by rich nations who have taken resources and people from the world's poorer nations. But we will see that this global competition does not benefit or harm everyone equally *within* each nation. Some people in poorer nations are made richer in this competition while many if not most of their fellow citizens remain poor. And many people within rich nations have much higher standards of living because of the exploitation of people in poorer nations, though many other people within rich nations are made poorer because half the world's population living on less than $2 per day is willing and able to work for much lower wages.

We will see, for example, that perhaps half of Americans are worse off because they must now compete with lower wage workers around the world as U.S. corporations move operations away from American shores to take advantage of this cheap labor. But we will also see that this economic harm to lower skilled American workers is not inevitable in today's global economy. European workers are much more protected by their governments, and such protection does not necessarily harm European economies.

Our main subject in this chapter, however, is how this modern world system developed about 500 years ago and how and why the wealthy nations of Europe and then North America came to dominate most other countries in the world by the 1800s. We will examine the characteristics of this modern world system and the characteristics of rich and poor nations within it. It is only with this understanding of the modern world system that we can then understand how some poor nations are hurt by this modern world system while others are not harmed. This will be the subject of the following chapter.

Characteristics of the Modern World System

Soon after the first industrial societies took root in the declining bed of European kingdoms about 250 years ago there was, no doubt, an increasing awareness that separate nations were more and more tied through economic exchange. But the extent of these economic ties grew more rapidly than the full awareness of their importance. In the early works of economists such as Adam Smith, for example, such awareness was not yet sufficient. In the mid-1800s Karl Marx did have something to say about the worldwide growth of capitalism, but he left the task of specifying how advanced capitalist nations would dominate others to Lenin (the "father" of the old Soviet Union) some 50 years later (Chase-Dunn, 1975:721–722; 1989). Still, Lenin's work on imperialism (or how rich nations would exploit poorer nations) remained incomplete in many details (Lenin, 1965).

It was not until after the middle of the twentieth century that an abundance of literature on what we know as the global economy or modern world system emerged (see, for example, Chase-Dunn, 2001; Chase-Dunn & Grimes, 1995; Chase-Dunn & Hall,

1997; Chirot, 2001; Grimes, 2000; Hall, 2000a, 2000b, 2002). Indeed, only in the last couple of decades has the full extent of what is now called globalization been widely recognized. While the magnitude of globalization is often exaggerated, there are abundant data on the impact of both economic and cultural globalization, a process bringing even the most remote people like the Jarawa tribe into the modern world system (Chase-Dunn, Kawano, & Brewer, 2000; Held, McGrew, Goldblatt, & Perraton, 1999).

To understand the basic nature of the modern world system, we must begin by recognizing the *worldwide division of labor.* In contrast to the traditional view of economic systems corresponding with political or national boundaries, an economic division of labor cuts across these boundaries, bringing national territories within a worldwide economic system (Wallerstein, 1974:348–349). Snyder and Kick (1979) summarize three main points in the modern world system perspective:

> First, the world system is the appropriate point of conceptual orientation. The behavior and experiences of its constituent geopolitical units depend fundamentally on features of the system as a whole (e.g., a capitalist world economy) which reflect transnational linkages. Second, the modern world system is composed of three structural positions: core, semiperiphery, and periphery. Third, these labels are not merely descriptive. They indicate an international division of labor in which the core is linked to the periphery (and semiperiphery) in dynamic and exploitative ways. (pp. 1099–1100)

Much like a class system or stratification system *within* a country, nations of the world today are divided into something like an international class system. Some nations own or control more of the world's resources, whereas other nations own little of the resources or control the resources (such as minerals, oil, or talented people) even when these resources are located within their country. Other nations are restricted to mainly doing the low-skilled work in the global economy, and receive much less of the world's income for their work. The richer nations of the global economy today are often able to prevent poorer countries from changing their position in the international stratification system, or modern world system, when changing this position may harm the interests of richer nations. Finally, because it is quite profitable for rich nations to dominate poorer nations, rich nations are often in conflict or competition among themselves to get as many poor nations as they can within their orbit, even when it means taking the poorer nation away from the obit of another rich nation. I must say again that there remain class divisions *within each nation,* each with differing interests with respect to these international ties. Americans in the top half of the income pile, for example, have certainly benefited from U.S. dominance of many poorer countries while Americans in the bottom half of the income pile have most often been harmed by this U.S. domination of poorer countries. But before we consider the differing class interests within the U.S. class system, we should proceed by examining the three primary class positions of nations within the world stratification system.

Similar to an upper class within a nation's stratification system are *core nations* in the modern world system (see, Bornschier, 1996; Bornschier & Chase-Dunn, 1985; Chase-Dunn, 1989; Chirot, 1986; Wallerstein, 1974:349–351). Core nations are more economically diversified, wealthy, and powerful (economically and militarily) in the modern world system. These core nations are highly industrialized; they specialize in information, finance, and other service industries, and they produce manufactured goods rather than raw materials for export. Core nations are more often in the forefront

TABLE 3.1

Examples of Core, Semiperiphery, and Periphery Nations in the Modern World System, 2000s

Core	Semiperiphery	Periphery
United States	Mexico	Chad
Japan	Argentina	Uganda
Germany	South Korea	Burma
Netherlands	Ireland	Laos
England	Chile	Bolivia
France	Thailand	Philippines
Italy	Taiwan	El Salvador
Canada	India	Haiti
Austria	Pakistan	Dominican Republic

Note: This table is a representative listing of contemporary nations in the structural positions in the world system from older data presented in research by Snyder and Kick, 1979. The partial list of nations in this table is from Snyder and Kick's study using trade relations, military interventions, and diplomatic and treaty ties as indicators of world system positions.

of new technologies and new industries, such as high-tech electronic and biotech industries today, or assembly-line auto production early in the twentieth century. Core nations also have a more complex occupational structure with generally less income inequality compared with the other nations. One of the most important characteristics of core nations is their complex and strong state institutions. These state institutions need a sufficient tax base so they can provide the infrastructure for a strong economy (such things as good schools, roads, and electric power), and they must be able to manage economic affairs internally and externally. Finally, these core nations have many means of influence over noncore nations but are themselves relatively independent of outside control (see Table 3.1 for examples of these nations).

Similar to a lower class or working class within a nation's class system are the periphery nations in the modern world system. Periphery nations are the least economically diversified and tend to depend upon one type of economic activity, such as extracting and exporting raw materials to the core nations. In recent decades, however, periphery nations have been targets for investments from multinational corporations from rich nations that come into the nation to exploit the cheap unskilled labor to make everything from automobiles to consumer electronic products for export back to rich nations. Because of their position in the global economy, periphery nations tend to have a high percentage of their people who are poor and uneducated. Inequality also tends to be very high in these nations because of a small upper class that generally owns most of the land and has profitable ties to multinational corporations that are in the country to take advantage of the mass of cheap labor. Most important, periphery nations have relatively weak state institutions with little tax base to support infrastructure development that can encourage more economic development and poverty reduction. Finally, core nations and their rich multinational corporations tend to have extensive influence over periphery nations, influence that often means that periphery nations are forced to follow economic policies that favor rich nations and harm the long-term economic prospects of periphery nations.

Semiperiphery nations tend to be midway between the core and periphery nations on all the above characteristics. They are much like a middle class within a nation's stratification system. Semiperiphery nations are often nations that have been able to achieve some economic development and are moving up the rank of nations because of more economic development, such as countries in East and Southeast Asia that have achieved rapid economic development in recent decades. Some of these semiperiphery nations, however, are on their way down the rank of nations, such as Argentina which has experienced several years of economic crisis. But for the most part, "While they are weaker than core societies, they are trying to overcome this weakness and are not as subject to outside manipulation as peripheral societies (Chirot, 1977:13).

Like a class system within a nation, class positions in relation to the modern world system result in an unequal distribution of rewards and resources. The upper-class or core nations receive the greatest share of income and profits, whereas periphery nations receive the least. Furthermore, because of the economic power of core nations, they are usually able to purchase raw materials and other goods from the noncore nations at low prices, while demanding higher prices for their exports to non-core nations. Some of the most important benefits coming to core societies from their domination of the periphery include (1) access to cheap raw materials, (2) cheap labor, (3) handsome profits from direct capital investments in periphery nations, (4) a market for exports, and (5) skilled professional people leaving periphery nations to use their skills and knowledge in and for the benefit of rich core nations. For non-core nations, and especially the periphery, there is typically an unequal exchange or exploitative relationship with core nations. It might appear (and the ideology pushed by core nations maintains) that periphery nations benefit from their relation with core nations. For example, the periphery nations get a market for their raw materials, military aid, factories built (and owned) by core multinational corporations providing jobs for their people, and technical equipment and expertise—all of which could help further economic development in the poor nations. However, although some benefits for periphery nations may be realized, the total impact of core domination often harms the economic and political well-being of people in periphery nations, especially in the long run. There are certainly differences among the noncore nations, especially in the noncore Asian nations compared with those in South America and Africa, as we will see in coming chapters. But these are outcomes common around the world's poorer nations.

We should conclude this section by again stressing the importance of economic factors behind the conflicts and changes in this modern world system. In his influential book *The Clash of Civilizations and Remaking of World Order,* Samuel Huntington has argued that civilizational divisions are again becoming more important after the fall of the old Soviet Union and at the end of the cold war (Huntington, 1996). No doubt these civilization ties are important in shaping national alliances. Most major nations have old cultural ties with either the Western/Christian civilization, Islamic civilization, Orthodox Christian civilization, Asian/Buddhist, or Hindu, to name some of the most important. But while such civilizational ties are important, a major point of modern world system theory is that economic forces are still most important and are becoming more important to what happens to nations and people in the world today.

A Brief History of the Modern World System

The founders of modern world system theory argued there have been only two types of world systems in history (see especially Wallerstein, 1974, 1980, 1989). The first type, world empire, existed in several periods of world history. Although never covering an area as large as today's world system, these world empires did include major parts of the world—for example, the Roman Empire, the Near Eastern empire of Alexander the Great, and the Egyptian and Babylonian empires much earlier. The major distinction between a world empire and today's modern world system is that a main goal of world empire was political, as well as economic, domination (Wallerstein, 1974:60). "In classical empires, a political elite, as opposed to a business elite, dominated policy. This elite was composed of soldiers, glory-seeking emperors, and learned but antibusiness religious officials" (Chirot, 1977:20). Core elites in the modern world system, by contrast, are economic elites concerned with economic profit. A subjected country in the modern world system is not usually controlled in every detail by core elites, occupied by a foreign army, or forced to pay taxes to the dominant country. These things would be rather inefficient in terms of the main goal, which is to extract profits for dominant core elites.

The original modern world system theory, it must be noted, had a strong Western bias because it neglected the extent that something much like the modern world system based upon economic principles existed in Asia for over 1,000 years. The Chinese and Indian economies dominated much of the world for that period, and the main objective of both countries was trade and not total cultural, political, or religious domination of other countries (Frank, 1998; Levathes, 1994; Menzies, 2002). We will consider this neglect of the earlier Asian economic systems in the next chapter because it has led to misunderstanding of Asian countries today. The distinction between world empires and the modern world system, however, is essential in understanding the development of the modern world system that led to European dominance of the world by the 1800s.

When conditions became ripe for a world economic system about 1450, Spain and Portugal took the lead. They were the first to establish extensive overseas colonies and explore the world for new territories. But Spain and Portugal soon lost their early lead, with other countries such as England, the Netherlands, and France becoming more powerful. These other nations learned a lesson that Spain and Portugal had not: It becomes too expensive to seek more than just economic dominance over many countries around the world (Chirot, 1977:18–20; Wallerstein, 1974:157–179). In short, Spain and Portugal became overextended with empire building and lost their earlier positions of power in the modern world system. This is not to say that some core countries within the modern world system today never attempt to gain extensive control over periphery nations, and to control them as their colonies. It is a matter of degree when comparing the control a dominant country tried to achieve in a world empire (say, the Roman Empire) with the modern world system. Since the 1600s there has been variation in the amount of control over periphery nations and colonization (Boswell, 1989). When the world economy is expanding and core nations are experiencing good economic times, there is less colonization, meaning core nations are not trying to achieve as much control over "their periphery nations." But during poor economic times these core nations tend to attempt more extensive colonial control to keep other core nations from having economic relations with their periphery nations.

Since the beginning of this modern world system there has always been a collection of core nations in competition with each other for economic dominance, hegemony over periphery nations, and access to the world's resources. At times the conflict is more overt and deadly, with shifting core alliances as nations try to gain better positions in the process of core conflict. At other times, however brief, there has been one core nation with clear economic dominance over other core nations in the world system. A core nation can be considered dominant over all others when it has a simultaneous lead in three economic rankings over an extended period of time (Wallerstein, 1980). First, *productivity dominance* is important. The nation with productivity dominance can produce products of higher quality and at a lower price compared with other nations. Second, productivity dominance can lead to *trade dominance*. In this situation the balance of trade favors the dominant nation because more nations are buying the products of the dominant nation than it is buying from them. Third, trade dominance can lead to *financial dominance*. With a favorable balance of trade, more money is coming into the nation than is going out. The bankers of the dominant nation tend to become the bankers of the world, with greater control of the world's financial resources.

When a nation achieves these three forms of economic dominance, military dominance is also likely. With a stronger economic base, and with interests tied to a world status quo worth protecting, the dominant core nation tends to build a strong military. In the modern world system, however, no country has been able to use military strength as a means to gain economic dominance. In fact, each of the previously dominant core nations has achieved economic dominance with relatively small levels of military spending as each rose to the top. Each of these dominate nations then lost economic dominance with later military expansion (Kennedy, 1987).

From the time this modern world system began in the 1400s to 1500s, there have been only three brief periods in which one core nation has come to dominate, with each period lasting less than 100 years (Wallerstein, 1980). The first country to have this clear dominance was the Netherlands during the 1600s. As Spain and Portugal tried to achieve this dominant position they failed when becoming overextended with too many military commitments and colonial territories to protect around the world (Kennedy, 1987:47–48). By the 1600s, however, the Dutch achieved this dominance after their political revolution led to a modernized state supporting capitalists, a new financial system some historians call "revolutionary," and the development of new technologies, especially with respect to efficient shipbuilding (Chirot, 1986:36; Kennedy, 1987:76). The Dutch shipbuilding industry also helped foster an economic lead through more exports to other nations, and the Dutch fleet provided an advantage in the race for colonies (Kennedy, 1987:67–86; Wallerstein, 1974).

By becoming the dominant core nation, however, the Netherlands set in motion a process that eventually led to its relative economic decline. First, other nations were able to copy the innovative production and banking methods created by the Dutch. With even newer production methods that were developed since the rise of the Dutch, and knowledge of what originally worked and did not work for the Dutch, other industrializing nations began to challenge Dutch economic dominance, particularly England and France. The productivity edge held by the Netherlands also declined with the rise in its standard of living, a result of its dominant core status. This relatively high standard of living pushed up production costs, making Dutch products somewhat less competitive

(Wallerstein, 1980:268–269). With loss of productivity dominance, the Dutch trade dominance was soon lost. And with trade dominance gone, financial dominance was eroded. Although the Netherlands continued to hold financial power, its bankers, seeking profitable investments, went outside the country to a greater degree than in the past. With the development of other industrial nations, Dutch bankers saw more profit potential in these other nations, and the flow of investment capital moved, especially to England (Kennedy, 1987:81). This outflow of investment capital further harmed the Dutch economic position even though it helped the profits of Dutch bankers.

With the Dutch in relative decline by the end of the 1600s, conflict among the core nations increased. There had always been wars among core nations, but now (1) the power of the Dutch to enforce world order was reduced, and (2) other nations were fighting for advantage to take the lead once held by the Dutch. The two main nations in this conflict at the time of Dutch decline were England and France. The Dutch had often fought the British, but by the early 1700s they were allies. It was Dutch financial investment that helped the English advance in productivity and trade, and it was Dutch military support that helped the English defeat the French. It should also be noted, however, that it was an outdated political structure and a rigid stratification system still dominated by the old agrarian aristocracy that hurt the French. The Dutch had what has been called the first "bourgeois revolution" in the 1560s that gave them more independence from the Hapsburgs in Spain, resulting in a new political system that favored the new capitalist class (Wallerstein, 1974:181). In England the capitalist class had achieved dominance over the old landed aristocracy by the 1700s, though this had happened more slowly, over an extended period of time compared with the Netherlands. But in France, the bourgeois revolution of 1789 came too late for French dominance in the new era of the modern world system and capitalist competition (Skocpol, 1979). Before 1789 the French government was still dominated by the old landed aristocracy, which resisted economic policies and financial reform that could have made its economy more competitive with England.

With British dominance of the modern world system by the 1800s there was again relative stability. It was especially a time of British expansion all over the world, with many colonies in Asia, Africa, and the Americas. But following the earlier pattern of the Dutch, the British also slid into a relative economic decline. The overextended colonial system placed a strain on the British military, the cost of which also contributed to British economic decline. Thus, like the Dutch, the British held clear dominance in the world system for a relatively short time—from about 1815 to the 1870s (Kennedy, 1987:226).

As in the 1700s, there was again extensive core conflict after the British lost their clear dominance. This time Britain and France were allies, with Germany, and later Japan and Italy, providing the new threat to their hegemony, or world dominance. Germany, and then Japan and Italy, were late developers among the industrial nations. It was German and Italian unification in the late 1800s that helped the rise of these two nations, and the Meiji Restoration beginning in 1868 that brought industrialization to Japan. The United States, of course, began its move toward achieving core nations status at this time, but there was a difference. By 1900 most of the periphery areas of the world had already been claimed by one of the older core nations (Chirot, 1986). In 1800 the old European core claimed 35 percent of the world's territory, whereas by 1914 this European core claimed an amazing 85 percent of the world's territory (Kennedy, 1987:150). The United States had thousands of square miles with plenty of natural resources it could steal from Native Americans. But if other new core nations wanted to expand and become stronger economically it meant they would have to take periphery areas from the older core nations. This the Germans, and then the Italians and Japanese, began to do in the first half of the twentieth century, setting the stage for World War I and World War II.

While the Germans, Italians, and Japanese were moving into core status in the world system in the late 1800s, of course, so was the United States. The defeat of the agrarian South in the American Civil War led to more power for Northern industrial elites who could pressure the American government for policies favoring industrial expansion. British bankers at this time were also directing more of their financial investment toward the United States as the British economy was in relative decline (as did the Dutch bankers when their relative decline was in process). And, like the Dutch and British at the time of their rise to core dominance, the United States had a very small military budget compared with those of all other industrial nations (Kennedy, 1987:248).

The United States began taking the place of Great Britain as the new dominant core nation after World War I. But with Europe and Japan in ruins after World War II, the United States was able to dominate the world system more than any other nation in the history of this world system. For example, soon after World War II, the United States alone accounted for over half of all the industrial production in the world, supplied one-third of all the world's exports, and owned two-thirds of the world's supply of gold reserves (Kennedy, 1987:358). Along with this economic dominance, the United States took over military dominance, becoming "policeman of the world" in protecting periphery areas seen as important to U.S. economic elites and their capitalist allies around the world. We currently hear the U.S. described as the only real "superpower" at the beginning of the twenty-first century. While this is basically the case when describing U.S. military power (though the Iraq War of 2003–2006 shows the United State has much less military power than it imagines), North America accounts for only about one-third of the world's economy, with Europe and East and Southeast Asia also accounting for almost one-third each.

Postwar Competition: The Rise and Fall of the Soviet Union

For most of the second half of the twentieth century there was the cold war: The United States took on the role as world watchdog for its capitalist allies in new core competition with the Soviet Union and its communist allied countries. By agreement at the end of World War II, the American and British forces met in Berlin, cutting Germany in half, with the American, British, and French forces occupying Western Europe while Soviet forces occupied Eastern Europe. At the very end of World War II in 1945 the Soviet Union also moved quickly to take parts of northeastern Asia from the defeated Japanese. It soon became clear that Soviet intentions were to create a new alliance against the capitalist bloc of core nations after World War II. Core competition in the modern world system had entered a new stage with the rise of the Soviet Union after their revolution in Russia in 1917. Soon after World War II the Soviet Union became the world's second largest economy after the United States, and of course a major military power.

By 1990, however, the Soviet Union had collapsed, bringing the cold war to a quick end. Almost no one had foreseen this collapse (for major exceptions, see Collins, 1981; Collins & Waller, 1992). But with hindsight we can see that the fall of the Soviet Union was not such a strange new event in the modern world system. Much like France in its wars and economic competition against Britain during the 1700s, the Soviet economy was weakened due to military competition with the United States. The Dutch, British, and Americans, you will remember, all had comparatively small military budgets when they were rising to core dominance: Military power came later. The Soviets, on the other hand, tried to achieve dominance in the modern world system through military might without first achieving the economic base to do so. The "house of cards" that once was the Soviet bloc in Eastern Europe fell as well. From the study of social movements, revolutions, and political violence, we know that these events do not occur only because people have become angry and fail to accept exploitation. Resource mobilization theory tells us, for example, that rebellions and revolutions usually become massive events and are successful due to changes in the balance of power between rebels and political authorities (Kerbo, 1982; McCarthy & Zald, 1977). During 1953, 1956, and 1968 there were major rebellions in East Germany, Poland, Hungary, and finally Czechoslovakia. During these rebellions against communism and Soviet dominance, Soviet tanks came in to crush the protest. In 1981, in the face of rebellion and the growing strength of the Solidarity movement in Poland, the Polish army itself stopped the movement and put leaders such as Lech Walesa in jail so that Soviet tanks would not come in again. But much had changed in the Soviet Union before the next round of east European rebellion occurred. By the late 1980s, the Solidarity movement was rising again in Poland. As East Europeans waited in fear, and the whole world watched in amazement, the Soviet tanks *did not* come in. Rather, Mikhail Gorbachev, who had taken over rule of the Soviet Union in 1985, began taking tanks out of Hungary in 1989. Before the end of the decade, the Berlin Wall had fallen, and so had communist governments all over Eastern Europe. As in previous centuries of the modern world system, international competition among the core had led to the downfall of a major power.

The United States did not come out of the cold war economically stronger, in contrast to the period right after World War II, even though the United States was the only military superpower after the fall of the Soviet Union. The American economy was badly damaged by years of focus on military spending, research and development for military production rather than consumer production, and a foreign policy oriented toward military competition rather than economic interests around the world. In a popular saying of the time, "The cold war is over; Japan won." In many respects, however, we should mention other winners as well, such as Germany. But with the cold war over the U.S. economic dominance returned—at least for a while. And of course the end of the cold war did not end U.S. action as the watchdog for capitalist industrial nations. Again and again, it was the United States that had to take the lead in protecting the capitalist nations' oil supplies in places like the Middle East, reestablishing stability in the former Yugoslavia, and now fighting terrorism directed against rich nations.

CASE IN POINT

Disappearing Foreign Aid

Most outcomes of the cold war between the United States and the Soviet Union were negative for the world, especially poor nations. The cold war meant that allies of one side in the superpower conflict were targets for the other superpower. The attempt was to pull them away from that alliance and bring the county into the other superpower orbit. If, for example, the country was on the U.S. side, the United States would support the government of that nation with military equipment and other aid, no matter how brutal, corrupt, and dictatorial that government might be. The Soviets would then support revolutionaries who would try to overthrow that U.S.-supported government. Millions of poor people in places like El Salvador, Indonesia, and Chile were killed when the Soviets back revolutionary movements. If the country was a Soviet ally then the United States would do the same, as it did in Nicaragua, Angola, Laos, and Cambodia. At times the superpowers became more directly involved in these wars rather than setting on the sidelines arming the government or rebels. For the United States, of course, this happened in Korea during the early 1950s and Vietnam from 1964 to 1973 where over 58,000 Americans and 2 million Vietnamese were killed. For the Soviets it was most bloody when they tried to defend a Soviet-backed government in Afghanistan through the 1980s. Then, as today, figures compiled by the World Bank show that about 90 percent of all cases of "civil war and strife" occurred in poor nations, with civilians much more likely to be killed than combatants (World Bank, 2000:50).

There were, however, a few positive outcomes of the cold war for poor nations. One of these was foreign aid. From the experience of "fighting communism" through rebuilding Europe after World War II with millions of dollars in Marshall Plan funds coming from the United States, foreign aid was seen as a tool of winning poorer countries to the side of the United States. But once the cold war was over in 1990 and communism no longer appeared a threat to global capitalism, American foreign aid began a dramatic drop. By 2002 U.S. foreign aid was at its lowest point since 1945 (*International Herald Tribune*, March 16, 2002). The following table shows just how far the United States is behind all other core nations in providing foreign aid. Americans tend to think they are a very generous people, and they certainly can be when it comes to private donations, as when millions were given to victims of the Asian tsunami after December of 2004. But these private donations pale compared to what rich governments give in aid. Because of its size, the United States provides more actual dollars in foreign aid than most other countries (Japan is number one here), though by far the biggest percentage of U.S. aid goes to Israel. On a per capita basis, or how much is given per person in foreign aid, however, the United States is the least generous of all major nations, though the United States retains its number one position as the world's biggest arms dealer, selling almost as much as all other countries combined (Table 3.2).

Many today have recognized that high levels of poverty are associated with the presence of global terrorist organizations in the country. International opinion polls also show a relationship between high levels of poverty and anger toward the United States.[1] So far, however, the idea that poverty can help breed violence against rich countries, especially the United States, has not led to serious discussions about increases in foreign aid from the United States.

(Continued)

(Continued)

TABLE 3.2

Shrinking Foreign Aid: Official Development Aid and Arms Sales by Rich Countries, 2000

Country by Rank in Giving	Foreign Aid as % GNP	Amount per Person in Donor Country (in U.S.$ equivalent)	% World's Arms Sales
Denmark	1.60%	$348	0.2%
Netherlands	0.84	221	1.8
Norway	0.80	276	0.2
Sweden	0.80	223	1.0
Belgium	0.36	91	0.5
Switzerland	0.34	137	0.3
France	0.32	80	8.6
Great Britain	0.32	79	6.6
Finland	0.31	80	0.0
Japan	0.28	102	0.0
Germany	0.27	71	5.4
Australia	0.27	56	0.5
Canada	0.25	55	0.9
Austria	0.23	60	0.1
Italy	0.13	27	1.7
United States	0.10	35	45.0

Sources: UNDP 2002:202, 216; World Bank, 2004d:262.

The Relative Decline, Then Reemergence of the United States

The 1970s came as a big shock to the United States. From the heights of world military and economic dominance during the 25 years immediately after World War II, the U.S. economy hit a period of relative decline, while in Vietnam the nation also lost its first war. This is not the place to go into all the details of this relative economic decline of the United States during the 1970s and 1980s (for discussions of this economic decline, see Bluestone & Harrison, 1982; Blumberg, 1980; Dietrich, 1991; Dore, 1987; Etzioni, 1984; Halberstam, 1986; Harrison & Bluestone, 1988; Reich, 1981; Thurow, 1991; Vogel, 1979, 1985). We have already seen the relative economic declines of previous core leaders that were never able to hold core dominance for as long as 100 years (and actually only between 50 and 75 years). Table 3.3 indicates the relative decline of U.S. productivity by the end of the 1970s. Looking at the base year of 1967 for all these countries in Table 3.3, we can see that U.S. productivity was growing, but not at nearly the rate as that of some of the other industrial nations in the world, especially Japan. U.S. corporate elites lost the competitive edge due to, among other things, a lack of real competition in a highly concentrated domestic

TABLE 3.3

Comparative Productivity Growth, 1970–1979
(base productivity in 1967 set at 100)

	1970	1975	1979
United States	104.5	118.2	129.2
Canada	114.7	133.3	156.3
France	121.2	150.7	189.9
West Germany	116.1	151.3	183.8
Japan	146.5	174.6	230.5
United Kingdom	108.8	124.2	133.0

Note: The base year of productivity in 1967 is set at 100 for every nation. Then each following year's productivity is compared with this base year. Thus, for the United States the 104.5 productivity figure in 1970
showed a slight increase over the 100 level for the 1967 base year.
Source: U.S. Bureau of the Census, 1980:913, Table 1591.

economy, a lack of reinvestment as well as research and development, and high production costs because the United States had the highest standard of living in the world.

After this relative decline in the U.S. economy became evident in the 1970s, the U.S. trade deficit grew to huge proportions in the 1980s. The U.S. trade imbalance was negative every year in the 1980s, and was well over $100 billion in the red for most years of the decade. Simply put, fewer and fewer countries were buying as many U.S.-made products while Americans were buying, and thus sending money to, other countries in the world. During the first half of the 1990s there was only slight improvement in this trade imbalance. Added to this was the United States' loss of financial dominance. At the beginning of the 1980s, the United States had the largest banks in the world, and more banks listed as among the 10 largest in the world than any other nation. By the end of the decade, however, the United States had only one bank among the world's top 10, while the top 8 banks in the world were all Japanese.

With the end of the cold war beginning in 1990, however, the U.S. economic decline was quickly reversed. Indeed, the United States began its longest economic boom in history that did not slow until 2001. As can be seen in Table 3.4, the United States led the seven largest industrial economies with annual growth in the economy (GNP), percent increases in domestic investment rate increases per year, and annual productivity increases while maintaining the lowest unemployment rate (with the exception of Japan which keeps unemployment artificially low even in times of economic stagnation). The U.S. stock market increased its value more than 100 percent in just a few years of the 1990s (Mishel et al., 1999:268). And as shown in Table 3.5, by 2002 the United States again dominated the list of the top 50 corporations in the world. It is especially striking that the world's top financial institutions were again American by the end of the 1990s compared to Japanese dominance of financial institutions at the end of the 1980s. Also, as indicated in Table 3.6 on page 77, the list of the richest 50 people in the world during 2001 was top heavy with Americans.

A primary question at this point is, how did the United States create this turnaround in its economic competitiveness relative to other industrial nations? It is time to

TABLE 3.4

Core Nation Economic Indicators, 1990s

Nation	% Growth GNP 1990–2000	% Average Investment Growth 1990–2000	% Productivity Increases 1995–2000	% Unemployment 1995–2000
United States	3.4%	7.0%	2.6%	4.5%
Japan	1.4	1.1	1.8	4.2
Germany	1.5	0.5	1.7	8.6
Great Britain	2.2	1.8	1.5	5.3
France	1.7	−1.6	1.4	11.1
Italy	1.2	−1.0	0.6	11.5
Canada	2.3	2.6	1.2	7.2

Sources: U.S. Bureau of the Census, 2001b; World Bank, 2000.

consider this question because it is directly related to the nature of poverty in the world as well as in the United States.

The Future of Core Competition

While poverty in America was higher than in other industrial nations, the gap between the rich, middle class, and poor in the United States was only about average compared to other industrial nations in the 1950s and 1960s (Kerbo, 2006). But the relative economic decline of the United States in the 1970s and 1980s set a trend of rapidly growing inequality in the United States that far surpasses the inequality of any other core nation. Because many U.S. industries were no longer as competitive compared with some in other countries, millions of well-paying working-class jobs were lost from the 1970s (Harrison & Bluestone, 1988; Reich, 1991; Thurow, 1991). But jobs were also lost due to automation and other labor-saving mechanisms that American companies were introducing into the workplace in an attempt to reduce labor costs, thus increasing global competitiveness. Other American workers had to accept lower pay because of domestic competition among workers for a smaller number of jobs, but also because of competition from low-wage labor in periphery and semiperiphery nations as U.S. multinational corporations began moving to other countries. By the 1990s, however, there was an important new element. The growing inequality in the United States was not a result of the relative U.S. economic decline but of the new national strategy by American business leaders, with U.S. government support, to "make America more competitive again." Lean production—cutting wages, cutting benefits (such as health insurance), making jobs temporary, with longer working hours for less pay to those who had the jobs—became an even greater reality during the 1990s (Mishel et al., 1999; Mishel, Bernstein, & Schmitt, 2001).

As a result of the U.S. economic decline the corporate elite became more politically active during the late 1970s and early 1980s (Kerbo, 2006: Chapters 6 & 7;

TABLE 3.5

Largest 50 Corporations Worldwide, 2002

Global 500 Rank	Company	Revenues ($ millions)	Country
1	Wal-Mart Stores	219,812.0	United States
2	Exxon Mobil	191,581.0	United States
3	General Motors	177,260.0	United States
4	BP	174,218.0	Great Britain
5	Ford Motor	162,412.0	United States
6	Enron	138,718.0	United States
7	DaimlerChrysler	136,897.3	Germany
8	Royal Dutch/Shell Group	135,211.0	Netherlands
9	General Electric	125,913.0	United States
10	Toyota Motor	120,814.4	Japan
11	Citigroup	112,022.0	United States
12	Mitsubishi	105,813.9	Japan
13	Mitsui	101,205.6	Japan
14	Chevron Texaco	99,699.0	United States
15	Total Fina Elf	94,311.9	France
16	Nippon Telegraph & Telephone	93,424.8	Japan
17	Itochu	91,176.6	Japan
18	Allianz	85,929.2	Germany
19	Intl. Business Machines	85,866.0	United States
20	ING Group	82,999.1	Netherlands
21	Volkswagen	79,287.3	Germany
22	Siemens	77,358.9	Germany
23	Sumitomo	77,140.1	Japan
24	Philip Morris	72,944.0	United States
25	Marubeni	71,756.6	Japan
26	Verizon Communications	67,190.0	Japan
27	Deutsche Bank	66,839.9	Germany
28	E. ON	66,453.0	Germany
29	U.S. Postal Service	65,834.0	United States
30	AXA	65,579.9	France
31	Credit Suisse	64,204.5	Switzerland
32	Hitachi	63,931.2	Japan
33	Nippon Life Insurance	63,827.2	Japan
34	American Intl. Group	62,402.0	United States
35	Carrefour	62,224.6	France
36	American Electric Power	61,257.0	United States
37	Sony	60,608.0	Japan
38	Royal Ahold	59,633.9	Netherlands
39	Duke Energy	59,503.0	United States
40	AT&T	59,142.0	United States

(Continued)

Global 500 Rank	Company	Revenues ($ millions)	Country
41	Honda Motor	58,882.0	Japan
42	Boeing	58,198.0	United States
43	El Paso	57,475.0	United States
44	BNP Paribas	55,044.4	France
45	Matsushita Electric Industrial	54,997.1	Japan
46	Home Depot	53,553.0	United States
47	Bank of America Corp.	52,641.0	United States
48	Aviva	52,317.6	British
49	Fiat	51,944.2	France
50	Assicurazioni Generali	51,394.3	Italy

Source: Adapted from the Fortune Web site, http://www.fortune.com/lists/G500/index.html.

Useem, 1984). Corporate elite pressure for more and more support from the government (through lower taxes, fewer labor laws, less government support for unions, etc.) continued throughout the 1980s but became even more focused after 1994 when conservative Republicans gained control of both the House and the Senate for the first time since the 1950s. Innovations in technology and improved production processes due to new high-tech manufacturing methods certainly helped the U.S. economic resurgence during the 1990s. But one of the most important elements in the U.S. economic resurgence and longest economic boom in American history was simply the ability of U.S. corporations to get more work from American workers at less cost compared to earlier periods and compared to other industrial nations. What is called the "total unit labor cost" (the cost of labor including wages, benefits, and taxes) dropped dramatically during the 1990s in the United States, falling below all the other seven largest capitalist countries except France by the end of the 1990s (Keizai. K.H., 2002:103). By the end of the 1990s the average wages of American workers were substantially below the average of other industrial nations, benefits (such as health care coverage) were lowest among major industrial nations, and the average work week and days worked per year for American workers finally became the longest of all industrial nations by the second half of the 1990s (Kerbo, 2006: Chapter 2; Mishel et al., 2001:400–401). In short, the conditions of work in America underwent a quiet revolution that allowed U.S. corporations to make and sell things around the world and at home for less than could be done by other major industrial nations.

American Inequality, Poverty, and Competing Forms of Capitalism in the Twenty-first Century

For the first time in American history the long economic boom in the 1990s did not lead to less inequality. The gap between the rich, middle class, and poor in America continued its steady growth even though less than 4 percent of Americans were unemployed in some years of the 1990s. The rate of poverty finally went down, however slightly,

T A B L E   3 . 6

The World's 50 Richest Individuals, 2001

Rank	Name	Worth ($ billions)	Country
1	Gates, William H. III	58.7	United States
2	Buffett, Warren Edward	32.3	United States
3	Allen, Paul Gardner	30.4	United States
4	Ellison, Lawrence Joseph	26	United States
5	Albrecht, Theo & Karl	25	Germany
6	Alsaud, Prince Alwaleed Bin Talal	20	Saudi Arabia
7	Walton, Jim C.	18.8	United States
8	Walton, John T.	18.7	United States
9	Walton, S. Robson	18.6	United States
10	Walton, Alice L.	18.5	United States
11	Walton, Helen R.	18.5	United States
12	Quandt, Johanna & family	17.8	Germany
13	Ballmer, Steven Anthony	16.6	United States
14	Thomson, Kenneth & family	16.4	Canada
15	Bettencourt, Liliane	15.6	France
16	Anschutz, Philip F.	15.3	United States
17	Kamprad, Ingvar	13	Sweden
18	Li Ka-shing	12.6	Hong Kong
18	Redstone, Sumner M.	12.6	United States
20	Kirch, Leo	12	Germany
21	Anthony, Barbara Cox	11.7	United States
21	Chambers, Anne Cox	11.7	United States
23	Kwok brothers	11.5	Hong Kong
24	Kluge, John Werner	10.9	United States
25	Slim Hel., Carlos	10.8	Mexico
26	Arnault, Bernard	10.7	France
27	Bertarelli, Ernesto & family	10.5	Switzerland
27	Dell, Michael	10.5	United States
29	Berlusconi, Silvio	10.3	Italy
30	Johnson, Abigail	9.1	United States
31	Mars, Forrest Edward Jr.	9	United States
31	Mars, Jacqueline Badger	9	United States
31	Mars, John Franklyn	9	United States
31	Rausing, Kirsten & family	9	Sweden
35	Ergen, Charles	8.8	United States
35	Turner, Robert E. (Ted)	8.8	United States
37	Takei, Yasuo & family	8.3	Japan
38	Olayan, Suliman	8	Saudi Arabia
39	Murdoch, Keith Rupert	7.8	United States
40	Rausing, Hans	7.7	Sweden
40	Saji, Nobutada & family	7.7	Japan

(Continued)

	(Continued)		
Rank	**Name**	**Worth ($ billions)**	**Country**
42	Premji, Azim & family	6.9	India
43	Del Vecchio, Leonardo	6.6	Italy
43	Ortega, Amancio	6.6	Spain
45	Grosvenor, Gerald Cavendish	6.5	United Kingdom
46	Kerkorian, Kirk	6.4	United States
47	Pinault, Francois	6.3	France
47	Schwab, Charles R.	6.3	United States
49	Landolt, Pierre & family	6.1	Switzerland
50	Al-Kharafi, Nasser & family	6	Kuwait

Source: *Forbes*, 2001.

during the last 3 years of the 1990s. As soon as the longest economic boom in American history was over in 2001 poverty quickly shot back up (Kerbo, 2006:Chapter 2; Mishel, Bernstein, & Schmitt, 2003). By the end of 2003 the United States reached another negative milestone: For the first time in history an economic recovery had progressed for over two years *with unemployment and poverty continuing to rise*.

The Japanese, but particularly the Europeans, have certainly taken notice of signs the U.S. economy has become more competitive compared to their own since the early 1990s, and of how American corporations have been doing it. Great Britain had been following the U.S. lead, with some economic improvement, following policies related to Reaganomics from the 1990s. (Reaganomics is the name give to tax breaks for the rich and corporations, welfare cuts, and the reduction of laws protecting American workers since President Reagan was in office from 1980.) By the end of the 1990s, Britain, like the United States, had the same trend of increasing income inequality, lower pay for workers, and fewer benefits (Mishel et al., 1999, 2000, 2002). As indicated in Table 3.3, compared to the 1970s and 1980s when Britain was often seen as the economically sick relative of Europe, the 1990s brought better economic figures, though not for the British working class. For Europe in general, however, the focus on economic unification had been the major strategy to improve economic competitiveness (Bornschier, 1994, 1995). The idea is that more economic cooperation among European Union nations will make their economies more efficient and competitive with other industrial nations. But with far greater welfare and unemployment benefits than the United States, more generous pay and benefits to workers, and much shorter working hours, Europeans are now becoming worried that they will be left behind in global competition if the more "corporate friendly and worker unfriendly" American strategy continues to succeed in making the U.S. economy much more competitive again. Whether or not the renewed American stress on cutting wages, benefits, and jobs, while increasing working hours for those with jobs, will in fact help maintain U.S. economic dominance in the long run, however, is far from certain. A growing, though still limited, number of scholars and economists in the United States have been arguing that America can regain economic strength, not to mention a society with

CASE IN POINT

American and German Workers Compared

By 2005 there were millions of Americans like John Chandler and his family.[2] Just before Christmas 2002, Chandler was laid off from his job at the Wrangler clothing factory. The company was closing several factories in Oklahoma, including the Henryetta branch where Chandler was employed, to move operations to an Asian country were wages are substantially lower than the U.S. minimum wage. Some 900 jobs in Wrangler plants in Oklahoma were lost in 2003 (*The Daily Oklahoman*, July 29, 2003). The average wage in Wrangler plants in Oklahoma was just over $10 per hour (*The Daily Oklahoman,* November 10, 2002; July 29, 2003). The U.S. Labor Department estimates that some 270,000 U.S. textile jobs, about 25 percent of the total jobs in this industry, were lost to foreign competition between just 2001 and 2003 (*International Herald Tribune*, July 26, 2003). No one knows the exact number of American factories that have moved overseas in recent years because the U.S. government does not keep the records as it does unemployment rates or wage rates. But we know that 2 to 3 million American jobs were lost between 2002 and 2005 as U.S. factories were being moved to low-wage countries such as China.[3]

Without much seniority, Chandler was making only $6.85 per hour at the Wrangler plant in 2003, not much above minimum wage. Unemployed and scared, his unemployment benefits would soon run out with little prospect of finding a steady job while unemployment

Unlike in the United States, labor unions in most European countries, such as members of IG Metel in Germany, are very strong and active. There is a direct link between the power of these unions and less poverty and inequality in European countries compared to the United States.

(Continued)

continued to rise throughout 2003. The Chandlers have a bright little 2-year-old boy and a new daughter born just a few months before John was laid off. Janet Chandler used to be able to work from time to time at a local fast-food restaurant but gave it up when their daughter was born. Before both became unemployed they had plans to finally move out of the dangerous mobile home they were renting for more secure lodgings in this tornado-prone part of the country. With both unemployed, of course, it is impossible. Their main hope is to keep any kind of roof over their heads.

The poverty line for 2002, established by government officials through estimates of the cost of basic necessities that year, stood at just over $17,000 for a family of four: Working at hard labor for 40 hours a week, 52 weeks a year, John *still could not bring his family out of poverty*. The $300 in monthly food stamps will be all they have left. Janet usually begins to cry when they discuss their future; John tries to appear strong and optimistic, hoping to make Janet feel better, but in reality John is just as scared.

In some states John and Janet could probably receive some money from the "reformed" welfare system of 1996, but at best that aid would last only a year or two because of the new time limits placed upon welfare benefits by federal law. As unemployment has risen in the United States since 2001, in the face of new time limits placed on receiving welfare benefits, and unemployment benefits lasting at best only 9 months, like many hundreds of thousands of other Americans, John, Janet, and their two children are likely to be hungry and homeless.

Helmut Urban and his wife Helga live with their two young boys in Duisburg, a city in Germany's industrial heartland known as the Ruhr. Situated along the Rhine River and close to the Dutch border, Duisburg obtained its central industrial status because it is next to the biggest inland port in all of Europe. Ships entering the Rhine from the Atlantic Ocean are seen daily loading and unloading along the docks on the west side of the city. From their apartment on the fifth floor of an old pre–World War II building in one of the city's many working-class areas, the Urban boys like to watch the dozens of cranes dancing up and down all day as they tend to the ships and smaller boats being loaded to take goods up river to other parts of Germany as well as other European countries along the Rhine. Their balcony can also provide a spectacular view at night when the sky is illuminated with an eerie red glow from ovens in nearby steel mills as they pour hot molten steel like lava flowing from a volcano.

The problem for Helmut Urban and others like him in the Ruhr area is that the red glow doesn't appear as often as it used to. Because of foreign competition the famous Duisburg steel mills are closing. The German economy remains fairly vigorous, and the biggest in Europe—the third largest in the world in fact. Germany has one of the world's leading export economies and runs a large trade surplus, unlike the U.S. economy with a decades-long trade deficit. The German economy still provides the highest wages and benefits, and one of the shortest work weeks in the world (Table 3.7).

Furthermore, far fewer German corporations are able to move factories to low-income countries because of laws making it more expensive than in the United States to close factories in Germany and lay off German workers. But the German economy is in the process of change, and moving away from the old industries such as steel production. A consequence has been rather high unemployment for more than 15 years—unemployment as high as 10 to 11 percent when including the higher unemployment of eastern Germany yet to make a full transition from communism.

Helmut Urban was a steel worker in one of the famous Duisburg steel mills until it was closed almost 4 years ago. He has been unemployed since. He didn't work much the year before he was unemployed, though, because of a serious knee and back injury he sustained when falling from one of the catwalks on the outside of the steel mill. Urban is worried

(Continued)

TABLE 3.7

Hourly Compensation for Production Workers, 13 Industrial Nations, 1999

Nation	Hourly Wage
Canada	$15.60
Great Britain	16.56
France	17.98
United States	19.20
Japan	20.89
Netherlands	20.94
Sweden	21.58
Austria	21.83
Denmark	22.96
Switzerland	23.56
Norway	23.91
Germany	26.18

Source: U.S. Department of Labor, 2000:Table 2.

about his future and hates staying at home. That old German work ethic remains strong. He does get some odd jobs from time to time, but nothing significant.

Unlike the Chandlers in Henryette, Oklahoma, at least the Urban family doesn't have to worry about putting food on the table, paying the rent, or taking care of medical bills. When he was working, like all Germans, Urban paid about 6 percent of his wages into the national health care system. When he hurt his knee and back 3 years ago all medical bills were paid. Had he needed longer hospitalization he could have even received as a normal benefit a month or two in a sort of hospital resort in the mountains. Now that Urban is unemployed, the state continues to provide him and his family with the same health care coverage as the rest of the German population. Also in Germany the unemployed can receive 53 to 67 percent of their working salary for several years. With German industrial workers holding the world's leading wage position, 53 percent is certainly enough to keep the family out of poverty. If Urban were still unemployed in a few more years he would then have to shift from unemployment benefits to a kind of welfare system that pays only 40 percent of the average German wage for the unemployed person, but with additional money for every other person in the family. The result for Urban and his family is that they are guaranteed something like 60 percent of his previous salary as a steel worker *for life*, plus full medical benefits. The Chandlers back in Henryette may soon be homeless and hungry because unemployment benefits last only 6 to 9 months and all other welfare programs except food stamps have been practically eliminated. A result of this German government action is that while the country has over 10 percent unemployment, its poverty rate is about 5 to 7 percent, depending on how poverty is measured. By the end of the 1990s the United States had only 4 to 5 percent unemployment, but 11 to 19 percent poverty, depending on how poverty is measured. Think about

(Continued)

(Continued)

this: Only 4 to 5 percent of Americans were not working, but more than two or three times as many are living in poverty. The reason poverty in European countries is lower can be clearly understood from Table 3.8 that shows how much governments reduce poverty.

TABLE 3.8

Comparative Impact of Government Welfare and Unemployment Benefits on Reducing Poverty

Country	Poverty (prewelfare payments) (%)	Poverty (afterwelfare payments) (%)	% Reduction (%)
Sweden	34.1%	6.7%	−80.4%
Denmark	26.9	7.5	−72.1
England	29.2	14.6	−50.0
Belgium	28.4	5.5	−80.6
Germany	22.0	7.6	−65.5
Netherlands	22.8	6.7	−70.6
France	21.6	7.5	−65.3
Italy	18.4	6.5	−64.7
Spain	28.2	10.4	−63.1
United States	26.7	19.1	−28.5

Note: Poverty is measured by income below 50 percent of median income in the nation. Data are available from 1989 to 1994.

Sources: Data from Mishel et al., 1999:377; Nieuwbeerta, 2001; Smeeding, 1997.

fewer social problems, only by moving in the opposite direction (see especially Reich, 1991; Thurow, 1991).

In a similar manner, others have argued that the United States should look closely at how Germany is able to train its workforce and obtain more worker involvement in corporate decision making as a way to improve competitiveness (Thelen, 1991; Turner 1991). The argument, in short, is that America needs a better-educated, better-trained, better-paid, and more motivated and loyal workforce in a world economy that increasingly rewards nations that are able to compete in high-tech industries. America must compete in a new high-tech world economy by worrying more about the education and motivation of the bottom 50 percent of workers and families, rather than by beating down wages and labor, as has been done in the past. In the view of many, it is the better-educated, more skilled, and more loyal workers (because of more labor participation and union involvement) of Europe and Japan who will give those countries the edge in future economic competition if the United States does not make big changes in these directions.

Whether or not the above is correct about competitive strategies for the future, an important point is that the political and economic systems in the United States,

TABLE 3.9

Competing Forms of Capitalism

	Corporate-Dominated Capitalism	Cooperative Capitalism	State Development Capitalism
Countries	United States Canada United Kingdom	Western European Union countries	Japan Developing countries in East and Southeast Asia
Characteristics	Small state, little government regulation, weak unions, low labor costs	Large welfare state, state regulation of the economy, economic planning, strong unions	Strong state intervention, extensive regulation and planning, weak unions
Outcomes	Cheap production costs, high inequality, low benefits to workers, less job security, low unemployment, high poverty, low taxes	High production costs, low inequality, high worker benefits, high job security, high unemployment, low poverty, high taxes	Medium production costs, low inequality, medium worker benefits, medium job security, low unemployment, low poverty, low taxes

Continental Europe, and Asian nations are significantly different, allowing differing economic classes to push through agendas favoring their interests relative to those in other class positions. There are what some refer to as competing models of "welfare capitalism," or simply different types of capitalist systems, with different relations between the government, the capitalist class, and the middle and working class (Esping-Andersen, 1990; Goodin, Headey, Muffels, & Dirven, 1999). The United States, and to a lesser degree Britain, have what some refer to as a neoliberal system or corporate dominated political economy in which the government stays relatively uninvolved in the economy (with little economic planning and almost no government ownership of industry), resulting in more freedom for a corporate class to run the economy as they see fit to do so. Implied in this description of a corporate-dominated political economy is a relatively weak working class, and especially a working class lacking influence in the government and in obtaining government protection (with labor laws, income protection, and social benefits).

A significantly different capitalist system found in varying degrees in Continental European countries (especially Germany and France) can be called "cooperative capitalism," also called a corporatist system. As shown in Table 3.9, in a cooperative capitalist system the corporate class and working class, in alliance with government, have arrived at a sort of power-sharing agreement so that the government helps organize the economy and protect the interests of all parties. Central components of cooperative capitalism in contrast to the U.S. corporate-dominated system are strong labor unions and labor laws restricting what corporate elites can do in the economy and political system.

Finally, while less studied by Western social scientists, the most rapidly growing economies of the world, especially in Asia, have what can generally be called "state development capitalism" (Fallows, 1994; Johnson, 1982; Kerbo & McKinstry, 1995;

WHY WE SHOULD CARE

Wal-Mart, Reduced American Wages, and the Loss of American Jobs

With more than $256 billion in sales during 2004, Wal-Mart is now the biggest corporation in the world. Its sales were almost twice as much as General Electric or Microsoft. As shown in Table 3.5, the five children of Sam Walton, the founder of Wal-Mart, have an estimated wealth of about $18 billion each, making them the 7th through the 11th richest people in the world. Not surprisingly, because of its size Wal-Mart establishes trends in American labor relations and shapes the production of goods all over the world. These trends in American labor relations are toward lower wages, fewer benefits, longer working hours, and the extermination of labor unions. The Institute for Industrial Relations at the University of California, Berkeley, in fact, estimated that the state of California must pay out some $87 million each year in health care and welfare benefits to Wal-Mart employees because the pay and benefits are so low (Associated Press, August 3, 2004). The company admits that you cannot raise a family on $8 per hour that it gives new employees, but adds that "working for Wal-Mart is maybe not right for everyone." During the mid-twentieth century the largest U.S. employer was General Motors where unions were strong, benefits were good, and with wages that would certainly put an American family above the poverty line. Now the trend is for more and more employers like Wal-Mart. For the first time since the U.S. Census Bureau began measuring poverty in 1959, by 2000 almost 50 percent of all people who were below the poverty line in the United States lived in the household of a full-time worker (U.S. Bureau of the Census, 2001:Table C).

Knowing that labor unions could help raise the wages and benefits of its employees, Wal-Mart has a strict policy of no union activity among its employees. If an employee so much as talks with a union representative he or she can be fired or denied any promotions. All new workers are required to watch a film depicting unions as corrupt and only out to take members' money. Managers of Wal-Mart branch stores are required to quickly report any union activity so the head office can rush out an "anti-union" swat team to make sure there is no further contact with a union.

Kerbo & Slagter, 2000a, 2000b; Vogel, 1991). In this model of capitalism the state has more independent, or autonomous, political power, as well as more control over the economy. As in the case of the second largest economy in the world, Japan, there is little government ownership of industry, but the private sector is rigidly guided and restricted by bureaucratic government elites. Indeed, these bureaucratic government elites are not elected officials and are thus less subject to influence by either the corporate-class or working-class through the political process. The argument from this perspective has been that a government ministry can have the freedom to plan the economy and look to long-term national interests without having their economic policies disrupted by either corporate-class or working-class short-term and narrow interests. We will especially consider this form of capitalism in more detail in coming chapters because of the success developing countries in East and Southeast Asia have had in using this model of capitalism to develop while protecting their national interests in the new global economy.

(Continued)

Wal-Mart's impact on working Americans, however, is not confined to its low wages, disappearing benefits, or union busting. Wal-Mart is a leader in helping move jobs from the United States to poor countries with low-wage labor. In the early days of Wal-Mart only 5 percent of goods bought in its stores were made in other countries. In 1985, founder Sam Walton launched his Bring It Home to the USA program. "Wal-Mart believes American workers can make a difference," he told his suppliers, offering to pay as much as 5 percent more for U.S.-made products. By 2002 around 60 percent of merchandise sold in Wal-Mart stores was made in other countries. So fierce is the cost-cutting pressure of Wal-Mart on its suppliers that companies who wish to remain a supplier to Wal-Mart are often forced to locate new factories in poor developing countries around the world. Wal-Mart now has more than 3,000 supplier factories in China alone, with many more moving to other poor countries, contributing a considerable portion of all factories moving from American shores.

Even in food retailing Wal-Mart has established new records in price cutting, largely through very low wages and benefits for its employees. A cart of groceries at one of Wal-Mart's superstores, for example, costs 17 to 39 percent less than in grocery stores that pay workers wages to keep them above the poverty line and allow union membership. To compete with Wal-Mart superstores, large corporations selling groceries, such as Safeway and Vons, attempted to impose new cost-cutting measures on employees in late 2003. These corporations wanted to cut health care benefits for current employees and offer no salary increases. Most important, the big companies wanted a new contract allowing lower entry wages for all future employees, severely reduced benefits, and the prohibition of any future union membership. This would bring the hourly wage and benefit cost for the super-market chains down from $19 per hour to the current $9 per hour for Wal-Mart employees. Employees of the big supermarket chains went on strike for 3 $1/_2$ months in an attempt to stop these demands. In the end the employees lost. Future employees will be offered pay and benefits close to those of current Wal-Mart employees, and prevented from joining unions. With no union pressure or U.S. government laws restricting any of the actions of Wal-Mart described above, and now big supermarket chains as well, all other U.S. retailers must follow Wal-Mart's lead if they are to stay in business.

Sources: Information cited comes primarily from a series of investigative reports appearing in the *Los Angeles Times*, November 23, 24, and 25, 2003. Also see *International Herald Tribune*, April 19, 2004.

The global economic competition of the twenty-first century will be played out under these differing forms of capitalism. Will the twenty-first century belong to a resurgent American economy with the new policies of cutting wages, benefits, and jobs, thus increasing inequality, while continuing to invest less in education and social welfare for families and children? Or will the better-educated and better-paid labor force of Western Europe, with more long-term commitment, authority, and loyalty in companies, be able to overtake the U.S. economic momentum to again become more competitive in the global economy in the long-term? Or, as Japan was able to do through the 1980s and before, will state development capitalism of government-guided and protected economies in East and Southeast Asia be the wave of the future? The stakes are extremely high for the world's poor in rich as well as poor countries. If the U.S. corporate-dominated form of capitalism continues to prevail, low-income workers in Europe and Japan will become much worse off and more like low-income American workers. If the corporate-dominated form of capitalism becomes more the model in developing countries around the world, if there is economic development at all, it will more likely be the kind of economic development found in Latin American rather than in East and Southeast Asian countries. We have already seen that economic development in Latin American countries tends to produce more poverty and wider gaps between the rich and poor compared to East and Southeast Asia. How countries in Asia have been able to achieve more evenly spread and sustainable economic develop will be the central issue in remaining chapters. On the subject of the modern world system and the dominance of core nations in the global economy, however, we have one more topic that must be considered in this chapter—the power and extent to which we have a global corporate class dominating the global economy today.

The Global Corporate Class

One of the most global of corporations today is certainly the Carlyle Group (Shorrock, 2002). It is an international conglomerate that specializes in investment funds in countries around the world. But it is also the 11th largest defense contractor in the world, securing arms deals in almost all the world's trouble spots. Carlyle is also a major real estate developer, operator of health care systems, and especially global telecommunications. The Carlyle Group, however, is probably most unique in its collection of top corporate actors. Carlyle's board chair is Frank Carlucci, former secretary of defense under Ronald Reagan, and also former deputy director of the CIA. Other board directors for the Carlyle Group are former president George Bush Sr.; former British prime minister John Major; former speaker of the U.S. House of Representatives Thomas Foley; former secretary of state under Reagan, James Baker III; and a former Thai prime minister, Anand Panyarachum. Other board members are also executives from Boeing, BMW, and Toshiba. As one might expect, the Carlyle Group has been doing quite well financially in recent years, pulling off profitable deals all over the world. If anyone is qualified to be a member of a global corporate class at the beginning of the twenty-first century, it would be the board members of the Carlyle Group.

A global stratification system as the modern world system has been described in this chapter implies that something like a global corporate class is likely. There are global class conflicts, and there are common interests for corporate leaders all over the world in keeping trade flowing, minimizing restrictions on investments and profits, and ensuring an ample supply of cheap labor and materials, just to name a few common interests. And with corporate mergers occurring across national borders in record numbers, there would seem to be a interconnected corporate structure ready-made for the development of a global corporate class watching over and maintaining international capitalism (Robinson & Harris, 2000).

There has unfortunately been very little research on the existence and power of a global corporate class despite the importance of the subject.[4] We know that economic and cultural globalization are moving ahead whether people like it or not, and we know that many social problems from extreme poverty to destruction of the environment are now global problems with global causes, and only global solutions. But we know too little about the interconnections and power of humans on top of this growing globalization. We can, however, apply some of what we have learned about the corporate class in individual nations such as the United States to shed some light on the subject, and organize some of what we do know about the humans on top of the global corporate structure of the twenty-first century.

As social scientists from C. Wright Mills to G. William Domhoff have shown us with respect to a domestic corporate class, we must examine (1) indicators of its existence and the unity of its individual members, (2) the institutions of the class established to maintain its power and control, and (3) the balance of power between a corporate class and classes below (Domhoff, 2001; Mills, 1956). The first two issues are rather straightforward. One must show that the people said to belong to the corporate class exist and have sufficient interaction to create enough unity for them to identify their common interests and work toward maintaining these interests. The difficult part is deciding how much interaction and unity is sufficient for a corporate class to maintain its power, but this must be considered a matter of degree and examined along with the strength of class institutions and the balance of power with classes below. With respect to corporate class institutions, as C. Wright Mills described, individuals (whether or not they are associated with others) can no longer maintain power without bureaucratic organizations or institutions that can effectively protect and carry out the common class interests. For a domestic corporate class, these institutions and organizations include the corporations they control, cross-corporate associations that coordinate the political and other activities of the capitalist class to protect its interests, and governmental institutions that the corporate class is able to influence.

Some people argue that multinational corporations are so numerous and the production processes are so global that a corporate class has emerged without loyalties to any particular nation (see, for example, Robinson & Harris, 2000). A few even argue that the nation-state is no longer a significant factor in the globalization of capitalism because of the power of multinational corporations across all countries. The global corporate class is so powerful that it "represents the transition from the nation-state phase to a new transnational phase of capitalism" (Robinson & Harris, 2000:16–17). The unity of a global corporate class is said to be furthered by the large increase in mergers between big corporations from different countries creating more common interests. Further, this global corporate class has sufficient institutional support to protect its common international interests. These organizations include the International Monetary Fund (IMF), World Bank, World Trade Organization (WTO), European Union, Asia Pacific Economic Cooperation (APEC), and World Economic Forum.

While we can agree that some of this is happening, one must still question the degree to which a global corporate class can exist. Beginning with questions of the existence and unity of a global corporate class, it seems that the degree of unity has been overestimated. As with the other problems, exaggerating global class unity is to a large extent related to the common assumption that national boundaries or even nation-states are no longer important considerations for a global class system. This assumption first leads to the neglect of cultural and value conflicts among a global corporate class. It further neglects the extent to which continued national identities and nationalism divides a global corporate class. One does not have to go to the extreme of Samuel Huntington in claiming a resurgence of cultural clashes, but there is abundant evidence that cultural divisions continue to exist and divide the world (Huntington, 1996). Nor are North Americans, Europeans, and Japanese who primarily make up any global corporate class able to experience anything like the common socialization experiences shaping shared worldviews and a "we feeling" described in the works on the domestic corporate class in the United States and Japan. As for the wave of cross-national corporate mergers, evidence shows that because of various types of national or cultural conflicts within the new corporations formed by such mergers, most have failed (dissolved after a few years) or one of the international partners ends up being almost completely dominant, as in the case of Daimler-Benz becoming the dominate force after the merger with Chrysler (*International Herald Tribune*, March 25, 1999). The only mergers that had a greater than 50 percent success rate have been among American and British firms.

For several years in Europe and Asia research colleagues and I have heard bitter criticisms of the executives from other countries (Kerbo & Slagter, 2000a, 2000b; Kerbo, Wittenhagen, & Nakao, 1994; Lincoln, Kerbo, & Wittenhagen 1995). Perhaps most important, they tell us of many barriers in working with each other due to differing perspectives on how work should be organized. One can imagine, for example, one simple cultural or national conflict behind the inside battles between the old Chrysler executives and Daimler-Benz executives that led to most of the Chrysler executives being pushed out and Daimler-Benz ending up the real power in the newly merged auto company. American corporative executives are by far the highest paid in the world, averaging almost $1 million annually in basic salary, and a total of about $10 million a year after stock options are included. German corporate executives, on the other hand, are paid about half of the basic salary of U.S. corporate executives, and they cannot receive the stock options under German rules. On top of this, the German executives have learned to work with powerful German unions and employees given extensive authority to pass judgment over all executive decisions (Kerbo, 2006: Chapter 15; Thelen, 1991; Turner, 1991). There are extensive corporate cultural clashes, in other words, and no doubt extreme jealousy when foreign colleagues with less authority are paid more than double the basic wage. In short, it seems that no matter how much their business has gone global, corporate executives still think of themselves as American, German, Japanese, British, and so on, and it can be difficult for them to escape feelings of national allegiance. American corporate executives and political leaders travel to Europe and find there is often a very different view of the world, not to mention when these people travel to Asia, or Africa, or elsewhere.

There are also questions about some of the international institutions who claim to protect and further the interests of a global corporate class. Some, such as the World Economic Forum, certainly bring an exclusive group of international corporate and political leaders together every year for discussion and consensus building. But the World Economic Forum has little power beyond that, and publications of their discussions every year continue to reflect important conflicts between national interests. Others, such as the World Trade Organization (WTO) which has ironically become the focus of international protest, are at least somewhat democratic in that most nations of the world are members and have representatives.

The WTO was created in 1995 out of the old General Agreements on Tariffs and Trade (GATT) which itself was created to help organize the world economy after World War II. There are more than 150 member nations of the WTO who are able to vote on trade issues, with no country able to veto any decision of the membership body. As one might expect, the rich nations are certainly able to bully the poorer nations into decisions, and the poorer nations often lack experience and knowledge about the world economy to allow them to protect their interests as well as the rich nations. But the WTO is not the ruler of global capitalism and exploiter of poor nations to the extent many would suggest. Of note is the recent dispute between rich and poorer nations over who would be elected as head of the WTO; the rich nations had to compromise and from 2003 the head of the WTO has been a representative from a developing nation—Thailand. This leaves the International Monetary Fund (IMF) and World Bank as clearly the most likely organizations protecting the interests of a global corporate class, but there are still some conflicts among the global corporate class about what these organizations will do and who will head them.

The IMF and World Bank grew out of what were called the Bretton Woods talks in 1944. The idea was to organize the world economy to prevent world depressions as occurred during the 1930s. The function of the IMF is to be the banker of crisis in the world, lending money to countries in economic trouble to keep them from sliding into collapse that would hurt other nations in the global economy. The World Bank is an organization that provides funds to poor countries for development projects. Most important, the IMF and World Bank are certainly not democratic organizations, and the corporate class members that run these organizations demand that recipient countries follow their rules and their views of how capitalism should operate (never going against the interests of rich nations that provide the funds for the IMF and World Bank). Since the founding of the World Bank and IMF after World War II there has been a "gentleman's agreement" between the American and European corporate class that the World Bank will always be headed by an American while the IMF will be headed by a European. Behind the scenes meetings are carried out, with power plays and demands and counterdemands made by the European and American corporate leaders. Japan, which has the world's second largest economy, is completely left out, as is Russia and all the other nations of the world. Thus, it can be said that both the IMF and World Bank are controlled by the American and European corporate class, and to a lesser degree, its political leaders. However, the most recent selection process for heading the IMF showed that it is the American corporate class that really dominates. The Europeans' selection was rejected by the United States and they had to put forth two candidates before the Americans would give their approval on one (*International Herald Tribune*, March 3, 2000).

Although several global corporate-class organizations bring these people together for socialization, discussion, and possible consensus building, it is difficult to say that a global corporate class, as opposed to an American corporate class, is in charge. All over the world English is the language of international business. To the extent there is a global corporate class, the people involved seem to mostly have American accents.

Whereas it is clear that a global corporate class does exist, one must be careful not to exaggerate its power and unity. Most often in the literature and research on the U.S. corporate class it has been the balance of power between a corporate class and other classes that has been disregarded. This neglect in recent decades is no doubt related to the sharp decline in American working-class influence in the second half of the twentieth century. Still, this neglect of a ratio of power between a corporate class and other class creates a serious American bias as well as a historical bias in current theory and research. One must remember that class implies class conflict, which also means there is a power ratio between one or more classes. We must recognize that power is always relative; the power of one group is enhanced as the power of other groups weakens. When we take this perspective of a balance of power, or a power ratio between two or more groups, to the global level we must recognize that the global corporate class is also in conflict with other interests in the world, particularly with people in less developed nations. One must not assume that a global corporate class can always rule unopposed, or that its decisions can never be countered by others in the world.

As we will see in coming chapters, a few nations have been able to protect the interests of their people against demands from multinational corporations. World poverty has been growing, but this is mostly so in some world regions rather than others. There are some solutions to growing world poverty, but these solutions require that one understand how the global stratification system operates. With this goal in mind, we must first turn to the place of poorer countries in the modern world system in the next chapter, and then consider how and why some poorer nations in the global economy, most often in Asia, are able to protect their national interests than others in our remaining chapters.

Notes

1. See recent international polls conducted by the Pew Research Center at http://people-press.org/. Also see *International Herald Tribune,* December 20, 2001, December 5, 2002.
2. The cases of the Chandler family in Oklahoma and the Urban family in Duisburg, Germany, are fictional but present accurate depictions of people in these areas based upon interviews with several people and contrasting economic and political conditions in the United States and Germany.
3. CNN commentator and analyst Lou Dobbs has been trying to track the number of U.S. jobs lost to low-wage countries. Information can be found online at http://www.cnn.com/lou.
4. One major exception is Leslie Sklair's book *The Transnational Capitalist Class* (Oxford, England: Blackwell, 2001). However, though multinational (transnational) corporations are spreading all over the world it does not necessarily mean there is a unified global corporate class. For data on the growing links among transnational corporations based in different countries, see Jeffery Kentor and Young Suk Jank, "Yes There Is a (Growing) Transnational Business Community: A Study in Interlocking Directorates 1983–98," *International Sociology.* 19, no. 3 (September 2004).

CHAPTER 4

The Global Economy and World Poverty: Attempted Explanations

Viewed from our television sets the mass protests, such as the one at the World Trade Organization meeting in Seattle during the fall of 1999, can sometimes appear irrational, with random, senseless attacks on people and property. One of the first people to study crowd behavior in 1897, Gustav Le Bon thought crowd behavior was the product of our animal instincts—the dominance of our "collective mind" over our "civilized mind."[1] While emotions of the moment can motivate people in large protest crowds, years of research on crowd behavior have shown there is almost always a logic to what is happening. We may not agree with it, or like it, but crowd behavior seldom involves mindless, irrational behavior: Peasants are hungry and direct their attacks toward people seen as hoarding bread; people living in a poor ghetto strike out at perceived symbols of their oppression (Couch, 1968; Tilly, 1978; Tilly, Tilly, & Tilly, 1975). Those who protest against globalization are targeting what they see as exploitation of the world's poor by rich multinational corporations—some of the more violent factions physically attack concrete symbols of these global corporations, such as Nike retail outlets, The Gap, McDonald's, and Starbucks (Gillham & Marx, 2000).

Ironically, the world's poor believed to be exploited by these symbols of global capitalism are less likely involved in the protests, even when antiglobalization protests occur in less developed countries. Too many of the world's poor are so desperate they are willing to take any sweatshop job that will put food on the table, however dangerous and temporary this job may be. Protestors from rich nations have the luxury of full stomachs and a broader view of the human conditions that affluence can bring. And while these protesters from rich nations may not be correct on all of the details, they are aware of cases in which global corporations *are* making some people poorer. Much of this evidence suggesting multinational corporations from rich countries *can* harm the world's poor comes from the relatively new perspective on international economic power, modern world system theory, outlined in the previous chapter (Kerbo, 2003: Chapters 14 & 17).

Although an earlier dependency theory provided some insights, Immanual Wallerstein is given credit for stimulating the development of modern world system theory in the early 1970s—many others have taken his lead in elaborating much of the theory (Bornschier & Chase-Dunn, 1985; Chase-Dunn, 1989; Chirot, 1977, 1986; Frank, 1969, 1975, 1978, 1998; Wallerstein, 1974, 1977, 1980, 1989). Some of the theory's details are yet to be worked out and earlier research findings appear contradictory. There are also charges of a Western bias in the theory (see especially Frank, 1998). But despite its flaws, one must still respect this new theory for helping organize and explain much of recent history, conflicts between nations, the current prospects for poorer nations in the world, as well as why some rich nations like the United States have continuing high levels of poverty. After outlining the basics of modern world system theory and recent world history in the previous chapter we are now ready to focus on how this theory can explain the growing gap between the world's rich and poor today. Before doing so, however, the fallacies of old views must be considered.

A Resurgence of Cultural Explanations

When contemplating the condition of poverty around the world many people in rich countries tend to wonder, "What is wrong with those people? They seem so slow, no one appears to work very hard, nor could they with all of those 'siestas.'" Comfortable people in rich nations know they have worked hard for what they have achieved. The question is, "Why can't these other people do the same?" Especially when contemplating the existence of poor people *within* rich nations, there is a tendency to blame the poor for their poverty. Those better off almost always assume other people have the same opportunities to better themselves through talent and hard work. They judge others from the realities of their own lives, from the logic of how human behavior brings rewards and punishment in their own day-to-day interactions. It remains difficult for the more affluent of this world to understand the everyday realities and options of the world's poor. If these people are poor it must be because "they do not behave as we do." The contrasting behavior of the poor, in other words, is often "explained" by suggesting there are different "cultural values" among the poor that prevent them from working hard, planning for the future, or doing other things believed to have helped people in affluent countries to become better off.

Max Weber, the sociological master who wrote his most important works some 100 years ago, was one of the first to suggest how cultural values can affect economic development and prosperity. In his *The Protestant Ethic and the Spirit of Capitalism,* Weber argued that the Protestant Reformation led northwestern European countries to reject Catholicism and establish values that drove people toward worldly achievements because of such things as the ability to delay immediate gratification for future rewards (Weber, 1958b). Hard work, saving to accumulate assets, and rational calculation, of course, are the essence of capitalism. By the 1950s others had expanded upon Weber's ideas to outline modernization theory and a process "all nations must follow" to become advanced industrial nations like the United States (Moore, 1974; Parsons, 1966). To make countries less poor, followers of this theory believe we must begin with change in values and attitudes that have perpetuated poverty. It is fatalism (the belief that life events are beyond one's control) and a focus on the present that makes people less able to delay present satisfactions, work hard, and save for the future. Likewise, modernization theory and its focus on culture has been used to explain why many nations of East and Southeast Asia have become richer because of "Asian values."[2]

In recent years, unfortunately, cultural explanations have made a comeback. To name just a few indicators of the renewed interest in cultural explanations, the World Bank is funding more projects guided by cultural theories, and a popular book first published in 1985, *Underdevelopment Is a State of Mind,* has been reissued. This book by Lawrence Harrison purports that Spanish Catholic values inherited by Latin American countries are the main cause of Latin American poverty (Harrison, 2000). The political scientist, Samuel Huntington, then collaborated with Harrison on an edited volume titled *Culture Matters: How Values Shape Human Progress,* also published in 2000 (Harrison & Huntington, 2000). At the same time, the World Bank suddenly started picking up the theme of cultural barriers to economic development, pouring millions of dollars into new books and international conferences on the subject, and aiding projects in developing countries designed to change cultural values believed to be detrimental to economic development.[3]

Popular explanations of poverty *within* rich nations from the 1950s began to follow what came to be known as the culture of poverty theory (see, for example, Lewis, 1966). The basic argument is that because of their poverty and the problems of living in poverty, the poor have developed a culture that helps them cope with their situation. This culture of poverty is significantly different from the culture of people who live in affluent sectors of the society because of such things as its "present time orientation" that creates an inability to delay gratification. These cultural traits are said to be coping mechanisms because it would be psychologically damaging to continually worry about and plan for a future that holds no promise of a better life. In the long run, though, these values reinforce conditions of poverty even if realistic opportunities to get out of poverty become available to the poor.

Abundant research has *rejected* the idea that culture is the most important cause of poverty in the United States. Among the reasons for rejecting a culture of poverty view is evidence that values are not as deeply ingrained as most proponents of cultural theories have assumed (for a summary of much of this research, see Kerbo, 2000:266–276). In addition, interviews with poor people in the United States indicate that most accept the dominant values—they simply find it difficult to live up to them in their present circumstance. Changing economic opportunities also have been found to explain most of the movement into and out of poverty, a movement of people into and out of poverty that cultural explanations have neglected. Those of us involved with the issue of poverty in the United States during the 1960s and 1970s can understand that the World Bank's new programs focused on "the values of the world's poor" mimic President Johnson's War on Poverty. During that time millions of U.S. dollars went into "service programs" to hire social workers (such as myself) to go into the homes of the poor and teach them how to "better raise their children and work harder" to find and keep jobs. American poverty went down in the 1960s and 1970s, but it did so because the poor got more cash directly from the welfare system and not because of millions of dollars paying social workers like me to "change the poor."

As for those Asian values many claim are responsible for the Asian economic miracles in recent decades, *not all East and Southeast Asian nations with these values have gotten themselves out of poverty.* We will see, for example, that Burma, Laos, Cambodia, and Thailand have almost identical cultural heritages. While Thailand has one of the best records of poverty reduction and economic development in recent decades, Burma, Laos, and Cambodia are among the poorest countries in the world, with few prospects of moving out of that status.

It is now time to pick up our examination of modern world system theory started in the previous chapter to see what it can help us understand about the causes of world poverty.

Why the World's Poor Often Remain Poor: Dependency, Uneven Development, and Economic Stagnation

For many years economists had assumed that nations in the world would follow a similar pattern of economic development. With some initial capital investment, nations could proceed on a path from preindustrial agrarian societies to industrialization as described in Rostow's "stages of economic growth" (Rostow, 1960). But we now know that these theories of economic development are highly misleading when applied to less developed nations today (Chase-Dunn, 1975; Johnson, 1982; Portes, 1976; Vogel, 1991). The realities faced by today's least developed nations are far different from those faced by the already developed rich nations when they were in their process of economic development two or three centuries ago. As Gunnar Myrdal noted years ago, today's poor nations often have fewer natural resources, larger populations, and a poorer climate (Myrdal, 1970:32–37). But most important, the nations that are now rich *did not have other already developed nations to contend with in their early process of development*. Today, core nations' influence on world commodity prices, interest rates, terms of trade and investment, and other economic forces restrict the opportunities and independence of poorer nations, all making it more difficult for poorer nations to achieve economic development. One of the biggest advantages of rich nations today is the subsidization their farmers and manufacturers receive so they can produce goods more cheaply and of better quality. Farmers in poor nations, for example, cannot compete in global economy where farmers in rich nations get billions of dollars to help with irrigation, fight crop and animal disease, and provide good transportation systems to get their products to market. One recent statistic is quite striking: Dairy farmers in the core of the European Union receive about $2 per day in subsidies for each cow they own. Almost half the world's population, we have seen, live on less than $2 per day.

Two other situations for many poorer countries in the modern world system make economic development with poverty reduction most difficult. The first involves *structural distortion* in their economies. In an "undistorted" economy, or normal economy, natural resources and human skills lead to a chain of economic activity promoting development. We can use the case of a core nation with extensive copper deposits. Mining the copper provides jobs and profits. The copper is refined into metal, again providing some people with jobs and profits. The metal is then used by other companies to make consumer products, again providing jobs and profits. Finally, the products are sold by wholesale and retail distributors, providing even more jobs and profits. From the mining process to the retail sales of the products, there is a chain of jobs and profits creating economic growth from a natural resource.

Now consider what may happen when the copper is mined in a poor nation with extensive ties to multinational corporations from core nations. The copper may be mined by native workers and even native companies, but the ore or metal is shipped to core nations where the remainder of the economic chain is completed. The additional jobs and profits from the chain of economic activities are lost to the periphery nation— they go to the rich core nations (Chase-Dunn, 1975). Leaders of poor nations should demand that such harmful relations with multinational corporations cease. They should demand that multinational corporations pay fair taxes and decent wages, and reinvest profits within the poor nations so the chain of economic activities creating development can occur within the poor nations. Political and economic elites in poor nations, however, often cannot or will not make these demands.

A second negative effect on the economy of periphery nations is related to agricultural disruption. Export agriculture often becomes an important economic activity of periphery nations brought into the modern world system. Before this time, traditional agriculture was directed toward local consumption with little incentive to introduce *capital-intensive methods of farming,* methods of farming that rely on more agricultural equipment and advanced farming methods. With traditional agricultural methods and a limited outside market for agricultural products, some land was left for poor peasants, food was cheaper, and jobs were more plentiful. More *labor-intensive methods of farming* were followed which meant more people needed in the fields to produce crops. But with export agriculture and capital-intensive farming methods, food for local consumption becomes more expensive and scarce because most land is used to produce export crops like soybeans rather than black beans, corn, potatoes, and other crops for local consumption. Richer land owners begin taking more and more land from poor peasants because the more land these rich land owners can hold the more they can produce and sell on the world market. Rich landowners buy more machines to increase farm production because it makes economic sense to do so, and they can afford these machines with the profits they acquired in global markets. In short, poorer farmers are losing their land and their labor is now being done by machines. This also means exaggerated urbanization as peasants who have lost their land and farming jobs move to cities in hopes of finding work (Kentor, 1981). As shown in Figure 4.1, it also means there is more hunger in the countries that ship a higher percentage of their food out of the country to the global markets.

The Class Struggle Within

The structural distortion and agricultural disruption in poor countries typically occur because governments in these less developed countries do not have the means to resist

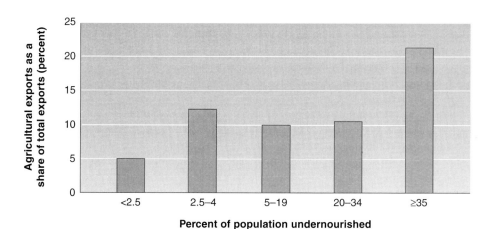

FIGURE 4.1   *Importance of Agricultural Exports from Countries with Hunger, 1996–2000*

SOURCE: United Nations Food and Agricultural Organization, 2003:17.

CASE IN POINT

Sweatshops and Child Labor in Latin America

An example from El Salvador is instructive. Six years ago, Abigail Martinez worked 18-hour days for 55 cents an hour sewing cotton tops and khaki pants. Martinez and several other workers employed by a small company making clothing for The Gap and other Western retailers finally began a strike. Normally the strike would have been put down with little effort or media attention. The timing of the strike was fortunate for the workers, however, because Western clothing firms such as The Gap were under heavy criticism from North American protestors and labor groups. Under this outside pressure The Gap gave in and demanded some improvements in working conditions and increased wages 5 cents an hour. However, representatives of The Gap reported that the small sweatshop (actually owned by Taiwanese investors) made few of the changes The Gap demanded. Local government officials made sure such strike activity did not happen again. Because of the negative publicity and potential for increased labor costs, several companies such as J.C. Penney, Eddie Bauer, and Target canceled contracts and moved to other locations with more controlled laborers (*International Herald Tribune,* April 26, 2001). Local El Salvadorian elites lost money, and many people like Abigail Martinez lost their jobs.

Conditions of child labor all over Latin America follow the same logic. Almost 10 percent of children aged 10 to 14 are working full time throughout Latin America. The average for poor countries all over the world is about the same, though many of course have much higher rates. It is highest in Brazil where almost 15 percent of these children work full time. The problem of child labor, however, is not as simple as demanding that it stop so that these children can be educated and grow up like "normal" children. In case after case, as demands from concerned people in rich countries lead multinational corporations to force there suppliers to stop child labor practices, children lose these jobs and their families have a harder time putting food on the table because these jobs have been

or prevent rich countries and their multinational corporations from doing these things. But, equally important, the political and economic leaders in these countries have economic incentives *not to stop these practices*. There are sharp *class conflicts within poor nations* because extensive ties to multinational corporations make the rich richer at the same time the poor are made poorer. That is, political and economic elites in poor nations often become more tied to, and accommodating to, corporate elites from rich nations who have investments in their country, and become less and less concerned with the welfare of all other citizens in their country. When we think about it this situation is not really surprising. The local political and economic elites receive handsome profits because multinational corporations have investments in the country. And these elites in poor countries are certainly smart enough to know that multinational corporations are making investments in the poor nation because labor costs are low, unions are nonexistent, taxes are low, and other things, such as lax environmental controls, are very favorable to multinational corporate interests. For self-serving elites in poorer nations this creates a direct *conflict between them and the masses of people in the nation*. The common people obviously want less poverty, better wages, more humane working

(Continued)

Workers in a Brazilian nut factory, Brazil Amazon River. As is typically the case, a high percentage of these workers are children, often making less than $2 a day.

taken from children (*International Herald Tribune,* July 16, 2002). The hard reality is that sweatshops and child labor are the only things keeping some families from starvation. Sweatshops and child labor will be eliminated in the world when there is no longer almost half the world's population living on less than $2 per day with no other opportunities to put food on the table.

conditions, and future economic development so their children will be better off. But if these things are realized it can mean multinational corporations will leave and local elites will lose their profitable ties to these corporations. Unfortunately, the poor often lose as well because of past agricultural disruption. Many of the poor crowded into urban slums have come to depend upon those extremely low-paid and miserable sweatshop jobs because there is nothing else for them.

Global Corporations Can Do Harm: Some Evidence

We must not get the impression that all periphery nations are equally hurt by investments from the core, or are hurt in the same way. Likewise, it is not being suggested that multinational corporate investments in poor nations cause all of their problems.[4] But research over the last 30 years has suggested that over the long run many periphery nations *are* significantly harmed by outside multinational corporate investments.

Soon after the utility of modern world system theory was recognized in the 1970s, it generated an impressive amount of quite sophisticated empirical research. One of the most important research questions, of course, is whether poor countries have *more or less* long-term economic growth when they become extensively tied to multinationals from rich nations. While there is certainly variability among periphery nations, especially in Asia, several early studies indicated that many periphery nations do have less long-term economic growth when overly dominated by outside multinational corporations (Bornschier & Chase-Dunn, 1985; Bornschier, Chase-Dunn, & Rubinson, 1978; Chase-Dunn, 1975, 1989; Nolan, 1983a, 1983b; Snyder & Kick, 1979; Stokes & Jaffee, 1982, 1985). Poor nations that receive extensive multinational corporate investments, of course, tend to have some economic growth in the shortterm. But the longer term prospects for growth (over 5 years or more) are in many cases actually harmed by the kinds of outside aid and investment these nations have received. Other research indicated that outside corporate investment increases income inequality within poorer nations. The historical pattern for rich nations has been one of reduced income inequality as economic development proceeds.[5] In the case of poor nations, however, the rich tend to get richer while the poor are either poorer or no better off (Chase-Dunn, 1975; Bornschier & Ballmer-Cao, 1979; Bornschier et al., 1978; Rubinson, 1976; Stack, 1978a).

After the first wave of research on the effects of multinational corporate investments in poor countries, however, more recent research has shown less consistent and even contradictory results. One new piece of research using a larger and more recent data set of poor nations has found extensive multinational corporate investment now tends to produce more positive economic growth in the long term, while another using recalculations of older data also finds outside investment results in more long-term economic growth (de Soysa & Oneal, 1999; Firebaugh, 1992, 1996). Other research has shown that outside corporate investment in poor nations does not lead to less economic development when the types of goods imported or exported to and from the poor nations are considered, or if the outside corporate investment is accounted for by several rich nations rather than just one or two (Bollen & Appold, 1993; Kentor, 2001; Kentor & Boswell, 2003). When many multinational corporations have smaller amounts of investment within a poor country they are less likely to be able to dominate the economy and political system, and in fact must compete among themselves giving workers in poor countries some advantage. Still other studies have questioned the negative effects of multinational investments in poor nations, such as increases in income inequality and a lower standard of living among the poor masses of people. They suggest a more complex relationship between multinational corporate investment and income inequality with evidence that the poor in many of these nations do have improved lives because of multinational investment (Alderson & Nielsen, 1999; Firebaugh & Beck, 1994). Some authors of original research showing that multinational corporate investment harms poorer nations have conducted research using data from the 1990s to conclude their original research was correct but that the negative effects on poor countries tend to be less today (see, for example, Herkenrath & Bornschier, 2003).

To help explain some of the new research findings we must consider several factors. First, it is quite possible that new forces in the world have produced some change in the balance of power between rich core nations and many less developed nations. For example, we know that more direct foreign investments going to developing nations today involve high-tech industries. These high-tech investments can lead to more sustainable economic growth for these nations than did previous low-tech investments.

Further, with the cold war over and rich nations focused more on profits and less on fighting communism, poorer nations are sometimes courted by rich nations, giving the poorer countries more leverage when playing one rich nation off another.

However, none of these new studies have so far considered that multinational corporate investments can have *different effects in different parts of the world*. For example, are there generally different outcomes when considering multinational corporate investments going to Asian nations in contrast to Latin American or African nations? During the 1980s and 1990s most East and Southeast Asian countries experienced rapid economic growth, while growth in Latin America was either negative or much slower, and slower yet in African nations. More multinational corporate investment has gone to Asian countries than other poor nations since the 1980s. Further, we know that nations with more human capital (i.e., a more educated population) are better able to use multinational corporate investment for positive long-term economic growth (de Soysa & Oneal, 1999). Recent research has confirmed that East and Southeast Asian nations are more likely to use outside corporate investment for their long-term benefit, but most remain puzzled as to why this is the case (see, for example, Hossein & Weiss, 2003; Jomo, 2001).

The next logical question follows: *Is there something different about East and Southeast Asian nations trying to maintain economic development compared to poorer nations in Latin America or Africa?* Using data from the 1970s and earlier, Barrett and Whyte have shown that Taiwan was an exception to the harmful effects of extensive outside multinational corporate investment. But this study did not attempt to make generalizations to other Asian nations. The first critiques of this study claimed that Taiwan had just recently (1960s and 1970s) started its attempt at economic development, and thus in the long run Taiwan would be no different in experiencing negative effects, a claim we know now is incorrect.[6] Research from the modern world system perspective has yet to consider that important aspects of political economy that interact with the effects of multinational corporate investment in East and Southeast Asian countries are generally different from those in Latin American and African nations.

The Western Bias: Why We Often Fail to Understand

Although basic statistics about economic development and income inequality in developing countries around the world demonstrate that something must be significantly different in East and Southeast Asia it is almost never mentioned in the modern world system theory and research.[7] One often gets the impression that Western social scientists become perplexed when faced with Asian nations that don't seem "to fit." The Asian "outliers" (that don't fit the usual pattern) are sometimes glaring. Yet, with few clues as to what might be happening in these Asian nations, social scientists usually note that they are different, sometimes offering vague comments on "Asian culture," before going on to other issues. But there have been a few exceptions.

In his recent book *ReOrient*, Andre Gunder Frank cites Marx, Weber, and others as central in developing Euro-centered sociological theory (see especially Frank, 1998:7–9, 323). He criticizes Marx for his concept of an "Asian Mode" as a rigid form of political dominance that serves only the interests of elites rather than acknowledging Asian traditions of political authority that may also restrict selfish elite exploitation of citizens. Much like the classic sociologist Max Weber, Marx was also misinformed about Chinese history, neglecting many periods of change and evolution over centuries of civilization (Golzio, 1985; Yawata, 1963). But in common with critiques of Western economic theory's failure to understand the rise of Japanese economic power in the twentieth century, Frank reserves most of his criticism for Weber's view that the development of capitalism follows the individualistic principles made possible with the Protestant ethic. Frank comments, "the contemporary East Asian experience does not seem to fit very well into any perceived Western theoretical or ideological scheme of things. On the contrary, what is happening in East Asia seems to violate all sorts of Western canons of how things 'should' be done, which is to copy how 'we' did it the 'Western way'"(Frank, 1998:7).

Somewhat earlier, James Fallows also criticized Western economic theory for its inability to adequately explain Asian economic development, particularly in Japan, because of invalid Western assumptions (Fallows, 1994). More precisely, though, Fallows argues that it is Anglo-American economic theory that is most biased toward Asian development and that it ignores the contrast between Asian and Anglo-American economic theory. He cites four main differences in the value orientations of Asian economic models:

1. The purpose of economic life: collective national strength rather than simply consumerism.
2. The view of power: a concentration of power is not necessarily bad as long as it is used for the long-term national interest.
3. A distrust of unpredictability: thus, free markets or "the hidden hand of the market place" are not trusted.
4. A focus on national borders: a view of us versus them and protection of the in-group. (p. 208)

Finally, it is worth noting that Fallows concludes that Western economic theory is good at "getting prices right," though if you are in a poor country without capital, rigging prices to acquire extra capital may be more in tune with your long-term interests (Fallows, 1994:203).

While Fallows's critiques of Western economic theory may be most sweeping when viewing Asian economic development, he is not alone. Chalmers Johnson has also been critical of the Western assumption that the state has only a limited role in developing and maintaining economic strength (Johnson, 1982). In his now classic work, *MITI and the Japanese Miracle,* Johnson chronicled the history of how through trial and error in the early twentieth century the Japanese government bureaucracy, particularly the Ministry of International Trade and Industry, learned how to manage the development of a modern economy in such a way that many Anglo-American economists still proclaim is impossible. Yet, it is this "Asian development model" that in one way or another is used all over Asia today. Even after the Asian economic crisis of 1997, we will see, there are no calls to throw out the Asian development model, only to fine tune it here and there.

Finally, we should consider a broader condemnation of Western sociological theory for its inability to understand critical differences in Asian cultures and social organization. In the introduction to the new 1985 paperback edition of his famous *Tokugawa Religion* (first published in 1957), Robert Bellah recounts how he was involved during the 1950s with famous sociologists such as Talcott Parsons in a project to understand

Japanese society and culture (Bellah, 1985:xi–xxi). Following Parsons's modernization theory and its related cultural explanations noted earlier (Parsons, 1951), Bellah recounts how there was broad agreement at the time that Japan must end up becoming much like Westerners if they are to achieve a fully modern, competitive industrial society. With 30 years of hindsight, Bellah now basically concludes, "we were wrong." Japan has become the second largest economy in the world, even with its stagnation of the 1990s, and it did so without altering many basic institutions or value orientations.

A major problem with Western social scientists is that they confuse their Western values with not just how they believe things *should be* but how things *must be.* There are opposing value orientations, and with issues such as achieving fair political institutions or strong economies, there are more than one way of doing things, and each way of doing things has its own set of negatives and positives; value orientations lead us to select the way of doing things that best fits our values (i.e., the positives).[8] Likewise, one must not assume that if something is done differently from the Western way it is somehow less rational. In a highly insightful analysis of Chinese values and group behavior, for example, Kwang-kuo Hwang shows how small-group behavior in China uses principles of rational-calculation, but does so from the perspective of values stressing group interests rather than individual interests. From these traditional Chinese values, actions should favor obligations stressing equality and sharing among people who are close peers (Hwang, 1987).

Until recently, none of this critical examination of Western bias had been applied to modern world system theory and research. In the late 1990s, in his book noted above, Frank finally picked up the charge of Western biases in this area of study as well. But Frank has done so mostly by showing how Western sociologists have almost completely neglected the fact that a powerful Asian world system existed long before the European-centered modern world system, which would actually copy many aspects of the earlier Asian world system (Frank, 1998). In the spirit of a "sociology of sociology" that existed long before the now popular postmodern deconstructionism, we need to examine the possibility that Western assumptions have led to a *neglect of how Asian societies may be able to counter the effects of outside investments from rich multinational corporations to achieve economic development* while many Latin American and African nations have had more difficulty doing so.[9]

Specifically, for our subject of the modern world system and economic development, the following points seem important:

1. Western individualistic assumptions often lead social scientists to conclude that what appears to be less democracy by Western definitions automatically leads to elite exploitation for elite self-interests. These assumptions *lead us to neglect other traditional restraining mechanisms on elites in Asian societies.*
2. Current theories have neglected how *Asian traditions of authority and state organization combine to create political structures better able to protect common national interests,* confront multinational corporations, and restrain elites so that common national interests rather than narrow self-interests of domestic elites are served.
3. Western, especially Anglo-American, values of individualism and mistrust of the state have led Western economists and many world system theorists to *neglect the degree to which state intervention can bring about sustained economic development.*

Other important factors affect economic development in Asia, and other biases contained in Western theories will be considered later. But these three points are among the most important in helping us understand some of the key differences in economic development in Asian versus non-Asian nations.

The Problem of Research Method

Before leaving this discussion of theory and research on the modern world system we have a remaining problem related to research methodologies. As noted earlier, from the very beginning of world system theory in the early 1970s there has been an impressive amount of empirical research to test and revise the hypotheses generated by the theory. This interaction between theory and research has come because the development of world system theory occurred as new statistical methodologies and computer driven data analysis made such research possible. Before that time one needed an extremely large data set, or many cases, for a statistically valid manipulation of data to test for the simultaneous effects of different things on the conditions you want to explain. When comparing periphery or less developed nations, of course, the unit of analysis is generally nations, so the researcher is limited to 100 or so nations at best. With the advance of "time-series analysis," however, some of these problems have been overcome.

The typical methodology of world system research today (time-series analysis) involves a sample of 50 to 100 less developed nations. Data on a number of independent variables are collected, such as the extent of outside multinational corporate investment in each country, the amount of foreign aid flowing into each country, outstanding debt to richer nations and international agencies, trade flows, and so on. Then, data on dependent variables are collected, measuring such things as growth in GNP, income inequality, and various indications of standards of living such as poverty levels, life expectancy, and infant mortality. Using lagged time intervals of 5 or 10 years to give the independent variables (such as multinational corporate investment) time to have their theorized effects, statistical correlations are made to see if relationships can be found among these variables (such as the connection between multinational corporate investments and higher levels of income inequality after 10 years).

This type of research has always been complex because there can be disputes over the correct measures of variables and even the correct indicators of important factors from world system theory such as what constitutes direct outside investments. Despite these problems, and despite all of the disputes and controversy, 30 years of research on the modern world system has shown impressive results. Much of the details of the theory have been supported and other parts revised in response to this research. But we must be clear on what this research has shown and has *not* shown, and we must be clear on the inherent limitations of the comparative time-series methodology generally used in the past 30 years.

First, a statistically significant relationship between, say multinational investment in one point of time and slower economic growth in a later time (10 years later) means quite simply that *most* nations with heavy amounts of multinational corporate investments have reduced economic growth rates later. It *does not* mean this happens in *all* nations. *Some* nations within the sample may have high levels of outside multinational corporate investments *and* strong economic growth in later years. Quite often in this research the authors will note that some countries (at times not even identified) are outliers, meaning they are located out on the margins of where the other countries line up on the variables. But then the subject is dropped. Why are they outliers? What is different about these countries that do not conform to the statistically significant relationship between the important variables studied? We will see that quite often in this world system research the outliers are Asian nations.

Second, we must recognize that the methodologies used by most world system research follow a Durkheimian tradition (see the critique by Ragin & Zaret, 1983; Smelser, 1976). It was Durkheim who first assumed there are "natural laws" of human behavior and social organization that span across all societies and then showed how these laws might be discovered in his masterful work *Suicide* in 1897 (Durkheim, 1951). Following this Durkheimian methodology the research can uncover important tendencies across nations, for example, but at the same time much of the detail about what is happening within each nation is ignored. This methodology has brought recent charges that world system research is missing "internal processes" within nations that help produce differing outcomes among these nations with the same level of outside multinational investments (Alderson & Nielsen, 1999). The comparative-historical research of Max Weber, in contrast, rejected such single-dimensional laws of the Durkheimian perspective and called instead for the recognition of complex and *somewhat unique combinations* of historical forces interacting to produce important outcomes for each nation. Further, Weber recognized that a certain outcome could even have different causes in differing nations (Smelser, 1976:142). To the extent this is true, it is obvious that a *qualitative* historical and comparative analysis of specific nations or groups of relatively similar nations is best suited to detect important differences within nations or groups of nations that affect their chances for economic development (as suggested in Ragin, 2000). Qualitative research does not rely primarily upon numbers or things that can be easily measured and compared across many nations. Qualitative research means the researcher must seek to uncover more specific details about each particular case (such as a nation's level of economic development) which is then studied before attempting comparisons to other nations that have also been studied with qualitative research methods. Along with some quantitative data such as that presented in our "Data File" boxes, I will primarily rely upon qualitative data in coming chapters to identify important characteristics and historical influences on less developed nations that result in economic development or stagnation.

We are not saying that current methods of world system research should be abandoned and previous findings rejected. In just 30 years there has been an impressive record of empirical research on issues related to modern world system theory. Much has been learned about the effects of holding a particular rank in this world system for specific countries and the people in these countries. In the second wave of research on the world system during the late 1980s and early 1990s much has also been learned about the internal processes (such as the nature of the state, type of trade, level of human capital) that interact with variables such as world system rank and level of outside multinational corporate investment to produce outcomes such as more or less economic development, or more or less income inequality.

To achieve a better understanding of the effects of the modern world system on the prospects of poverty or economic development for the world's masses, however, it seems a third wave of research should include a greater number of case studies using a more qualitative historical and comparative analysis. Research on economic development in Taiwan by Richard Barrett and Martin King Whyte published in 1982 started world

DATA FILE

Foreign Direct Investment and Contrasting Outcomes
by Patrick Ziltener

Despite a clear lack of evidence, the leaders of rich capitalist countries and global capitalist organizations like the IMF (International Monetary Fund) tell us again and again that open markets are good for the world's poor. One of the few leading economists to point out this lack of evidence is Joseph Stiglitz who won a Noble Prize for his work in 2002. The call for open markets in less developed countries is like "trickle down economics" preached by conservative politicians since the time of Ronald Reagan in the 1980s. As Stiglitz (2004) puts it:

> Trickle-down economics became discredited for an obvious reason: it was not true. Sometimes growth helps poor people, but sometimes it does not. By some measures poverty increased in Latin America in the 1990s, even in many countries where there

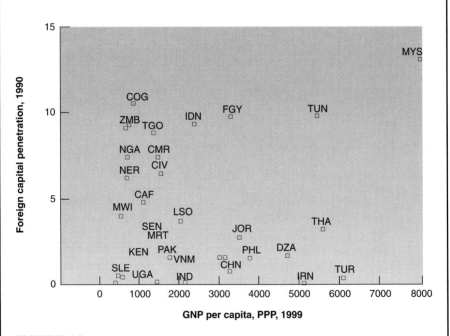

FIGURE 4.2   *Foreign Capital Penetration and GNP per Capita*

NOTE: The following are World Bank country codes used in the figure.
Algeria = DZA, Angola = AGO, Botswana = BWA, Cameroon = CMR, Central African Rep. = CAF, Chad = TCD, China, P.R.: Mainland = CHN, Congo, Republic of = COG, Ivory Coast, Côte d'Ivoire = CIV, Egypt = EGY, Ethiopia = ETH, India = IND, Indonesia = IDN, Iran, I.R. of = IRN, Jordan = JOR, Kenya = KEN, Lao People's Dem. Rep = LAO, Lesotho = LSO, Malawi = MWI, Malaysia = MYS, Martinique = MTQ, Mauritania = MRT, Mauritius = MUS, Mexico = MEX, Moldova = MDA, Mongolia = MNG, Morocco = MAR, Mozambique = MOZ, Niger = NER, Nigeria = NGA, Philippines = PHL, Sierra Leone = SLE, South Africa = ZAF, Tanzania = TZA, Thailand = THA, Togo = TGO, Tunisia = TUN, Turkey = TUR, Vietnam = VNM, Zambia = ZMB.

(Continued)

was growth. It was not just that well-off people gained disproportionately from growth: some of their gains may even have been at the expense of poor people. (p. 80)

Given this lack of evidence that open markets almost always produce economic development and poverty reduction around the world it is easy to understand why some people assume there is some kind of capitalist plot to take advantage of the world's poor. This is especially so when the evidence is clear that rich countries profit from these open markets in poorer nations.

As already shown in our Chapter 1 Data File, the relationship between economic development as measured by GNP per capita and poverty reduction is quite varied and complex around the world. The scatter plots in Figures 4.2 and 4.3 support Stiglitz's view that there is no real relationship between open markets and either economic development or poverty reduction. Open markets can be indicated by the amount of foreign direct investment (FDI) coming into a nation. As we see, FDI is not strongly related to either growth in GNP or poverty rates.

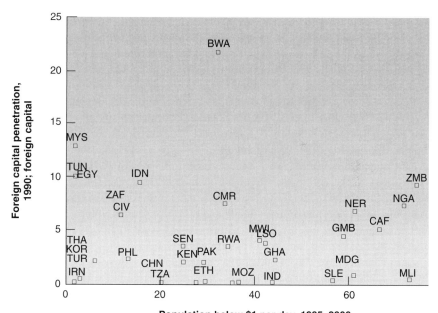

FIGURE 4.3   *Foreign Capital Penetration and Percent Below $1 Per Day*

NOTE: The following are World Bank country codes used in the figure.
Algeria = DZA, Angola = AGO, Botswana = BWA, Cameroon = CMR, Central African Rep. = CAF, Chad = TCD, China, P.R.: Mainland = CHN, Congo, Republic of = COG, Ivory Coast, Côte d'Ivoire = CIV, Egypt = EGY, Ethiopia = ETH, India = IND, Indonesia = IDN, Iran, I.R. of = IRN, Jordan = JOR, Kenya = KEN, Lao People's Dem. Rep = LAO, Lesotho = LSO, Malawi = MWI, Malaysia = MYS, Martinique = MTQ, Mauritania = MRT, Mauritius = MUS, Mexico = MEX, Moldova = MDA, Mongolia = MNG, Morocco = MAR, Mozambique = MOZ, Niger = NER, Nigeria = NGA, Philippines = PHL, Sierra Leone = SLE, South Africa = ZAF, Tanzania = TZA, Thailand = THA, Togo = TGO, Tunisia = TUN, Turkey = TUR, Vietnam = VNM, Zambia = ZMB.

system research in this direction but failed to lead to a broader analysis of Asian nations that could have shown Taiwan is not so much of an exception. In 1988, York Bradshaw published a case analysis of Kenya which specified how that country experienced very uneven economic development with outside multinational corporate investment that made the elite much richer without benefiting the poor (Barrett & Whyte, 1982; Bradshaw, 1988). But much more qualitative, comparative research on specific nations and groups of similar nations must be done if we are to better understand why some nations are able to overcome their extensive poverty and develop economically while others are not. This is a task of this book with respect to Southeast Asian nations.

A Rich Nation Bias

We must confront another type of bias when attempting to understand the world's poor today. There is all too often a common though unstated assumption that "those people" should somehow be more like "us." *At this moment* these people should have better wages and better living conditions, and refrain from sending their young women and children to work in factories. These poor people should no doubt also be "neater," clean up their cities, and of course stop polluting the environment around them. In essence, it seems people from the rich nations expect some kind of magical jump from poverty to affluence almost over night, a jump that skips the stages people must move through to achieve decent wages, a clean environment, and the prohibition of child labor.

Perhaps above all, this rich nation bias involves an ignorance of history. During the industrial expansion of Europe some 150 to 200 years ago, conditions were at best no better, and perhaps worse, when compared to many of the developing nations today. The novels of Charles Dickens, such as *Oliver Twist*, were all too accurate. In the British cotton industry during 1835, for example, 74 percent of the labor was made up of women and children below the age of 18, with 13 percent of the labor force younger than 13. Comparable figures are found for the United States in 1831: Some 60 percent of all laborers in the cotton industry were women (Kuczynski, 1967:51–63; Tilly & Tilly, 1998:Chapter 3). Factory owners preferred the labor of women and children because they were considered more docile and easily controlled. It took more than 100 years before labor laws, pushed by labor organizations, were finally effective in improving the situation in Europe and North America.

This is not to say that the outcry against sweatshops today should stop. Far from it. A similar outcry against the sweatshops of North America in the late nineteenth and early twentieth century paid off quite well in time, and helped found the profession of social work and the famous Settlement House movement. But with over 1 billion people in the world living on less than $1 a day, ending sweatshops will be a formidable task in the near future. Effectiveness in stopping sweatshops will also come only when we in rich nations realize their appeal to those living in periphery countries. I remember living in Bangkok when a news story came out about the rescue of Thai people who had been held as slave laborers in Los Angeles. The response of poor Thais was, "Wow, they made that much money?" As the middle class in rich nations aspire to things such as a college education and well-paid professional jobs for their children, those living on less than $1 a day aspire to sweatshop jobs for their children—it is a considerable step up for them. Sweatshops around the world will be easier to eliminate when they are considered a step down for everyone.

In the chapters that follow I will first present something of Asia as a general case in and of itself using a type of qualitative historical and comparative analysis I have argued for above. Later chapters will be more directly devoted to a qualitative historical and comparative analysis of Southeast Asian nations themselves, particularly the Theravada Buddhist countries of Southeast Asia (Thailand, Burma, Laos, and Cambodia) to control for the supposed impact of culture on economic development. There will also be chapters on poverty in African and Latin American countries. With this analysis it is hoped that we can better understand why many Asian nations have been something of exceptions to the tendency for poorer nations to experience economic stagnation with extensive outside multinational investments from the rich core nations, or uneven economic development. Finally, it is also hoped that this analysis will contribute to eliminating at least some of the many Western biases in North American and European sociology that have rendered these theories not only weak in attempts to understand a majority of the world's population, but also weaker than they otherwise would be in providing us with a better understanding of the causes and possible cures of world poverty.

Notes

1. When people are in large crowds, according to Le Bon, the excitement and emotion of it all can allow the collective mind of our "animal nature" to overtake our civilized mind. Also, according to Le Bon, the lower orders of society, as well as women and children, were more susceptible to being overcome by the collective mind. Today, Le Bon's view is known as the "aristocratic view" or the "balcony view" of crowd behavior. See Gustave Le Bon, *The Crowd: A Study of the Popular Mind* (Dunwoody, GA: Norman S. Berg, 1897/1960).
2. See, for example, Max Weber, *The Religion of China* (New York: Free Press, 1951). This use of Weber in explaining Asian miracles is ironic because in his original works about 100 years ago Max Weber attempted to explain why Asian nations could *not* develop economically like the Protestant nations of Western Europe. We now know that Weber, having never traveled to Asia, was misled by many accounts of Asia written by Westerners of his day. By the last decades of the twentieth century, Asian values seemed a good place to look for explanations of Asian economic miracles.
3. All of these projects, as well as dozens of conference papers, can be found on the World Bank Web site, http://www.worldbank.org.
4. For example, some research suggests that the relationship between core involvement and less economic development in poor nations over the long term can be affected by such things as the type of goods imported or exported. Also, the level of technology within the periphery nation at the time it is brought into the modern world system is important in influencing whether or not the periphery nation can achieve economic growth. Periphery nations that have more advanced agriculture when brought into the modern world system through core investments, for example, are more likely to have some economic growth. See Kenneth Bollen and Stephen J. Appold, "National Industrial Structure and the Global System," *American Sociological Review* 58 (1993), pp. 283–301; Gerhard Lenski and Patrick Nolan,

"Trajectories of Development: A Test of Ecological-Evolutionary Theory," *Social Forces* 63 (1984), pp. 1–23; Gerhard Lenski and Patrick Nolan, "Trajectories of Development: A Further Test," *Social Forces* 64 (1986), pp. 794–795.

5. Robert Jackman, *Politics and Social Equality: A Comparative Analysis* (New York: Wiley, 1975); Christopher Hewitt, "The Effect of Political Democracy and Social Democracy on Equality in Industrial Societies: A Cross-National Comparison," *American Sociological Review* 42 (1977), pp. 450–463; Steven Stack, "The Effect of Direct Government Involvement in the Economy on the Degree of Income Inequality: A Cross-National Study," *American Sociological Review* 43 (1978), pp. 880–888; Erich Weede, "Beyond Misspecification in Sociological Analysis of Income Inequality," *American Sociological Review* 45 (1980), pp. 497–501. More recent research, however, has shown a new pattern of inequality increasing again in Western industrial societies, especially following the pattern of the United States in recent decades: Francois Nielsen and Arthur S. Alderson, "The Kuznets Curve and the Great U-Turn: Income Inequality in US Counties, 1970 to 1990," *American Sociological Review* 62 (1997), pp. 12–33. But this change in the pattern of income inequality for the most developed of North America, Europe, and Japan is primarily related to internal causes not found in the poorer countries today.

6. Richard Barrett and Martin King Whyte, "Dependency Theory and Taiwan: Analysis of a Deviant Case," *American Journal of Sociology* 87 (1982), pp. 1064–1089; Heather-Jo Hammer, "Comment of 'Dependency Theory and Taiwan: Analysis of a Deviant Case," *American Journal of Sociology* 89 (1984), pp. 932–936. Another limited study by Tsai (Pan-Long Tsai, "Foreign Direct Investment and Income Inequality: Further Evidence," *World Development* 23 [1995], pp. 469–483) seems to be the only research that considers Asian effects separately. This research found foreign direct investment increases income inequality in Asia more than in other regions, but notes this is likely due to Asian inequality already being less than in other developing nations, and thus has more room to rise. The research does not consider this effect could be due to the fact that multinational corporate investment generates more growth in Asia. This is a likely possibility we must consider in later chapters.

7. One exception to this as we have seen and will see in more detail in the next chapter is an analysis of Taiwan by Barrett and Whyte, "Dependency Theory and Taiwan." However, they do not take their analysis beyond Taiwan to other Asian nations. Also, in his analysis of Taiwan's economic development, Gold notes that modern world system theory is biased toward Latin American when trying to explain problems of economic development (Thomas B. Gold, *State and Society in the Taiwan Miracle* [Armonk, NY: M.E. Sharpe, 1986]). But as we will see in the next chapter, no other work has expanded upon this bias in world system theory with a broader analysis of East and Southeast Asian nations.

8. This is also to say that elites in any type of society must select from these value orientations in the society to seek legitimation for what they are doing. And to maintain their popularity elites must try to at least show that the values held dear by the people are being followed in reality, such as the attempts to show how "equality of opportunity" exists in the United States.

9. For the much earlier and extensive tradition of a "sociology of sociology" directed toward "deconstructing" sociological theory, see for example, Alvin Gouldner, *The Coming Crisis in Western Sociology* (New York: Basic Books, 1970); Robert Friedrichs, *A Sociology of Sociology* (New York: Free Press, 1970); Andrew Effrat, "Power to the Paradigms," in *Perspectives in Political Sociology*, ed. Andrew Effrat, pp. 3–34 (New York: Bobbs-Merrill, 1972).

The Roots of "Asian Miracles": Ancient Traditions and Development States

In the last decades of the twentieth century we became accustomed to television scenes of starvation and desperate poverty in Africa. For most of the twentieth century, though, it was actually China and India, rather than Africa, that first came to mind when the subject of third world hunger was mentioned. In the mid-twentieth century, mothers like mine all over America told their children to clean their plates by saying, "think of all the starving children in China." If we had the calculations I am quite certain they would show that during the twentieth century many more millions have died of hunger and diseases in China and India than the rest of the world combined. China, the world's most populous nation, was devastated by European colonialism. The last Imperial Dynasty fell into a massive revolution in 1911 that did not really end until the communist government became more stable after 1975. In the middle of it all was Japanese invasion, World War II, communist revolution, and Mao's bloody Cultural Revolution. In the end, however, one must admit that almost no one is starving in China today. As we enter the twenty-first century it is China that has more rapid economic development than any other county.

With mass poverty and starvation in much of Asia through most of the twentieth century we can perhaps understand Western ignorance of the past glories of China and India. It is this ignorance, however, that tricks people into assuming that the West has always led the world and "no doubt always will." Nothing could be further from the truth. As we have already seen, in the last 1,000 years Asian countries (mainly India and China) accounted for more than half of the world's economy (GNP) until just 200 years ago (Kristof & WuDunn, 2000: 29–31; Maddison, 1998). In the early twenty-first century Asia is poised to regain a dominant share of the world's GNP, with China likely overtaking the United States as the world's largest economy before 2025 (*International Herald Tribune,* May 23, 2001). But it was not just the size of Asian economies during 80 percent of the last 1,000 years that was important. China was also ahead of the West in science and technology during much of this period (Needham, 1983).

India and China, however, were not alone in their economic expansion in this early age. Going back more than 1,000 years there were important trading empires in what we consider to be Southeast Asia today, empires sending their merchant ships out and receiving those of other nations throughout Asia (Osbourne, 1995:17–32; Reid, 1988, 1993, 1999). In his recent critique of modern world system theory, we have seen that Andre Gunder Frank, in his recent book *ReOrient: Global Economy in the Asian Age,* has claimed that the modern world system actually began in Asia long before the Europeans emerged as dominant. Evidence of this can be seen today in the beautiful

Economic growth and poverty reduction in Vietnam is even more impressive than in China. During my first visit to Hanoi about 10 years ago, this same street was only filled with bicycles with almost no motorbikes or cars. It is now almost impossible to cross the crowded streets on foot. In the next picture, we see a large modern shopping mall with expensive French and Italian designer shops in the center of Hanoi in 2004 that were not there when I visited two years earlier.

little city of Hoi An, on the central coast of Vietnam. Declared a United Nations historical site in 2000, there are well-preserved Chinese and Japanese sections of the city, as well as Dutch and Portugese sections, where merchants from all over the early Asian world system came together some 500 to 1,000 years ago. As Frank notes, we can more accurately say that the Europeans copied many features of the Asian world system, in essence, buying into it with the silver and gold they were stealing from the Americas. During the 1500s and 1600s most of that silver and gold taken out of the Americas did in fact end up in Asia as the Europeans were buying valued goods they were unable to produce themselves (Frank, 1998:65–67).

Most people in the West are surprised by figures showing Asia will soon overtake Europe and North America in overall size of GNP; and they marvel at the "economic miracles" of East and Southeast Asia producing much more rapid economic development and poverty reduction than ever seen in the West. But the West had better get used to giving more credit and respect to Asia, for Asians are more and more in a position to demand such credit and respect. Likewise, the West had better get used to the fact that commerce and *economic development can be achieved in ways Western economists think impossible,* because many Asian nations are doing it.

Asian "Economic Miracles"

During the early 1990s Japan began what we now know was a long stagnation that has lasted into the twenty-first century. Then, in early July of 1997, with growing economic problems the Thai government decided to allow the currency (baht) to float after long denying it would take such action. Previously tagged at around 25 baht to the U.S. dollar, the baht immediately plunged and continued to plunge until it hit a low of 55 baht to the U.S. dollar only 6 months later. This drop in the value of the Thai currency

T A B L E   5 . 1

Percentage Growth in GNP by World Region, 1965–2002

	1965–1988	1990–1999	1998–1999	2001–2002
East Asia and Pacific	5.2	7.4	7.2	6.7
Latin America and Caribbean	0.2	3.4	−0.9	−0.5
South Asia	1.8	5.7	6.2	4.3
Sub-Saharan Africa	0.2	2.4	2.0	3.2

Sources: World Bank, 1990:179; World Bank, 2000:277, 294; World Bank, 2004d:253.

set off panic across East and South East Asia, creating what came to be called the Asian economic crisis.

Given that the Asian economic miracles were not supposed to happen according to accepted economic theories, many, if not most, American and British economists felt exonerated by the Asian economic crisis—but only briefly (see especially Fallows, 1994). Equally remarkable was the speed in which the Asian economic crisis began to resolve itself when most East and Southeast Asian nations made their economic adjustments (though not always ones specified by the IMF) to return to positive growth figures by the end of 1999. And while it seems accurate to say that most Asian nations have not achieved enough reform of their financial institutions, looking back at the episode in 25 years or so it might be said that the Asian economic crisis of 1997 was a positive stimulus to needed economic corrections after almost 20 years of rapid economic expansion. No other world region in modern history has grown so fast, including North America and Europe during their early years of industrialization. Table 5.1 shows that there was certainly nothing like the Asian economic boom of the 1980s and 1990s in Latin America or Africa. Latin American countries, in fact, are the ones most following the "Washington consensus" of open markets. Although there has been some economic development in South Asia and Sub-Saharan Africa, there has been much less or no poverty reduction compared to East and Southeast Asia, nor has the standard of living shown much increase because of continued high rates of population growth.

The situation for the world's poor cannot be shown with simple economic growth rates. Economic growth does not always mean poverty reduction—in fact, far from it in many countries. For example, the most dominant economy in Latin America, Brazil, had a per capita income of almost $8,000 (measured in Purchasing Power Parity) at the end of the twentieth century. At the same time, the poorest 20 percent of the people in Brazil received only 2.5 percent of the income while the richest 20 percent of the people received more than 68.3 percent of the income in 1996. Over 5 percent of the Brazilian population lived on less than $1 per day. Currently, the percentage of the population in Brazil with what the World Bank defines as access to sanitation is only 67 percent, whereas it is 96 percent in Thailand. The per capita GNP of Thailand (just over $6,000) is a bit lower than that of Brazil, but even with growing inequality from the bubble economy of the early 1990s, in 1998 the bottom 20 percent of the people in Thailand received 6.8 percent of the income while the top 20 percent of the people received 48.4 percent (Slagter & Kerbo, 2000:66–69). Moreover, only 1 percent of the

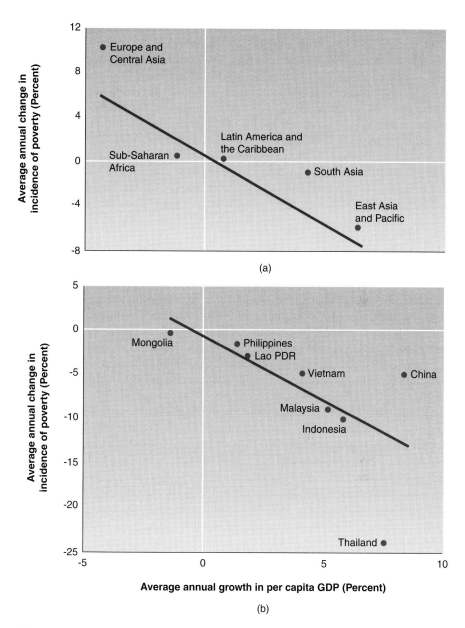

FIGURE 5.1 *Economic Growth and Poverty Reduction (a) across Regions of the World; (b) across Regions in East Asia.*

SOURCE: World Bank, 2000:48.

Thai population lived on less than $1 per day at the end of the twentieth century compared to the 5 percent in Brazil.

The World Bank's *World Development Report 2000/2001* includes calculations indicating East and Southeast Asia have the best records for poverty reduction per each percentage increase in GNP of any of world region. Figure 5.1 shows the country's rate of GDP growth across the bottom and the rate of poverty reduction along the left side of the figure. Putting the two together we find Asian nations fall along a line going down as we move to the right (toward higher levels of economic growth), thus showing poverty reduction and economic growth are strongly related for most Asian nations. In the second figure indicating poverty reduction per growth in GDP for Asian nations only, we find that Thailand had the best rate in the early 1990s—the Thai poverty rate reduction was far off the line shown for the other Asian nations (indicating much more poverty reduction per growth in GDP). The World Bank likes to claim that open markets and multinational corporate investment reduces poverty all over the world. With stagnation in Latin America, however, a closer look at World Bank figures shows this is the case only in most of East and Southeast Asia (Hossien & Weiss, 2003; Jomo, 2001; Stiglitz, 2004; Weder, 1999).

Returning to the expanding protest against multinational corporations' exploitation of poor people around the world, it is important to stress that the *solid economic development and poverty reduction in East and Southeast Asia has been happening despite (and often because of) the extensive corporate investment coming from the outside*. Of the 29 nations described as "leading" developing nations by the World Bank, in 1999 alone the private capital in flows totaled more than $136 billion, with 60 percent going to Asian countries (*International Herald Tribune,* January 4, 2000). There was over $64 trillion in foreign direct investment in East and Southeast Asia by 1998, which according to exploitation theories and modern world system theory should mean less long-term economic development and growing poverty (World Bank, 2000:315). Obviously something is wrong with these theories, at least with respect to much of Asia. We know now that a high amount of FDI going into a developing nation will be less harmful and more positive to future economic development and poverty reduction if the FDI comes from many different rich countries rather than a few (Kentor, 2001; Kentor & Boswell, 2003). But this begs the question of how a developing nation is able to achieve this healthier mix of FDI, as more Southeast Asian nations such as Thailand have done.

Why are developing nations in Asia often different from those in Latin America and Africa? Why has there been more solid economic development spread more equally among people in Asia? How is it possible that most East and Southeast Asian nations have relatively less poverty and inequality than developing nations in other world regions?

Even though the predictions of modern world system theory don't seem to fit in most of East and Southeast Asia, modernization theory, with its focus on culture, at first seems well suited for explaining the Asian economic miracles. In reality, however, *modernization theory has even more shortcomings*. First of all, there is much more cultural variation among Asian nations, even among the Asian nations that have had solid economic growth and poverty reduction, than modernization theory would recognize. Second, and more critical, *groups of Asian nations that have almost identical cultural traditions have very different development outcomes today*. As will be explored in later chapters, Vietnam shares key cultural characteristics with the Chinese "tiger nations" such as Taiwan and Singapore. Vietnam, of course, is only now showing strong signs of economic development and poverty reduction. We will see that Burma, Thailand, Laos, and Cambodia share the same traditions of Theravada Buddhism: One of these nations has an excellent record of poverty reduction with economic development, while the others are among the world's poorest nations with no immediate prospects for significant economic development.

What can generally be called *development theory* is more likely to focus on the mechanisms or techniques used to bring about economic development in poor countries. Significant progress in some countries has been achieved by international development agencies with new methods and technologies in agriculture, empowering women, and simple programs such as "microloans" for small projects such as a water pump to help irrigate crops. Interesting research has also suggested that traditional forms of social organization must be considered in understanding what type of investments and trade can be most successful for bringing economic success to a nation (see, for example, Biggart & Cuillen, 1999). But development theory has paid little attention to *what allows these new techniques for development to be used in the first place.* What are the broad social characteristics of societies that allow for the introduction of these techniques of economic development? What characteristics of poor countries motivate people to employ these techniques of economic development? And more important, *what social characteristics lead the rich and powerful in the poor nation to help rather than block programs for economic development?*

With few exceptions, none of these theories and research traditions have paid much attention to the broader characteristics of societies, or the general characteristics of countries in whole world regions, that may have important effects on the success of economic development. In other words, none of these research traditions are adequate in helping us understand why many East and Southeast Asian nations have been much more successful in achieving sustained economic development, economic development that brings a higher standard of living for most people in the region, compared to Latin America or Africa. There is little or nothing said about how cooperation of the elite in poor countries can be forthcoming so that economic development techniques are not blocked by powerful people in these countries. Modern world system theory, of course, is much more aware of political power and conflicts of interest between the rich and poor of developing countries. But modern world system theory also has its problems. We have seen economic figures suggesting that outside investments from rich multinationals (a focus of world system theory) tend to help rather than harm poorer Asian nations. With one partial exception, almost none of this is found in the world system literature. We must consider this exception before we examine the characteristics of Asian nations more broadly.

The Development of Underdevelopment: Taiwan as an Exception

One of the few cases in which research from the world system perspective has been focused on an Asian country appeared in 1982 with Richard Barrett and Martin King Whyte's article titled, "Dependency Theory and Taiwan: Analysis of a Deviant Case" (Barrett & Whyte, 1982). Following world system theory, which suggests that less developed countries can be harmed and their economic development stunted by extensive foreign multinational corporate investment, Barrett and Whyte examined why Taiwan was able to achieve strong economic development despite this outside intervention. At the time of their analysis South Korea was the only other country that could have served as a "deviant case" because Singapore and Hong Kong were rather unique in being small city-states left over from the old British empire.[1] In 1982 they had no way of knowing that some other nations in Southeast Asia would take off economically, and then China, providing other deviant cases throughout East and Southeast Asia. Before we turn to these other countries, and characteristics of Asian nations more generally, it is useful to begin with the case of Taiwan.

A bit of history first. For hundreds of years the island now referred to as Taiwan moved between independence and being a province of China. Japan took Taiwan as a colony in 1895 after a short war with China and then kept Taiwan until Japan was defeated in 1945. From the beginning of Japanese occupation there was extensive development of agriculture to supplement Japan's inadequate resources. But soon after liberation from the Japanese the Chinese mainland anticommunist party led by Chiang Kai-Shek fled Mao's successful communist revolution on the mainland to set up their government in exile on Taiwan in 1949. Most of the upper-class Chinese who had supported Chiang Kai-Shek and his Kuomintang Party did not follow him to Taiwan, settling instead in other locations, particularly Hong Kong (Gold, 1986: 70). But there was enough of a middle and upper class to follow Chiang to Taiwan, which in combination with the preexisting infrastructure for agricultural development, gave Taiwan an economic basis for potential economic development.

But this provided only the *potential* for economic development. One of the most important factors lacking in many if not most poor countries is the *political organization and motivation of elites* to promote policies that can bring about sustained economic development which benefits everyone in the nation. In the case of Taiwan, from the 1950s there was a national political elite within Chiang's Kuomintang Party that was strongly motivated to achieve such development. As all accounts of the Chinese Revolution point out, to a large degree Mao and the Communist Party were victorious on the mainland because of the Kuomintang Party's short-sighted corruption and economic policies favoring only the affluent in China before 1949 (Fairbank, 1986; Skocpol, 1979). Realizing they had lost the revolution to Mao for these reasons, Kuomintang Party elites resolved to overcome the corruption and promote rapid economic development that would benefit all of the Chinese on the island of Taiwan so as not to lose the allegiance of these people again (Gold, 1986:57, 67). The place of Taiwan in the United States' conduct of the cold war, of course, was also crucial in that the United States gave Taiwan extensive aid and special treatment as a show case against communism. But it seems evident that this alone would not have enabled Taiwan to develop among the ranks of the four tigers without the other resources and a national elite ready to follow development policies and overcome corruption within their ranks. This is in contrast to South Vietnam during the 1960s, for example, which received extensive aid from the U.S. government but was unable or unwilling to overcome corruption and self-serving policies among the political elite. The contrast is even greater when considering the Philippines and its slide into economic stagnation and greater poverty during the 1960s and 1970s under Ferdinand Marcos despite extensive U.S. aid and support (Karrow, 1989).

We find some relatively unique details in Taiwan such as an agricultural infrastructure and a large government transported from mainland China. There are nonetheless some important factors setting the stage for Taiwan's strong economic development that are common among several other East and Southeast Asian nations, including factors setting the stage for Japan's economic expansion earlier. Among the most important of these factors was *low material inequality* among the general population and a *strong state* with *elites motivated and able to protect national interests.*

Many development experts have stressed the need for limited inequality to promote unity and allegiance among the general population. Lower inequality can also help provide more domestic consumers able to spend money and sustain economic development. Further, low levels of inequality and poverty help promote the expansion of an educated middle class needed to staff and run a modernizing economy.[2] In Taiwan the foundation for relatively low inequality was first established by extensive land reform (redistribution) carried out by the Kuomintang Party from 1949 to 1953. Then, as economic development took hold, the Taiwanese government used its influence to reduce income inequality. The income gap between the top 20 percent of the population and the bottom 20 percent of the population dropped from 12 to 1 in 1960 to 4 to 1 by 1980 (Gold, 1986:112).

This action to reduce inequality by the state brings us to another important characteristic. As described in more detail below, a strong state, or *development state,* with the means and the will to bring about sustained economic development is one of the most important factors, and one of the most difficult to achieve.[3] In the case of Taiwan after Mao's revolution on the mainland, not only did the old Kuomintang Party elites realize their survival depended upon creating popular allegiance through economic development, there was the "means" in the form of a strong state the Kuomintang Party had transported from the mainland.

With this strong state in place the Kuomintang Party elites began working out their *economic development policies*—that is, the technical means of establishing economic development that would protect national interests and bring about sustained, less uneven economic development. There was the now common policy first favoring *import substitution.* With import substitution the development state limits imports into the country so that consumer goods and material needed for domestic industries could be produced within the country. This works to limit "structural distortion" in the economy when jobs and profits are lost to rich countries. Then there was the common policy favoring *export industries.* With this policy the government helps stimulate the production of goods for export to the rich nations to obtain a favorable balance of trade and the inflow of capital or funds for further investment (Barrett & Whyte, 1982; Gold, 1986). During this time the Taiwanese state also promoted policies that would help create *economic diversity.* Economic diversity gives flexibility and economic stability when world market conditions hurt some industries or outside economic actors attempt to manipulate prices or supplies. Likewise, from the 1960s onward the state enforced policies of savings and fiscal restraint. There was relatively little foreign borrowing after this time and 20 to 30 percent of GNP was saved and reinvested (Gold, 1986:4–7).

Before these policies could be successfully carried out, the strong state, or development state, had to maintain some control over (1) the powerful multinational corporations wanting to exploit the resources and market within Taiwan and (2) the more affluent among the domestic population who wanted to maintain a high standard of living with quick economic returns that could harm long-term national economic interests. The development state dominated by the reformed Kuomintang on Taiwan was able to control both of these interest groups by funneling almost all foreign economic investment through the state (Gold, 1986:73).

It is important to note again that Taiwan was the first, and still primarily the only country to be analyzed by researchers following the modern world system perspective. The Asian studies literature, of course, has considered the process of economic development from an Asian perspective, and much of it seriously questions basic assumptions of Western economic theory. Specifically, what is commonly called the Asian development model has been instrumental in all cases of rapid development in Asia (Chang, 1999; Cumings, 1999; Johnson, 1982, 1999; Kerbo & Slagter, 2000a; Lau, 1996; Pempel, 1999; Woo-Cumings, 1996, 1999). This Asian development model was conceptualized and first implemented in Japan as far back as the late 1800s with the Meiji Restoration, then perfected more and more from the 1920s in Japan (Aoki, 1996; Chang, 1999; Fallows, 1994; Johnson, 1982; Okazaki, 1996; Vogel, 1991). Before examining this Asian development model in more detail we must consider other major characteristics of Asian nations related to the use of the model.

Asian Traditions and Social Organization: Some Commonalities

In contrast to the image held by most Westerners, Asian nations are not "all alike." In fact, while moving from, say, Japan to Korea, from Korea to China, and then from China into Southeast Asian nations, one encounters more variety and contrast of cultures than if one were to travel through modern Europe. For one example, as we move from Japan to Korea and China we find only little change in the subservient position of women outside the home. But as we move into some of the mainland Southeast Asian nations (with the exception of Vietnam) we find regions with traditions of matrilocalism where daughters have historically inherited the land and their husbands must come to live with the wifes' families (Osborne, 1995; Slagter & Kerbo, 2000). When we move further south into Southeast Asian nations dominated by Islam, of course, we again find major changes in the role of women. Similarly, Westerners tend to assume that all Asian religions are rather alike; Confucianism, Buddhism, Shinto, and Taoism seem to blend into one mass of Asian religions in Western minds. But Confucianism exists only in East Asian nations (with the exception of Vietnam in Southeast Asia), and Buddhism varies significantly between East Asia and most of Southeast Asia.

Having said all of this, among the variety of Asian cultures, forms of social organization, and other historical traditions, we can identify some characteristics of Asian societies that are *relatively* common and in contrast to Western societies. But it is useful to think in terms of degrees rather than neat, simple categories. Asian nations, for example, tend to have collectivist rather than individualistic value orientations. That is individual desires and interests are judged as secondary when the needs of a broader group such as the family, local community, work group, or nation come into conflict with these individual desires and interests. However, not all Asian nations equally value the suppression of the individual, nor do Western nations equally value individualism. When considering individualism versus collectivism as a continuum we find that Western nations are clustered toward the individualism end (with the United States, Britain, Canada, and Australia close together) and Asian nations clustered toward the collectivism end of this continuum. There are similar clusters of Western versus Asian nations on values such as "avoidance of uncertainty," "power-distance" (power and respect for authority), and a "long-term orientation" (Hampden-Turner & Trompenaars, 1993; Hofstede, 1991). When we think in terms of degrees of differences in social organization and value orientations we find rather distinct clusters of Western nations and Asian nations on many characteristics despite the fact that there are still differences of degree among Western nations themselves and differences of degree among Asian nations.

Keeping all of this in mind, especially the most important caution that all Asian nations are not alike, we can consider the broad similarities that exist among Asian nations for what they may help us understand about why East and Southeast Asian nations tend to be deviant cases for world system theory. My comparative analysis of Asian nations suggests three characteristics are important for our subject of economic development and poverty reduction. It is time to describe these characteristics before considering how they interact with the varied legacy of colonialism among Asian nations and in Latin America and Africa. Also, after examination of these three Asian characteristics we will give some consideration to the question of Asian values said by many to be important for economic development. While these values may have some positive effects on economic development, it is clear that they are not enough in and of themselves, or even most important for the rapidly developing East and Southeast Asian countries today.

Ancient Civilizations

This general characteristic of Asian nations can be suggested by Hanoi's Temple of Literature, which is in fact one of the first "universities" in Vietnam. In the large court-yards of what remains of the original structures are what look like many tombstones. Upon closer inspection these "tombstones" are in fact engraved records of graduates who had obtained their degrees in the first centuries of this university. What is most remarkable to contemplate are the dates; it turns out this university dates back some 1,000 years, a fact that should humble Oxford graduates, or graduates of the University of Salamanca in Spain who think of themselves as graduating from the oldest universities in Europe. Similar Chinese universities are far older than Vietnam's Temple of Literature.

Placed in this context we can begin to imagine some of the underlying differences between developing nations in Asia, Latin America, and Africa. Latin America and Africa, of course, are continents that once contained ancient civilizations; but the key words are "once contained." About all that exists of the ancient civilizations in South and Central America are old stone pyramids. Just a few hundred years ago Europeans began carving out new national boundaries with colonialism so that the nations of South and Central America today are only some 200 years old. These are infant nations by world standards, with none of the traditions of the old lost civilizations. In Africa, too, we find ancient civilizations and the cradle of human evolution. But again, except for a few cases in northern Africa and the horn of Africa, these old civilizations were mostly destroyed or radically altered by the European colonialists. With the Berlin Conference of 1884–1885 European nations partitioned Africa into what would become nations that make no sense socially, culturally, or ethnically. These are the roots of African political instability today with ethnic group conflicts helping spark one civil war after another (Mazrui, 1978, 1986).

About 300 years before the Europeans had their first universities, in many ways Vietnam was more advanced. The Temple of Literature pictured here was the site of one of Vietnam's first universities about 1,000 years ago.

In contrast to Latin America and Africa, we find throughout most of Asia countries that are the direct descendants or were once central parts of ancient civilizations. To be sure, none of these were as dominant as the Chinese or Indian civilizations, but most Asian nations today have strong roots in ancient civilizations dating back at least a thousand years ago (Fairbank, Reischauer, & Craig, 1970; Frank, 1998; Osborne, 1995; Sardesai, 1989). In contrast to Latin America and Africa, colonialism in Asia was also less likely to result in new countries with boundaries cutting across old civilizations or ethnic groups. Asian nations today are therefore more likely to make "sociological sense" with respect to rather natural societal and cultural boundaries (Myrdal, 1970:64).

There are nations in Asia today that do not fit this general rule, but these are in most cases precisely the Asian nations with most instability and least economic development. Indonesia, for example, has had higher levels of political violence in recent years, political violence that has harmed economic development. Indonesia today is in reality a collection of many old civilizations put together by the Dutch during their colonial dominance of the region. Laos, now one of the poorest countries of Southeast Asia, was in large part created by the French in the 1800s. The national boundaries of Burma, or Myanmar as the military dictators now demand it be called, were largely a construct of British colonialism. Before giving up Burma after World War II, the British fashioned national boundaries that included many people from old civilizations historically opposed to the dominant group. Since independence Burma has remained contested territory with several groups fighting for independence. An ancient civilization, Cambodia is just now regaining some

DATA FILE

The Legacy of State Building and State Efficiency Today

by Patrick Ziltener

One of the strongest correlations in our data set is between precolonial state building and efficiency of state functioning today. The level of state building before the impact of colonialism in less developed nations was measured by the number of levels of government that existed a couple of hundred years ago. In other words, to what extent were there city governments, district-level governments, state-or prefectural-level governments, along with national governments *before* colonial powers took over the country? The scatter plot in Figure 5.2 shows a strong tendency for countries to have more efficient governments today that had more levels of government in their past. The high rankings shown for Asian countries on both scales *clearly indicate the importance of ancient civilizations in many Asian countries*, especially countries such as China, Thailand, and Vietnam. The cases indicated at the bottom are all countries in Sub-Saharan Africa.

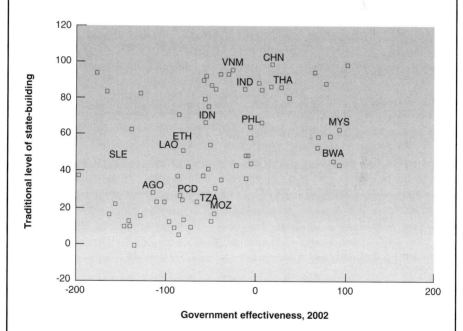

Government effectiveness, 2002

FIGURE 5.2   *State Development 200 Years ago and Government Effectiveness Today*

NOTE: The following are World Bank country codes used in the figure.
Algeria = DZA, Angola = AGO, Botswana = BWA, Cameroon = CMR, Central African Rep. = CAF, Chad = TCD, China, P.R.: Mainland = CHN, Congo, Republic of = COG, Ivory Coast, Côte d'Ivoire = CIV, Egypt = EGY, Ethiopia = ETH, India = IND, Indonesia = IDN, Iran, I.R. of = IRN, Jordan = JOR, Kenya = KEN, Lao People's Dem. Rep = LAO, Lesotho = LSO, Malawi = MWI, Malaysia = MYS, Martinique = MTQ, Mauritania = MRT, Mauritius = MUS, Mexico = MEX, Moldova = MDA, Mongolia = MNG, Morocco = MAR, Mozambique = MOZ, Niger = NER, Nigeria = NGA, Philippines = PHL, Sierra Leone = SLE, South Africa = ZAF, Tanzania = TZA, Thailand = THA, Togo = TGO, Tunisia = TUN, Turkey = TUR, Vietnam = VNM, Zambia = ZMB.

stability after the Indo-China wars involving the French, then the Japanese, then the French, and finally the Americans. The Philippines is the nation in the region with least claim to an ancient civilization and most dominated and changed by Western colonialists, the Spanish, and then the Americans, losing comparatively more of its indigenous culture.[4] When I first visited the Philippines after spending much more time in other Southeast Asian nations I was amazed at the lack of old native traditions. There are no ancient native Philippine capital cities to visit as there are in other Southeast Asian nations. The oldest urban structures one can tour were built by the Spanish colonists. Today the Philippines includes extensive Muslim areas among the dominant Christian areas, creating the roots of the Islamic separatist rebellion that continues to break into open warfare from time to time.

Traditions of Authority and Elite Responsibility

In addition to a greater sense of national identity among the population that comes with ancient civilizations, the older civilizations of Asia are more likely to have retained ancient traditions of authority, elite responsibility, and elites who strongly identify with national interests as well. In Myrdal's description, European colonialism in Asia was less likely to harm "the indigenous system of rights and obligations among the population" (Myrdal, 1970:212). As noted in the previous chapter, outside intervention by rich multinational corporations often presents a situation in which wealthy and powerful elites within less developed nations can enrich themselves, often at the expense of long-term economic development and the continued poverty of people in their country.[5] In contrast, when faced with the dilemma of pleasing outside multinationals or pushing for some protection and benefits for their nation and the common people, elites in countries with these ancient traditions of obligations will more likely temper their narrow self-interests to protect the nation and people.

Even in the ancient Asian civilizations, throughout history and today, elites at times ignore these traditions of elite responsibility. But in the long run they ignore these traditions at their own peril. As noted sociologist and historian Barrington Moore demonstrated in his masterful book *Injustice: The Social Bases of Obedience and Revolt,* throughout history, when these elite obligations were violated, various types of protest or even revolutions were likely forthcoming. The three obligations most important for elites to uphold, Moore's historical works suggest, are (1) protection from outside forces, (2) internal peace and order, and (3) material security (Moore, 1978:21). Much the same is described in the historical analysis of political violence and rebellion in European feudal societies by Charles Tilly (Tilly, 1978, 1981; Tilly et al., 1975). As European nations moved from old feudal societies to industrial societies, Tilly shows that rebellion was most often related to state building and changes (such as taxation) that violated the old elite obligations. Finally, Gerhard Lenski's historical examination of elite rule suggests that elite-sponsored ideologies to some extent can modify what the common people think about the specifics of such obligations (Lenski, 1966:180). But over the long run, more or less blatant violation of these obligations will eventually bring political violence directed against elite rule.

Much the same can be found in the ancient civilizations of Asia. In his comparative history of the mandate to rule and modernization in Europe and Asia,

Reinhard Bendix noted that from at least 2000 BC there was the idea of a "heavenly mandate" for emperors in China. But emperors were obligated to take care of the nation and "perform," in a sense, or the mandate would be lost. The earliest emperors were believed to deserve their rule because they alone had the power to control ancestor spirits for the good of the nation (Bendix, 1978:49–56). By 500 BC, however, Confucius worked out his philosophy of rights and obligations between rulers and subjects in response to almost 200 years of social disorder. These old traditions of rights and obligations in China held the nation more or less together and maintained emperor rule for centuries until emperors began to have greater difficulty meeting their obligations with social change and European colonialism. These were the changes that led eventually to massive revolution in China throughout most of the twentieth century (Fairbank, 1986).

In Japan, rule by an emperor or a military clan called a *shogun* involved similar obligations and rights established through centuries of social evolution. There is a myth today of Japan as a nation of harmony and obedience to authority. In reality, Japanese history is full of rebellion by subjects when they felt the obligations of ruling elites were not fulfilled (Bowen, 1980; Eisenstadt, 1996; Gluck, 1985; Hane, 1982).

Most kingdoms in Southeast Asia are relatively more recent when compared to those of India and China. Some of the first were found in Cambodia (Angkor), Sumatra (Srivijaya), and Burma (Pagan) around AD 800. But like other Asian empires, these "Buddhist kingdoms," along with Vietnam's Confucian model inherited from China, also had strong traditions of obligations and rights developed and amended over the centuries. Most of these traditions of elite obligations survived European colonialism, though there are some relative exceptions, such as in the Philippines without the kind of ancient civilization found on mainland Southeast Asia, and which was more dominated and changed by Spanish rule (Osborne 1995:17–27, 45–50).

Development State

In Volume II of his famous work *Asian Drama: An Inquiry into the Poverty of Nations*, Nobel Prize–winning economist Gunnar Myrdal (1968) wrote in reference to South Asia:

> [T]hroughout the region, national governments require extraordinarily little of their citizens. There are few obligations either to do things in the interest of the community or to avoid actions opposed to that interest. Even those obligations that do exist are enforced inadequately if at all. (p. 896)

Myrdal was referring to the problem of "soft states" primarily in India, Pakistan, and Sri Lanka (Ceylon) soon after independence from British colonialism. He was not yet aware of how multinational corporations spreading more widely in poor countries in the early 1960s could be harmful to the long-term development interests of these poor nations. But his idea of the need for "hard states" has become one of the most important aspects of his massive work on the problems of poor nations.

What is also given more recognition since Myrdal's time is that late-developing nations, or nations that have achieved economic development since the nations in Europe and North America, have required extensive state intervention, planning, and even some state ownership of many industries if they are to have significant economic development (Fallows, 1994; Thurow, 1991). One of the best examples of this late development is found with Germany. The many German territories were not even united into a single nation until the late 1800s under the leadership of Bismarck. Already behind most of Europe by this time, the German state used extensive intervention in the economy in the form of planning, state-directed loans, economic incentives to businesses, and extensive government ownership of corporations, to push Germany rapidly into the position of Europe's largest economy (Chirot, 1977, 1986; Craig, 1991; Dietrich, 1991; Kennedy, 1987; Raff, 1988).

Nations trying to develop in the second half of the twentieth century, nations Vogel calls "late, late developers," are even more in need of state assistance in overcoming obstacles created for them by the new global economy. The four Asian tigers (Taiwan, South Korea, Hong Kong, and Singapore) achieved rapid economic growth in the 1980s, Vogel shows, with extensive state intervention (Vogel, 1991). As many other scholars have shown, it was Japan that led the way as an Asian late-developing nation with extensive state intervention from the late 1800s to become the second largest economic power in the world after the United States. It was Japan that perfected what is now known as the Asian development model that has been copied in one form or another by Asian nations recently achieving at least some success with economic development (Johnson, 1982).

Specifically, what is meant by a *hard state,* or now more commonly called a *development state,* is a government with sufficient organization and power to achieve its development goals (see Chang, 1999; Cumings, 1999; Johnson, 1982, 1999; Kerbo & Slagter, 2000b; Lau, 1996; Pempel, 1999; Woo-Cumings, 1996, 1999). There must be a state with the ability to prove consistent economic guidance and rational and efficient organization, and the power to back up its long-range economic policies. All of this is important because the state must be able to resist external demands from outside multinational corporations to do things for its short-term gain, overcome internal resistence from strong groups trying to protect short-term narrow interests, reduce corruption, and control infighting within the nation pertaining to who will most benefit from development projects. What this hard state comes down to primarily is leadership and bureaucracy—bureaucracy that is honest, efficient, and has the power to back up policy decisions.

In a useful piece of research described briefly in Chapter 2, Evans and Rauch created what they called a Weberianness Scale, referring to the most important characteristics of rational and efficient bureaucratic organizations defined in the famous works of Max Weber some 100 years ago (Evans & Rauch, 1999). These researchers first designed a questionnaire that measured key aspects of efficient bureaucracy, and then asked several experts on each of 37 developing nations in their data set to rate the nation's government in terms of bureaucratic efficiency. Of the 37 nations in the sample, 7 were Asian, and with the exception of the Philippines, all ranked above average on their Weberianness Scale. The four tigers (Taiwan, South Korea, Hong Kong, and Singapore) clustered at the top four positions. Evans and Rauch also found the Weberianness Scale positively related to economic development. Unfortunately, the interesting fact that the four Asian tigers are at the top was mentioned but no consideration was given as to why the Asian nations tend to rank so well on this scale.

In other work Evans has developed the concept of "embedded autonomy" which is similar to the earlier concept of a development state described here (Evans, 1995). He recounts how Japan's economic development must be understood with state intervention and he explains how specific political interventions in some industries within developing nations have been successful. But critical questions remain: What preconditions make the development state possible? Why are many Asian nations more likely to have a development state? Why is the development state able to bring about more evenly spread development in some countries and not others? These are questions we will consider in more detail in coming chapters. But we already have some partial answers.

The characteristics of Asian nations described already (respect for authority and old traditions of obligations for elites) should be recognized as the stuff making a development state more likely in East and Southeast Asia. The scatter plot in Figure 5.2 strongly suggests *why* these ancient civilizations of Asia have a hard state or development state today: One aspect of having an ancient civilization is *more government complexity before colonialism,* before the European colonials came to disrupt poorer countries all over the world during the high point of colonialism in the 1800s. This greater state complexity, or levels of government, before European colonials came to exploit poorer countries, indicates these countries were in a better position to protect themselves during colonial times, minimize the disruption, and recover from colonial exploitation after the colonials were kicked out. But while these characteristics can help make this development state possible, it is not inevitable. We will see that several nations in Southeast Asia have been unable to achieve anything like a development state with good governance. In the next chapter we must consider in more detail how countries in Asia were treated differently during the dark years of colonial dominance.

It is important to underscore what is not a key or required component of a hard state or development state. A hard state is *not* to be equated with a military dictatorship, and in fact it is generally the opposite. Military dictatorships in third world countries often develop because the state is unable to provide basic support for the health, welfare, and infrastructure needs of the nation. It is in response to the resulting political instability that an oppressive military dictatorship may come into existence. The Burmese military dictatorship, in other words, does not represent a hard state and cannot become a development state in its current configuration. It is also important to stress that the U.S. or Western view of a military government always backing the interests of capitalists over the masses in the country is inaccurate. In fact, during the 1960s, research showed that military coups were as likely to bring about change favorable to workers over capitalists as the other way around (Brier & Calvert, 1975). It is more accurate to say *U.S.-backed military coups* of the period were more favorable toward capitalists. Consider the hard states of South Korea and Taiwan, and the *relative* hard state of Thailand in some detail.

Until its turn toward democracy in the 1990s, South Korea had been a repressive state with strong military backing if not direct military involvement in the government. There is no doubt that from the 1950s until the mid-1990s the South Korean government was strongly behind the interests of big capital (Kim, 1997). Unlike Japan, which eliminated the wealth and power of the big capitalist families behind the *zaibatsu* soon after World War II, the similar *chaebol* remain firmly in the hands of extremely rich families in South Korea (Abegglen & Stalk, 1985; Kerbo & McKinstry, 1995; Roberts; 1976). Despite the strong backing of big business and wealthy families, however, South Korean governments followed long-term development policies and protected national interests from outside multinational corporate exploitation. One of the best examples to site is the South Korean ban on Japanese car imports for decades. South Korea successfully follows import substitution policies to build up their own auto industry and are now selling millions of highly rated automobiles in the United States and Europe. Policies like this have resulted in rapid economic development and poverty reduction for the nation as a whole.

It was a military coup in Thailand that eliminated the absolute monarchy in 1932, and from that time until the 1980s there were military-backed governments in Thailand.[6] But more often than not, these military governments had strong populist elements with anticapitalist leanings and concerns for protecting peasants and workers. To make sense of this one needs to see how the split between the military and rich capitalists goes back many years.

As is the case all over Southeast Asia, the most powerful and wealthiest capitalists tend to be from Chinese immigrant families. From the 1932 military takeover in Thailand the military saw its role as protecting Thai peasants and workers from the dominance of these wealthy Chinese families. However, unlike Indonesia and Malaysia where the antagonisms remain strong, the Thais made their compromises. The military governments and wealthy Chinese families learned to cooperate with each other; the deal was that rich Chinese families received protection from the government while top Thai military personnel were brought into the corporate boards of the Chinese-owned corporations. Likewise, the Thai military started many of their own businesses, with one of the largest banks in Thailand today still owned by the military. However, Thai military governments never sided completely with capitalists. Populist elements always remained because the military was one of the main avenues of social mobility for poor peasant boys. Moving to the top of the business world is much more difficult, but a poor Thai boy can hope to join the military, move up the ranks, and in this indirect root be brought into the capitalist class where the top military and Chinese corporate interests merged (Muscat, 1994:57, 83; Pasuk & Baker, 1998:22; Slagter & Kerbo, 2000:71–72; Wyatt, 1984:273). Even today, all but two of the richest 25 business families in Thailand are of Chinese ethnic origin, as are two of the largest three banks, and 12 of the top 15 banks (*International Herald Tribune,* April 17, 1998; Kulick & Wilson, 1996:85, 90; Muscat, 1994:117).

Taiwan, as we have seen, was taken over by the Nationalist Party fleeing from Mao's revolution on the mainland. From that time it was certainly a repressive, hard state. To a large degree the newly formed Republic of Taiwan needed state building, and in the minds of the ruling Nationalist Party this required crushing any opposition, especially from the native Taiwanese who were not happy about the invasion of their island by rich and powerful mainlanders.[7] As already described, the Nationalist Party realized after defeat by the communists that their survival as a government on Taiwan required popular support, and thus economic development. It was not until 1987 that martial law was eliminated in the Republic of Taiwan, with the first national elections for president held in 1996. From the beginning of 1949 Taiwan had a hard state, but one that changed from repression to a continuing hard state that is much more democratic today.

Finally, the case of Vietnam today is worth brief mention. Soon after the north was victorious in 1975 there was certainly political repression directed toward opponents and reestablishing social order. As is typical of postrevolutionary situations, the political leaders in Vietnam after 1975 were still military leaders and communist ideologues; they

DATA FILE

State Effectiveness and Economic Development Today

by Patrick Ziltener

We discussed earlier that one of the strongest correlations in our data set was between the extent of state building (or "state complexity") before colonialism in poorer countries and the level of state effectiveness today. There is another positive correlation in our data set, though not as strong, that pertains to this issue of the Asian development state. As shown in the scatter plot of Figure 5.3, state effectiveness in 1996 is strongly related to the level of gross national product (GNP) per capita in 1999. We find strong evidence for

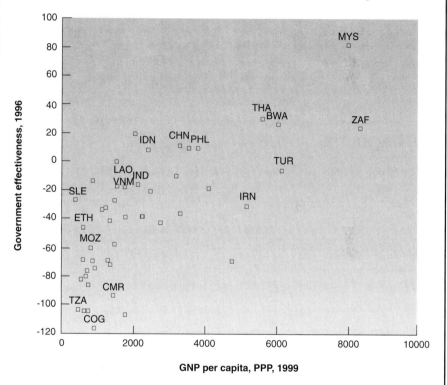

FIGURE 5.3 *Government Effectiveness and GNP Per Capita*

NOTE: The following are World Bank country codes used in the figure.
Algeria = DZA, Angola = AGO, Botswana = BWA, Cameroon = CMR, Central African Rep. = CAF, Chad = TCD, China, P.R.: Mainland = CHN, Congo, Republic of = COG, Ivory Coast, Côte d'Ivoire = CIV, Egypt = EGY, Ethiopia = ETH, India = IND, Indonesia = IDN, Iran, I.R. of = IRN, Jordan = JOR, Kenya = KEN, Lao People's Dem. Rep = LAO, Lesotho = LSO, Malawi = MWI, Malaysia = MYS, Martinique = MTQ, Mauritania = MRT, Mauritius = MUS, Mexico = MEX, Moldova = MDA, Mongolia = MNG, Morocco = MAR, Mozambique = MOZ, Niger = NER, Nigeria = NGA, Philippines = PHL, Sierra Leone = SLE, South Africa = ZAF, Tanzania = TZA, Thailand = THA, Togo = TGO, Tunisia = TUN, Turkey = TUR, Vietnam = VNM, Zambia = ZMB.

(Continued)

(Continued)

the following pattern: The less developed countries that are getting richer today are those with more efficient governments. Then, as shown earlier in this chapter, the countries with the most efficient governments today are the ones that had more state complexity 100 or 200 years ago—in other words, before European colonial powers took over the country. Another indicator is that countries with ancient civilizations are more likely to have a development state today, which in turn helps increase their level of economic development. In the scatter plot in Figure 5.3 we find Thailand high on both dimensions. China and Vietnam are fairly high in state effectiveness but not so high on level of economic development yet. These two countries have just overcome some of the disruption set in motion by colonialism to have more recently become successful in their drives for economic development. There are some surprises, though: South Africa and Botswana are high on state efficiency and economic development. As we will see in a forthcoming chapter, state efficiency is one of the biggest problems for African countries, but as South Africa and Botswana indicate, it is not impossible to overcome the obstacles to development found in most African countries.

wanted the well-ordered anticapitalist state for which their ideology led them to fight. But as economic realities set in, hunger and joblessness spread, and the old aging revolutionary leaders lost some of their grip on power, the state turned its attention to economic development. The reform and liberalizing policies called *doi moi* which were established by 1989 began having their effects by the early 1990s (see Duiker, 1995; Hiebert, 1996; Jamieson, 1995; Kamm, 1996; Kolko, 1997; Morley & Nishihara, 1997). It can be argued that there is less political repression in Vietnam today than in some other countries in Southeast Asia, but there is certainly the hard state. And although there is still much corruption and infighting making the Vietnamese government much less effective than it could be, Vietnam can be said to have a development state. The attention of the state is now focused on regulating economic activities, promoting development, and attracting foreign capital. But Vietnam is attracting this foreign capital on its own terms, with rules it believes are more likely to ensure the long-term development of the country's economy.[8]

Despite all the evidence of the importance of a hard state first described by Myrdal almost 40 years ago, some international aid agencies are just now publicly recognizing the fact. The United Nations Development Program, for example, published a report in April of 2000, *Overcoming Human Poverty: UNDP Poverty Report 2000*, which focused on good governance in poor countries as a key to economic development and overcoming the selfish interests of wealthy elites often behind state actions in developing nations. The report concludes that "Without good governance, reliance on trickle-down economic development and a host of other strategies will not work" (*International Herald Tribune*, April 6, 2000; UNDP, 2000b). It seems it has taken quite some time for the Western-dominated international development agencies to acknowledge that bad governing and the collusion between Western multinationals and third world governments have been part of the problem. Many Western economists still find it difficult to acknowledge that an Asian development state that has been used throughout Asia can be a model of development both in Asia and in other poor countries today. It is time to examine this development model in more detail.

The Asian Development Model

It is important to specify what is meant by the "Asian development model" because there are variations throughout Asia (Raphael & Rohlen, 1998). There are enough commonalities, however, for a *general* description, primarily in contrast to its Western counterpart (Chang, 1999; Cumings, 1999; Johnson, 1982, 1999; Lau, 1996; Pempel, 1999; Woo-Cumings, 1996, 1999).

Two separate aspects of the model must be distinguished—the *purpose of economic development* and the *means of economic development*—though to a large degree the purpose shapes the choice of means. Fallows provides a simple description of contrasting development models: "In the Anglo-American model, the basic reason to have an economy is to raise the individual consumer's standard of living. In the Asian model, it is to increase the collective national strength" (Fallows, 1994:208). Fallows's contrast is perhaps a bit extreme. Asia, too, has consumers who also want a higher standard of living. But when considered as a relative contrast, Fallows's point is well taken. Fallows goes on to suggest that the focus on national strength for Asia is in reaction to the long repression of Asians by European colonialism, though I would in part disagree on this point. A broader look at history suggests that the same Asian goals for an economy and political system existed long before colonial repression (Frank, 1998). From the perspective of Asian values the *purpose* of development is, at least in large part, historically and culturally determined. In the Western model, "economic development means more. . . . If people have more choice, more leisure, more wealth, more opportunity to pursue happiness, society as a whole will be a success" (Fallows, 1994:209). This definition of the purpose of development reflects an individualist value orientation in which individuals are largely responsible for themselves and individual goals are emphasized. In contrast, the more collectivist value orientation of Asian societies emphasizes group goals to a greater extent. It is interesting to note that in contrast to American and British social scientists, Asian social scientists seem to be more aware that the theoretical underpinning for an Asian development model can be traced to the early-nineteenth-century German economist Friedrich List who viewed collective rather than individual interests as more important for national economies (Fallows 1994:179–196; List, 1983).

It is important to stress again that in Asia, people are *relatively* more concerned about how well the group is doing—the family, the work group, the company, the nation—than with purely individual material success. The emphasis is on the *relative* aspect of this difference; Asian people as individuals certainly want more material goods, but it is a matter of degree and relative priorities when reference groups are considered. In addition, we must remember that Americans tend to have even more focus on material economic success goals than Europeans.[9] Thus, again we must speak in relative terms with respect to the purpose of economic activities. Doing so, however, makes sense and is required if we are to understand how differing value orientations shape the goals of economic development.

With respect to the *means* of economic development, it logically follows that in a more collectivist nation some agent representing the group or nation should have some authority over the economy. At the national level this agent is always the polity in one form or another (king, emperor, president, parliament, bureaucracy, military, etc.). Pye convincingly shows that power and authority in Asian nations have been viewed differently when compared to Western nations. Asian nations are of course in the process of change, but still there is "the common denominator of idealizing benevolent, paternalistic leadership. . . . Thus, although Europe did succeed in imposing on Asia its legalistic concept of the nation-state, the Asian response has been a new and powerful form of nationalism based on paternalistic authority" (Phy, 1985:vii). Others writing about the nature of the state in the Asian development model generally agree (Fallows, 1994; Kim, 1997; Pye, 1985:Chapter 1; Vogel, 1991). Johnson prefers the phrase "capitalist development state" (Johnson, 1982). In essence, both Pye and Johnson are saying that an important element of the Asian development model is a hard state, which has been described earlier.

To be a capitalist development state, or to follow the Asian development model, also means extensive state intervention in the economy. Such intervention usually involves long-term economic planning, coordination of research and development, economic policies believed to be good for national interests that are imposed upon corporations, and in some cases even government ownership of major industries. Most of the practical details of how an Asian development model actually operates, Johnson shows, were worked out through trial and error by the Japanese bureaucratic elite from the 1920s, through World War II, and even after the war (Johnson, 1982). A brief review of the history of Japanese economic development and details of the Japanese capitalist development model will be helpful at this point.

Japan's Economic Development

In 1868, when the rebellious army from the Satsuma and Choshu regions of Japan marched into what is now Tokyo, the revolutionary coup, or what was called the Meiji Restoration, had finally come. The primary concern of the new Meiji government was the threat of either European or American colonization and economic exploitation. As noted, every other country in Asia except Thailand was being colonized by Western powers so the new Japanese government knew it had to act fast. As this new government saw it, only a powerful economy and military of its own would bring security and equal treatment with the Western powers.

In effect, a kind of forced industrialization and modernization took place, all orchestrated by the new government (Johnson, 1982). With this early form of a capitalist development state, the Japanese first sent many of their best and brightest to Europe during the late 1800s to study the institutions of the West, later reporting back as to what could best work for Japan. (They especially liked and copied many aspects of Bismarck's Germany.) They then began to create a capitalist industrial economy, skipping many stages of the more gradual development that had occurred in the West. In the process, the new Meiji government also created an upper class of wealthy families called the zaibatsu which soon came to almost completely dominate the Japanese economy in the pre–World War II era. All of the big zaibatsu families, in one way or another, developed and grew in the late 1800s and early 1900s through sponsorship and protection by the political elites. In some cases the government granted them exclusive rights to certain economic activity, as with Mitsui's first role as banker to the new government. In other cases the new government started its own industries, especially when it was judged that these industries were most important for rapid industrialization. Being rather inept in this activity, however, the government-run industries usually did not operate very efficiently, and were soon sold to private owners. Few Japanese had the money or access to government loans for such purchases, but some of the old merchant families had enough money, as did many former *daimyo* (feudal lords) and *samurai* (literally "those who serve," or warriors) who were given government compensation when losing their old positions after 1868. Thus, through very low-cost deals on struggling government companies, then more government protection, others became wealthy zaibatsu families (Morikawa, 1992). Once Japanese economic development took off in the late 1800s these zaibatsu families themselves created many types of corporations in several industries, all linked to the central family stock holding company and a main bank. The biggest of these old zaibatsu included many corporate names well known today, such as Mitsui, Fujita, and Sumitomo (Morikawa, 1992).

The Japanese Bureaucratic Elite and the Technical Means of the Development State

One of the most important elements of Japan's rapid economic development from the late 1800s as well as again after World War II was a relatively independent government ministry with the education and power to establish and enforce economic policies. From the early years of the Meiji Restoration a bureaucratic ministry was established with a constitution giving elected politicians little influence over this ministry. With Japan's defeat in World War II, however, came a new constitution written by the American occupation forces under MacArthur. This postwar constitution continued to allow for extensive bureaucratic power, though does not require it. The American occupation forces unwittingly made it almost certain that the bureaucratic elite would not only maintain their power, but actually expand it. First, because the American occupation force did not fully understand the prewar Japanese political system, it was assumed that the military and politicians had most power before the war, and were therefore responsible for the war. These people were promptly purged. Of all purges, over 79 percent involved military officers and 16 percent involved politicians—less than 1 percent involved the bureaucratic ministry elite (Halliday, 1975:173–174). Second, the remaining, untainted politicians placed into positions of power by the occupation forces were inexperienced and mostly incompetent (Johnson, 1982:44–45). The resulting power vacuum was filled by the bureaucratic elite.

During the second half of the twentieth century the most important ministries were the Ministries of Justice, Foreign Affairs, Finance, and International Trade and Industry.[10] The prime minister selects the minister for each of these ministries, as well as the heads of a few other agencies. These people then make up the prime minister's cabinet, much like in the United States. However, it is the administrative vice-minister in each of these ministries who is considered most knowledgeable and powerful. As political appointees, compared to the vice-ministers who are career civil servants, the ministers of these bureaucracies are inexperienced outsiders to the agencies, and to a large extent at the mercy of the vice-ministers. The vice-ministers spend their entire careers in the ministry, working their way to the top after college graduation. The vice-ministers, therefore, have wide experience and training in the agency, extensive knowledge of the particular aspects of the Japanese society the agency is to regulate, and the loyalty of thousands of other ministry officials in the agency. Politicians and temporary outsiders coming in as ministers are at a disadvantage.[11]

The vice-ministers of these government agencies and their assistants have several means of influence to go along with their extensive knowledge gained over the years of their careers as unelected civil servants. One of the most important has been their ability to write legislation. Like the U.S. Congress or the parliaments of Europe, of course, the Japanese Diet is the legislative branch of government. But in reality, most Japanese laws are written by ministry officials, then handed to the Diet for passage. Estimates suggest that about 80 percent of the ministry-sponsored bills pass the Diet, compared to 30 percent or fewer of the Diet-sponsored bills (Kishimoto, 1988:66; Koh, 1989:206). It is not only that most legislation is written by ministry officials, it is also how laws are written; they are often vague, leaving wide gaps for interpretation. The bureaucratic ministry administer the laws, and in the process, have the luxury of interpreting the laws. The most famous source of ministry influence, however, has been "administrative guidance." The basis of administrative guidance comes from Japanese law giving the ministries the authority to issue directives, requests, warnings, offer suggestions, and encouragements to private organizations and individuals. As Johnson describes it, "Administrative guidance is constrained only by the requirement that the 'guidees' must come under a given governmental organ's jurisdiction" (Johnson, 1982:267).

Finally, one other influence held by the economically related ministries (particularly the Ministries of Finance and International Trade and Industry, or MITI) must be mentioned. A key ingredient in this economic guidance is the control these ministries have had over commercial loans. In contrast to the United States, corporations in Japan are more likely to expand through bank loans rather than new stock issues (Abegglen & Stalk, 1985). These ministries can target industries for development and carry out their plans by influencing which corporations and industries are able to secure the capital for their growth or survival through administrative guidance to private banks, and their control over the Japan Development Bank and the Bank of Japan, both government agencies (Johnson, 1982:205–217; Vogel, 1979:73–75).

The Japanese government ministries have not always followed the best policies for economic development—and they have certainly made mistakes. For example, over 30 years ago MITI demanded that Honda not get into the automobile industry. Honda defied the ministry and ended up making some of the best cars in the industry's history. The successes of MITI and the other ministries, however, have been numerous. Japan's success in overtaking the United States in consumer electronics, auto quality, and computer chips are among the many before the 1990s. Then there was Japan's huge reduction in energy consumption in the 1970s after the first big worldwide "oil shock," together with the way the economy was managed to minimize the disruption from big price increases in oil at this time. All of this has been attributed to the ministries. Also of note is that Japan had one of the biggest problems of industrial pollution and industrial accidents in the 1960s. Today, these rates in Japan are among the lowest of all industrial nations.[12]

Although the Asian development model has helped Japan and now other Asian nations develop their economies quite rapidly, one of the drawbacks of this model of political economy is the restrictions on quick adjustments to changes in the global economy (Kerbo & Slagter, 2000a, 2000b; Pempel, 2000). There is also the common problem of too much power in the hands of relatively unaccountable elites. Plenty of evidence suggests that the Japanese ministry bureaucrats have become more self-serving compared to earlier decades, especially in contrast to the decades after World War II (Kerbo & McKinstry, 1995). But we must understand that it was the Japanese development state and the bureaucratic ministry elite that got Japan to the position of the world's second largest economy after WWII, a feat achieved after much trial and error to develop its development model before WWII. We must also recognize flaws in the Asian development model after the Asian economic crisis of 1997. However, it can also be argued that these flaws need not be fatal or permanent, as we will try to show later in this book. As should be obvious, the world's poor would *love* to have Japan's problems. Japan is a stagnating rich country with a continuing high standard of living and very little poverty. Even if the case of Japan today were to show there are fatal flaws in the Asian development model once a nation becomes rich, the world's poor would no doubt prefer to worry about that aspect later.

The Asian Development Model: A Conclusion

Table 5.2 summariges the key arguments about the preconditions for economic development made above. But some final points about the Asian development model are necessary. While it can be said that Japanese bureaucrats were most responsible for

---

TABLE 5.2

The East and Southeast Asian Advantage: A Path to Economic Development

Ancient Civilizations

Help promote a sense of nationhood, national identity, and more state complexity,

Which Can Promote . . .

Traditions of Elite Responsibility

With norms of reciprocity and feelings of obligations toward nonelites, rooted in the development of ancient traditions codified in philosophies, religions, which

Help to Make Possible . . .

A Hard State

Or the development of a capitalist development state with the motivation and power to enact and enforce development policies against domestic and international opposition,

All of Which Have Not Been Negated by the Impact of . . .

The Specific Experiences of Colonialism

Which are related to:
- the economic and political strength of the nation before it was colonized
- the presence or lack of infrastructure development during colonialism
- the construction of national boundaries by colonial powers (relative presence or absence of contested territory by smaller kingdoms or ethnic and tribal minorities)
- and how the colonial power left the country (such as the extent of planning and preparation for independence)

developing the Asian development model, this is not to say that all Asian nations can or should follow this model exactly. The problem with much of the past literature and theories of economic development has been a "one size fits all" approach when attempting to explain the lack of economic development and what to do about it. Even within Asia such thinking will simply render development policies useless at best, and often harmful to the prospects of a better life for the world's poor. The case of Thailand provides us with one of the best examples of why the one-size-fits-all approach is highly misleading. The approach Thailand has taken toward economic development in recent decades could in fact be called the "Thai Third Way"—that is, a third way between the more bureaucratic ministry-driven development policies of Japan and the *laissez faire* capitalism of little government involvement in the United States.

Before we examine the Thai development model in action, however, we must return to a comparative analysis of Asia, Africa, and Latin America, with a greater focus on Southeast Asian nations after comparing these regions. Many Southeast Asian nations that are mired in extreme poverty today might have used this Asian development model but never had the chance. Likewise, we cannot say that the characteristics of Asia outlined in the previous chapter are the only important factors for economic development in countries like Taiwan, South Korea, or Thailand. Several of Thailand's neighbors, for example, have virtually identical Asian characteristics. Even Vietnam with Confucian Asian values more in line with the rapidly developing East Asian nations is just now showing strong potential for sustained economic development. Obviously, we need to return to our exploration of what factors separate these nations despite similar Asian traditions. One of the most important of these factors is the varied impact of colonialism on less developed countries around the world.

Notes

1. Unlike South Korea and Taiwan, of course, Singapore and Hong Kong were rather unique little city-states containing the remnants of the British colonial financial centers. Much the same can be said for Vogel's analysis of economic development of the four tigers, though unlike Barrett and Whyte's work Vogel does not specifically address issues raised by the modern world system literature. (Ezra Vogel, *The Four Little Dragons: The Spread of Industrialization in East Asia* [Cambridge, MA: Harvard University Press, 1991]; Richard Barrett and Martin King Whyte, "Dependency Theory and Taiwan: Analysis of a Deviant Case," *American Journal of Sociology* 87 [1982], pp. 1064–1089). It should also be noted, however, that Japan can be examined as a deviant case even though Japan started its economic development in the late 1800s. We will consider the case of Japan extensively in Chapter 5.

2. Most important, see the work of Nobel Prize–winning economist Myrdal who devoted much of his life's work to the problems of world poverty. (Gunnar Myrdal, *The Challenge of World Poverty: A World Anti-Poverty Program in Outline* [New York: Pantheon Books, 1970], pp. 50–58.)

3. Again it was Myrdal (ibid.) who first and most effectively explained the importance of a hard state in leading the economic development process among third world nations.

4. For a good summary of the impact of the European powers upon Southeast Asia see Osborne (Milton Osborne, *Southeast Asia: An Introductory History* [Brisbane: Allen and Unwin, 1995], pp. 61–80).

5. This is often the case, it will be remembered, because multinational corporations are in the country because of low wages, low taxes, the absence of labor unions, and few restrictions on other things such as how much of the profits can be taken out of the country. If domestic political or economic elites take some of these benefits away from foreign corporations, the corporations can leave the country and many sources of wealth and power for these domestic elites are then also lost.

6. In fact, 1991 was the first time Thailand had a nonmilitary prime minister. For this history see Charles F. Keyes, *Thailand: Buddhist Kingdom as Modern Nation-State* (Boulder, CO: Westview Press, 1989); Pasuk Phongpaichit and Chris Baker, *Thailand's Boom* (Chiang Mai, Thailand: Silkworm Books, 1996); David K. Wyatt, *Thailand: A Short History* (New Haven, CT: Yale University Press, 1984); John L. S. Girling, *Thailand: Society and Politics* (Ithaca, NY: Cornell University Press, 1981); Robert Slagter and Harold Kerbo, *Modern Thailand: A Volume in the Comparative Societies Series* (New York: McGraw-Hill, 2000).

7. Native Taiwanese had hoped to receive independence when Japanese colonialism was eliminated instead of being pushed back to Chinese mainland control. Thus, when mainland China took control in 1945 there were riots in which 10,000 to 20,000 Taiwanese were killed. See Thomas B. Gold, *State and Society in the Taiwan Miracle* (Armonk, NY: M.E. Sharpe, 1986), p. 51.

8. A final example can be useful. During April of 2000 newspapers all over the United States and the world were filled with stories of the fall of Saigon 25 years earlier. There were the usual assessments of how far Vietnam has come or not come since that time, but of course many of the stories replayed America's part in the Vietnam War with questions of what America achieved or did not achieve with its involvement. Some of the most interesting news stories reanalyzed U.S. military tactics, as is also being done in U.S. military academies, to ask how the U.S. military might have won the war, and how the most powerful military in the world could have possibly lost. Of course there was also the inevitable comparison to the Gulf War of the early 1990s where the United States and its coalition partners so easily and quickly defeated the Iraqi army. These commentators and military specialists *still* have not gotten the point. There are certainly the important variables of terrain, comparative military size, military technology of the opponents, and possible allies of both sides. But it seems Americans, from news commentators to military tacticians, still cannot understand how differences of social structure, social organization, and cultural traditions impact military strength—just as they impact economic development chances. The comparisons between the Gulf War and the Vietnam War could not be more polar. In Vietnam there was a traditional social order with a strong sense of unity, purpose, and support for its leaders and the goals of the war. Vietnam's people felt a strong sense of nationalism and pride in their ancient homeland, and anger that their homeland had been violated by Western colonial powers. Except for an ancient civilization, all of this is in contrast to Iraqi where people had much less respect for their current leaders or the aims of Saddam Hussein. Since 2003 when the United States began its new war in Iraq, it is becoming clearer to Americans

why a nation disrupted by colonialism with many ethnic groups is almost impossible to govern. The point is that aside from specific military strategies and technology, the characteristics of societies such as some of those analyzed here can also be useful to analyze the military strength of a nation. (Many newspapers ran such stories 25 years after the fall of Saigon, but for a good example see especially the *International Herald Tribune* and *The New York Times*, April 29, 2000.)

9. Despite the common charge of oversimplification, we have seen that there is rather strong empirical support for these differing value orientations. Hofstede's data from over 50 countries show the United States highest on his "individualism vs. collectivism scale," with Britain, Canada, New Zealand, and Australia close behind, while most Asian nations line up toward the other end of the scale. Hampden-Turner and Trompenaars found much the same thing with their questionnaires to business people around the world, as did Verba in his study of national elite attitudes toward inequality and the goals of government between the United States and Japan. While other national opinion polls seldom include data from Asian nations other than Japan, most questions involving the purpose of government and government regulations of the economy generally show North Americans most opposed (with the British usually closer to the American view) and Japanese more in favor. See Geert Hofstede, *Cultures and Organization: Software of the Mind* (New York: McGraw-Hill, 1991); Charles Hampden-Turner and Alfons Tompenaars, *The Seven Cultures of Capitalism* (New York: Doubleday, 1993); Sidney Verba et al., *Elites and the Idea of Equality* (Cambridge, MA: Harvard University Press, 1987); Everett Carl Ladd and Karlyn H. Bowman, *Attitudes Toward Economic Inequality* (Washington, DC: American Enterprise Institute, 1998). For a review of these contrasting American and European materialist values see the *International Herald Tribune,* April 10, 2000.

10 The other ministries include Education; Health and Welfare; Agriculture, Forestry, and Fisheries; Transport; Posts and Telecommunications; Labor; Construction; and Home Affairs. Not among the main 12, it is interesting to note that these are considered only as agencies: Defense, the National Public Safety Commission, and the Economic Planning Agency (Kōichi Kishimoto, *Politics in Modern Japan: Development and Organization* [Tokyo: Japan Echo Inc., 1988], p. 82).

11. There has been debate within Japan over the extent to which some Diet members are gaining more influence in relation to the bureaucratic elite. While clearly overstated, a new phrase appeared in the Japanese media, *tōkō kantei* (party predominant-bureaucracy subordinate), which would have been unthinkable a couple of decades ago (Leonard J. Schoppa, "Zoku Power and LDP Power: A Case Study of the Zoku Rule in Education Policy," *Journal of Japanese Studies* 17 [1991], p. 79.

A major part of the argument for expanded Diet power was that a few new groups of LDP politicians in the Diet, called zoku, had gained sufficient expertise on particular policy issues (such as education policy) to enable them to counter the ministry elite, actually making important decisions themselves, and dictating these decisions to the ministry (Yung H. Park, *Bureaucrats and Ministers in Contemporary Japanese Government* [Berkeley: University of California, Institute of East Asian Studies, 1986]; Karel van Wolferen, *The Enigma of*

Japanese Power [New York: Knopf, 1989]; Gary D. Allinson, "Politics in Contemporary Japan: Pluralist Scholarship in the Conservative Era—A Review Article," *Journal of Asian Studies* 48 [1989]; Schoppa, "Zoku Power and LDP Power." There are still questions such as how often this happens, with how many policy issues, and who the zoku are really serving, the LDP or the bureaucratic elite. A number of issues can be discussed on this question of who has most power. For example, much depends upon the policy area, for in some cases, such as education and agriculture, it can be said that the LDP is more in control (see B. C. Koh, *Japan's Administrative Elite* [Berkeley: University of California Press, 1989], pp. 204–218; Schoppa, "Zoku Power and LDP Power"). Many of these zoku members in the Diet are, in fact, retired bureaucratic officials. Finally, the loss of power by the LDP in 1993, and the continuing general disarray among politicians before and since the fall of the LDP, brings this notion of "zoku power" into serious question today.

12. By the beginning of the twenty-first century, of course, in some ways Japan looked like a different country. Perhaps no country in recent decades has faced such a dramatic turnaround. In 2004 the economy had been stagnant for more than 13 years, with three official recessions along the way. Japanese unemployment had grown to post–World War II highs. Only 2 Japanese banks remained on the list of the world's top 10 compared to 8 Japanese banks in the 1980s. Collectively Japan's banks held from $115 billion to $169 billion in bad loans. Government debt was 130 percent of annual GNP in 2000, unprecedented among industrial nations, and expected to rise to 200 percent of GNP by 2007. Overall corporate debt in Japan stood at an incredible level of $2 trillion by 2001. And of course, the political scandals continued through the 1990s; now, however, they have brought down many ministry bureaucrats who were perhaps the most respected individuals in Japan before the 1990s. (Statistics in this paragraph come from various recent issues of *Japan Times* and the *International Herald Tribune,* as well as the World Bank, *World Bank Development Report 2000/2001* (New York: Oxford University Press, 2000).

Understandably, in contrast to the early twentieth century, and especially the postwar recovery, Japanese ministry bureaucrats are condemned rather than praised. The Japanese political economy is badly in need of change to keep up with competition in the global economy, but it seems clear that little change can be forthcoming until the bureaucratic ministry elite is forced to give up its control, or at least recognize that change is necessary (Harold R. Kerbo and John McKinstry, *Who Rules Japan?: The Inner Circles of Economic and Political Power* [Westport, CT: Greenwood/Praeger, 1995]; Bai Gao, *Japan's Economic Dilemma: The Institutional Origins of Prosperity and Stagnation* [Cambridge, England: Cambridge University Press, 2001]; Edward J. Lincoln, *Arthritic Japan: The Slow Pace of Economic Reform* [Washington, DC: Brookings Institution Press, 2001]; T. J. Pempel, *Regime Shift: Comparative Dynamics of the Japanese Political Economy* [Ithaca, NY: Cornell University Press, 2000]). Several attempts by elected politicians to reform the political system and reduce bureaucratic ministry power, including reducing the number of government bureaucracies, have failed. The Japanese corporate elite has increasingly broken ranks with the traditional power elite to challenge bureaucratic ministry dominance, but so far this has also failed to bring about much change.

Colonialism and Its Aftermath: Fractured Nations, Wars, and Recovery—For Some

With the violent twentieth century behind us and almost all of the world's population now living in independent nations, a sweeping revisionist history of colonialism should be written. One can imagine it to start with something like, "What were those people thinking?" "How did they expect to walk into other people's nations and simply claim them as their own, then continue to believe they could get away with it for decade upon decade?" It is one thing to move into lightly inhabited territories to steal from relatively defenseless indigenous people as was the case in most of North and South America. Immoral and inhumane, to be sure, but one can see a cold rationale of how European Americans could get away with it. It is quite another thing to move onto land where an ancient and comparatively more powerful civilization continued to maintain control of the territory, even if some of these ancient civilizations had been in decline for a century or more. Besides being simple thievery as in the first case, one must question the sanity of thinking the people being robbed would not someday be able to mount a successful rebellion to take back what was stolen from them. It is the latter case that best describes the history of colonialism in most of Asia.

Compared to the Americas, colonialism came late to Asia and Africa. The Western powers had been slowly moving into Asia and Africa from the 1600s. But it was not until the 1800s that colonialism in most of Asia and Africa was consolidated, and in some cases not until the late 1800s. It is important to remember that in Asia these were mostly ancient civilizations where people still had a strong sense of national identity, and where traditional ruling elites were still in charge of relatively strong governments. Western powers could not simply walk ashore Christopher Columbus–style and claim territory for the king or queen of whatever European nation. Except for places such as Australia where the situation was more like the Americas, colonization in Asia had to progress piece by piece, and war by war.

Most commonly, in contrast to Latin America and Africa, the emergence of European colonialism in East and Southeast Asia was driven by merchants looking to get rich with traditional commerce. There were some brilliant characters such as Thomas Raffles who is most responsible for establishing Singapore as a wealthy asset for Britain, a city-state that remains the wealthiest in Southeast Asia today. There were other characters, such as Alexander Dalrymple and the "White Raj" James Brooke. Dalrymple was sent by a British trading company to found a city port that was to be what Singapore ended up being. Dalrymple chose territory in what is today eastern Malaysia, close to the southern Philippines. But he and his "alcoholic officials" wasted

CASE IN POINT

British Drug Pushers, the Opium Wars, and the Colonization of China

One of the best examples of how colonialism slowly swept over Asia is the British move into China. With India already subdued, the British began advancing into East and Southeast Asia more seriously by the 1800s. In China, as elsewhere in Asia, it started with trade. The problem that perplexed the British, however, was that while there were many things they wanted to import from China (the proverbial tea and spices, for example), the Chinese were not much interested in anything the British had to offer. Leaving all of that silver behind in China to pay for the tea and spices was creating a serious balance of payments problem for the British. But in a most pragmatic fashion, the British came up with a brilliant solution. The British-controlled territories in India had excellent poppy-growing fields, so a triangular trade system was arranged to make the British opium pushers in China. For a time it worked quite well; the British shipped opium from India to China in exchange for the tea and spices they shipped back to Britain. I remember reading a biography of the famous writer George Orwell and discovering that he was born in India while his father worked for what could be called the British government's "Ministry of Narcotics." Without knowing the history one would conclude that Orwell's father worked for something like the current U.S. government programs to stop drug cultivation in Colombia or somewhere. Actually, Orwell's father worked for a British agency in charge of *pushing drugs* in Asia.

Growing drug addiction, however, led the Chinese emperor to demand that the British stop selling drugs to the Chinese. The British refused the demand and a brief war called the Opium War ensued. The British won handily, and as compensation for "causing the war," the British demanded and received Hong Kong as compensation. As the British flag was being lowered over Hong Kong for the last time during the summer of 1997, Prince Charles and other British officials stood with tears in their eyes. The fact that Britain obtained Hong Kong in a manner uncomfortably close to Colombian drug warlords was never mentioned.

huge amounts of money on "wine, women, and (presumably) song" before the company gave up on them and moved their plans to what is now Singapore. In a contrasting case, James Brooke spent all of his money on a second-hand schooner to make his fortune in the East Indies. Through luck in chasing away some pirates, Brooke fell into favor with the Sultan of Brunei. Following an Islamic tradition that resembled a feudal lord in control over a large area of land as a small kingdom, in 1839 the Sultan decided to make James Brooke a minor sultan as a reward, resulting in a sultanate ruled by a White Raj passed down in the Brooke family until after World War II (Keay, 1997:46–58).

Whatever the details, however, British, Dutch, and French trading companies—some large, some quite small—were sending their employees into the region to find valuable goods to ship back home. In most cases there were handsome profits in it, at times as high as 1,000 percent (Keay, 1997:16). Once these goods were found, the merchant houses would plead with their political leaders back home in Europe for protection, a declaration of protectorate status over another piece of land, and little by little almost all of East and Southeast Asia was claimed by European nations by the end of the 1800s.

There were a few lingering colonies such as Hong Kong until 1997, but after World War II the long history of Western colonialism in Asia was basically over. Its legacy, however, will last much longer. We must recognize that the general characteristics of Asian nations outlined in the previous chapter only give these nations *the chance* to bring about economic development and reduce poverty among their people. Many of these nations, in one way or another, are still saddled with political or economic institutions shaped by their former colonial masters, or are just now removing the effects of colonialism from these institutions. Less developed nations with similar ancient histories and even identical cultural traditions find themselves with very different prospects for economic development because of differing colonial experiences.

To understand economic development chances today one must consider how these nations were changed in varied ways during colonialism. We must consider how these changes were related to *who the colonizers were, how they ruled the colony,* and *how they left* throughout the second half of the twentieth century. Put another way, we must consider the degree to which a developing nation has been successful in removing legacies of colonialism that have been *impediments to economic development,* as well as when and how these impediments were removed or reduced.

All industrial nations at one time had various impediments to development and modernization that in one way or another had to be cleared away before the development process could proceed. But throwing off these impediments, as usually is done in some form of revolution, is not enough for sustained economic development. The tricky thing about revolutions is that they often end up putting in place a political economy worse than the one that proceeded it. Further, even if the new political economy is able to bring about economic development, there is no assurance that it will be equitable development benefiting all in the society.

In the previous chapter we have seen that ancient civilizations, Asian traditions, and the Asian development state have been instrumental in the sustained and more evenly distributed economic development achieved by many of the East and Southeast Asian nations by the end of the twentieth century. But we must recognize that the colonial experience of these Asian nations was also fundamental in shaping their current destinies. The European colonials at times erased the impact of ancient civilizations and old traditions, but more often in Asia, colonialism delayed economic development or made it more difficult. In Africa the colonial experience severely harmed development chances whereas in Latin America the colonial experience created the seeds of development; in most cases economic development was spread unevenly. In this chapter we will consider these varied experiences of colonialism after reviewing how all of the currently developed nations had to clear away their own impediments to development in an earlier age.

Clearing Away Impediments: Preindustrial Europe, North America, and Japan

Looking around the world and throughout history we find that major, lasting change toward more development and modernization has seldom occurred without first clearing away the impediments of the old social order. The process can be slow and nonviolent, though more often relatively quick and violent. But in one way or another the old impediments must be removed. Adam Smith was clear on this in *The Wealth of Nations*. Today Smith is usually depicted by political conservatives as antigovernment. In reality, Smith was antifeudal government. He knew it was the old kingships and landed aristocracies of Europe that were blocking changes. These old feudal elites suspected that if a new class of capitalists were given their freedom to prosper, their own positions of wealth and status based in the old order would be threatened. In England, the destruction of the old impediments began early and progressed slowly. Before they were finished, however, the Dutch already had their first "bourgeois revolution" in the 1500s to throw off Hapsburg aristocrats, bringing in a new state that supported the emerging bourgeoises (Chirot, 1986:36; Kennedy, 1987:67–86; Wallerstein, 1974). As a result, Holland became Europe's dominant capitalist nation by the early 1600s.

During the late 1600s and early 1700s new competition for dominance arose, primarily between the British and French. The economic and military battles went on for years, with the British finally winning out by the late 1700s to be the dominant European and world power during the 1800s. What had started slowly with the Magna Carta of the 1200s was rather gradual change, though heating up during Cromwell's Glorious Revolution of the mid-1600s. But the change no less removed impediments present in the old feudal regime. In the case of England, many of the old aristocracy recognized their fate and began to form alliances with the new urban capitalists to save themselves.

While this was occurring in Great Britain, France was desperately trying to defeat the British both militarily and economically *without* fundamental change to their old social order. They failed, of course, but what they did accomplish was to bring the old order crashing down with the French Revolution of 1789. The French Royal Government had become bankrupted, and their peasants had become desperate for bread, all because France tried to defeat the British without major reform of the old order (Skocpol, 1979; Soboul, 1974). A dictatorship under Napoleon eventually followed the turmoil of the French Revolution of 1789 to initiate the process of modern state building which later allowed France to industrialize and join the other newly industrialized nations of Europe.

The rise of the United States also occurred only after impediments were cleared away, but cleared away in a fashion that has more application to the world's poorer countries today. The first task, of course, was to rid itself of British colonial dominance from 1776. Unlike the French Revolution of 1789, this was a less bloody affair and should best be called a "nationalist revolution" rather than a true *revolution* which involves a class struggle between upper classes and lower classes to defend the old class system or change it. A *nationalist revolution* has the more limited goal of throwing out foreign domination; the internal political economy and class structure in the country is less the issue. Internal contention over the future political economy of the United States, however, did come to a head by the mid-1800s when a choice again had to be made. The issue was whether the U.S. government would favor economic policies more supportive of elites in the industrializing north or elites of the agrarian, feudal south. In this second task it took one of the bloodiest wars the world had yet seen to settle the dispute. But once settled, political and economic dominance of the northern industrialists began to move the United States to a dominant economic position in the world economy.

At about the same time, on the other side of the world, Japan was providing another example of clearing away impediments from the old order to create conditions favorable for modernization and industrialization. But in comparison to the European and North American examples, this case presents some interesting Asian differences. The "top down" or elite-sponsored revolution in Japan that helped bring about a new social order occurred from 1868 with what is known as the Meiji Restoration. In reality, the Meiji Restoration was a revolutionary coup in which a group of lower samurai overthrow the old Tokugawa shogun (ruling military clan) to rapidly modernize Japan's political economy (albeit in an Asian manner) and bring about industrialization (Bendix, 1978; Eisenstadt, 1996; Jansen, 2000; McClain, 2002; Reischauer, 1988; Reischauer & Craig, 1998).

The process can be traced back to 1600 when Japan, threatened by the emerging European colonial powers, closed off its country. It was at this time that the nation was finally unified under one powerful shogun ruling clan referred to as the Tokugawa shogunate. From this time until 1853, when the United States began forcing Japan to open the country to foreigners, this Tokugawa shogunate maintained its power and worked to create a sense of national identity throughout the main Japanese archipelago. There was some slow economic development during this Tokugawa Period (or Edo Period), but it was minuscule compared to what had happened in Europe during this time (Collins, 1997; Gluck, 1985; Halliday, 1975; Kerbo & Mekinstry, 1995). To a much greater and systematic degree than during European feudalism before modernization and industrialization, the Tokugawa shogunate from the early 1600s specifically kept the merchant class from becoming too wealthy and powerful, in large degree with the development of a stratification system somewhat like the Indian caste system. Under this Tokugawa system of social stratification the emperor was officially considered to be in the highest rank, but in reality the top position of power was occupied by the ruling Tokugawa clan. Ranked below the Tokugawa shogunate were the local landed aristocratic families (or daimyo), followed in order by the samurai, then peasants, merchants, and finally an outcaste group called *burakumin* at the very bottom. Members of the merchant class, in other words, were specifically restricted in what they could do and placed in a low status so they could not threaten the power of the ruling shogun, daimyo, and samurai elites. To a much greater degree than in feudal Europe, therefore, Adam Smith's call for eliminating the impediments of feudal state restrictions blocking economic development applied to Japan and other states in Asia.[1]

By the early 1800s the feudal system created by the Tokugawa shogunate was in stagnation and only a small push by the United States led to its destruction. Before this time, a lower ranked samurai group, a group less occupied by warfare during the long stability of Tokugawa rule, had been one of the only sectors of the society to obtain "Dutch learning," or knowledge of world history, math, and modern science through books smuggled from the region close to Nagasaki where the small community of foreigners (mostly Dutch) were allowed during the long period of Tokugawa closure. It was this lower samurai who brought about the revolutionary coup in 1868 that overthrew the Tokugawa shogunate and set about rapidly changing Japan's political economy. It was the group of samurai with Dutch learning that most clearly understood Japan's situation in the world at the time; Japan had to quickly modernize to be strong enough to resist colonial domination from Europe that all of Asia, with the exception of Japan and Thailand, was experiencing by the mid-1800s. It was from this period that

Japan's new state-driven capitalism emerged, then the Asian development model which to some degree has become the model for development used by all of the rapidly developing Asian nations during the later decades of the twentieth century (Johnson, 1982; Kerbo & Slagter, 2000a, 2000b; Vogel, 1991).

The most important point is that the clearing of old impediments happened in different ways around the world and throughout history, but it no less happened in all nations that became modern industrial powers. China, for example, lost out in the new global competition when it was able to keep its merchants under stricter control so they would not threaten old aristocratic class rule. Compared to 200 or 300 years ago, however, the modern world system today is a different place for those countries that find themselves poor and dominated by rich nations, as did the Chinese by the beginning of the twentieth century. The European nations able to modernize and industrialize first did not have other rich nations already there to take advantage of their preindustrial economic weakness. The primary task of these European nations was to clear away the internal impediments to economic development. Poor countries today are often faced with a more difficult challenge of trying to clear away the impediments to economic development that come from both within the country and richer nations in the modern world system.

Overcoming the Legacies of Colonialism

At the high point of colonialism during the late 1800s the Western powers controlled some 85 percent of the world's territory (Chirot, 1986). In Asia, China was divided into spheres of influence by European powers, and only Japan and Thailand remained free from colonization, though even Japan and Thailand were burdened with unequal treaties forced upon them by Western powers. As we will see, much has been written about the Thai advantage for economic and political development because of this relative freedom. For all the colonized countries, getting rid of colonial domination was only the first step. In one way or another, they had to overcome the effects of colonialism to begin their move to economic development.

The nations of East and Southeast Asia had to quickly alter old or even very new postcolonial political economies if they were to achieve economic development before their people fell into more extreme poverty. For many the process is incomplete or has stagnated. For example, Burma's attempt was short-lived: A military dictatorship stepped into power and stopped all change needed for development. Cambodia and Laos were stymied by major internal disruptions related to cold war era superpower conflicts; and Vietnam is only now moving forward, however slowly and with many wrong turns, after a nationalist revolution and class revolution beginning even before World War II finally ended in 1975 (Evans, 1998, 1999b; Jamieson, 1995; Kamm, 1996; Osborne, 1995; Stuart-Fox, 1996, 1997). We have seen how Taiwan's Nationalist Party was able to drastically change policies after losing the mainland to Mao's communist revolution. In Korea, the South was able to achieve a new political economy favorable to modernization with the help of a colonial era infrastructure left by Japan, then the superpower support of the United States, while the north stagnated under one of the most repressive communist dictatorships in the world. Among these and other cases in East and Southeast Asia, though, one of the most interesting is presented by twentieth century China.

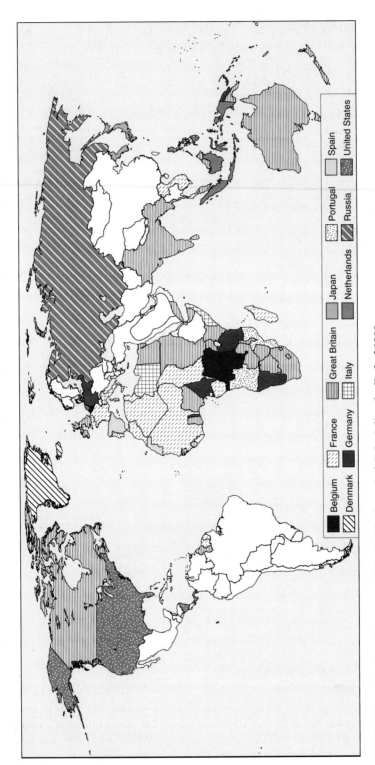

MAP 6.1 *This Map Illustrates the Worldwide Spread of Colonialism by End of 1800s.*

Belgium | France | Great Britain | Japan | Portugal | Spain
Denmark | Germany | Italy | Netherlands | Russia | United States

China: Opting Out of the Modern World System

Following theory and research suggesting poor nations tied to rich nations in the modern world system are primarily harmed by these ties, many have concluded that "opting out" of the modern world system is the best solution for these nations (Chirot, 1999, 1986). After the break from dominance has been made, the idea is that poor countries must focus their attention on nation building, establishing political authority, building the infrastructure needed for development, and taking control of their own resources. Scholars have never argued that anything as radical and hopeless as that tried by the Khmer Rouge is required. From 1975 to 1979, the Khmer Rouge tried to completely purge Cambodia of anything modern and Western to start from the ground up with a new agrarian society, what the Khmer Rouge called "year one." Nor has any serious scholar suggested that a country close itself off and remain closed as has happened in North Korea. But the argument following modern world system theory and earlier dependency research is that the nation must become relatively independent long enough to reshape its own social structure to provide an environment supportive for economic development. In this process the country must establish a sufficient amount of unity and political legitimacy allowing a development state to enforce policies bringing about economic development.

One of the more difficult parts of opting out of the world system, of course, has been resistance from the colonial or former colonial powers. Even after colonialism, these old powers continue to seek exclusive rights over trade and resources in their old colonial possessions. During the cold war, however, support from the old Soviet Union made opting out more possible because former colonies were able to get countersupport in the form of economic and military aid from the anticapitalist alliance in the world. The danger, of course, was becoming a "colonial" subject of the former Soviet Union. But there is the case of China that provides some encouragement to the poor nations of Asia, and the world.

For China the attempt to break from colonialism began long before World War II, but was not complete until Mao's communist victory in 1949. The struggle began in earnest from 1911 with the fall of the last imperial dynasty weakened even before colonial powers began carving up Chinese territory and demanding numerous economic concessions (Fairbank, 1986; Skocpol, 1979). What followed was a very long and bloody struggle between political parties and armies with different concepts of what the new China should be, ending as we have seen with the Nationalist Party's defeat and exile to Taiwan soon after the Japanese were thrown out of the country at the end of World War II. On the Chinese mainland, however, numerous struggles continued with different factions who had different ideas about how to develop China, struggles that in some ways followed those of the United States' Civil War a few decades after independence from British colonialism in 1776. But in contrast to the United States of earlier centuries, the Chinese had many more old class antagonisms and regional differences that required drastic internal changes before economic development could proceed. Also in contrast to the United States after 1776, China chose to opt out of the modern world system in an attempt to bring about internal changes without superpower manipulation. It was not until the mid-1970s and the end of the Cultural Revolution that China had achieved extensive unity under a very hard state, but a state that was finally able to reenter the world to negotiate with rich nations from a position of strength. Now

China is again letting the rich nations and their multinational corporations back into the country, but it is in a position to demand terms from multinational corporations that favor China's long-term development interests, such as the taxes they will pay to China for infrastructure development, the percent of profits that must be reinvested in China, how much of a joint venture will be Chinese owned, and so on. One of my favorite recent examples is the deal China made with Wal-Mart in 2004; The Wal-Mart stores coming into China will be the only ones in the world that allow labor unions (BBC News, 2004b).

Clearly China's development policies are not necessarily the best, and the revolution and then Cultural Revolution need not be as bloody as they were. Although the repressive state is still present in China, it can be argued that continued oppression and resistance to change in China by communist party elites in the late twentieth and early twenty-first centuries are growing more and more detrimental to China's long-term development potential. But, for China to develop economically and overcome the vast starvation among Chinese people in the late nineteenth century and first half of the twentieth century, China had to begin by gaining freedom from colonialism and getting its own social structure in order. Put another way, however horrible the process was for China, it was one means of setting the stage for economic policies that could work with some degree of success in reducing poverty, hunger, and the lack of economic development prospects for China. Despite all of the horrors of the Chinese Revolution through most of the twentieth century, it is important to put the process into perspective: Today in China, millions are not starving.

India and China Compared

It is in this context that the contrast between China and India is often noted. India also obtained independence after World War II. It is the largest democratic country in the world (in terms of population), a country with more PhDs and scientists than all but a few other countries, a country with a middle class larger than the whole U.S. population, and a country that has been granted extensive aid from rich nations and international organizations. Yet, during the final decades of the twentieth century India's prospects for further economic development and reduction of its vast amount of poverty grew only slowly compared to the rapid rate of economic growth in China. By 2004 China's economy was growing at more than 10 percent a year compared to India's 4 percent. By 2001 China had reached $3,976 per capita income compared to India's $2,358. Between 1990 and 2000 the percentage of China's population living on less than $1 per day dropped from 33 percent to 16 percent. During roughly the same period the percentage of people living on less than $1 per day in India dropped from 42 percent to 35 percent (UNDP, 2003:73).

A critical point is that though both China and India gained their independence after World War II, India had no comparable break from the old impediments blocking further development. As pointed out by Myrdal in his groundbreaking research, during the 1960s India had weak state structures unable to contend with old interest groups who preferred to keep a status quo that was not conducive to long-term and more evenly spread economic development (Myrdal, 1968, 1970; Sekhon, 2000). Relative democracy in a huge nation with many local elites with opposing interests has resulted in many elite veto groups paralyzing progress. India also retained a colonial bureaucracy established by the British in an earlier age of colonialism which operates somewhat efficiently as suggested by a relatively high score on the Weberianness Scale described in Chapter 2 (Evans & Rauch, 1999). But a detailed comparison of the Indian government bureaucracy with that of present-day South Korea shows it is not a strong development state able to restrain conflicting elite interests so that consistent development policies are carried out (Chibber, 2002). India had its nationalist revolution to end British exploitation, but India failed to achieve a real revolution that could clear away the old impediments and class interests blocking policies necessary for economic development. India is finally achieving better economic growth and poverty reduction after some economic reforms began in 1991, but at the current pace of change China will be way ahead of India in poverty reduction for many years to come.

Other comparisons can be instructive. During the 1990s both Russia and China, two "former" communist countries, were struggling to develop economically. A central problem for Russia has been extensive disorganization and loss of central authority. In the early 1990s there was serious talk in Russia about trying to copy Japan and the Asian development model. Free-market economists from the United States and the IMF, however, prevailed to impose their economic and political theories upon Russia. Since then Russia has mostly survived on IMF loans, with indications of economic growth showing up only in 2002, while China's economy has been moving forward quite rapidly. In hindsight we can see that Russia tried to reform its political system first, and then its economic system. China, in contrast, has focused on economic reform first and has yet to achieve any political democracy. In Russia there was nothing like a hard state or development state that could carry through development policies in the face of resistance from many old factions within the country and a rapidly emerging capitalist class that had become superrich and corrupt. China has retained a development state better able to control opposing interests in the new economy to achieve long-term and rapid economic development. China's problem, in contrast, will come with increasing demands for democracy from a population becoming much more affluent, educated, and independent in coming years.

The Colonial Experience of East and Southeast Asia

It is particularly important within East and Southeast Asia to compare how each country was treated by the colonial powers and how these colonial powers left the country. The end of British colonialism, for instance, was at first comparatively tame for both Malaysia and Burma. In Malaysia, the British stayed on for several years to provide advice on running the newly independent nation and to fight communist insurgents. Burma, however, became mired in conflict after the British abruptly left the country. Primarily because of internal conflicts the British helped rekindle as they left the country, Burma immediately degenerated into political violence and remains in suspension with a military dictatorship repressing any needed reforms.

Compared to Vietnam, Indonesia needed a less violent and less disruptive struggle for independence when the Dutch elected to reoccupy the country after the Japanese were pushed out at the end of World War II. But the shear size and multiethnic, multinational nature of the country we know of as Indonesia has proven very difficult to govern. True, Malaysia was created by the British from many semi-independent sultanates. But there was enough common culture and identity among these sultanates to make nation building possible. What is now Indonesia was composed by the Dutch from a mix of dramatically contrasting ethnic and cultural groups with no sense of national identity. The difference became clear after the Asian economic crisis of 1997: Thailand, which remained independent of colonialism, and Malaysia, which was able to regain social order relatively soon after colonialism, could act quickly (though following different strategies) to recover from the economic crisis. As the twenty-first century began, Indonesia was only slowly making steps toward economic recovery because of needed attention to a multitude of violent separatist movements stimulated by economic crisis.[2] The December 2004 earthquake and tsunami devastated Indonesia more than any other country in the region, killing over 100,000 people in the western part of the island chain. Aid to the victims and development aid was hampered because of the ongoing separatist revolution in Aceh, the region most affected by the tsunami.

To the east, the French left Indochina in a mess: Rather than exit somewhat gracefully as the British elected to do after World War II, the French chose to retake their colonial possessions.[3] Throughout the second half of the twentieth century Indochina has been a region of revolution, civil war, and economic stagnation in large degree because of French actions. Vietnam was finally establishing social order and economic development by the 1990s, with Laos still to make much progress, and Cambodia finally taking some slow steps toward enough social order to hope for some economic development at the beginning of the twenty-first century.

Korea and Taiwan were colonies of the Japanese through the first half of the twentieth century, and although the experience was particularly cruel and brutal for Korea, both Korea and Taiwan did gain independence from Japan after World War II with more infrastructure development than other people colonized in Asia.[4] Cold war struggles both harmed and helped Taiwan and South Korea for most of the second half of the twentieth century, but similar strong development states in Taiwan and South Korea helped direct successful policies for economic development.

The Philippines had the most unique experiences with colonialism in Southeast Asia, with colonization first by Spain and then by the United States. The Spanish began taking parts of the Philippines from the 1500s. In many ways the Philippines has become the most Westernized country in Asia because of the longer colonial domination by Spain and because there was no ancient empire in what is now the Philippines before the Spanish took control. The Philippines is also a country left with national boundaries that do not make cultural or social sense after colonialism, primarily because of the Christian dominance in the north and Islamic dominance in the south. An important result has been less national unity which has made economic development more difficult.

A more detailed examination of the interaction between Asian characteristics (outlined in the previous chapter) and the effects of colonialism among each of the countries of Southeast Asia will be taken up later. But a primary point is that even countries with Asian characteristics somehow predisposing them to economic development could not always activate these characteristics because of lingering effects of colonialism in the second half of the twentieth century. Some Asian nations, such as Indonesia, have been unable to benefit from ancient civilizations because of how old areas with such diverse traditions were put together during colonialism. Other Asian nations, such as China and Vietnam, have only recently been able to activate these Asian characteristics to employ a development state for economic development after getting over the aftereffects of colonialism. But despite this Asian diversity, the contrast of the colonial experience for Africa and Latin America is even greater.

CASE IN POINT

The Dishonor Roll of the World's Most Corrupt Dictators

Nations formed without the ancient traditions and philosophies restraining elites are prone to big-time corruption, not just the more common petty corruption of government officials and business leaders. In 2004 Transparency International, a nonprofit watch agency for corruption around the world, compiled a list of the most corrupt political leaders of the last decades of the twentieth century. The list contains the usual suspects from countries without a strong sense of national unity and ancient traditions restraining elites or countries disrupted by colonialism.

Heading the list was Suharto, president of Indonesia from 1967 to 1998. He was able to steal between $15 and $35 billion for his personal use during his rule. Second was Ferdinand Marcos, president of the Philippines from 1972 to 1986. His take was from $5 to $10 billion. Third was Mobutu Sese Seko, dictator of Zaire, now the Democratic Republic of the Congo, between 1965 and 1997. His take was at least $5 billion, but many suspect it was much more. In many ways, Mobutu's corruption was greater simply because there was more to steal in richer countries like Indonesia and the Philippines. As we will see in the next chapter, all agree that Mobutu was one of the most masterful of corrupt dictators.

Colonialism and the Division of Africa

As in Asia, the Portuguese were the first to explore African coastal areas from the early 1500s, and the Dutch established trading ports in what is now South Africa from 1652. But there was no serious attempt at colonization at this early date because the primary goal of Europeans was to establish ports to take on supplies for their ships sailing around Africa to reach Asian trade destinations, especially India, Southeast Asia, and China. The 1800s brought more European interest in Africa, and extreme exploitation. There was first the slave trade in a triangular route between Europe, Africa (with ships carrying slaves), and the Americas with ships loaded with goods bound for Europe again. From 30 million to 100 million Africans were captured and sent to the Americas as slaves during the 1700s and early 1800s, with about *9 million dying* on the voyage to the Americas (Clark, 1969:323; Genovese, 1974:5).

Formal colonization by Europeans began in the late 1800s. Already the various European powers had begun fighting each other for pieces of Africa, so a conference was called in Berlin during 1884–1885. It was here that the Europeans decided, without consultation from Africans of course, the division of Africa into European colonies (Hochschild, 1999; Mazrui, 1986; Pakenham, 1991). Except for Ethiopia in northern Africa and Liberia (a country established by former slaves returning from the Americas), all of Africa became dominated by European powers. Some of the worst forms of colonial exploitation and violence occurred in Africa. One of worst forms ever recorded was in the Belgium Congo. Technically this west central African region was not a colony of a European state but the actual property claimed by King Leopold of

The modern world system began about 500 years ago as Europeans spread around the world, taking land and resources from other people and forcing them into the emerging global economy. As shown here, Europeans first took over all of the Americas, and only later began stealing Africa and Asia.

Belgium (Wrong, 2001). Extreme forms of terror were used to control the natives of the area and make them work for Belgium companies seeking elephant ivory and Belgium-owned rubber plantations. Men, women, and children were chained day and night as they worked and slept, and small infractions of rules brought the punishment of hands or feet chopped off. The novelist Joseph Conrad captured the horror of the Belgium Congo in his novel *The Heart of Darkness*, written after Conrad worked briefly on a boat transporting ivory down rivers to the coast where it could be transported to Europe.

The most lasting of the detrimental impacts of colonialism on Africa, however, was the way the Europeans cut up the continent at the 1884–1885 Berlin Conference. The current nations of Africa were formed with European interests in mind, not African interests. The countries that make up Africa today cut across several traditional ethnic boundaries. Sociologically and culturally the map of Africa should have been drawn differently, with national boundaries following old ethnic and cultural boundaries. As it stands most African nations are almost impossible to govern because of the internal tribal conflicts they contain. I say almost impossible because we will see there are some positive examples in Sub-Saharan Africa. But they are few.

Colonialism and the Creation of Latin America

In contrast to Sub-Saharan Africa, there were some powerful ancient civilizations in what is now Latin America. The Maya, Aztecs, and Incas had relatively advanced agricultural societies with large cities of several thousands of people some 2,000 years ago (Lenski, 1966; Pfeiffer, 1977:349 –401). There were elaborate temples and central governments that resembled bureaucracies. But these civilizations were in severe decline when the Europeans arrived, and the Europeans finally destroyed them.

We commonly read in our history books that the Europeans brought diseases that killed off more than half of these Native American populations. What is less often described was the brutality of the Europeans and the systematic murder of these people (Diamond, 1999). It began with Columbus. His Spanish soldiers thought nothing of massacring the Native Americans while taking hundreds of women as sex slaves. If Columbus were doing his business today he would be tried in the World Court for genocide instead of having a national holiday in his honor in the United States. In some areas of Central America thousands of Native Americans died while working as slaves of the Spanish soldiers looking for gold and silver. One of the first cases of mass slaughter by Columbus's men occurred on the island that contains the Dominican Republic and Haiti. In two years after the Spanish arrived the island's population of 250,000 was cut in half. Later the deaths of Native Americans on the island were due mainly to disease and overwork as slaves. By 1515 there were only 5,000 of these Native Americans left alive, and only 500 by 1550 (Zinn, 1995:4). Much the same happened throughout Central and South America as more and more Spanish soldiers continued to arrive in the 1500s and 1600s. The Spanish and Portuguese established their colonies in Latin America with almost all influences of these ancient civilizations eliminated.

As the Spanish and Portuguese quickly lost power in the modern world system from the 1600s and 1700s they could no longer maintain their colonial empires in Latin America, with most becoming independent in the 1800s. The new nations that emerged in Latin America were *almost completely based on values and traditions of these Europeans* who settled in the new world. The descendants of these European conquerors are now in the upper and middle classes of the nations in Latin America while the descendants of the conquered Native Americans are found in the lower classes. This dominance by European descendants in Latin America today is so complete that it was front-page news when a man from mostly peasant Native American ancestry became president of Peru in 2000.

We can sum up the contrasting colonial situations of Asia, Africa, and Latin America in this way: In Asia the European colonists were there to exploit the people and resources before being kicked out by Asians. The disruption to most Asian civilizations by the Europeans was comparatively less. In Africa the European colonists were there to exploit the people and resources before leaving after World War II. The disruption to the African continent was extensive, especially because of the way boundaries to new African nations were created by the Europeans. When the Europeans left, with the exception of countries like South Africa and Rhodesia (Zimbabwe), Africans were primarily back in control, though in control of nations and economies that were almost ungovernable. In the Americas the Europeans came to exploit the people and resources—but they also came to stay. Both North and South America essentially became a new Europe with the native peoples completely subjugated and mostly exterminated. There is one simple indicator of this: In most of the larger Latin American countries today over 50 percent of the population is made up of people with European ancestry. At one extreme is Argentina where 97 percent of the population is of European ancestry, and Chile where it is 95 percent. Brazil is more typical with 55 percent of its population of European origin and 38 percent mixed European and black from unions of former slaves from Africa. Mexico and smaller Latin American countries have more of a mixed population of Native Americans and people of European origins (U.S. CIA, *2003*).

Because of their history, few countries outside Asia have been able to use anything like the Asian development model as a motor of economic development. In the next two chapters we will examine why this has been so in Africa and Latin America. Then we will return to Southeast Asia to consider why some countries have been able to achieve more even economic development and poverty reduction compared to most countries in Africa and Latin America.

Notes

1. With respect to Japan versus other Asian nations, especially China, it is interesting to note that Japan had a feudal system that was much closer to that of preindustrial Europe (Edwin O. Reischauer, *The Japanese* [Cambridge, MA: Harvard University Press, 1987]; Reinhard Bendix, *Kings or People: Power and the Mandate to Rule* [Berkeley: University of California Press, 1978]; S. N. Eisenstadt, *Japanese Civilization: A Comparative View* [Chicago: University of Chicago Press, 1996]). With a less powerful imperial feudal state in Japan, a shogun that was able to unite and control the local feudal aristocracy for only a relatively brief time, the shogun state was less able to maintain its control over the centuries, thus blocking change that would help bring about industrialization. In part, this is the argument used to explain why it was Japan that has been the first Asian nation to industralize.

2. While Singapore and Hong Kong are of course considered among the Asian tigers and analyzed along with the other East and Southeast Asian nations by many social scientists (for example, see Ezra Vogel, *The Four Little Dragons: The Spread of Industrialization in East Asia* [Cambridge, MA: Harvard University Press, 1991), their situation as small city-states makes for many differences, especially differences in governability and the development provided during British colonialism. I have chosen to focus less on these two cases in the present analysis for these reasons.

3. Though, of course, French political leaders at the end of World War II were undecided about such a return to Indochina, and the United States was pressuring France to give up Indochina. Local French military commanders in Indochina, however, decided to make their own policy and moved to retake Indochina.

4. Taiwan was colonized by Japan after a short war with China in 1895 and Korea was taken from Russia by Japan after a short war with Russia in 1904–1905.

Africa and the Middle East: Fractured Nations in the Global Economy

A posi Lakwemwe is a boy of 16 living in Kampala, the capital city of Uganda, one of the world's poorest countries in Sub-Saharan Africa. About 75 percent of people in Uganda live on less than what $2 per day would buy in the United States. When Aposi caught the attention of reporters in 2002 he was homeless, living under a plastic sheet in one of the huge slums of Kampala. The boy owned nothing but the old T-shirt and tattered jeans he wore, and the plastic sheet. Thousands of other children are homeless and living alone in the streets of Kampala, "begging and robbing their way from one day to the next" (*International Herald Tribune, The New York Times,* March 26, 2002). Aposi told reporters, "Most of us are thieves but not all of us. You have to be careful around us. The problem is that not enough people give to us. What are we supposed to do?" Most of these children have lost their parents to the AIDS epidemic in Uganda. Children such as Aposi exist in the streets of almost all the major cities in Sub-Saharan Africa, but many are worse off. At least things are improving in Uganda where a ruthless dictator not too many years ago destroyed the economy, stole much of the government's money, and killed hundreds of thousands of people. The World Bank has recently listed Uganda as one of the recent "success stories" because of the prudent use of foreign aid to improve conditions (World Bank, 2002a).

The most common situation for people in Sub-Saharan Africa, however, is not like that of Aposi. Most of Africa's poor live in small villages and farming areas. The problem is, even if they have some land, the soil is so poor very little will grow, there is little water, or they have no money for seed or tools to work the land. There is some agricultural investment coming into a few African countries like Kenya, where new farms in the Rift Valley are growing vegetables and flowers for the European markets. About 250,000 landless peasants now live around this Rift Valley area of Kenya helping to grow these crops. There are many "horror stories of pitiful pay and abuse," and illnesses from the toxic chemicals used in the fields (*International Herald Tribune, The New York Times,* June 5, 2003). There is no environmental protection agency for these people. A bouquet of flowers these poor people help to grow cost about $3.20 in a British supermarket. None of these people make even close to that much money in their 46-hour work week. Poor peasants in countries all over Sub-Saharan Africa are growing such vegetables and flowers for the European market now, but these African countries must obtain food aid to feed their people. They export food while large percentages of their people are malnourished.

Alexandra Township, Johannesburg, South Africa.
Poor black South Africans sit among shacks in
Alexandra Township with a view of the wealthy
white suburb of Sandton City in Johannesburg,
South Africa.

Considerable evidence shows that poverty reduction in less developed countries usually begins with land reform or policies that help small farmers. Sub-Saharan Africa has a greater percentage of its population living as poor farmers than Thailand (IFAD, 2001). It is logical, therefore, to expect African countries to have many aid programs for small farmers so they can grow food for themselves and for other Africans instead of exporting food to Europe. But it seldom happens. Studies of this problem in Africa note that while three-fourths of Africans are farmers, there are *almost no policies* attempting to boost agricultural production. We can again use Kenya as an example: With the vast majority of its people living off the land, only 4 percent of the Kenyan government budget goes to agricultural programs, and 75 percent of this 4 percent goes to support wasteful state farms (*International Herald Tribune,* September 6, 2001). And there is the case of President Mugabe of Zimbabwe in the late 1990s until 2002. With falling political support Mugabe jumped on the bandwagon of land redistribution for Zimbabwe. The problem was that it was land reform only for his political supporters and carried out in such an irrational manner that agricultural output dropped (*International Herald Tribune,* August 1, 2001). Taking land from white land owners and giving it to Mugabe's political supporters in fact made 70 percent of Zimbabwe's agricultural workers jobless.

More common, though, is simple old-fashioned corruption, though on a grand scale, by national leaders of Africa. In Liberia, for example, in 2003 the deposed leader Taylor took $100 million out of the country, money from aid programs for the country's poor (*International Herald Tribune,* September 2, 2003). Mozambique provides another example. In the early 1990s Mozambique finally overcame war and failed Soviet policies to establish some "market capitalist" policies for economic development. The economy has been growing by around 10 percent since 1997. Mozambique is now producing enough food to feed its population, but people are still malnourished. One estimate is that 66 percent of the population still lives in poverty. Corruption and even mafia-style killings are common. For instance, the largest bank in Mozambique siphoned $14 million from corporate investment and aid programs (*International Herald Tribune,* December 24, 2001).

In country after country in Africa, why are obviously sound development policies seldom attempted? When they are attempted, why do they most often seem to go terribly wrong? And why is corruption by national leaders so rampant?

A key answer to these questions seems to be the lack of what the World Bank calls good governance. Or perhaps even more to the point, the problem is often a lack of any governance at all. As noted briefly in previous chapters, the flow of African history is in dramatic contrast to the history of most nations of East and Southeast Asian. To begin with, we find very few old civilizations in Sub-Saharan Africa that could hand down traditions of government support for its people and moral codes encouraging elite responsibility to the people of the whole nation. There are *certainly admirable moral codes and a sense of responsibility* to fellow human beings in Africa. In fact, this is one of Africa's strengths. But such codes of responsibility to others are almost exclusively rooted in the family structure and within specific ethnic groups. A sense of nationalism, moral responsibility between elites and masses, simply did not follow the development of nation-states in Sub-Saharan Africa as much as it did in most of Asia.

Of course, there were also the effects of colonialism in Africa. Unlike in Asia, there were no strong civilizations still able to confront the European colonials in Sub-Saharan Africa. The colonials could, and did, do almost as they pleased. The colonials did relatively little to develop the infrastructure of their colonial possessions in Africa as was done in, say, Vietnam, Malaysia, or Hong Kong. In Africa the colonials only wanted land for some of their own settlers and natural resources, including the people as slaves to work the new American plantations where the local populations were too small to enslave for agricultural purposes. It is time to look at some of this history a little more carefully before we examine the situation of Sub-Saharan Africa today.

A Brief History of Africa in the Modern World System

Africa was the cradle of human evolution. From time to time there are discoveries in places like China where someone claims to have found earlier human remains, but upon closer examination these claims have never been upheld. Indeed, we can go even further to say that it was in Africa where our great-, great-, great-grandmother lived—literally. The evidence from genetic tests suggests there was one woman some 120,000 to 220,000 years ago from whom all humans today have descended. There were other mothers around 250,000 years ago, of course, but for one reason or another these other mothers had their genetic line stopped after several generations. It was the descendants from this common grandmother several generations later who began moving slowly out of Africa some 35,000 to 89,000 years ago to eventually populate the whole planet

CASE IN POINT

Colonialism and Hunger in Africa

In the African country of Malawi, Lucas Lufuzi was recently interviewed by reporters as he waited for a distribution of food aid (*International Herald Tribune,* May 11, 2002). He had not eaten anything in 3 days, and then it was only some small cobs of unripened corn he found dying in the fields. He was most concerned about feeding his two grandchildren: His 29-year-old son had already died of hunger, leaving him with the children. In this part of Africa the estimate was that 20 million people were close to starvation in 2002. The U.N. World Food Program has been feeding some 2.6 million people in this part of Africa but needs much more food to forestall starvation. The 2002 round of famine was set off a few months before with flooding and then drought. U.N. World Food Program officials say the problem is made worse by corrupt governments and political instability. That was the key problem in Chad during 2004 as civil war caused dislocations and farmers to flee their fields from fear of being massacred like thousands of their neighbors.

Such stories repeat the all too common pattern in Africa, a pattern depicted on our TV screens for years. The latest U.N. *Food Security Report* tells us that about 60 percent of people in central Africa are malnourished, whereas other sections of Sub-Saharan Africa are only a little better off at about 40 percent. We have already seen that in less developed countries all over the world the number one killer is lack of food, while for Americans in 2005 the previous number one killer—tobacco—was surpassed by too much food.

Seeing all of those terrible pictures of wave after wave of starvation in Africa we tend to assume it is due to too many people living on dry unproductive land. A friend of mine who is a respected soil scientist tells me that Africa has the worst soil of any continent. We know there has been some climate change and desertification as the desert creeps further and further through central parts of Africa. And of course most people know of the political instability and mass murders, making people flee from their fields that remain unplanted.

All of these causes of famine in Africa are beyond question. But the fact remains that people had lived well in Africa for hundreds of centuries before colonialism. What we must understand is that many of the problems in Africa are related to changes brought by European colonization. For example, people who had lived reasonably well as hunter-gathers were forced into farming by Europeans seeking cash crops. More and more of the land was taken for farming, land that could not sustain their farming methods, or the increasing lack of water. In addition came social changes that brought rapid population growth. Finally, as we have seen, much of that political instability keeping people from their fields in Africa is related to how the map of Africa was created to almost ensure perpetual conflicts among differing ethnic factions. As the next wave of starving faces appear on our TV screens, we should pause to consider what Africa would have been like without European colonialism before we rush to judge Africans for having too many children, destroying their environment, and forming too many corrupt and unstable governments.

Sources: United Nations, *Food and Agriculture Organization,* 2003; IFAD, 2001.

(Boyd & Silk, 2003). New DNA studies also show that all males on this planet are related to Africans who came out of Africa at this same time, some 35,000 to 89,000 years ago (Gibbons, 2001). These humans migrating out of Africa became the dominate groups all over the world, replacing other humans in these regions who did not survive for many more generations.

Those who stayed in northern Africa, more specifically in northeast Africa, eventually formed one of the most ancient civilizations about 5,000 years ago, Egypt. Ethiopia, south of Egypt in the horn of Africa, was part of an ancient civilization with a large Christian population long before Christianity moved into Europe. There were other civilizations or empires in Sub-Saharan Africa, but they were small and had only a comparatively short existence. One such empire that existed in what is now Zimbabwe became extinct about 500 years ago. In the usual manner, it fell into decline with too many people and animals for the environment and agricultural methods of the time. The people of this old empire reverted to a smaller tribal village existence spread throughout that area of Africa. Almost all people in Sub-Saharan Africa were practicing rather simple agriculture or were hunter-gathers when traders and conquerors from other parts of the world arrived. Arabs brought Islam to Africa about 1,300 years ago, and much of Africa was already Muslim when the Chinese first started trading with some East African villages in the early 1400s. The Europeans first showed up about 100 years later.

While Arabs had a major impact on all of Africa, it was the Europeans who came to more completely dominate the continent at the high point of European colonialism during the late 1800s and early 1900s. Though this colonization lasted only briefly, with most of Africa becoming independent soon after World War II, the legacy of European colonization lasts to this day. As stated earlier, a key problem for Africa is that the European powers cut up Africa to form the present countries in a manner that did not make social or cultural sense. To this day most Sub-Saharan African countries cut across old ethnic areas to form nations containing ethnic groups that have been in conflict for centuries. In addition, in many African countries the European colonials encouraged further ethnic rivalries as a means of divide and rule. A result has been that many African countries are almost ungovernable, with one ethnic faction holding power and others trying to remove their ethnic rivals from power to take control of the government for themselves. There has been almost endless political violence in many Sub-Saharan Africa countries since independence. We will see below that there are exceptions: Some Sub-Saharan countries have achieved stability, some have relatively good governments, but these are too few in a region badly needing stability for economic development and poverty reduction.

To make all of this worse, African independence unfolded in the early years of the cold war between the United States and the Soviet Union. Many African countries were caught up in the superpower conflict that further encouraged ethnic rivalries and made them even bloodier. If a country was alined with, and receiving aid from one side in the cold war, the other side would supply arms and training to their ethnic enemies, making civil wars and revolutions more likely and costly. The American Central Intelligence Agency (CIA) was active in the 1960s supplying arms and even organizing assassinations of African leaders to counter the activities of Soviet agents. We know the details of some of these CIA activities because of a U.S. Senate investigation published in a booklet titled *Alleged Assassination Plots Involving Foreign Leaders* in 1975.

WHY WE SHOULD CARE

Blowback

We have already seen international opinion polls showing high levels of anti-Americanism today. Surprisingly for most Americans, more people in the world blame the United States for the world's problems, from terrorism to hunger and poverty. Most Americans are puzzled over why so many people in the world seem to hate us. While the blame may be misplaced, one must acknowledge that the United States has a severe image problem in the world and that there are many, many harmful implications from this negative image.

Blowback is a term used by the U.S. Central Intelligence Agency to describe the negative consequences of its foreign activities. Some of the better known blowbacks these days are the results of U.S. aid and support to Osama bin Laden and Saddam Hussein in Iraq during the cold war days. There are many others.

It was not always so, however. Soon after World War II, the United States took the moral high ground by demanding that the Europeans grant their former colonies independence. (Of course, there was some self-interest involved because the United States had no dependence on a colonial empire and wanted an open world for U.S. corporations.) The French and Dutch, for example, both went back into their old colonial territories after the Japanese were kicked out in 1945. The United States was successful in removing the Dutch by threatening to cut off their Marshall Plan funds if they did not leave Indonesia. But by the time the United States was trying to get the French out of Vietnam the cold war began. The Soviet Union was threatening Europe and communists had taken over China. The Nationalist leader in Vietnam, Ho Chi Minh, had worked with the United States to defeat the Japanese in Vietnam. U.S. Army intelligence officers had been sending back reports that Ho Chi Minh was a leader the United States should work with. Ho Chi Minh himself was asking for American support because he so admired the United States and feared the Chinese. Ho Chi Minh even included the opening paragraphs of the American Declaration of Independence for that of his own country. But the cold war and an almost

As well as covert actions in Africa, the booklet outlines other assassination plots against leaders like Castro in Cuba, where (among other things) the CIA tried to give him poison cigars, attempted to drug him before giving a speech, or tried to dust him with powder that would make his famous beard fall out.[1]

Not all consequences of the superpower conflict in Africa were negative, of course. It brought more attention to Africa in the United States and Soviet allied countries, resulting in more foreign aid, much more than Africa receives from the United States today. One of my students from the University of Vienna, for example, spent some years growing up in Lybia because her father was posted there as a medical doctor by the former communist country of Czechoslovakia. As we will see in some detail later, though, much of this aid was wasted on corrupt dictators who hid billions of dollars in Swiss banks. There were also big development projects, such as huge dams, that were not needed or only went to help U.S. multinational corporations take more resources and profits out of Africa. Most of these corrupt dictators were warmly supported by the U.S. government simply because they were anticommunist.

(Continued)

complete lack of understanding of Asia dashed all of these possibilities. The U.S. government changed its mind and began *financing* France's return to Vietnam and its fight against Ho Chi Minh's nationalists. When the French were defeated in the early 1950s the United States slowly begin sending in U.S. troops, only to be defeated as well, with more than 58,000 Americans killed in that war by 1973.

It was during the cold war days that John Foster Dulles, the U.S. secretary of state in the 1950s, and his brother, CIA director Allen Dulles, worked out their strategy of overthrowing foreign governments they did not like and replacing them with pro-American governments. Their first success in this activity in Iran during 1953 so pleased these cold warriors that they used the strategy in other parts of the world, such as the Chilean coup in 1973. We now have a rather detailed account of how the CIA pulled off the overthrow of the Iranian prime minister in 1953 written by the CIA station chief in charge of the operation, Kermit Roosevelt. As the Dulles's biographer also found, the British came to the CIA requesting assistance because the newly elected prime minister of Iran was trying to get control of some of British Petroleum's operations in Iran (taken while Iran was a colony of Britain) and charge higher prices for oil. The British knew they were too weak after World War II to carry out the operation themselves, so the U.S. government secretly agreed to help. The CIA operation overthrew the democratically elected Iranian government and placed the Shah (king) back in power. The country was again open for easy U.S. and British corporate investment, and the Shah began a campaign of political repression in Iran. By 1979, anger against the Shah and the United States reached the point of revolution, putting in power an extremist Islamic leader who began openly calling for attacks on the United States. These are the kind of situations most American never knew about, or have forgotten, that people in places such as the Middle East and Africa have never forgotten. And these are the situations that have made the majority of people in the Middle East distrust and feel resentful toward the United States today.

Sources: Leonard Mosley, 1978; John Keay, 1977; Duiker, 2000; Roosevelt, 1979; Yergin, 1991; Chalmers Johnson, 2000; U.S. Senate Select Committee, 1975a.

African Social Organization: The Big Man and Predator States

We saw in Chapter 2 that African countries tend to rank among the world's least democratic, but more importantly seem to rank among the world's least efficient state bureaucracies. African countries tend to have the most unstable governments, changing from one military dictatorship to another, year after year. We see in Table 7.1 that African countries are among the world's most corrupt. Transparency International, a nonprofit organization that conducts various surveys of this nature, relies primarily upon interviews with people doing business around the world when ranking countries from the most to the least corrupt. In the 2001 ranking, Bangladesh was the most corrupt, receiving a score of 8.8, with Denmark being the world's least corrupt at 0.5. The United States' score was 2.7. Of the world's 10 most corrupt nations, 6 were in Africa. The average score for all countries was 5.5,

TABLE 7.1

Government Corruption in Africa

Country (most corrupt to least)	Corruption Score*
Nigeria	8.4
Angola	8.3
Madagascar	8.3
Kenya	8.1
Uganda	7.9
Cameroon	7.8
Zambia	7.4
Cote d'Ivoire	7.3
Tanzania	7.3
Zimbabwe	7.3
Malawi	7.1
Senegal	6.9
African Average	**6.8**
Egypt	6.6
Ethiopia	6.5
Morocco	6.3
Ghana	6.1
World Average	**5.5**
South Africa	5.2
Tunisia	5.2
Namibia	4.3
Botswana	3.6

*The higher the corruption, the higher the score. The world average corruption score is 5.5, with most advanced industrial societies having scores ranging from 2.7 to 0.5.

Source: Transparency International http://www.transparency.org and http://www.global-corruptionreport.org

with the African average score 6.7. Table 7.1 shows that all African countries in the study were above the world average except four nations.

The political instability and corruption in so many African nations have always brought attempts by social scientists to figure out why Africa seems so ungovernable compared to other world regions. There is still much disagreement, though there is agreement that Africa's predicament is related to a mix of precolonial African culture and the effects of colonialism. A primary impact of colonialism, as we have seen, was the division of Africa into colonies and later nation-states that did not make social and cultural sense. With hostile ethnic groups somewhat equally balanced in the national territory the ability to achieve stable and efficient government institutions is very difficult. Also, it is argued that ethnic identities were made more important to African people in response to colonial rule.[2] In opposition to European rule, in other words, Africans reverted to traditional ethnic-based social networks to take care of themselves, which also produced greater ethnic identity. At times the colonial powers intentionally stimulated these ethnic rivalries to keep Africans fighting each other and not the European colonials. However, the mode of social organization called the *big man* system that existed in many regions of Africa even before European colonialism was not one conducive to long-term development and national goals (Wrong, 2001:281).

A couple of years ago I remember talking with young African academics who, like most African social scientists, are highly critical of the government inefficiency and corruption in Africa. In reference to the higher standard of living of us Western social scientists, one young man, reverting in jest to this African tradition, told me how someday when he was a "big man" he too could have a more comfortable standard of living. The big man in African society is the dominant local power because it is he who has amassed the most wealth or valued goods that can be distributed to others as a reward for loyalty and protection. A key to becoming a big man is letting people *know you have extensive wealth to pass around for this support*. One makes this known with an extravagant lifestyle—many expensive cars, jewelry, a huge mansion, and so on. The big man system is easily transferred to national politics, especially in ethnically diverse countries. A result is a political system in which patronage and the distribution of rewards for support becomes primary. The big man system, in other words, has become national with *predator states* used in the same way: One ethnic group tries to gain control of the state which then becomes a means of handing out spoils for support from other groups. It is a system based upon the display of wealth and immediate gratification, which is a barrier to long-term savings, investment, and thus economic development. It is a system played for short-term personal gains and ethnic group rewards, with those in power often having no short-term incentive to change it. In fact, the incentive is *not* to change it because one would lose power and achieve nothing even if long-term development goals were desired. This is combined with the problem of little national identity among elites and masses in Africa, in contrast to most of Asia, because of very recent and illogical national boundaries drawn by the colonial powers. This means there is less motivation by African leaders to look to long-term national interests for all in the society. There have been many youthful, idealistic African leaders who have tried to challenge this system. But under its logic, these idealistic leaders cannot gain or hold much of a following because they have not amassed a pool of wealth to buy loyalty to enough of their fellow citizens.

There are, of course, local patronage systems in all nations. In the United States it is called "pork barrel politics." A similar system is widespread in Japan, for example, with all national politicians fighting to get more bridges, schools, and roads built in their district so they can get reelected. But the contrast in developed countries and throughout most of Asia is that such pork barrel politics *has limits*. A broad sense of national identity in the country leads to criticism of pork barrel politics that harms national security and economic development. In Asian countries, while local communities want such political spoils, they also come together on a higher, national level with interest in protecting and developing the nation in general. In Africa, by contrast, stashing money away in a secret Swiss bank account could be seen as a prudent means of protecting wealth that will be given out for patronage. In Asia it would more likely be seen as national betrayal, except in those countries, such as Indonesia, that have national boundaries that also produce regional ethnic conflicts (Chabal & Daloz, 1999:107). Another way to consider the African difference is to compare Africa to China in the early twentieth century. Colonial exploitation of China finally led to a collapse of the old imperial government in 1911. For a few decades after 1911 China fell into a system of many separate "warlord governments" that operated much like Africa's big man system. The difference, however, is that China has an ancient civilization that still promotes national identity and unity that could be reasserted by future leaders to reestablish a national government more devoted to long-term national goals. Having achieved independence from European colonial dominance and overcome serious internal divisions, this national unity has now made China one of the most rapidly developing economies in the world.

As noted earlier in this book, many people often like to revert to an argument based upon values that tends to blame poor people for their poverty. What exists in Africa is not cultural values blocking efficient government and economic development; it is a fractured system of loyalties based upon ethnic groups that prevents long-term development for broader national interests. There is an internal logic to the big man system. In the face of many barriers to long-term economic development in Africa, the big man patronage system provides a means of at least enhancing the standard of living for you and your ethnic group, though unfortunately this is a logic that has only short-term vision (Chabal & Daloz, 1999). International development agencies have been unable to change the system: Loans from the World Bank, International Monetary Fund, and international NGOs (nongovernmental organizations devoted to economic development) are often "captured" by big men and used as wealth to distribute to their supporters to keep themselves in power.

Africa Today and Future Prospects

Although there are some bright spots, we have seen in previous chapters that the current situation and future prospects for Sub-Saharan Africa are grim, the world's worst. Almost half of the population live on less than $1 per day, and that percentage is expected to grow by 20 percent between now and 2015 (World Bank, 2000). Sub-Saharan Africa has the highest percentage of people living on less than $1 per day of any world region, and the only world region expected to have an increase in the percent of its population living on less than $1 per day. As shown in Table 7.2, the average yearly growth in the economy (real GDP) was only 2.2 from 1991 to 2000, with an average 3.7 percent growth between 2004 and 2010. But this growth meant a reduction

TABLE 7.2

Sub-Saharan Africa: Past and Future Prospects

	1991–2000	2004–2010
Real GDP growth	2.2 %	3.7%
Consumption per capita	–0.6	1.1
GDP per capita	–0.4	1.5
Population growth	2.6	2.2

Source: World Bank, 2002b:205.

CASE IN POINT

Mobutu's Congo

An all too common case of dashed hopes and government corruption is found in the Democratic Republic of the Congo, or what was called Zaire after Belgium gave independence to the Congo. As many Sub-Saharan African countries were gaining their independence in the late 1950s and early 1960s there was much hope that finally new nationalist African leaders with concern for their people would bring much needed economic develop with their leadership. After the horrors of Belgian rule in the Congo this hope was especially strong. The first leader of independent Zaire, Lumumba, was seen as too close to the Soviet Union and was assassinated with clear evidence of involvement by the American CIA. U.S. support was given to the energetic and seemingly devoted Mobutu Sese Seko who became Zaire's president in 1960. He was to win wide popular support after he bravely stood up to drunken army troops who were rioting in the capital during this period of political instability. For a few years after becoming president, Mobutu did seem to try to bring about reform and economic development in his country. Eventually, however, he turned into the typical big man devoted mostly to enriching himself and tribal relatives, and hanging on to power with terror over his citizens.

Reports suggest Mobutu's change began around 1973 when he started nationalizing corporations in Zaire. Thousands of businesses with assets totaling more than $1 billion were nationalized and given to Mobutu supporters. He kept the best for himself, as well as 14 plantations employing 25,000 people. Before long Mobutu had a dozen mansions in Zaire, as well as a palace in Switzerland, and, among other things, a Boeing 707 always at his disposal. The World Bank could not fail to notice the growing corruption in Mobutu's government and began attempts to reduce it. Being practical, World Bank officials insisted that Mobutu could take only about $2 million per month from grants and aid going to development projects in Zaire. Mobutu was furious and demanded more. In the end he reached an agreement that allowed him to take $36 million a year for his personal family and household expenses, a sum that was 20 percent of his country's total budget at the time. All of this, of course, was on top of the millions of dollars, some say billions, that he gained illegally in other ways. At one point in the 1970s the International Monetary Fund (IMF) discovered $100 to $200 million missing from grants to Zaire. In 1989 one IMF auditor found another $600 million missing. This was about the same time Mobutu was being hosted by President George Bush Sr., who praised Mobutu for his (anticommunist) leadership of Zaire.

Before Mobutu began nationalization of the economy in 1973 the economy was growing at an excellent rate of 7 percent a year. The economy has never returned to anything close to that rate since. Now the Democratic Republic of the Congo (what was Zaire) has one of the world's lowest per capita GNPs, just $580 per person a year.[3] Of 173 countries ranked on the U.N. Human Development Index, the Congo is ranked 155. The World Bank has been unable to obtain poverty figures for this country, but it is obvious that a majority of the people live on less than $1 per day. Since Mobutu was overthrown in a popular revolt in 1997 there has been almost constant fighting with terrible massacres committed by all sides in the conflict. While claiming lofty goals for helping people in the Congo, the battle among rebellious factions today is over who becomes the next big man.

Source: Most of the above information comes from Wrong, 2001. Information on the CIA involvement in the assassination of Lumumba and putting Mobutu in power can be found in U.S. Senate Select Committee, 1975a.

in per capita consumption and per capita GDP in the 1990s, with only very small gains expected to 2010. The reason for negative gains in the 1990s and only small gains in per capita consumption and per capita GDP to 2010 is continued high population growth figures per year. The slight reduction in population growth between 2001 and 2010 is why per capita consumption and GDP will grow slightly, unfortunately because of the high number of deaths from AIDS. In 2002 the per capita GDP for Sub-Saharan Africa was only $1,620, the worst for any world region and half the per capita GDP of second place South Asia (World Bank, 2004d). It is AIDS, of course, that is the biggest crisis of the region. As described earlier, in 10 years the number of AIDS-related deaths in Africa will exceed all of those killed in both World War I and World War II, and many times more than the 20 million people that were killed by the infamous bubonic plague that devastated Europe in the fourteenth century.[4]

Oil Wealth

There is the corruption in Africa. One ray of hope, but only a small one, has come with the discovery of oil along the Atlantic coast in central Sub-Saharan Africa. There are billions to be made. But the usual question is, who will benefit?

One of the most important cases is Angola. Only six other countries in the world produce more oil than Angola. At 800,000 barrels of oil a day, Angola is ahead of Kuwait. But despite this oil wealth, about three-quarters of Angola's population live in extreme poverty and some 2 million would probably starve without food aid from international agencies. The United Nations estimates that 2.7 million Angolan children are malnourished. Like many Sub-Sahara African countries, Angola has been in a civil war for years, 27 to be exact. About half of government spending had gone to cover the costs of this war, including half of its oil revenues. Thus, there is some hope with relative peace coming to the country. But the corruption is huge. In 2001 it was estimated that international oil companies paid Angola about $900 million for exploration rights. Half of that money went to the war, but $450 million went missing. The IMF estimates that about $1 billion was missing from all state revenues. Over the last 5 years the IMF figures that about $4 billion has disappeared from state revenues. Two years ago one outside auditor figured that Angola spent more money on cars for cabinet ministers, legislators, and their wives than on health care and education for all its people.[5]

Another case is from Equatorial Guinea, a small country on the Atlantic coast north of Angola. A few years ago Equatorial Guinea was found to have huge oil reserves onshore and offshore. Still, except for a few elites, almost all of the people in this small country live on less than $1 per day. In 2003 it was discovered that $300 to $400 million of government oil revenues had been hidden away in a small bank in Washington, DC. Later it was discovered that the dictator of Equatorial Guinea has $16 million in another account, and he and his family have a Washington, DC. home worth $2.6 million and one in Beverly Hills worth $7.7 million, plus dozens of expensive sports cars. Mobil Oil recently admitted to paying him personally hundreds of thousands of dollars to drill for oil in his country, plus a cut in much of the profits (*Los Angeles Times,* December 18, 2004). With about 500,000 population, that $400 million alone (and there is no doubt much more hidden away) would have put about $800 into the hands of each person in the country, putting everyone way above the $1 day extreme poverty line, and even above the $2 per day line.

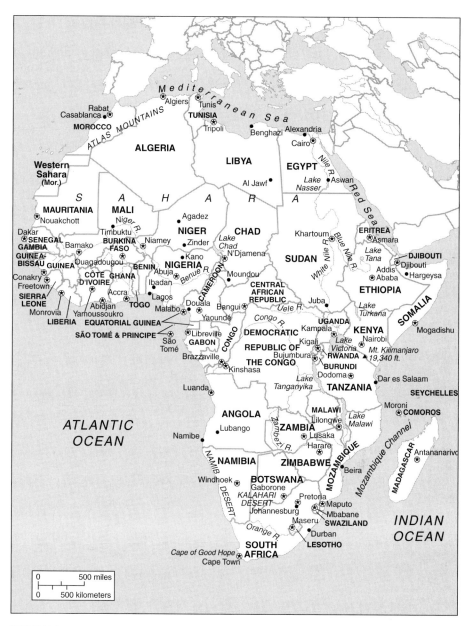

MAP 7.1 *Map of Current National Borders in Africa.*

One possible solution to all of this corruption suggested by the nonprofit agency, Global Witness, is to pass laws in rich countries like the United States requiring their oil companies to disclose publicly all payments made to governments for such things as oil exploration in the country. At least people in the country and agencies like the United Nations and IMF could then keep better track of what happens to this money.

Such laws could help reduce the level of corruption in places such as Angola. Prospects for these laws, however, are slim.

Another approach recently began in Chad, a landlocked country in the heart of Sub-Saharan Africa. Like countries around it, Chad is one of the poorest in the world and has a highly corrupt government dominated by one ethnic group. Per capita income in Chad is just over $1,000 and Chad ranks 165 out of 173 countries on the U.N. Human Development Index. About 80 percent of the population is estimated to live in poverty. Huge amounts of oil have just been discovered in Chad, and American and Canadian oil companies are rushing into the country. In this case, however, the World Bank has set up its first ever agency to manage the oil investments itself (*International Herald Tribune, The New York Times,* February 18, 2004). The first oil royalties have brought about $100 million to be controlled by the World Bank agency, though another $100 million in taxes from this oil wealth is still controlled by the Chad government. So far about $6.3 million has been distributed directly to local villages by the World Bank agency, though it lacks control over how the village elders spend the money. There have been some small improvements in these villages, but the overall impact is yet to be determined. The American oil companies like the project because it helps clear them of any responsibility for the corruption. But the situation for the World Bank agency is still difficult and conflict with the Chad government is increasing.

Contrasting National Conditions in Africa

All of these figures for Sub-Saharan Africa, of course, are averages for the whole region. Some countries are doing much worse than others, and some are doing better. It is useful to consider a few of the worst and best cases in more detail.

Worst Cases

Rwanda

For many reasons one of the worst cases in Africa today is Rwanda, in west central Africa. Almost 85 percent of the people in Rwanda live on less than $2 per day. Per capita GDP is just over $1,000 per year. Rwanda is 162 out of 173 countries ranked on the U.N. Human Development Index. About 9 percent of Rwandans have HIV infection, and not surprisingly the life expectancy is only 40 years. Over 90 percent of Rwandans are subsistence farmers who do not make enough to feed themselves, requiring substantial food aid. Rwanda was a German colony from 1895, but was given to Belgium after Germany was defeated in World War I. A central problem for Rwanda is that since independence from Belgium in 1962 there has been almost constant warfare. The conflicts, as in most African countries, are the results of national boundaries created by colonial powers that do not make sociological sense and render the countries almost ungovernable. Within Rwanda there are two major ethnic groups that have been at war from many years, Hutus and Tutsis. The fighting hit its worst level in 1994 when 800,000 Tutsis and moderate Hutus were massacred by Hutu rebels in an attempt to kill all Tutsis. About 2 million Hutus are now refugees in neighboring countries. Rwanda continues to be listed as one of the most violence prone, corrupt, and least democratic countries in the world. The country is close to the bottom of the world's rankings for civil liberties and human rights, education, many health indicators, and economic exports.[6]

Sierra Leone

As bad as Rwanda has become, Sierra Leone is worse. Until 1961 the country was a British colony. But like Rwanda the country fell into civil war among rival tribes soon after independence. In 1991 the civil war became more serious, resulting in tens of thousands of deaths and about 2 million refugees in neighboring countries. The civil war was effectively over by the beginning of the twenty-first century and the country had national elections in May 2002. There is a chance to finally overcome the cycle of fighting and political instability with a U.N. peacekeeping force in place. But the country is a mess and will take years to recover.

In Sierra Leone today about 75 percent of the population live on less than $2 per day and in 2002 the GNP per capita was only $490. Almost 30 percent of children are malnourished and 316 out of every 1,000 children die before 5 years of age. Sierra Leone is 173 out of 173 countries ranked on the U.N. Human Development Index. On top of this, Sierra Leone has the highest level of income inequality in the world. The bottom 20 percent of people get only 1.1 percent of the extremely low national income, while the top 20 percent of the people get over 63 percent of the income. All of this is despite the fact that Sierra Leone receives one of the highest levels of foreign aid in the world. Foreign aid accounted for 45 percent of all national income in 2001.

Somewhat Successful Cases

Despite all of the pessimistic figures on such things as poverty growth and AIDS in Sub-Saharan Africa, there is some hope. Things are not always destined to be bad in Africa. Economic development and poverty reduction can be achieved, but it will take much effort and international concern and involvement. A few cases support this conclusion.

Tanzania

The situation of Tanzania in southeast Africa represents another type of poor African country that is making slow improvements. Tanzania was a British colony until 1961. But rather than fall into a cycle of civil war as much as many other Sub-Sahara African countries, by 1964 Tanzania was a one-party socialist state trying to develop the country through a state-controlled economy. It didn't get very far. By 1995 Tanzania changed its policies to more free-market development. In a recent case study of 10 African countries, the World Bank listed Tanzania as one of the emerging success cases (World Bank, 2002a).

Tanzania has a long way to go, however. Almost 60 percent of the population lived on $2 per day before the end of the 1990s, and per capita GNP was only $550. Almost 30 percent of children are malnourished, and 165 of 1,000 children die before they are 5 years old. In 2004 Tanzania was only 162 out of 177 countries on the U.N. Human Development Index. At least Tanzania seems to be going in the right direction and is improving compared to many others in Sub-Saharan Africa. Still, how much and when will this improvement in the country's economy and political system reach down to the poorest people in the country?

Uganda

One of the most noted success cases cited by the World Bank will surprise many people. Uganda received a reputation as one of the most horrifying cases in all of Sub-Saharan

Africa before the more recent genocide of 800,000 people in Rwanda. Uganda was also a British colony until 1962, but a cycle of civil war was lessened by the infamous dictator Idi Amin between 1971 and 1979, followed by another ruthless dictator Milton Obote between 1980 and 1985. During the rule of Idi Amin some 300,000 of his opponents were massacred, though with a twist that after Idi Amin was deposed it was discovered that some of these people were stored in his palace kitchen freezer for his personal consumption. (I remember one young Ugandan social scientist who tried to put it nicely to me and a small group of European social scientists by saying that Uganda was "recovering from a dictator called Idi Amin who was not a very nice person.") In the 5 years of Obote's rule another 100,000 were massacred.

In its recent analysis of successful and unsuccessful cases of the use of foreign aid for reform and development in Sub-Saharan Africa, the World Bank now lists Uganda as one of the recent success stories (World Bank, 2002a). The horrors of the 1970s and early 1980s seem to have brought a shock to the country and international community. U.N. assistance came in, as did much foreign aid. Economic reform was set in place, corruption has been reduced, and solid economic growth has been forthcoming. Between 1987 and 2001 the economy grew by 6.4 percent a year. During 1992 there were still about 75 percent of Ugandans living on less than $2 per day. But by 2002 the per capita GNP of Uganda was $1,320, about three times that of Sierra Leone and more than double that of Tanzania. In 2004 Uganda was ranked 146 of 177 countries on the U.N. Human Development Index—still low, but a considerable improvement in 10 years. In a big contrast to Sierra Leone, income inequality in Uganda today is actually lower than it is in the United States. This is not saying that Uganda is out of trouble; children are still dying of malnutrition, and the AIDS crisis still exists. The point is that Uganda is now moving in the right direction and seems to have a stable enough government to keep it on a better course.

Mozambique

Another country that has shown at least some development success in recent years is Mozambique, on the southeastern coast of Africa. This area of Africa was one of the first to be colonized by Europeans, and one of the last to achieve independence. The Portuguese began settling in the area during the 1500s, using it as a port of call for its ships moving around Africa to India, Southeast Asia, and China. It was not until after a revolution against a fascist government in Portugal in 1975 that Mozambique gained its independence. During all the centuries of colonization by Portugal, little was done to develop the country.

Like many other African countries, independence brought civil war among competing groups to see who would come to control the country. In the high point of cold war conflicts, Mozambique ended up with a Marxist government supported by the Soviet Union. Mozambique rejected the Soviet model in 1989, about the same time that East European communist countries were rejecting Marxist governments. A higher level of democracy and an open invitation to foreign investment has brought a surge of economic growth. During 2001 and 2002 this growth rate was still moving ahead at about 9 percent.

Still, the per capita GNP in 2001 for Mozambique was just over $1,000. Like most other cases in Africa, this World Bank and IMF induced reform has yet to significantly filter down to the poor. About 78 percent of the population continue to live on less than $2 per day, though mortality for children below 5 years of age has dropped from 88 per 1,000 during 1990 to only 44 per 1,000 by 2001. But Mozambique is still ranked 171 out of 177 countries on the U.N. Human Development Index in 2004. Corruption remains extensive. Much like the oil riches siphoned out of the African countries with newly found oil, the profits from increased multinational corporate investments in Mozambique often find their way into hidden bank accounts of the rich in places like Switzerland. Over $14 million from the country's central bank was found to be missing in 2000 (*International Herald Tribune,* December 24, 2001). Even the IMF has now admitted that for now "any gains to the poor in Mozambique will likely be modest."

South Africa

South Africa, on the other hand, is in a completely different category of success. It is by far the richest country in Sub-Saharan Africa, with a per capita GNP of $9,870 in 2002, almost 10 times the level of most other Sub-Saharan Africa countries. The percent of South Africa's population living on less than $2 per day, 24 percent, is also lower than all the others. In 2004 South Africa was ranked 119 out of 177 nations on the U.N. Human Development Index.

South African history in the realm of European colonialism explains much of this difference. From the late 1500s there was a European presence at the Cape of Good Hope, the southern tip of Africa, due to its vital location in the European trade route to Asia. The Dutch were the first to settle in South Africa, but the British seized the Cape of Good Hope in 1806 as they became the clearly dominant colonial power in the world and wanted to make sure the route to its colonial prize, India, as well as its other "Far Eastern" colonies was secure. This action, however, led to the costly Boer War (1899–1902) between the British and the Dutch in South Africa. The British won the war but a sizable population of Dutch remained. Most important for South African history, the infamous apartheid system of rule was established giving complete power to the small white majority of new European settlers over almost 90 percent of the African native population in South Africa.

As European settlers came to take over the best lands of South Africa, there was extensive infrastructure development, much like what the British brought to their small colony of Hong Kong which became a center of British commerce in East Asia. But revolution by native South Africans, and increasing international condemnation, finally brought down the apartheid system by the early 1990s. With a democratic government now in place, one that is among the least corrupt in Africa, economic development was allowed to spread more evenly to the majority African population of South Africa. Zimbabwe, to the north of South Africa, presents an important contrast. Zimbabwe was also a British colony (called Rhodesia at the time) that overcame apartheid even before South Africa. But Zimbabwe is now mired in civil strife as President Mugabe has tried to maintain power by pitting his supporters against the few white farmers still in the country.

With its stability, less corruption, and more democratic government, South Africa is now in a position to sustain solid and evenly spread economic growth with more modern industries. With some 40 percent of the whole Sub-Saharan African economy accounted for by South Africa, there is a trend for South Africa to be the economic modernizer of other countries in Sub-Saharan Africa. About $1 billion from South African companies have been invested in other African countries (*International Herald Tribune,* February 19, 2002). There is the problem that some of these corporations from South Africa investing in other African countries are white owned, producing a new sense of colonialism in the rest of Africa. But the fact remains that South Africa has a democratic government that is clearly dominated by native Africans. This dominance of South Africa will likely be one of the important issues in the twenty-first century, with the pros and cons of this dominance debated as South Africa becomes more and more influential.

Africa in the New Global Economy

Despite all the negative statistics, there is some hope for Africa. South Africa's successful fight against apartheid and then more even economic development is one example. The revival of Uganda after the horrors of Idi Amin's dictatorship is another. There is perhaps even some hope for the future of Rwanda if crisis can bring enough international attention and reform.

But the biggest legacy in most of Sub-Saharan Africa is bad governance, and simply unstable and corrupt governments. We come again to some key questions: How do you get good governance? How does a country obtain a state bureaucracy that has dedicated government officials and rational organization to carry out successful development programs? We will see in more detail below that a major contrast to East and Southeast Asian countries is the lack of national identity in Sub-Saharan Africa. Unlike in East and Southeast Asia, there have been few ancient civilizations in Africa to create the sense of nationhood, unity, and willingness on the part of elites to work for the good of their nation and its people rather than a particular ethnic group. Sub-Saharan Africa was a region of economic and political weakness in the modern world system when the Europeans moved in to take control. All Sub-Saharan African countries had only simple forms of agriculture, and no governments strong enough to protect the people of Africa as the colonials moved in. These Europeans did with Africa as they pleased, taking out the natural resources as well as its people as slaves. Perhaps the most lasting negative impact of colonialism is the way Europeans cut up the continent into nations that made no sociological sense. One solution to this legacy would be to drastically redraw the map of Sub-Saharan Africa, but that will never happen. Too much is at stake for those who already rule African nations.

There is also, however, the more subtle impact of neocolonialism—a form of exploitative relationship short of the old formal control of a country during colonialism. There are means of setting the stage in global economic conflicts so that poor countries in Africa mostly lose and rich countries mostly win (*International Herald Tribune,* October 19, 2000, May 14, 2001). The current push for open markets by itself will not help most Africans, and in fact hurt most of them (*International Herald Tribune,* October 2, 2000, July 15, 2003). Most people in rich countries do not realize, or do not want to realize, that when their economies were developing, open markets were almost nonexistent. These now rich countries could develop their industries and agricultural specialities without concern for countries who could do it better coming in to nip their infant industries in the bud. Furthermore, there is currently an imbalance of open markets (*International Herald Tribune,* March 28, 2001). As we will see in our concluding chapter, poor countries in this world have been forced to have more free trade than have the rich countries today (*International Herald Tribune,* May 16, 2001).

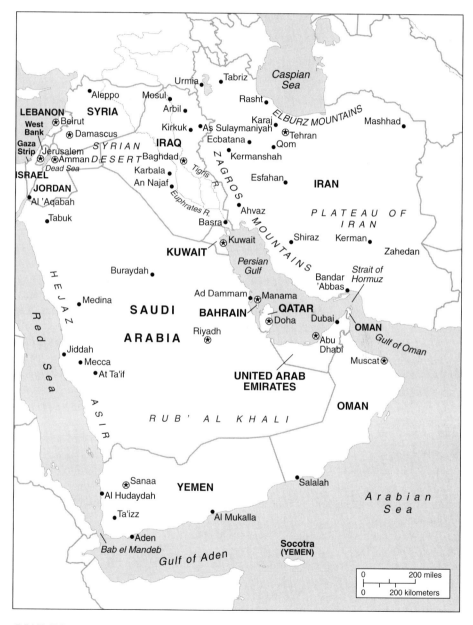

MAP 7.2   *Current National Borders in Middle East.*

The Middle East: Oil Wealth and the Poverty of Disruption

We now turn to a world region of ancient civilizations and modern contrasts. As noted in Chapter 2, this area contains some of the world's oldest civilizations, some older than 6,000 years, and the seeds of Western as well as Arab civilizations. This region is commonly defined as east of Northern Africa, west of South Asia, and south of Central Asia. Afghanistan is often not included in this Middle East region, but will be included in what follows. The central themes of this region today are oil, the impact of colonialism, the rise of fundamentalist Islam, and disruption. The contrasts of wealth and poverty in the area are primarily explained by varying combinations of these forces.

Contrasting Nations in an Ancient Land

As the various Islamic empires began their decline relative to the reemerging nations of Europe a few hundred years ago, the stage was set for deadly conflicts. The crusades of almost a millennium ago were the first of these bloody conflicts. But a major defeat for the Ottoman Empire on the verge of destroying Vienna in 1683 was a first major step in the decline of Islamic empires. It was an alliance of European nations that saved this capital of the Hapsburg Empire based in Austria, pushing the Ottomans further and further out of Europe (Brook-Shepherd, 1996; Mansfield, 2003). In the process, Western civilizations took more and more of Islamic culture into its own, symbolized in the tons of Ottoman coffee captured on the fringes of Vienna when the Turks were forced to retreat. This huge surplus of coffee led to the famous Vienna coffeehouses of today. But the final stage of Islamic decline relative to Europe came when the Ottoman Empire based in Turkey was defeated along with their German allies at the end of World War I.

It was about this time that the developed world became more and more desperate for cheap oil. The move by European nations, particularly Britain and France, to control much of the Middle East began in the 1800s. From the early 1900s European control of Middle Eastern oil regions became more serious. Most countries in the region were not formal colonies of European powers, but they were no less controlled by these powers. Middle Eastern governments unfavorable to European interests were overthrown, and European and American oil companies did as they pleased with knowledge their governments, backed by military power, would protect their interests in the region (Blair, 1976; Mosley, 1978). And much like Sub-Saharan Africa, many Middle Eastern countries had their borders shaped by European powers in such a way that ethnic and religious rivalries make some countries almost impossible to govern without bloody dictatorships. It has been only since World War II when European powers were no longer able to maintain their colonial-type dominance that some countries in the Middle East have been able to raise the standards of living for their people, especially after the Organization of the Petroleum Exporting Countries, or OPEC, gained influence in the global oil market. Established in the 1960s, during the 1970s OPEC finally achieved enough internal cooperation to keep oil prices up, and thus profits, by collectively regulating oil output.

Countries in the Middle East today can be divided into those with no or little oil, those with oil but who have been unable to use it for their own national interests, and

TABLE 7.3

The Richer and Poorer Countries of the Middle East

	GDP per Capita PPP, 2002	Percent Malnutrition under 5 1990	2001	HDI*	Percent of Population Living on Less Than $1	$2
Syria	$ 3,250	—	—	106	—	—
Iran	6,340	—	11	101	<2%	7.3%
Iraq	2,400	—	—	—	—	—
Jordan	4,070	6	—	90	<2	7.4
Egypt	3,710	10	4	120	3.1	—
Afghanistan	822	—	—	173	—	—
Yemen	750	30	—	149	15.7	45.2
Saudi Arabia	11,400	—	—	—	—	—
Kuwait	16,240	—	—	44	—	—
Oman	13,340	—	—	74	—	—
Lebanon	4,470	—	—	80	—	—
Qatar	28,634	—	—	47	—	—
UAE	22,051	—	—	49	—	—
Bahrain	17,170	—	—	40	—	—

*United Nations Human Development Index ranking countries with respect to per capita income, levels of education, health, and levels of poverty.

Sources: UNDP, 2004b; World Bank, 2004d; UNDP, 2004a; U.S. CIA, 2003.

those that have oil and have been able to control the resource for their own economic interests. Most of these latter countries are kingdoms with rather small populations and fewer internal conflicts based upon old ethnic and religious rivalries. We have less extensive data on most Middle Eastern countries for several reasons, mostly related to political turmoil or dictators who will not let the World Bank or other international agencies gather information. But much of the relevant data we do have is presented in Table 7.3.

The wide variation shown in Table 7.3 is mostly related to oil, or lack of it, and political turmoil. Yemen has had both a lack of oil wealth and political disruption. Much the same can be said for Afghanistan. It was only in late 2004 that the United Nations could get enough information to construct a human development score for Afghanistan, giving it a ranking of 173 out of 178 countries, the only non-Sub-Saharan African country in the world's lowest 10 (UNDP, 2004a). During the mid-twentieth century Afghanistan had a standard of living higher than several other countries in the region. The country's decent into poverty began during the 1970s when superpower conflicts led to a Soviet invasion, followed by the United States' economic and military support for groups organized to counter Soviet influence. The result for Afghan people, of course, has been a decline into destruction and poverty (UNDP, 2004a, 2004b). Iraq is currently in a similar situation, though not yet at levels of poverty found in Afghanistan. Despite having huge oil reserves, Iraq has never been as wealthy as other countries with

substantial oil reserves in the region, though during the early 1980s, per capita GNP
was about four times what it is today.

At the other end of the scale, the oil-rich nations of Kuwait, Qatar, and the United
Arab Emirates are rather wealthy. Saudi Arabia is among this group, though we have
less complete data for reasons listed above. But we do know that in contrast to most
Latin American countries, in these oil-rich nations income is distributed more equally,
almost certainly resulting in less poverty when compared to equally developed Latin
American countries with much higher levels of inequality (UNDP, 2004a, 2004b).

To understand the history and current situation of countries in this region it is best
to focus upon some specific countries, particularly countries currently on the minds of
people in Western nations. We will begin with more detailed consideration of Afghanistan,
then Iran, and finally Iraq. All three countries have been negatively impacted by colonialism and superpower conflicts. Only Afghanistan has not been directly affected by a
rush among industrialized nations to dominate oil resources—resources that are scarce
in Afghanistan.

The Case of Afghanistan

People have lived in what is now Afghanistan for at least 100,000 years. About 2000
BC a nomadic group called Aryans established a major civilization in the region. These
non-Arab peoples were then conquered by Persian rulers (now Iran) in the sixth century
BC. Alexander the Great briefly took control of the area in early 300 BC, followed by
control from Central Asian nomadic tribes from 135 BC. During the seventh century
AD Arabic armies conquered what is now Afghanistan, bringing Islam to dominate the
area as it does to this day. What continued was dynasty after dynasty, some bringing
cultural and economic advance, others bring decline.

As the various Islamic civilizations went into steep decline in the face of European
industrialization, it was the British who moved into most of what is now Afghanistan.
The primary British interest by the early twentieth century was to secure as much of the
Middle East and neighboring territory as possible as it became evident that oil would be
found in huge quantities. But after World War II, the British were in decline and had to
give up control in the region. Afghanistan went through a few decades of peace and
development, though the country was still subject to instability and internal conflicts due
to national boundaries earlier redrawn by the European colonials. Like much of Sub-
Saharan Africa, the country contains major ethnic groups who have historically been in
conflict, making governance of today's Afghanistan extremely challenging.

More serious trouble for Afghanistan, as noted, came with superpower conflicts
during the cold war. In an attempt to acquire more dominance in the region and to prevent Islamic rebellion in the Central Asian territories that were part of the Soviet Union,
the Soviet Army marched into Afghanistan in 1979. What followed was a guerrilla war
against Soviet domination that was supported and largely funded by the United States.
This is how many of the present-day Islamic terrorist groups directing their anger
toward the United States originally acquired their weapons, and groups such as al
Qaeda came into existence.

After the Soviet Union fell apart in 1991, much of Afghanistan was in ruins
and extremely poor. But it was also a country without a central authority, creating

Once one of the most advanced countries in the region, the effects of colonialism and the cold war have left Afghanistan among the five poorest countries in the world today. This disruption has also made Afghanistan a magnet for some of the most radical terrorist groups throughout the region.

a haven for all types of Islamic fundamentalists from outside Afghanistan. Civil war to gain control of Afghanistan was slowly won by one of these Islamic groups called the Taliban (or students). Islamic "fundamentalist schools" through the region, particularly in Pakistan, taught young men angry over their fate during colonialism and the recent superpower conflicts. Their countries' honor and restoration, they came to believe, would be achieved only with radical Islamic states hostile toward the West. As the Taliban took control over most of Afghanistan it encouraged and protected other radical Islamic groups such as Osama bin Laden's al Qaeda. The September 11, 2001, attacks on the United States finally brought in a coalition army of primarily Western nations lead by the United States to eliminate control of Afghanistan by the Taliban. There were American promises of rebuilding Afghanistan after the U.S. led bombing further destroyed the country, but little follow-through as the George W. Bush administration quickly changed focus toward its next war in Iraq.

As previous tables have shown, colonialism, superpower conflicts, then control by the Taliban and more war has left Afghanistan one of the poorest countries in the world. It now ranks 173 of 178 countries in the world on the U.N. Human Development Index, the only non-African country in the world's bottom 10 (*The New York Times*, February 22, 2005; UNDP, 2004a). Over half of all Afghans are considered poor by United Nations' estimates, and over 20 percent of Afghans in rural areas do not have enough to eat. The per capita GNP (PPP) is just over $800, and life expectancy is only

44 years. Without adjusting for Purchasing Power Parity (PPP), per capita GNP is an amazing $190 per year.

The Case of Iran

Iran is today a much richer country compared to Afghanistan, but it is a country that has also experienced extensive disruption and exploitation by outside powers in recent decades. Iranian history goes back some 6,000 years when an advanced civilization called Elamites emerged (Farr, 2000; Mansfield, 2003). As in Afghanistan, Aryan tribes arrived about 3,500 years ago to form a more dominant and advanced civilization. The first real Iranian, or Persian, empire was Acaemenian from 559 BC. Also like Afghanistan, Iran was conquered in the seventh century AD by Arabs who brought Islam. Non-Arab Iran regained its independence in 1501, though Islam remained the dominant religion.

By the early 1800s the British began taking control of the region. Russia, too, was in a colonial mode at the time, taking the northern regions of what is now Iran. There was no formal colonial control of Iran by the British, but British power over Iran came through a series of concessions forced on Iranian kings (shahs) who became wealthy from British rewards. British dominance increased after World War I, especially as oil became more important. After World War II a declining Britain could no longer maintain control over Iran. During the 1950s an Iranian nationalist movement began, resulting in a popularly elected prime minister, Mossadeq. This new prime minister and his alliance in the Iranian parliament began passing laws limiting British control of Iranian oil fields, and taking British Petroleum (BP) assets within Iran as compensation for past inequities in the prices paid for Iranian oil. As oil prices were pushed up in Iran, the British, who were too weak to intervene militarily to protect cheap oil and BP assets, secretly turned to the United States for help (Blair, 1976; Mosley, 1978; Roosevelt, 1979). The United States responded with a CIA operation leading to the overthrow of the elected Mossadeq government, and then placed the shah (king) back in complete control of Iran. Thousands were killed in the aftermath. Oil companies came back, as did other multinational corporations. Iran became more prosperous, but it was a Latin American style of economic development that left many Iranians in poverty.

It was anger over the rising gap between the rich and poor, as well as increased Westernization and secularization, that brought revolution in 1979. Unsurprisingly, it was a revolution directed against the United States which was recognized as putting the shah and multinational corporate dominance back in Iran after 1953. Ayatollah Khomeini, who led this Islamic revolution, came to dominate the country, remolding it into a strictly Islamic state.

With Iran now in control of their own resources again, Table 7.3 indicates that it is no longer an impoverished country compared to Afghanistan. GNP per capita in Iran is substantially above that of Afghanistan, and only some 7 percent of Iranians live on less than $2 per day. Life expectancy is over 70 years and literacy is almost 80 percent (UNDP, 2004a, 2004b). It is interesting to note that inequality in Iran, in contrast to Arab countries, is rather high. But even though the bottom 20 percent of the population receives 2 percent of the income while the top 20 percent of the population receives 49 percent of the income (about the same as the United States today), Iran still has less inequality than many Latin American countries, and thus a bit less of the uneven economic development more common in the developing world (UNDP, 2004a: Table 2.8).

As is typical throughout history, a few years of political control by radical revolutionaries brings less economic progress and a people tired of it all. We will see in Chapter 9 that this stage occurred in Vietnam during the late 1980s. Wide support for a more moderate government has formed within Iran, but resistance to reform from Islamic fundamentalists who still have most control in the government remains strong. The next several years of the twenty-first century, and trends within the United States that can increase or reduce support for moderation within Iran, will help determine whether or not Iran can finally turn is focus toward economic policies that can lead to further economic development and poverty reduction.

The Case of Iraq

One of the most ancient civilizations in the region, Iraq's origins go back to Mesopotamia of biblical times. While identified as a continued civilization from this time, borders have been altered and serious divisions have existed for centuries. These divisions are centered on the Sunni–Shiite division in Islam today, with Shiites in the majority. But Kurds in the north account for a significant part of the population, with Christians making up a small minority.

In the early 1500s Iraq became part of the powerful Ottoman Empire based in Turkey (Brook-Shepherd, 1996; Mansfield, 2003). But because Turkey gambled in World War I with an alliance with Germany, German defeat in 1918 brought Britain and France into the region with something much closer to colonialism than the weaker control by European powers in the region before World War I. The British called their control of Iraq after World War I a "mandate." With the world more opposed to old colonial rule in the intrawar period, the League of Nations was able to persuade Britain to give up its official mandate over Iraq in 1932. But with substantial oil discovered in 1927, it was clear that the British Iraq Petroleum Company would continue to dominate Iraq for British interests. With substantial oil in Iraq territory, even though British corporations got cheap oil, there was still money to promote some economic development in Iraq.

Increasing conflicts between the new state of Israel and surrounding Islamic countries from 1948 brought more and more changes in the region, as did the superpower conflict as we saw in the case of Afghanistan. Major change for Iraq came after Iraq and its neighboring countries were defeated by Israel in the 1967 Six-Day War. The major change for Iraq was the rise of Saddam Hussein who took over from humiliated Iraqi leaders after this war. As we know so well from U.S. mass media hype during the run-up to George W. Bush's 2003 Iraq War, Hussein was a ruthless dictator who killed thousands of his opponents, especially his critics among the majority Shiite community and Kurds. As the United States learned after the 2003 Iraq War, these divisions or "centrifugal forces" have made Iraq a difficult country to govern for centuries (Mansfield, 2003:197). Despite a reasonable level of development and improving standards of living in Iraq during much of Saddam Hussein's rule, his grand schemes to bring Iraq back to ancient glory finally destroyed the country. There was war between Iran and Iraq (due to attacks by Iraq when Iran was weakened after its 1979 revolution) through most of the 1980s, then the Gulf War of 1991 after Hussein invaded Kuwait (when he miscalculated in thinking the West would not intervene); and finally the 2003 war with the United States when the Bush administration, long before September 11, 2001, decided Saddam Hussein was not to be trusted with all of his potential oil power.

CASE IN POINT

The Israeli–Palestinian Conflict

Throughout this region the ancient conflicts are complex with many overlapping claims to territory. Unfortunately, many Americans do not understand more than the immediate details of a recent conflict, such as the Gulf War or current Iraq War. This makes it difficult for Americans to develop a full understanding of what is happening in this region and why.

The Israeli–Palestinian conflict is a prime example. The complexity is certainly there, and both sides have legitimate claims and concerns for their well-being. But given other conflicts the United States currently has with several Middle Eastern countries, Americans mostly hear about the Israeli side of the story.

The Israeli side of the story is that Israel was created in ancient Jew lands after they fled discrimination in Europe from the early twentieth century. Especially after the Holocaust of World War II and the murder of some 6 million Jews by the Nazis, Jews flocked to what is now Israel to found a modern state where they could protect themselves against future attacks on their people and heritage. But there is an equally legitimate Palestinian side to the story.

I remember seeing the Palestinian side clearly one day almost 25 years ago. I was in the mail room of our department office, looking over my mail which had just arrived. I had just received a postcard from an Israeli friend at the University of Haifa. The front of the postcard showed the city of Haifa from the sea, with nice houses lining the hills above the beach. One of my colleagues who was about to retire saw the postcard and said, "Oh, right about there is my old house. I haven't been back in many years, not since the Israelis took away our homes." My colleagues was a Palestinian who had lived in the United States since the development of the state of Israel in 1948.

When trying to explain the Palestinian side of the current conflict to my students, I like to say, "Consider this: What if Mexico was the stronger country and one day said 'We are taking California. All you Gringos get out. We're taking your homes and moving you

Since the 2003 war with the United States, child malnutrition has jumped from 4 percent to at least 8 percent and poverty has rapidly increased (*Los Angeles Times,* November 23, 2004; UNDP, 2004b). While we did not have precise data in recent decades, all indications are that per capita GNP in Iraq was substantially higher in previous years.

Prospects for the Middle East in the New World Disorder

The Middle East is a very diverse and mixed region of the world with respect to poverty and economic development today. Some of these nations are oil rich and have the stability to continue their economic development and poverty reduction. But old colonial boundaries (much like Sub-Saharan Africa) have made many countries in the region difficult to govern, as have superpower conflicts during the cold

(Continued)

into camps in the Arizona desert.'" I then ask, "So what would you feel after growing up in desert camps knowing your beautiful homes were now occupied by richer Mexicans who had moved north?"

Of course many details of my California story are different, but the situation is fairly close to that of Palestinians today. Like most other countries in the region, the ancient country of Palestine was controlled by the British before the fall of colonialism. Because of British control some European Jews were allowed to move there more than 100 years ago. As more and more Jews moved from Europe to what was then the state of Palestine they began to make up a large percentage of the population. After World War II, as more Jews fled the massacres of Europe, and as Britain was weak from the war, the Jews began a revolt to create their own state, fighting both the Palestinians and British to do so. The state of Israel was created from this revolt of 1948, eliminating the old state of Palestine, and Palestinians began losing their homeland. Today Israelis want to protect their new state and prevent future holocausts against their people. But Palestinians are stateless, many very poor, without their old homes, and living as mostly unwelcome guests in other countries in the region, many still in refugee camps.

Many displaced Palestinians, like my old colleague, have found a place in other countries where their education and talent have done them well. But many remain stateless refugees in other Middle Eastern countries. About 3.2 million Palestinians now live in Israeli territories more recently taken from Arabs in other wars since 1948. The World Bank has finally included some of these territories in its economic analysis, particularly the West Bank and Gaza Strip. Per capita GNP for these Palestinians was only $930 in 2002, though these figures are not in PPP estimates, so likely not quite as low as this seems. In 2004 the United Nations ranked the Occupied Palestinian Territories as 102 in the world on its Human Development Index. Despite their misfortune, Palestinians remain talented and educated people, with a literacy rate over 90 percent. But without stability and a return of at least some of their homelands for a new Palestinian state, these people are unlikely to have substantial improvements in their lives. And war between Palestinians and Israel will certainly continue.

war. Most are ancient civilizations, but these problems have created so many divisions that any positive benefits from a sense of national identity are difficult to achieve. Afghanistan and Iraq are good examples of these problems. A sense of elite responsibility, however, has had some positive effects; there have been some economic development and poverty reduction in most of the countries in the region, and levels of inequality have been kept much lower compared to Africa and Latin America. Finally, we must recognize that Islam is not always a barrier to strong economic development as many people in the West tend to assume. We will see that Malaysia with more than 60 percent of its population Islamic is the richest country in Southeast Asia, and continues to be included among the second wave of Asian tiger economies rapidly developing today. The good news is that if violent internal conflicts within the Middle East are ever overcome, prospects for economic development and poverty reduction are good. The bad news is that these conflicts are unlikely to be reduced for many decades.

Notes

1. U.S. Senate Select Committee to Study Governmental Operations with Respect to Intelligence Activities, *Alleged Assassination Plots Involving Foreign Leaders* (Washington, DC: U.S. Government Printing Office, 1975). I am not making up this stuff. On page 72 you can read that U.S. agents "impregnated a box of cigars with a chemical which produced temporary disorientation, hoping to induce Castro to smoke one of the cigars before delivering a speech. The Inspector General also reported a plan to destroy Castro's image as 'The Beard' by dusting his shoes with thallium salts, a strong depilatory that would cause his beard to fall out." Or on page 73 you can read testimony about attempts to give Castro a box of his favorite cigars they had contaminated with a botulinum toxin that would have killed him instantly if they had not failed in getting the cigars into Castro's hands. As for Africa, much of the Senate investigation was centered on the CIA involvement in a successful plot to assassinate Lumumba, the leader of the Congo after independence who was moving too closely toward the Soviets in the eyes of the CIA.

2. Patrick Chabal and Gean-Pascal Daloz, *Africa Works: Disorder as Political Instrument* (Bloomington: Indiana University Press, 1999). Much of the following is based on the idea of Chabal and Daloz in an important new book, *Africa Works: Disorder as Political Instrument,* which summarizes and critiques previous ideas about African societies and states.

3. These are PPP gross national income per capita figures from World Bank, *World Development Report 2004,* http://www.worldbank.org.

4. Information comes from the United Nations, World Health Organization, and other international health and aid agencies. Recently summarized reports from these agency reports can be found in the *International Herald Tribune* (October 5, 1999, December 13, 1999, July 6, 2000) and the *Los Angeles Times* (July 11, 2000).

5. All data about recent scandals involving oil wealth in these countries can be found in several BBC online news articles in 2002 and 2003, as well as the *Los Angeles Times* (January 20, 2003); *International Herald Tribune* (September 19, 2000, June 20, 2002). Other data are from the World Bank, *World Development Report 2004,* http://www.worldbank.org.

6. See data from several academic research reports and international agencies from Nation Master, on the Web at http://www.nationmaster.com.

Latin America: Stagnation and Uneven Development

As one travels the world of less developed countries some scenes seem to be repeated again and again in country after country. One of these scenes is that of the homeless street vendors hustling to sell anything they can, legal or illegal, to keep from starving. In Hanoi and Saigon most street orphans are organized to sell chewing gum and postcards. In Bangkok fresh fruits and vegetables are the big items. Some countries, of course, have more of these homeless street vendors than others. A particularly large concentration are found in major cities all over Latin America. In the Spanish-speaking countries of Latin American these people are called *ambulates*. No one knows exactly how many ambulates there are throughout Latin America, but estimates are in the millions. There are about 50,000 of these ambulates in Lima, the capital city of Peru (*International Herald Tribune*, January 7, 2002). Peru is not one of the poorest countries in Latin America. With a gross domestic product (GDP) per capita of almost $5,000, though, the country is richer than all the Sub-Sahara African countries except South Africa. But over 40 percent of the people in Peru live on less than $2 per day, a higher rate than many African countries.

These ambulates may look like the many street vendors I have talked with in Bangkok, but there is a major difference. Upon closer analysis, the street vendors in Bangkok are seldom homeless. They may live in temporary shanty towns in Bangkok, but they usually have village homes to return to on the weekends or days they are not hustling whatever they have been selling on the streets. We have already seen the figures on land inequality in East and Southeast Asia compared to Africa and Latin America—it is by far highest in Latin America. This means that former peasants are more likely homeless in the big cities of Latin America, forced to sell whatever they can with no place to sleep except in some plywood and sheet-metal hovel thrown together to keep out the rain and cold.

Too often these landless peasants end up as actual slaves. They are sometimes recruited by unscrupulous employers with promises of good jobs if they relocate, only to find they are thrown into slavery—seldom paid for their work and constantly watched by armed guards so they cannot escape. In Brazil there are thought to be about 25,000 such slaves. One of these former Brazilian slaves, Bernardo Gomes da Silva, described his plight to a *New York Times* reporter investigating this condition: "We were forced to start work at 6 in the morning and to continue sometimes until 11 at night, but I was never paid during that entire time because they always claimed that I owed them money" (*International Herald Tribune, The New York Times*, March 26, 2002). Slaves or not, many of the children of landless peasants in Latin America

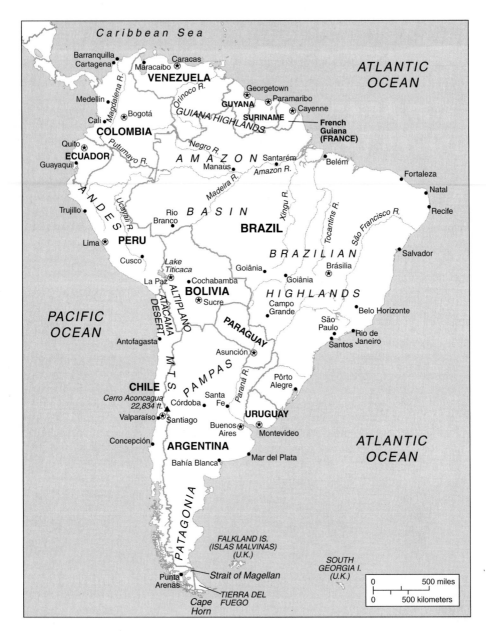

MAP 8.1 *Map of Latin American Nations.*

must work in similar conditions to feed themselves. In Brazil about 14 percent of all children between the ages of 10 and 14 must work to survive. The average for all Latin American countries is over 8 percent of children this age (*International Herald Tribune*, July 16, 2002).

A Brief History of Elites and Masses in Latin America

As we have seen, colonialism came very early in Latin America compared to Asia and Africa. But we have also seen that the European colonials left Latin America much earlier than they did in Asia or Africa. By the early 1800s most Latin American countries were independent states, though with societies that were almost completely Europeanized. The old civilizations of Latin America were in severe decline as the Europeans arrived, then almost completely dissolved by future waves of European settlers. But the impression that these new nations in Latin America were "independent" from the 1800s, however, is highly misleading. They quickly entered a new form of colonialism called *neocolonialism.*

In the case of Latin America, of course, this dominant neocolonial power was the United States before the end of the 1800s. In essence the United States has had veto power over Latin American political leaders, and U.S. corporations have had almost complete freedom to do as they please in Latin America. A kind of Anglo-Saxon political philosophy exists, an individualistic free-market economic model, also called a "neoliberal" political economy, that prohibits the kind of development state common in most of East and Southeast Asia today. We will see that it is this characteristic of Latin America that helps explain the uneven economic development with less poverty reduction found in the region. A good example of the free-market economic model is the North American Free Trade Agreement (NAFTA) created by elites of America and Mexico.

The poor of Mexico were given much hope in 1994 when NAFTA was signed. Other people of Latin America have similar hopes as discussions are being held to expand NAFTA into a free trade zone including other Latin American nations. In Mexico the number of new factories coming into the country bringing new jobs to the poor increased by more than 10 percent every year for the first few years of NAFTA. Cesiah Ruiz Brena was one of the rural poor who went to Tijuana in 1989, "deliriously happy to get a job at a new Japanese factory. Her work space was grand, the lights were bright, and the pay was unimaginably good: $100 a week to start" (*The Washington Post,* June 21, 2002). Neither NAFTA nor the Mexican government, however, could keep those jobs in the country. The Mexican government has been unable to sustain the initial economic stimulus that NAFTA originally provided to create new jobs. By 2000 these new NAFTA jobs were beginning to disappear—mostly to China where wages are much lower with an even more educated labor force and a Chinese government able to provide better infrastructure to attract multinational corporations. Between 2001 and 2002 Mexico's per capita GDP growth was –0.8 percent. In 2000 alone some 250,000 of the jobs originally created by NAFTA left Mexico. Many more have left since.

Like Brazil, Mexico is a much richer country than all Sub-Saharan African countries except South Africa. Both Mexico and Brazil have a per capita GNP of almost $8,000. But Mexico has about 26 percent of its population living on less than $2 per day while Brazil has 22 percent. Most countries in Latin America have comparatively advanced economies with their own companies making typewriters, appliances, and even airplanes. We saw in Chapter 2 that the per capita GNP of Latin American countries is significantly higher than the per capita GNP of East and Southeast Asian countries, $6,750 compared to $4,160 for East and Southeast Asian countries in 2002. But the percent of the population living on less than $1 per day is about the same in both world regions. More important, this extreme poverty rate is going down rapidly in East and Southeast Asia compared to almost no poverty reduction in Latin America (World Bank, 2004d). The World Bank likes to tell us that open markets lead to economic expansion, and economic expansion leads to poverty reduction. But this does not occur equally in all countries, and least so in most Latin American countries (Altimir, 1998; Fields, 2001).

Equally important is the inability of most Latin American countries to thrive in the new global economy as well as many East and Southeast Asian countries. Of the countries achieving significant and sustained economic expansion between 1975 and 2000, only one major Latin American country, Chile, has made it into the top 25 countries. Most countries on the top 25 list for economic growth are from Asia. The average annual economic growth rate for major South American countries between 1975 and 2000 was an anemic 0.6 percent (World Bank, 1990, 2000). We have already seen that between 2000 and 2015 East and Southeast Asian countries are expected to reduce the number of their people living on less than $1 a day by some 60 percent. Latin American countries are predicated to reduce their extreme poverty by 5 percent at best (World Bank, 2000). These predictions made by the World Bank in 2000, however, are probably overly optimistic for Latin America. In 2002 and 2003 some of the major Latin American countries such as Argentina had huge economic declines and major poverty increases (*International Herald Tribune,* August 7, 2002). Argentina's GDP growth between 2001 and 2002 was −10.9 percent. Will Argentina go the way of many East and Southeast Asian countries that recovered in a couple of years after the Asian economic crisis of 1997? It is too early to tell, but the answer is probably not. Argentina will likely have economic recovery, but nothing like the 7, 8, and 9 percent growth rates of Southeast Asian countries. Again the question is, why have most Latin American countries not been able to thrive and protect themselves in the new global economy as more East and Southeast Asian countries have been able to do?

It is time to consider how historical forces in Latin America have helped reduce their chances of more even economic development with poverty reduction.

Theories of Latin American Economic Stagnation

When looking for explanations of Latin American economic stagnation or development without significant poverty reduction, we are not going to focus on technical economic policies. Those are certainly important but the first question is, why have almost all of them failed and others not tried? We need to understand the broader explanations first.

One of those broad explanations now being revived can be put rather simply at first: North America is rich and Latin America is poor because North America got the Protestants and Latin America got the Catholics. The revival of this type of cultural thesis is related to the tendency to cite Asian values as also the key to greater economic success in East and Southeast Asia. As noted, both North and South America were totally taken over by the Europeans. As we all know, of course, mostly Protestants from Britain, Germany, France, and a few other countries in Europe were the first to spread over North America. The Catholics from Spain and Portugal went south.

The thesis of why Protestantism is a religion more conducive to economic success goes back to the master sociologist Max Weber in his book *The Protestant Ethic and the Spirit of Capitalism.* In short, the argument is that Protestant values promote insecurity about the afterlife and therefore make people want to feel more secure in this life by being successful. Soon after Protestantism emerged in the 1400s it was economic success in the new capitalist world system that became the focus of many Protestants. This religion encouraged people to take the initiative, rationally plan for the future, and of course save or invest for the future. Catholicism, it is said, did not promote the insecurity that encouraged people to save and work hard in this life as much as Protestantism. Nor did Catholicism encourage as much individualism or initiative in people to take on new capitalist ventures. Thus, the argument goes, all over Europe and the new world, Catholic countries tend to be less wealthy than Protestant countries. While we might agree there is something in Weber's thesis, the correlation to economic success is far from perfect.

One of the most influential writers pushing this cultural thesis for Latin America is Lawrence Harrison, with a newly revised book first published in 1985, *Underdevelopment Is a State of Mind: The Latin American Case* (Harrison, 2000; Harrison & Huntington, 2000). In this book we are told that Latin American intellectuals are also condemning Catholic values and calling for Protestantism to spread through the region. Harrison tells us that the reason some countries in Latin America are doing well, such as the small island country of Barbados, is that they inherited "progressive British values and institutions" (Harrison, 2000:xxxii). Considering the problems with cultural explanations by simply comparing countries such as Thailand, Burma, Cambodia, and Laos, countries with basically identical cultures, it is hard to accept the idea that Catholicism is mostly to blame for Latin American poverty. Recent research has shown that there is considerable variation in economic development today among the countries of Latin America colonized by the Spanish because of how these countries were treated differently during Spanish colonization (Mahoney, 2003).

Another point Harrison makes on Latin America problems is more convincing. He quotes an earlier work that notes "the British came to North America to plant colonies and rear families and build, while the Spaniards and Portuguese came to Central and South America to conquer and kill, to extract and exploit" (Martin, 1966). We have already seen some of the murder and exploitation brought by the Spanish and Portuguese. Although there were certainly atrocities committed by the Europeans in North America, it is accurate to say that at first the Spanish and Portugese came only to kill and exploit, not to settle. It can be argued that these Europeans who first came to control Latin America were much more corrupt than the British settlers who came for a new life. In the 1500s, for example, the Spanish King Philip II sold positions of authority in the new colonies to the highest bidders in Spain (Skidmore and Smith, 2001). These people then came to the Americas to steal as much as they could to recoup their investment and then go home. We saw in Chapter 2 that Latin American governments today are among the most corrupt and much lower than Asian countries on the Weberianness scale which measures government rationality and efficiency. It is quite likely that the current "bad governance" in most Latin American governments is related to the early traditions brought by the Spanish and Portuguese conquerors.

Another line of argument for Latin American problems is related to the kind of free-market capitalism or neoliberal economic model that most Latin American governments have taken (or were forced to accept) from the United States. We have seen in earlier chapters that later developing countries such as Germany and Japan had to

WHY WE SHOULD CARE

Global Migration

A world with huge inequalities creates a world with millions of people in migration. When they are able (and they are often able in many illegal ways) people move from poverty areas to affluent areas. During the 1990s the United Nations estimated there were 120 million people voluntarily working or seeking employment in foreign countries. At the end of the twentieth century there were 70 million more migrants on the move. Since the cold war, European Union nations probably have a greater problem from poor immigrants flooding into their countries than does the United States. No one knows for sure the exact number of illegal immigrants in the United States or European countries, but we do know that about 30,000 people applied for asylum in the United States in 1999 compared to 365,000 in European Union countries. The estimates of illegal immigrants in the United States range widely, from around 1 to 2 million. Europeans, however, have been shocked with their rate of increase since 1990: Illegal immigration into the European Union countries has increased from 30 thousand to half a million people between 1993 and 1999. Throughout its history the United States considered itself alone as a nation of immigrants. Indeed, the number of foreign-born Americans increased from 10 million in 1970 to 30 million by 2000. The number is expected to reach 38 million by 2020. However, some European countries now have a larger foreign-born population than the 9 percent found in the United States.

One should not assume that immigration from poor countries to rich countries is only bad for people in rich countries. There is much evidence that recent immigrants into the United States take jobs that would go unfilled if they were not in the country, and it is even clearer that the United States has received some of the best and brightest people from all over the world in the last two centuries. Immigrants from poorer countries are even more important to European countries. With birth rates way below sustaining the populations of European countries today, if there were no immigrants the economy would crash for lack of workers, and social security systems would go broke with too many older recipients and too few workers paying into the social security system and health care systems. Japan is the rich country least able to accept foreigners and it is in serious trouble. Its birth rate is even lower than most European countries and the country will soon have about 35 percent of its population over 65 years old.

But there are problems for rich countries from all of this legal and illegal immigration. The education and medical care for immigrants can be expensive. Perhaps most troubling, the flood of immigrants usually brings down the wages for low-skilled Americans. There are some solutions: A realistic minimum wage law like most European countries have would certainly help. The most effective solution, however, would be to dramatically reduce world poverty. There would be no more sweatshops if people all over the world had opportunities for something better, and lower skilled Americans would not have to compete with about half of the world's population living on less than $2 per day.

Sources: All of these figures can be found in U.S. Central Intelligence Agency, 2001.

develop economically with more state intervention and guidance than in the first developed European countries (see, for example, Fallows, 1994; Kerbo & McKinstry, 1995; Vogel, 1991). The "late, late developing countries" in East and Southeast Asia, as we have seen, had to have even more state intervention with a hard state or development state to achieve economic development and poverty reduction. The free-market capitalism (what Europeans today like to call "cowboy capitalism") pushed by the United States is the opposite of the Asian development model with a development state. In free-market capitalism the state is involved minimally in the economy and makes little effort to reduce inequality (Esping-Anderson, 1990; Goodin et al., 1999). Private corporations are given much more power and independence to do as they please both within and outside the country.

The problem for Latin America is especially that the state cannot work to protect its national economic interests against the demands of richer nations and their multinational corporations with this free-market capitalism. This presents a major contrast to the rapidly developing countries of East and Southeast Asia who are better able to protect their long-term national economic interests in the new global economy. Not surprisingly, we have seen that America's only colony in Asia, the Philippines, which was also dominated by the Spanish longer than any other Asian country was dominated by Europeans, has a weak economy and levels of poverty like most Latin American countries (Karnow, 1989). They, too, have been encouraged to accept this U.S.-style free-market capitalism. It is time that we examine the U.S. dominance of Latin American countries more closely.

The Latin American State: For U.S. Corporations and by U.S. Corporations

The twentieth century saw comparatively little economic development for Latin American countries, and in fact many losses. Argentina, for example, was among the 10 largest economies in the world at the beginning of the twentieth century. Today the Argentine economy is ranked along with the rapidly developing Asian countries of Thailand and Taiwan, and they are rising while Argentina is sinking. In a similar situation, the Philippines was the richest country in Southeast Asia during the 1960s. But with the free-market capitalism model from the United States the Philippines is now far below Malaysia, Thailand, and even Indonesia and Vietnam. A central problem is that the free-market capitalism largely forced upon Latin American countries by the United States is not one that is able to protect weaker economies in the new global economy of the twentieth and twenty-first centuries. Table 8.1 indicates just how anaemic the Latin American economies have been since 1975 compared to East and Southeast Asian countries. As noted earlier, the more free-market capitalism of the Philippines puts them last in Southeast Asia, even behind the very poor countries of Burma, Cambodia, and Laos.

The contrast is even more striking between Latin American and East and Southeast Asian countries when comparing per capita GDP in 1900 and 2002. Most Asian countries were far behind Latin American countries in 1900. (We do not have 1900 data for Singapore, Hong Kong, or Malaysia, but other indicators show these countries were similar to Taiwan and South Korea in 1900.) By 2002 East Asian nations had raced way ahead of Latin American countries. Some Southeast Asia countries are now close to Latin American countries in per capita GDP. Figures in Table 8.1, however,

TABLE 8.1

Growth in Gross Domestic Product in Latin America and East and Southeast Asia, 1975–2000

Latin America	Average % Growth
Chile	4.1%
Colombia	1.6
Uruguay	1.4
Brazil	0.8
Paraguay	0.7
Argentina	0.4
Guyana	0.3
Ecuador	0.2
Suriname	–0.1
Bolivia	–0.5
Peru	–0.7
Venezuela	–0.9
East and Southeast Asia	
China	8.1%
South Korea	6.2
Thailand	5.5
Singapore	5.2
Vietnam	4.8
Hong Kong	4.6
Indonesia	4.4
Malaysia	4.1
Laos	3.2
Japan	2.7
Cambodia	1.9
Burma	1.3
Philippines	0.1

Source: NationMaster at http://www.nationmaster.com; original data from World Bank (2002c).

show that some of these Southeast Asian countries are growing much faster since 1975 and will clearly move further ahead of Latin American countries in coming years. The effect of free-market capitalism on the Philippines is dramatically indicated in Table 8.2 as well: The Philippines was the richest country in Southeast Asia, only slightly behind Japan in East Asia, and ahead of several Latin American countries in 1900. By 2002 the Philippines had dropped dramatically in rank.

A chapter subheading such as the one for this section is of course an overstatement. But it proclaims a partial truth that has had a major impact on all of Latin America for over a century. This U.S. dominance of Latin American countries began in 1823 with proclamation of the Monroe Doctrine which in essence told the European colonial

TABLE 8.2

Per Capita GDP in Major Latin American and East and Southeast Asian Nations, 1900 and 2002

Latin America	1900	2002*
Argentina	$2,756	$10,340**
Chile	1,949	9,871
Colombia	973	6,218
Venezuela	821	6,019
Peru	817	4,722
Brazil	704	7,612
East and Southeast Asia		
Japan	$1,135	$27,958
South Korea	850	19,265
Singapore	—	23,872
Hong Kong	—	24,646
Taiwan	759	17,119
Philippines	1,033	3,963
Malaysia	—	8,825
Thailand	812	6,575
Indonesia	745	2,969
Burma	647	1,491

*Figures for 2002 are in Purchasing Power Parity (PPP) estimates. PPP is not available for 1900.

**As we will see, this figure for Argentina is probably much lower with the economic crisis of 1999 to 2003.

Source: NationMaster at http://www.nationmaster.com; original data from World Bank estimates.

powers to "stay out of Latin America, it is ours" (Roberts, 1993:616–661). From that time on, the United States intervened in the affairs of Latin American countries many times when these countries followed policies the United States did not like, often with military force. A U.S. State Department study concluded that from 1798 to 1945 the United States had intervened in other countries some 103 times, with the vast majority of these interventions in Latin American countries (Zinn, 1995:290–291). There were to be many more interventions during the cold war from 1949 to 1990. For Latin America specifically, one estimate shows that the U.S. military intervened 29 times in Latin American nations between 1806 and 1940 (Johnson, 1973:6). Table 8.3 presents only a *partial list* of military action by the United States in Latin American nations between 1850 and 1965.

Another study sponsored by the Pentagon found that the U.S. military was involved in a "show of force" in other nations (for example, sending the navy within striking distance or building up troops in the area) a total of 215 times between 1945 and 1975 (*The Washington Post,* January 3, 1979). The only other nation close to the

TABLE 8.3

U.S. Military Interventions in Latin America, 1850–1965

Year(s)	Nation
1852–1853	Argentina
1853–1854	Nicaragua
1855	Uruguay
1856	Panama
1858	Uruguay
1865	Colombia
1867	Nicaragua
1868	Uruguay
1869–1871	Dominican Republic
1890	Argentina
1891	Chile
1894	Nicaragua
1896	Nicaragua
1898	Nicaragua
1899	Nicaragua
1903	Honduras
1903	Dominican Republic
1903	Panama
1904	Dominican Republic
1907	Honduras
1907	Nicaragua
1910	Nicaragua
1910	Honduras
1912	Cuba
1912–1925	Nicaragua
1914	Haiti
1914	Dominican Republic
1915–1934	Haiti
1916–1924	Dominican Republic
1919	Honduras
1920	Guatemala
1924–1925	Honduras
1926–1933	Nicaragua
1965	Dominican Republic

Sources: Table constructed from data in L. Gordon Crovitz, "Presidents Have a History of Unilateral Moves," *The Wall Street Journal*, January 15, 1987, p. 24; Zinn, 1995:291.

United States in such activity was the old Soviet Union, with 115 cases of military display in that time period. But this study also showed that overt military threats by the United States were decreasing, while such activity by the Soviet Union was increasing in the 1970s. There was an average of 13.4 per year during John Kennedy's presidency, 9.7 during Johnson's, and 5 or fever per year during the Nixon and Ford years. For whatever reason (counterpressure by the Soviet Union, lack of success, a counterproductive image, or the Vietnam disaster for U.S. foreign policy), it seems that the threat and use of overt military action to prevent changes unwanted by the United States in other countries was being reduced. However, the covert action approach remains.

Covert actions are secret operations to achieve political or economic objectives. Included in such actions were assassination of political actors seen as a threat to U.S. interests, bribes to periphery politicians or other people who may further U.S. interests, helping stage coups, propaganda, rigged elections, and all kinds of "dirty tricks" that are limited only by the imagination—such as plans by the CIA in the 1960s to "hurt Castro's public image" by giving him LSD before a major speech or secretly dusting Castro with a chemical to make his beard fall out as noted earlier (U.S. Senate Select Committee, 1975a:72). When these types of covert action are successful they can achieve political and economic objectives at much less expense—less expense in the use of military resources, lives lost, and world opinion. The extensive use of covert actions by the United States against nations such as Nicaragua, Cuba, Chile, Iran, the Congo, the Dominican Republic, and Vietnam became widely known through the release of government documents and congressional investigations (Kolko, 1988; U.S. Senate Select Committee, 1975a, 1975b).

The objectives of covert action can be quite varied, but they generally fall into three main categories. First, and no doubt most common, covert action can be directed toward suppressing opposition groups attempting to change governments in the less developed nations supportive of U.S. interests. Second, covert action can be directed more specifically toward supporting governments favorable to U.S. interests. Third, and more complex, are actions directed toward disrupting an unfavorable government to place in power a more favorable government—one that will help U.S. interests and is more receptive to U.S. multinational corporate investment and trade.

Because of the importance of complex covert action to disrupt governments unfavorable to U.S. interests it is worth considering in more detail. We can use the case of Chile to show (1) the extent of dependence of many Latin American nations and (2) how the United States is able to make sure these nations remain economically dependent on U.S. interests (Kerbo, 1978).

The Case of U.S. Covert Action in Chile

The increasing political violence in Chile during 1970–1973 preceding the military coup in September 1973 is important for several reasons. We now know that the plan of action described below to overthrow the Chilean government was used many times before by the CIA and was first developed to overthrow the prime minister's government in Iran in 1953 (Kolko, 1988; Roosevelt, 1979). Another reason to focus on the case of Chile is that we have more information pertaining to the CIA-sponsored coup. Because of the political debate in the United States at the time and the subsequent U.S. Senate investigations, and because of the Allende government's willingness to help with research in that country, much is now known about the political and economic conditions leading up to the political violence in Chile that helped bring about the 1973 military coup (U.S. Senate Select Committee, 1975a, 1975b; Zeitlin, Ewen & Ratcliff, 1974).

Also, for two other reasons Chile is probably one of the best cases that can be used. Chile had one of the strongest traditions of democracy in Latin America. We can suggest that a foreign power will have a more difficult time helping create and exploit conditions leading to a rejection of that constitutional government (Goldberg, 1975; Petras & Morley, 1975; Zeitlin et al., 1974). In addition, Chile provides us with an example of a country highly dependent on economic actors from the outside. For example, before Allende (the socialist president) took office, Chile had the second highest foreign debt in the world. In terms of foreign aid, "Between 1961 and 1970, Chile was the largest recipient of any country in Latin America, on a per capita basis, of U.S. Alliance for Progress loans, approximately $1.3 to $1.4 billion." Further, "U.S. direct private investment in Chile in 1970 stood at $1.1 billion, out of a total estimated foreign investment of $1.672 billion" (Petras & Morley, 1975:22; U.S. Senate Select Committee, 1975b:32). Most U.S. corporate investment in Chile was in the mining and smelting sector (over 50 percent). "However, U.S. and foreign corporations controlled almost all of the most dynamic and critical areas of the economy by the end of 1970." The foreign-controlled industry included machinery and equipment (50 percent); iron, steel, and metal products (60 percent); petroleum products and distribution (over 50 percent); industrial and other chemicals (60 percent); rubber products (45 percent); automotive assembly (100 percent); radio and television (nearly 100 percent); and advertising (90 percent). "Furthermore, U.S. corporations controlled 80 percent of the production of Chile's only important foreign exchange earner—copper" (above quotes from Petras & Morley, 1975:8–9).

Before discussing how the preconditions for political violence in Chile developed with the help of foreign influence, we must look at the relative absence of these preconditions before 1970. The consensus has generally been that Chile had one of the most stable political systems in Latin America up to 1970, with the longest history of constitutional democracy of any Latin American country (Needler, 1968:891–896).

While relatively a democratic country, however, Chile was dominated economically by wealthy nations, particularly by U.S. multinational corporations. It was a country in which these outside interests could apply pressures that had the potential of seriously disrupting that country's economy and government. Rather than simply sending support for one side in the conflict after it had broken out, these foreign interests had the potential to exacerbate chronic economic imbalances already existing due to its periphery status, as well as help create new ones that could lead to serious political violence. The only thing lacking in Chile before 1970 was the motivation for outside interests to apply these pressures. With a newly elected president unfavorable to U.S. interests, one who moved toward policies viewed as highly unfavorable by the United States, that motivation soon materialized.

Not long after Allende was elected president in 1970 a concerted effort was mounted from outside to disrupt the highly dependent economy and government. These foreign interests alone did not create the conditions leading to political violence in Chile, but as a Senate investigation maintains, these outside pressures were very important (Goldberg, 1975:116; Petras & Morley, 1975:6; Sanford, 1976:150;

TABLE 8.4

Foreign Aid to Chile from Selected U.S. Agencies and International Organizations

Agency	Millions of Dollars							
	1966	1967	1968	1969	1970	1971	1972	1973
U.S. AID	$93.2	$15.5	$57.9	$35.4	$18.0	$1.5	$1.0	$0.8
U.S. Food for Peace	14.4	7.9	23.0	15.0	7.2	6.3	5.9	2.5
U.S. military assistance	10.2	4.2	7.8	11.7	0.8	5.7	12.3	15.0
U.S. Export-Import Bank	0.1	212.3	13.4	28.7	—	—	1.6	3.1
World Bank	2.7	60.0	—	11.6	19.3	—	—	—
Inter-American Development Bank	62.2	31.0	16.5	31.9	45.6	12.0	2.1	5.2

Sources: U.S. Senate Select Committee, 1975b:34; Petras and Morley, 1975:166–167.

U.S. Senate Select Committee, 1975b:32). After an attempted coup supported by the United States first failed to prevent Allende from assuming office in 1970, the efforts, mainly from the U.S. government and private industry, were directed toward two goals: to disrupt the economy and then aid segments within the country mobilized and mobilizing to oppose Allende's government (U.S. Senate Select Committee, 1975b:2).

Several actions were taken by multinationals and the U.S. government that helped disrupt the Chilean economy.

1. The various types of foreign aid coming from the United States before Allende took office were cut back severely, as shown in Table 8.4 (Sanford, 1976:147–148, U.S. Senate Select Committee, 1975b:33–35).
2. Short-term credits to Chile from American commercial banks were virtually cut off (Goldberg, 1975:109; U.S. Senate Select Committee, 1975b:33–35).
3. Funds from the World Bank and Inter-American Development Bank were cut (Petras & Morley, 1975:94; U.S. Senate Select Committee, 1975b:33–35).
4. Multinationals such as ITT worked with other multinationals and the U.S. government to organize these pressures (Sampson, 1973:283; U.S. Senate Select Committee, 1975b:13–14).
5. Supplies necessary to Chile's industry were withheld, such as parts for the primarily U.S.-made machinery (Goldberg, 1975:109; Petras & Morley, 1975:98; U.S. Senate Select Committee, 1975b:109).
6. Pressure was applied to other countries to prevent them from trading with Chile (Farnsworth, Feinberg, & Leenson, 1976:362; Petras & Morley, 1975:111; Sanford, 1976:149).

The above measures contributed to limiting industrial output in Chile severely by 1972. In Goldberg's words: "The United States' credit blockage aroused intense consumer dissatisfaction which the opposition parties succeeded in mobilizing against the government. . . . Producers whose imports were also curtailed joined newly deprived

Estado do Parana, Brazil. A peasant father builds a fence around his portion of Fazenda Padroeira. The fazenda, or farmland, was taken over and settled by landless peasants in a fight for agrarian reform in Brazil.

consumers in protest strikes and demonstrations against the government" (Goldberg, 1975:109–110).

The next step for foreign powers working within Chile was fairly simple—to provide support for old and newly emerging protest groups. In this regard, the CIA was authorized to spend $8 million between 1970 and 1973, $3 million of this spent in 1973 alone (U.S. Senate Select Committee, 1975b:1, 29–30). It is interesting to note that while all other aid to Chile from the United States was cut, the aid going specifically to the military in Chile was maintained at a high level, as shown in Table 8.4 (Petras & Morley, 1975:126; Sanford, 1976:149; U.S. Senate Select Committee, 1975b:37–39). In line with this the U.S. military also attempted to cultivate stronger personal ties with the Chilean military in an attempt to make it known that the United States would not look unfavorably on a coup (Petras & Morley, 1975:119; Sanford, 1976:52, 78, 192; U.S. Senate Select Committee, 1975b:26–28).

In conclusion, what we find in the case of Chile is a concerted effort by U.S. government officials and U.S. corporate leaders that contributed to the disruption of Chile's economy and society. This disruption helped create the preconditions for political violence. Three main factors were important in the development of political violence in Chile during President Allende's term in office. Due to the vested interests of those favored by the previous status quo of Chile's dependent relationship, opposition groups developed (aided by the CIA) as soon as Allende was elected. Newly deprived groups later arose to oppose Allende because of the economic disruption promoted by the U.S. government and multinational economic actions against Chile. Then both of these opposition groups were aided by CIA covert actions, which further contributed to an increasingly vicious cycle of political and economic breakdown.

The result was the coup of September 1973 that killed President Allende and thousands more in Chile. A military dictatorship took power that reopened Chile to economic investment and trade from U.S. multinational corporations, and reestablished the place of wealthy Chilean elites tied to these U.S. corporate interests. The U.S. government more than restored the aid and loans that were cut or eliminated when Allende took office in 1970, and top U.S. banks sent huge loans to revitalize the economy (Letelier & Moffitt, 1980; Petras & Morley, 1975:141; Sanford, 1976). Chile was welcomed back to its place in the world economic system. With foreign investment flowing back in, Chile had more economic growth between 1975 and 2000 than other Latin American countries (see Table 8.1). But it was very uneven development, helping the Chilean rich and U.S. multinational corporations more than the poor. Chile has one of the highest levels of income inequality in the world (as we saw in Table 2.2). With respect to overall GNP per capita, several nations in East and Southeast Asia passed Chile by since 1975. Even South Africa now has a higher GNP per capita than does Chile.

The Reform Approach of the Late 1970s

From 1976 to 1980, President Jimmy Carter's human rights campaign, gestures such as returning the Panama Canal to Panama in 1979, and in the same year some weak support for rebels in Nicaragua (in hopes they would not turn to communists) are other examples of core management techniques. Showing more sympathy for the poor of Latin America, and reacting to the very low international opinion of the United States after the Vietnam War, President Carter did try to help reduce Latin American poverty with more enlightened policies. The hope, of course, was that Latin American countries would become less fertile ground for anti-American and pro-Soviet social movements that were becoming widespread during that phase of the cold war.

One of the most ambitious policies was President Carter's policy promoting land reform in Central America. We know from many cases (such as greater land equality in Thailand) that getting more land into the hands of peasants is one of the best methods to reduce poverty in developing countries and help set the stage for sustainable economic development in the country (IFAD, 2001; UNDP, 2001). There was a multistage policy pushed upon the Central American dictatorships to reduce the huge inequalities in landownership in the region. The first stage would buy up land from the biggest landholders and distribute the land through low-interest loans to poor peasants. Subsequent stages of Carter's land reform policy would take parts of the land from rich landowners (paying them reasonable prices for some of their land) to make this land available to landless peasants.

The land reform policy did not get beyond the first stage in Central America. Wealthy landowners who are the power brokers behind most Central American governments became more politically active to resist the land reform policies. As the wealthy landowners became successful in this resistance, peasants whose hopes had been raised by the promised land reform became angry, with many joining left-wing and socialist movements. Wealthy landowners responded with right-wing death squads, in some countries like El Salvador killing 40,000 people in the process. Revolutionary movements became widespread all through Central America in the later years of the 1970s and early 1980s. In Nicaragua a socialist revolution succeeded in taking over the country for a few years. But mostly there was just killing from both sides—

peasants joining antigovernment movements trying to get some land and jobs, and wealthy landowners setting up right-wing death squads killing mobilized peasant farmers or anyone else (such as Catholic priests, nuns, and even some U.S. aid workers) who supported land reform.

It all came to a stop soon after Ronald Reagan was elected president in 1980. Newspaper stories told of celebrations among the rich in Central American countries the day afer Reagan was elected president in November of 1980. The U.S. government was back into covert operations to oppose governments or social movements that were against U.S. corporate interests. Some of these U.S. covert operations were illegal since laws passed by the U.S. Congress in the mid-1970s, but they proceeded anyway. The Iran-Contra scandal caused some trouble for the Reagan administration when it was discovered that surplus U.S. military equipment was being sold illegally to the Iranian government then fighting a bitter war with Iraq and the money from the sales were being used illegally to finance contrarevolutionaries fighting the new socialist government in Nicaragua. But in the end the peasant movements calling for more land equality failed and rich landowners held onto their land and control of most Central American governments. Poverty remains relatively unchanged in most Central American countries today.

IMF Structural Adjustments

From the first years of the Clinton administration in the United States, there was again a turn from CIA covert actions around the world. This is not to say that the United States will never again be involved in such actions, but international organizations dominated by Western industrial nations in North America and Europe are often able to change economic policies in developing countries with financial muscle and threat. The international bankers leading such agencies as the IMF (International Monetary Fund) no doubt think they are doing good in the world (Easterly, 2001). But because these agencies are run by U.S. and European bankers and economists who often do not understand the predicament of poor countries today, often because of their free-market ideological blinders, they are wittingly or unwittingly participating in a new form of neocolonialism that opens less developed countries to foreign multinational corporate advantage.

One of the chief means the IMF has of forcing changes in less developed countries is called "structural adjustments." When the IMF bankers or economists go into a country that has some kind of financial crisis they always require the government to make changes in economic policies before the IMF will lend the country money to overcome its crisis. These structural adjustments most often mean that the country can no longer protect some of its industries and must allow more foreign investment. In reality it means that multinational corporations from the United States and Europe can come into the country and buy up corporations in the less developed country at bargain prices (*International Herald Tribune,* October 23, 2000; *Los Angeles Times,* January 4, 1998). Further, as a requirement for loaning money, the IMF usually requires a country to cut its spending on things like social welfare programs and reduce taxes on the rich. In other words, in exchange for borrowing money from the IMF (mostly controlled by the United States) the country must make its political and economic system conform more to the free-market or neoliberal model led by the United States. What this also

CASE IN POINT

Crisis and Decline in Argentina

People have gotten quite desperate in Argentina in recent years. A couple of years ago, for example, a cattle truck overturned on a busy highway. People in the area rushed out and slaughtered the cattle, taking all the meat home before the police could arrive. In May of 2003 Norma Albino, a woman of 59, stepped into her bank branch in this Buenos Aires suburb of cobblestone streets, famous for its affluence and the tall spires of its 100-year-old church. She asked—for the third or fourth time since December—for her family's money. When the teller told her that he couldn't help her, she blurted out: "I'm going to kill myself." She then poured alcohol over herself and set herself on fire. Mrs. Albino had seen most of her family's life savings disappear in just a few months. Mrs. Isabel Andres, a 56-year-old woman now alone and dying of a rare form of cancer, represents another common case in Argentina today. While Mrs. Andres now "lives in the cozy house that her grandparents bought when Argentina was as rich as France and had more cars than Japan," she can no longer afford the money to buy the drugs that are keeping her alive. Neither Argentina's national medical care system nor the country's social welfare system can help her; they too are out of money.

More than any other developing country in the 1990s, Argentina followed the free-market policies pushed by the United States and the IMF. But even more than in other countries in Latin America, these policies brought economic crisis and more poverty to Argentina. About 100 years ago Argentina was among the 10 richest countries in the world, and the richest in Latin America. But as we have already seen, Argentina like the rest of Latin America failed to keep pace with the growth of other countries in North America, Europe, and Asia. When the economic crisis hit Argentina in 1999 the per capita gross national income (GNI) per capita was just under $9,000; by 2000 it was just over $7,000 per capita. After the full effect of the economic crisis, in 2002 Argentina's GNI was an amazing $4,060 per capita, less than half the 1999 figure.[1] Overall, the Argentine economy shrunk by 21 percent between 1999 and 2002. Unemployment remained over 20 percent in 2003. People with life savings of, say, $42,000 saw the value of their money shrink to $11,600. The Argentine government now estimates that about half of its people live in poverty.

In return for IMF loans, Argentina had to open the country for even more foreign investment and sell off almost all state-run agencies. Foreign corporations quickly took advantage of the situation to buy the national telephone company, water and gas companies, the railroads, the national post office, and the national airline. The government oil company and its reserves in the southern region of Patagonia were also sold to foreign corporations, mostly American. Electric Services of Greater Buenos Aires was divided up and sold to Chilean, Spanish, and American investors. Most bank branches in Argentina are now owned by either U.S. or European banks.

Argentina will recover; by 2003 there was again some economic growth. But Argentina will almost certainly *not recover like the countries in Asia that quickly regained their previous level of wealth and growth 2 or 3 years after the Asian economic crisis of 1997.* When Argentina regains some economic stability and has less unemployment, it will be a country in which more of the economic assets are owned and controlled by corporations from the United States and Europe.

Sources: International Herald Tribune, October 23, 2000, November 10, 2001, January 4, 2002, August 7, 2002, July 30, 2003; *Los Angeles Times,* January 4, 1998; various World Bank reports.

means is that a country borrowing money from the IMF is *less able to follow an Asian development model* with a strong development state directing its economic development. We have seen that an Asian development model with a hard state or development state has been most successful in achieving economic development for Asian countries. Thus, it is not surprising that several studies have charged that the IMF has made developing countries worse off with its policies (*International Herald Tribune,* October 23, 2000, November 10, 2001, January 4, 2002, August 7, 2002, July 30, 2003; see also *Los Angeles Times,* January 4, 1998). Although the people might become poorer because of IMF structural adjustments, these people get more multinational corporations moving into the country buying up the weak companies.

Conclusion

The central problem for most Latin American countries today is that they have an individualistic, free-market economic model (what is also called a neoliberal economic model) pushed on them by the United States, the region's dominant power for over 150 years. This economic model is not suited to protect less developed countries in today's global economy. Because of extensive influence from U.S. multinational corporations and the benefits these corporations rain upon the rich in Latin American countries, the elites in Latin America are more inclined to take care of their individual interests instead of the long-term interests of their nations as a whole. This means that Latin American countries have few of what are called development states in Asian countries.

When there is economic development in Latin America, however, as in the United States in recent decades, the economic growth is unevenly spread around the country. The United States has yet to attain the level of inequality of most Latin American countries, but it is moving in that direction. This is again an outcome of economic models: The free-market model in today's global economy can produce some economic growth, but it does so by producing more inequality in the country and at expensive of the poor. The more cooperative approach of economic growth found in most European countries (often called a corporatist model, or cooperative capitalism, where government, corporations, and workers have a balance of power) has led to somewhat less economic growth compared to the United States in recent decades, but with much less inequality and poverty (Alderson & Nielsen, 2002; Goodin et al., 1999; Mahler, 2001, 2002). In less developed countries, however, we have seen evidence from Asia that a development state is the best solution. In the rapidly growing economies of East and Southeast Asia there has been sustained poverty reduction and much less growth in inequality. It is time to turn to Southeast Asian nations for more detail about how this has been accomplished.

Notes

1. These are figures from World Bank's *World Development Reports,* 1999 through 2004, and are gross national income figures *not* using PPP estimates so we can have comparable figures across these years.

Development and Poverty in Southeast Asia: A Region of Extremes

From Vietnam and the Philippines in the east, to Burma in the west, and the vast country of Indonesia in the south, perhaps no other world region has such a varied record of economic development and poverty reduction (see Map 9.1). Indeed, few world regions have the cultural variation and contrasting political histories as do the countries of Southeast Asia. Because of their unique situations of wealth, the small city-state and center of British investment, Singapore, and the little oil-rich sheikdom of Brunei will not be considered here. All of the others, however, will be considered, but with a focus on the Buddhist countries of Southeast Asia. In contrast to much of the literature about Asian economic miracles, a central point of our analysis has been that Asian values, or any particular cultural orientation, are not enough for economic development. With this in mind we should begin with a "cultural tour of Southeast Asia."

A Cultural Tour of Southeast Asia

Leaving Bangkok on one of the new elevated highways, heading due west for about 45 minutes, one arrives in the city of Nakorn Pathom. A rather typical, small provincial city, much like those seen all over Thailand today, Nakorn Pathom holds claim to one of the earliest cities in what is now Thailand. There is also the claim that it has the tallest Buddhist monument in the world. Not quite into the mountains that line the border between Burma and Thailand, Nakorn Pathom is on the fringe of Thailand's agricultural heartland. Coming into the city from a few miles out in any direction, after noticing pamelo orchards and pig farms mixed among rice paddies, one sees the towering orange-gold dome of the Phra Pathom Chedi. Once inside the city the Chedi is truly impressive. Not only is the Chedi tall, higher than a 10 story building, it is also massive. It takes over the center of the city and the lives of its people. There are monks in bright saffron robes chanting most hours of the day and blessing the devoted, and busloads of tourists (almost all Asian) walking around the Chedi. All important religious ceremonies are conducted inside the grounds of the Phra Pathom Chedi, secular carnivals and political rallies are carried outside the gates, and every night there is a kind of bazaar going on late into the night where people can buy all kinds of food, music CDs, clothing, and household goods. While all of this and more is going on outside the grounds of the Chedi, public buses and trucks hauling the locals and farm produce circle the massive structure seemingly competing with each other to see which can blow out the most black smoke and make the loudest noise.

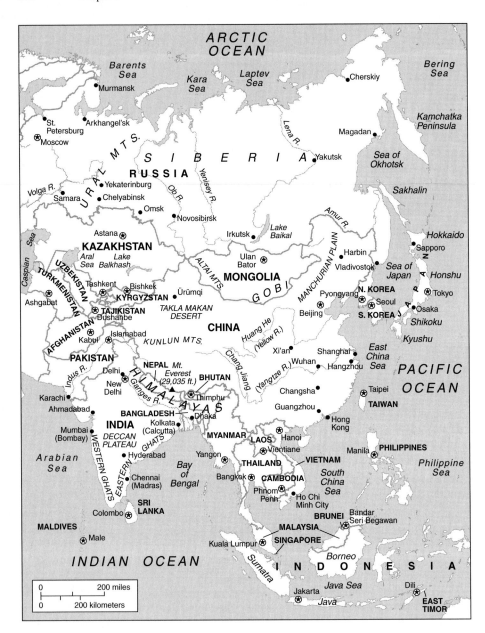

MAP 9.1 *Map of Asia Nations.*

The claim that Phra Pathom Chedi is the biggest Buddhist structure in the world, however, is perhaps less important for the history of Southeast Asia than is the estimate that it is here Theravada Buddhism first arrived in Southeast Asia from Sri Lanka some-time during the seventh century. It was Theravada Buddhism that carried the particular Buddhist culture that came to dominate the mainland of Southeast Asia, down to the

Phra Pathom Chedi pictured here is one of the largest Buddhist structures in the world and estimated to be the site where Theravada Buddhism first arrived in Southeast Asia from Sri Lanka and India sometime during the seventh century.

Muslim areas just above Malaysia and over to the Vietnamese border today (De Casparis & Mabbett, 1999:294). During the seventh century, Nakorn Pathom was part of the Davaravati kingdom that was destroyed in the early eleventh century by the Khmer king, Suryavarman I, during the Angkor (Cambodian) dominance in Southeast Asia. A Hindu Brahman prang was then built over the original (and much smaller) Buddhist monument by the Khmer who were at the time more influenced by Hinduism. A few years later (AD 1057) the Pagan king (Burma) destroyed the city again and the religious monument lay in ruins until the famous King Mongkut of Thailand built the towering Chedi on top of the original structures in 1860. By this time Thailand had been the dominant country in most of Southeast Asia (with the exception of Vietnam) for almost a century. The once powerful kingdoms of what are Burma (Pagan) and Cambodia (Angkor) today had long been in decline. But even before the sharp decline of these other kingdoms, for several centuries Theravada Buddhism had been the dominant religion for the ruling elites and the common people alike. Elements of Hinduism were embedded in the practice of Theravada Buddhism as is still the case today. Throughout these countries, Hindu gods can be found in Theravada Buddhist wats (temples). A few of the most popular shrines are essentially Hindu, such as the Erawan Shrine in the middle of one of the busiest sections of Bangkok, which is believed to be the best location to pray for good luck. (This explains why there are always many vendors selling lottery tickets just outside.) Elements of animism and spirit worship as well are mixed with the Theravada Buddhism practiced by the less educated and rural people of Thailand, Laos, Cambodia, and Burma. But the main tenets of the religion followed by the vast majority of people in these Southeast Asian nations for the past several centuries are found in Theravada Buddhism. It must be stressed that these people are devoutly religious. There are likely more wats per square mile than there are churches in small towns in Oklahoma, Texas, or Mississippi. In Thailand today some 80 to 90 percent of young men or boys still follow the tradition of becoming novice Buddhist monks for a few months of their life to honor their families and receive religious training.

Traveling from Thailand to Burma, then back to the east into Laos and down to Cambodia, the wats look strikingly similar, the monks follow the same scriptures, wear rather similar saffron-colored robes, and the organization of their religious orders (*sangha*) is almost identical. The religious monuments in the wats of Thailand, Burma, Laos, and Cambodia mostly have a mixture of Khmer, Sri Lankan, and traditional Thai artistic styles. The temples of Angkor, which were the center of the Khmer empire from AD 800 to 1432 and then abandoned, have a distinct architecture and show more Hindu influence than the wats of Cambodia today (Higham, 2001). Before Angkor Wat was abandoned, however, some of the Khmer kings had favored Theravada Buddhism. Touring these massive temples today one can see many places where Theravada Buddhist images replaced Hindu images, and where other Hindu images have been destroyed. The most important religious monuments still in use today in Cambodia, such as the Silver Pagoda on the grounds of the Royal Palace in Phnom Penh (the nation's capital), though poorer and less grand, look remarkably similar to the Grand Palace and attached Wat Phra Kaew in contemporary Bangkok.

As the above scenes suggest, and as scholars specializing in the region confirm, Southeast Asian culture and the strength of Buddhism in people's lives have survived colonialism (Evans, 1998:168). In Burma, Cambodia, and Laos, though communist governments or military dictatorships tried to eliminate or substantially reduce the hold of the sangha (religious hierarchy) over the hearts and minds of the people, Theravada Buddhism remains strong. For centuries, as today, Buddhist monks in Southeast Asia have been at the forefront of protest movements. Their resistance to military dictators, communism, and corrupt governments has continued to shape the history of these countries since the middle of the twentieth century. The People's Democratic Republic of Laos, for example, like its communist brothers and sisters in Vietnam, tried to eliminate the moral force of Buddhism as dictated by communist doctrine. By the 1990s it was evident that it had failed completely. Taking the practical way out, the Laotian communist elite reversed policies and revived Theravada Buddhism and the sangha as important symbols of the nation in an attempt to recoup the legitimacy of their communist rule. Important Buddhist monuments, especially the one next door to the Communist Party's odd "socialist realist" building headquarters in Vientiane (the capital city of Laos), became locations for prominent party functions and national holidays (Evans, 1998, 1999a, 1999b). Monks in Laos continue to receive much more respect than communist leaders, and since Laotian royalty has been rejected from the country, the dominant "lowland"people of Laos (in contrast to the hill tribe people who make up some 40 percent of the population) have increasingly adopted Thai royal figures as their own. Likewise, from the 1960s the Burmese military dictators, following their Burmese way to socialism, tried much the same with much the same results. By the end of the 1990s, with their rule increasingly seen as illegitimate within the country and international community, the military dictators began a new campaign to restore the historic Buddhist monuments and seek support from the sangha. Buddhism is as strong as ever in Burma, but it hasn't helped the dictators' status: Referring to Buddhist beliefs regarding reincarnation based upon merit achieved in this life, and in response to the attempts of the military dictators to restore their legitimacy through the biggest effort to rebuild historic wats in all of Southeast Asia, one old monk high in the Burmese sangha told a reporter secretly visiting Burma, "they are still coming back as rats" (*International Herald Tribune*, November 15, 2000).

As one travels down the peninsula that connects southwestern Thailand to other countries of Southeast Asia, the striking contrast begins when entering the four south-ernmost provinces of Thailand that were once attached to what is now Malaysia. The religious landscape rapidly changes from Buddhist to Muslim. More and more mosques begin to dominate the center of villages and fewer and fewer Buddhist wats are to be seen. Most women in the streets wear the traditional Muslim chader covering their heads, and few restaurants serve beer or any other alcoholic drinks.

Islam arrived relatively late to Southeast Asia. The Islamic empire that emerged in the Middle East after the fall of the Roman Empire, then spread through much of north-ern Africa and southern Europe, was already in decline when Islam began to spread in southern Southeast Asia during the 1400s (De Casparis & Mabbett, 1999: 330). But Islam rapidly replaced (or perhaps one should say, mixed with) many earlier centuries of Buddhism throughout what is now Malaysia, Indonesia, the little sultanate of Brunei, and southern regions of the Philippines.

In the far eastern regions of Southeast Asia two other religious–cultural influ-ences complete our picture of Southeast Asia today. The Philippines experienced the overpowering urge of the Spanish to impose their Catholic religion as they did in Central and South American at about the same time. Southeast Asian scholars agree that more than any other country in Southeast Asia, the people of the dominant northern half of the Philippines have had their culture transformed by a European power (Cheong, 1999; Karnow, 1989; Osborne, 1995). The majority of northern Filipinos are devout Catholics. Catholic churches are everywhere, and probably half of the strange-looking buses on the streets of Manila (the nation's capital city), called "jeepneys," have reli-gions slogans painted on the front and sides. It is this overwhelming dominance of Christianity in the north that of course has set the stage for violent conflict between northern Filipinos and southern Islamic Filipinos to this day.

Back on the mainland of Southeast Asia, Vietnam is the only Southeast Asian country to be heavily dominated by Confucian culture and a Buddhism different from Theravada Buddhism. In essence, Vietnam can be described as a Northeast Asian nation located in Southeast Asia. Vietnam's unique position among Southeast Asian nations is due to some 2,000 years of Chinese influence as the Chinese moved south along the eastern coast of Southeast Asia to take advantage of important seaports and trade routes (Hall, 1999:263; Taylor, 1999). As the old temples of Vietnam suggest, the consensus among scholars today is that Vietnam shares more cultural orientations related to the Confucianism that spread through Northeast Asian countries of China, Korea, and Japan than the Theravada Buddhism of Vietnam's closest Southeast Asian neighbors.

As we finish our little religious–cultural tour of Southeast Asia, there is a remain-ing question: To what degree can one speak of common Asian values as did Malaysian Prime Minister Mahathir when explaining why Malaysia and its neighbors prefer to do things differently from the West? Thailand, Burma, Laos, and Cambodia are dominated by the values of Theravada Buddhism, with a dose of Hinduism mixed in. Malaysia, Indonesia, Brunei, and the southern Philippines are predominately Muslim. The Chinese who make up most of the population of Singapore (a country created in the

1960s when it was kicked out of Malaysia because of this Chinese dominance) have strong Confucian roots, as does Vietnam. Thus, can we speak of Pan-Asian values in Southeast Asia?

As typical with such questions, the answer is probably yes, but also no. Because of the preexisting Southeast Asian culture before Islam arrived there are significant differences between the behavior of Malaysian and Indonesian Muslims when compared to Muslims in Northern Africa and the Middle East (Kathirithamby-Wells, 1999; Ricklefs, 1993; Sardesai, 1989; Turnbull, 1999). As with Theravada Buddhism in Thailand, Burma, Laos, and Cambodia, the Islam of Malaysia, Indonesia, and southern Philippines has been mixed with old animist beliefs that predated both Theravada Buddhism and Islam in Southeast Asia. In the last 600 years how much has Islam changed the originally Buddhist-and Hindu-based cultures of what is now Malaysian and Indonesian that preceded Islam by some 1,000 years? Then again, how different is the Theravada Buddhism of the rest of Southeast Asia compared to the Chinese–Confucian Buddhism of Vietnam?

To answer such questions one must ask, compared to what? Compared to Western Christianity the Theravada Buddhists and Chinese–Confucian Buddhists are quite similar. There is extensive comparative evidence from around the world indicating that East and Southeast Asian nations (Buddhist, Confucian, as well as Islamic) tend to cluster together on important value scales such as collectivism and "power distance"—respect for and dominance of authority figures (Hofstede, 1991; Slagter & Kerbo, 2000). Further, there is strong evidence that traditional values from different world regions have been less altered by a global mass media in recent decades than most people assume. Studies indicate that economic development has produced more rationalism and tolerance, but core traditional values remain (Inglehart & Baker, 2000). So despite some important differences, and despite clusters of cultural orientations within Southeast Asia (for example, Burma, Thailand, Cambodia, and Laos versus Malaysia and Indonesia) it seems reasonable to conclude that there is a base of Asian values in Southeast Asia.[1]

It is also reasonable to conclude from a comparison of wealth, poverty, and economic growth (or the lack of it) throughout East and Southeast Asia that the *Asian values don't really matter all that much*. This will be especially evident when we compare the strong Theravada Buddhist countries of Thailand, Burma, Cambodia, and Laos. The revived cultural theories of economic development would have us believe that culture matters more than anything else in determining why some countries stay poor and others have economic development. Latin American countries, we have seen, are claimed by some to be less developed than North America because of the Catholic culture inherited from Spain. Interestingly enough the Philippines seems to fit this view as well. But what about Burma, Thailand, Laos, and Cambodia? All four countries have very similar cultural values but have had dramatically different economic development outcomes in recent decades. These differences in economic development must be explained by factors other than culture. Specifically, we will see how the influences of *ancient civilizations, traditions of authority and elite responsibility*, and the *characteristics of the state* described earlier for Asian nations have been affected by the legacy of colonialism. I have chosen a method of qualitative historical-comparative analysis that allows us to control for the impact of culture, or in other words, hold the impact of culture constant across the countries to be compared. Thus, it has been important to establish that the four Theravada Buddhist countries of Thailand, Burma, Cambodia, and Laos have similar cultural bases so we can look for other causes when economic development records are very different. We can include Vietnam in our analysis with only a little less confidence that culture is not a major factor in economic development compared to the other four nations. Finally, we will consider the Philippines, Malaysia, and Indonesia in the comparative analysis, including two Islamic countries and one that is primarily Catholic and Islamic.

The Impact of Colonialism and Southeast Asia Today

Southeast Asia was a quite different place before the age of European colonialism. Among the most obvious changes, there were 40 "nations" before colonialism compared to 10 by the twentieth century. Most of those swept away were in what is now Indonesia, Malaysia, and Laos. Of those states that still existed by the twentieth century, however, all had at least some alterations in their traditional national boundaries (Osborne, 1995:38). But while all of the nations were touched in one way or another, colonialism had a significantly different impact on each of the nations of Southeast Asia. The colonial actors on the mainland of Southeast Asia were the French and British. The Dutch had the large chain of southern islands that make up Indonesia today. And, of course, the Spanish took the Philippines during the early stages of colonialism, with the United States taking the Philippines away from Spain after the Spanish-American War at the end of the nineteenth century. Thailand was the only nation in the region to remain independent through the colonial years, though even in Thailand the British influence was extensive and national borders were slightly altered.

The British arrived to the west and south of Thailand, in Burma and Malaysia, after the British had secured India for their empire, their "jewel in the crown" and most important prize in the colonial land grab. The French were to focus on what was (inaccurately) called Indochina—Vietnam, Laos, and Cambodia, to the east of Thailand. It was the luck of the Thais to have favorable geography and astute leadership. The Thais were able to manipulate fears the French and British had about each others' intentions in the region to negotiate for themselves a pledge of independence from both Western powers (Girling, 1981; Wyatt, 1984). But as we will see, it was more than just the fact that Burma, Laos, Cambodia, and Vietnam, as well as Malaysia and Indonesia, were colonized and Thailand was not. One must consider differences in *how these countries were colonized, what was done during colonization,* and *how the colonial powers left the scene* in the second half of the twentieth century. Further, we must consider the level of economic and political development in each nation before the European colonials arrived on the scene. Previous research has indicated that the level of agricultural technology in the country before multinational corporations came to dominate the country had an impact on long-term economic development (Lenski & Nolan, 1984, 1986). The Zurich data set introduced in this book in Chapter 2 indicates in a similar manner that government complexity, or levels of government before the colonials arrived, has had an impact on long-term economic development and poverty reduction. In the case of Southeast Asian nations, history indicates that the nations that were politically stronger before colonialism arrived were better able to overcome the effects of colonization after World War II.

TABLE 9.1

Standards of Living and Poverty in Southeast Asia, 2001

Country	U.N. Human Development Index Score*	Real GDP per Capita**	Percent living on $1 a Day or Less**
Malaysia	0.79	8,750	Under 2
Thailand	0.76	6,400	Under 2
Philippines	0.75	3,840	20
Vietnam	0.69	2,070	18
Indonesia	0.68	2,940	7
Cambodia	0.56	1,860	—
Burma	0.55	1,027	—
Laos	0.53	1,620	26

*The United Nations Human Development Index is based upon life expectancy at birth, adult literacy, and adjusted per capita income in PPP.

**Figures are calculated in Purchasing Power Parity (PPP).

Source: UNDP, 2003:238–239, 245–246.

As Table 9.1 indicates, of the first five countries involved in this analysis (Burma, Thailand, Laos, Cambodia, and Vietnam), Thailand is by far the richest nation. The military dictators of Burma will not let international agencies such as the United Nations or World Bank obtain some estimates such as the percentage living on less than $1 per day. But other agencies, such as the World Health Organization, estimate Burma to be next to the bottom among 191 nations in providing for the health of its people (*International Herald Tribune,* November 15, 2000). All the World Bank can do is include a footnote for Burma saying it is among the poorest nations in the world. Traveling through Southeast Asia one can agree that Burma must indeed have a per capita GNP close to or lower than that of Laos and Cambodia. Vietnam, on the other hand, is certainly a more developed country compared to Laos, Burma, or Cambodia, and even the Philippines. I spent a few weeks in Vietnam in 2004, and then a few days in the Philippines. The contrast between Saigon (now Ho Chi Minh City) and Manila could not have been greater. High-rise buildings of all kinds are going up around Saigon. There is a new shopping mall with European high-fashion boutiques in the middle of Saigon, with new four-star hotels everywhere. In Manila it seems nothing is changing. There are old shopping malls of 1960s vintage, and that is about it. The most recent data reported by the World Bank show that Vietnam has cut its poverty rate from around 70 percent in 1990 to 30 percent by 2000 (Gwatkin et al., 2000). Similarly, health indicators such as infant mortality rates tend to correspond to levels of economic development and poverty. For Vietnam in 1999 the infant mortality rate was 69 per 1,000 births, compared to 102 for Cambodia, 96 for Laos, 78 for Burma, and 29 for Thailand (World Bank, 2000). Life expectancy in Vietnam as of 1999 was 69 years, while it was 54 in Cambodia, 54 for Laos, 60 for Burma, and 73 for Thailand. One standard indicator for the level of economic development in a country is electric power consumption per capita, which in 1999 stood at 203 kilowatt hours for Vietnam, 57 for Burma, and 1,360 for Thailand (with no estimates given for Laos and Cambodia).

Any attempt to understand such variation among these nations must step further back into history. We must consider what was happening in the countries, how far they had developed, and the relative power before the European colonials came to dominate Southeast Asia.

A Brief History of Southeast Asian Nations

With the overwhelming dominance of the old Asian civilizations of China and India, few people give much thought to Southeast Asia when considering ancient civilizations. But we know that Southeast Asia from 1,000 to 400 years ago was one of the busiest trading areas in the world. In the middle of trade routes between China and India, port cities in what are now Vietnam, Thailand, Malaysia, and Indonesia were at times more active than those of Europe during the same period. There is also evidence that some 40,000 years ago tribal peoples of Southeast Asia were making the first voyages into the Pacific, reaching far Pacific islands and Australia (Bellwood, 1999:55).

With the "rediscovery" of Angkor Wat by the French colonials in the 1800s, and especially since its opening to more tourist travel by the late 1990s (after final surrender of the Khmer Rouge communist forces made the area safe), more people recognize there was at least one ancient civilization in Southeast Asia (Higham, 2001; Osborne, 2000). (As we will see, the high point of Angkor Wat was from 802 to 1432.) A few veterans from the American part of the Vietnam War may also know there were some other ancient civilizations. Not far from the famous "China Beach," just outside Da Nang, there are strange-looking and crumbling remains of old temples in central Vietnam. These were built by the Champ civilization of Hindu–Buddhist sea traders and part-time pirates who are traced back some 2,000 years, long before the high point of Angkor Wat (Taylor, 1999:153–157). In what was once the Champ city of My Son (a U.N. historical site since 2002) one can still see the remnants of these beautiful old temples rising from the valley in a mountainous area a few miles inland. Sadly, of the 68 original structures studied by the French almost 100 years ago, only 20 remain. During America's involvement in the Vietnam War these structures at times provided shelter to the Viet Cong and were thus bombed by the U.S. military.

Another important legacy of the ancient people of Southeast Asia was discovered as recently as the 1970s. In the northeast of Thailand today, about an hour's drive from the provincial town of Udon Thani, is the archaeological site of Ban Chiang. It is only now being excavated among the contemporary rice patties to reveal how some of the early humans in the region lived and died. We know they ate and stored rice; domesticated pigs, dogs, chickens, and cattle; and that they hunted for meat, killing such animals as crocodiles, deer, and even rhinoceros. We know their lives were probably rather short (an average of 31 years) and that malaria killed many of these people. Walking around the hot plain from site to site one can see the remains of these people, their homes, and pottery that go back at least 5,000 years. Most remarkable, there is evidence at this site that bronze was made by these people about 4,000 years ago. If confirmed with further research this means these people were among the first humans anywhere in the world to smelt bronze (Bellwood, 1999:98).

Some 2,000 years ago there was probably a common Pan-Southeast Asian culture among the people in the region (Wyatt, 1984:4). Today, however, we find that

2,000 years of development and influence from peoples outside Southeast Asia have resulted in more variation. We need to understand how these countries are both similar and different if we are to understand their current situations of economic success or failure. With each of these countries we will summarize what scholars know about their ancient origins and the evolution of their civilizations, then trace their history through colonialism and the postcolonial era up to the present to help explain their level of economic development and poverty today. As we begin this review of history for each Southeast Asian nation, starting with Thailand, it will be useful to remember Table 5.2 which summarized the impact of Asian characteristics (described in previous chapters) and colonialism on the ability of these Southeast Asian nations to bring about economic development. Table 9.2 at the end of this chapter will again summarize these characteristics and place each of these countries in the table. We must consider the impact of ancient civilizations and traditions of elite responsibility and national identity on chances of economic development today. We must also consider how a development state has been made possible and the impact of colonialism if we are to understand differing levels of economic development and poverty reduction today.

Thailand: The Preconditions for Economic Development and Poverty Reduction

With Thailand the wealthiest of the Buddhist countries of Southeast Asia today, and the country with the best record of poverty reduction, it is perhaps fitting that we begin with a short examination of Thai political and economic history. Because of this success we must also look more closely at the specific policies and techniques Thailand was able to use for its more equitable economic development in the second half of the twentieth century. But this will come later, in the next chapter. For now, a look at early and contemporary aspects of the Thai civilization and political system, and the influence of colonialism in the region, will be the focus.

A concrete image of Thai political and economic history can be gained by looking at the archeological record on display around the country today. Two of the most important spots are the ruins of the old capitals of Sukothai, toward the middle of the country, and Ayudhya, closer to Bangkok further south. While not as exotic and impressive as the ruins of Angkor Wat, still, they are impressive. These remains of wats (temples), palaces, and huge Buddha images cover many square miles in both of these old capitals, though the ruins of Sukothai are more impressive because much of Ayudhya's remains were either taken by invading Burmese or removed to help construct Bangkok's Wat Phra Kaew about 200 years ago. The spires, stupas, and walls of the old wats and palaces remain partially intact, though the once elaborately decorated plaster that covered the structures is gone, exposing the underlying brick construction. Walking through the remains of Ayudhya a few years ago with a Thai historian who helped design the museum on the grounds, I was told at one point that we were standing where the royal kitchen existed some 600 years ago. For many yards in every direction we could see thousands of broken pieces of fine Ming dynasty pottery imported to serve the royal family and their guests. One can imagine the grandeur of the place several hundred years ago as the kings of Thailand, their court nobility, and foreign dignitaries dined not far from where we were standing.

By Middle Eastern and Asian standards, of course, the old capitals of Thailand are not really so ancient. Even the Europeans were already well into their Renaissance when the older of the Thai capitals was constructed from the mid-thirteenth century. Still, in contrast to most other developing nations today, there was an unbroken continuity for the kingdom of Thailand going back some 800 years. The civilization was strong and still in its emergent phase when Western colonialists arrived, giving Thais an important advantage compared to, for example, Burma and Cambodia.

People identified today as Thai, like many other people in Southeast Asia, originated in China. We know that Tai people (the original tribal name of Thai people) began migrating out of China almost 2,000 years ago, some going to India and others going south into Southeast Asia (Osborne, 1995; Wyatt, 1984). As Pagan kings (now Burma) were weakened by Mongol invasions from AD 1250 and rival kingdoms within the area, and as Angkor (Cambodia) was in decline, the Thai people began their long process of nation building (Taylor, 1999:168–169). National boundaries are something of a Western concept, so no exact national boundaries can be described for the early Thai kingdoms. But their first capital, Sukothai, was in the northern center of what is now Thailand, with the kingdom extending as far out as the kingdom had the strength to defend. The Sukothai period lasted from only 1253 until 1350, but it was an extremely important period in which the Thais were able to establish the kingdom as a political system dominated by a king with strict obligations to the people. It was a time in which the great King Ramkamheng (who is believed to have established the written language Thailand has today) provided a philosophy of justice which some claim was first inscribed on a stone lintel found in the ruins of Sukothai (Keyes, 1989:25; Wyatt, 1984:54).

In 1350 it was decided that the capital city should be moved further south for better access to trade routes on the Chao Phaya River and a richer agricultural area. At the new capital of Ayudhya Thai nation building continued until 1767, with the king's power strengthened along with that of a central government, during a time of renewed threats from the Khmers (Cambodia) and Burmese. It was in Ayudhya that the patriarch model of king was dropped from the Hindu concept of divine king, a king that was both political and religious leader. A system of government ministries was also instituted for more efficient running of the government (Akin, 1996:31). As was often the case in early feudal empires, Western or Asian, the kings' control was never complete and infighting within the court was frequent. It was during such a period of infighting that a weakened Thailand was unable to defend itself from Burmese conquest in 1767. But this was to be the last conquest for a declining Burmese kingdom. The Thai capital was again moved. For a few years the new Thai capital was on the west bank of the Chao Phaya River (in Thonburi), then it was completely rebuilt across the river by 1782 in what is now Bangkok. In relatively short order Thailand regained its power to counter Burma, then dominate as well what is now Cambodia. During the Bangkok period the current royal line, now up to Rama IX, began, with the current king reining for more than 55 years, still the world's longest reining monarch as of 2005.

By the middle 1800s Thailand and Vietnam had become dominant regional powers as Burma and Cambodia were in decline. But then came the threat of colonialism, described in the 1860s by the great King Monkut (Rama IV) as a choice between swimming upriver to make friends with the crocodile or swimming out to sea hanging onto the whale, referring to the French and British respectively. It was King Monkut and then his son King Chulalongkorn (Rama V) who astutely led the nation during this most crucial period of confrontation with the West from the 1850s until the turn of the century—a period in which the kingdom began its transformation into a more modern nation-state. The Western powers, and Britain in particular, forced Thailand into a world economic system dominated by the West (Chaiyan, 1994). The French stripped away some Thai territory for their new colonies in Laos and Cambodia. But unlike all other countries in Southeast Asia, Thailand kept its independence, and even strengthened and modernized Thai institutions in the process.

Much like Japan at about the same time, Thailand began sending some of its best and brightest abroad to acquire Western education and expertise (Eisenstadt, 1996; Reischauer, 1988; Reischauer & Craig, 1978). Under the leadership of King Chulalongkorn, the government administration was transformed from the old household system to a modern bureaucratic form with civil servants, and a modern and permanent military force was established. By the early 1900s the corvee system (periods of forced labor by peasants) and slavery were also abolished, and over time many Western cultural practices were introduced into the population (such as the requirement that family names be adopted).

By the early 1930s, as the effects of the worldwide economic depression were felt in Thailand, tensions brought on by confrontation with the West and the creation of a more modern nation-state came to a crisis point. Most affected was the small middle class, government civil servants, military officers, and a small urban commercial group. The last Thai king to end his rule in a normal transition, Rama VI, was known as the "literary king" who showed little interest in authoritarian reign. Rama VI was more the British gentleman with a passion for producing and translating British and French plays. His rather strange summer palace in Nakorn Pathom, built in a mix of European and Thai design, is today a museum where his literary works and pictures of his theatrical productions are displayed (along with a large statue of his favorite dog reportedly shot by one of his palace guards as a nuisance).

Finally, in June of 1932, there was a military coup that deposed King Rama VII as the last absolute monarch of Thailand. The coup leaders, the "promoters" as they called themselves (49 military officers and 65 civilians), were mostly educated in the West and motivated by their conviction that the absolute monarchy was an obstacle to further modernization and development of Thailand. But their justification of the coup under the guise of democracy set the stage for a period of Thai history where the country often had the *form* of democratic government but not the substance. Between 1932 and 1938, first the civilian faction and then the senior military officers lost in the struggle to control the new government. It was the middle-level nationalistic and antimonarchical military officers among the original promoters, particularly the army, who dominated the government in alliance with civilian officials in the bureaucratic ministry. The appearance of democracy in the form of a constitution and a parliament were maintained, in line with democratic justification of the original coup, while Thailand was actually governed by the military with bureaucratic ministry officials taking care of details. It was with this form of government that Thailand survived the turmoil of World War II and moved to establish policies for economic development from the 1950s.

At the beginning of World War II in Europe, Thailand was able to regain its honor by quickly attacking the French in Indochina when they were weakened by German occupation at home. Thailand was thus able to regain territory in the east taken by the French for their colonies in Laos and Cambodia about 100 years earlier. (A huge Victory Monument stands today in the middle of Ratchawithi Road in northeastern Bangkok to commemorate this victory.) Thailand then basically sat out the rest of World

War II in relative safety after capitulating in a few hours to the Japanese attack from across the Mekong River by quickly declaring war on Britain and the United States to make itself a Japanese ally. After 1945 it was able to convince the United States and Britain that its declaration of war was made only under duress and to save itself from disaster at the hands of the Japanese. (The Thais never fought against the Western Allies in World War II, and gave only grudging material support to the Japanese occupying Thailand.) Like King Monkut and King Chulalongkorn in the second half of the nineteenth century who saved Thailand from becoming a colony, the Thai government again pulled off an impressive feat while in the grip of superpowers, escaping any significant punishment during *or* after World War II (Wyatt, 1984).

During the second half of the twentieth century military control of the government continued until 1973 (Prudhisan, 1992; Wyatt, 1984). It was at this time that elected civilian officials began exerting more influence in the government, but it was not until 1992 that a national government completely free of military influence became a reality. This was the year in which the "cell phone mob" of mostly middle-class Thais took to the streets of Bangkok to soundly defeat the last attempt by the military to manipulate the civilian government (Callahan, 1998; Murray, 1996; Pasuk & Baker, 1996).

The image of a "banana republic" run by and for corrupt military generals, however, is inaccurate for Thailand from 1932 to 1992. The Thai military has been nationalistic, often populist, and some factions even socialist. Because the military has been one of the most open institutions for the poor and rural people in Thailand its reputation is that of protectorate of the common people against the affluent and urban educated elites. Military coups have at times occurred because the general population as well as the military resented the amount of corruption in government. As we will see in the next chapter, it was during the 1950s and 1960s that successful economic development policies started Thailand on the road to solid economic development and poverty reduction. None of this is to praise Thai military governments, nor to say they have been free of corruption themselves. But unless one recognizes that Thai military governments have not always been negative for the interests of Thai people, the economic achievements of the last 40 years cannot be adequately understood.

In contrast to the Western image of governments, particularly the American image, it is also important to consider the independent influence of the highly educated career civil servants in running the Thai government. Often seen as a representative of the king or emperor in other Asian countries, the government ministry typically has had broad power in Asian societies, and generally continues to have extensive powers today. Elected officials seldom have expertise or sufficient staff, are often corrupt, and usually spend most of their time trying to get themselves reelected. The Thai political system was best characterized as a bureaucratic polity (Riggs, 1966). In many policy areas even today the Thai parliament can pass only general legislation with implementation left to the government bureaucracy. An example might be a particular tax where the parliament can set the maximum rate but the bureaucracy manages the rate anywhere below that level. On most details of government, these unelected government bureaucrats have extensive power and independence, sometimes allowing them to take actions they believe are in the interests of the country as a whole rather than the narrow interests of one group of politicians or big business. While the Thai bureaucracy has never been as powerful as in some Asian countries such as Japan, and while the Thai bureaucracy is finding its power falling with more influence by elected officials under the new constitution of 1997, it remains power-ful. The Thai bureaucratic elite, educated in some of the best universities in Thailand and the West, continue to have a heavy hand on the economic policies that helped guide Thailand out of the Asian economic crisis of 1997 more quickly than most other governments in East and Southeast Asia.

What we find in Thailand today would *not* look very familiar to Thais alive more than 100 years ago. The growing affluence, the extensive Western influence, and smaller things like the disappearance of almost all the klongs (canals) in favor of paved roads all make for a very different Thailand today. But many more things are quite con-stant: Thais have maintained their own government and independence, their national boundaries have changed very little over the past few hundred years, the ethnic mix of the nation is little different, and the Buddhist religious and cultural influences have not changed much. Like the majority of young men in Cambodia, Laos, and Burma, Thai men in their late teens and early 20s continue the tradition of becoming monks for a period of time so that everywhere the country remains dotted with the saffron-colored robes of monks.

Thailand, in summary, is a country that provides us with a case of relative economic success in a region of many failures. The Thailand of today was passed down from an ancient civilization firmly influenced by the Theravada Buddhism that came to dominate the region long before the kingdom of Thailand emerged. While not quite as ancient as some of its neighbors, the kingdom of Thailand was on an *ascending* trajectory when European powers came upon the scene. This position of relative strength, and astute kings, allowed Thailand to escape being colonized, though to some degree they had to compromise their national sovereignty. But with relative independence and a sufficient sense of elite responsibility and a hard state (or a *semihard state* which I will describe in the next chapter), Thailand has been able to institute and carry out reasonably successful plans for economic development. These development plans can be traced back to the reform kings Mongkut (Rama IV) and his son Chulalongkorn (Rama V) during the sec-ond half of the nineteenth century. In an attempt to modernize at this time, Thailand fol-lowed a path somewhat similar to Japan's Meiji Restoration, though with less success. However, a relatively modern state bureaucracy finally emerged that was able to guide development policies that led to significant economic development with dramatic poverty reduction in the second half of the twentieth century.

A Visit to a Thai Village

In attempting to understand conditions of poverty in less developed countries we most often need to turn our attention to rural villages. As we have seen, a majority of all the world's poor reside in small villages that continue to shape their life chances even in the age of globalization. Small villages in some parts of the world can encourage their peo-ple to take advantages of new economic realities and provide protection when things do not go well. In other parts of the world village culture and social organization can make people fearful of the outside and withdrawn, and at times village support disintegrates when faced with social change. Most of East and Southeast Asia are fortunate because of their village organization. In many cases the poor in this part of the world have the advantages of protection through a village clan that make their lives more secure than many of the American poor.

This is in part why figures showing Thailand has a relatively low rate of inequality and poverty are sometimes difficult to believe. When arriving in Bangkok, especially by train, one cannot miss what seems to be appalling conditions of poverty. All along the train tracks are squatters' shacks of scrap tin, plywood, and cardboard. Whole families can be seen crowded into these small spaces, sitting on the floor, cooking on little charcoal burners, with filthy polluted water all around for children to fall into. Affluent urban Thais, but especially tourists from rich countries, find it difficult to believe people can live in such conditions. These slum people "must be" very poor, likely hungry, and one can imagine all kinds of illnesses from living in such conditions. While there are far too many people in Thailand who fit such descriptions, the overall impression given by these "shanty towns" along the roads and train tracks can be quite misleading. A trip to the Thai countryside can help us understand this point, along with several others about the relatively low rates of rural poverty in Thailand.

A few years ago I began periodic visits to a small village in Thailand about one and a half hours' drive north of Bangkok. A Swiss friend of mine had been spending a lot of time in the village for a couple of years and invited me along. During my first visit I stayed a few days in the home of a family my friend had gotten to know well. The village, I will call it Ban Sue, is quite standard for central Thailand. The family I stayed with, as is the tradition, is part of an extended family or clan (about 600 people in this case) who all live close together in the village. There are 5 separate clans in Ban Sue, each clan living in a separate area of the village. The specific household of my hosts consisted of an elderly grandfather and the families of two of his children (one divorced daughter with her single-mother daughter and child, one married daughter with her husband and daughter). The

Villages such as the one pictured here (above, left) have been important in Thailand's good record of poverty reduction. The village people have control over land, which has improved their standards of living as government programs stimulated agricultural development even before urban industry. The people of this Bangkok slum (above, right) are mostly from the village pictured to the left. Visits to this village help one understand the connection between rural development in Thailand, as well as why people who seem desperately poor and homeless in these Bangkok slums are actually not so poor.

house, as almost all others in the village, is simple—a roof of tin and ceramic tile, wooden floors, and walls that have many cracks and holes where the rain can blow in during the monsoon season. There is very little furniture and people sleep on mats thrown on the floor in the evening. They had yet to get running water during my first visit and had only "outdoor toilets." They bathe in the front yard area in "Thai style" using stored rainwater or filtered river water wearing a cloth (called *pakhaoma* for men and *mathung* for women) covering important body parts while throwing water over your head. When I visited the village in 2002, about 2 years after my first visit, a crude fresh water delivery system had been installed, but the outhouses and outdoor Thai-style showers remained. Electricity is now in every house and some of the better-off families have small refrigerators, electric rice cookers, and even TV sets and stereos. Meals are usually prepared on small stoves using bottled gas, though charcoal braziers are also common. Food is plentiful, and I should add, the dinners I enjoyed were as good as in most Thai restaurants. When I last visited this village in 2004 not much had changed, though the people were somewhat better off. Some in the village clan had started a new wholesale greenhouse business on their lands to supply some landscaping companies in Bangkok.

As is the case in every Thai village (except in the four southern provinces with a majority Muslim population), the Buddhist wat (temple), with beautiful architecture and bright colors, dominates family and community life. In Ban Sue, in fact, there are two competing wats, with differing clans supporting one or the other. All important events take place there—weddings, funerals, festivals—though now there are government-funded schools so secular education is no longer a main task of the monks. Each clan, no matter how poor, competes to provide most to the wat, often organizing the clan to build a new structure for some function. (The clan of my host family had recently built a small library or reading building within the wat compound.)

I have described conditions in this typical Thai village, in part, to convey the impression of an absence of extreme poverty. People from rich countries would of course consider themselves poor without running water or if they lived in any of the houses found in the village. But while living conditions might be relatively crude by rich nation standards, these people have security in knowing they will not want of basic necessities, especially food, housing, and government-provided health care. My informants and I estimated that half or more of the people in this village live at or perhaps below the average daily wage for Thailand ($4 to $6 per day depending on the recently fluctuating exchange rate, though closer to $9 per day with the new Purchasing Power Parity index). But again, it is hard to think of these people as extremely poor, nor do they consider themselves so.[2] In the household of my hosts, for example, of the seven people, only the young single mother and the married couple had outside income, though there was occasional income from selling rice when the harvest was good. The three people with relatively stable incomes earned their money from selling things in Bangkok. The single mother, however, had recently helped start the wholesale greenhouse business of the clan which has good promise for more income.

It is also important to recognize that villages such as these in Thailand have several advantages when compared to other people in developing countries around the world. First, and very important for rural people, is that the land is under their control (though short of actual ownership). The Thai king and religious organizations own much of the land in Thailand and it is distributed somewhat equally to peasant families for many generations. One of the local wats of Ban Sue actually owns the land where my host family built their home many years ago, but it was leased to this family indefinitely for a one-time cost of $2. In addition, each family in the clan has farmland provided for their use, enough land to grow rice, vegetables, and fruit for their own needs, with some left to sell in the open market for cash in good years. This is also the land where some of the clan members have started a new wholesale greenhouse business. Second, much like the advanced industrial nations (except for the United States), all people of Thailand are provided health care at very low cost (currently about $0.75 per doctor or hospital visit). While some villagers in remote areas of Thailand may at times find it difficult to get to these services, this is not the case for most villages such as Ban Sue.

A third major asset of village life in Thailand is a strong, extended family system with traditions of taking care of their own, or what Phillips (the respected anthropologist who studied village Thailand many years ago) called the "practical reciprocity of benefits in the family" (Phillips, 1965). As is the norm, the 600 or so clan members in the village where I was hosted are obligated to take care of each other. One young woman with a small child, for example, had recently been abandoned by her husband and had no money or a home. She was given a place to stay and food for as long as it was needed, and clan members nursed her back to health after a suicide attempt. There was also the seemingly typical clan (town) drunk, tolerated and taken care of by other clan members. (He liked me for some reason and often followed me around the village.) The elderly, of course, are also taken care of by the extended clan. In a few cases where the grandfather or grandmother no longer have a living spouse or adult children in the village, the clan compound had a ready solution: One of the larger houses had been turned into a sort of in-family "old folks home" where five widows and one widower live together. More common was the household of my host family: Grandfather was a widower who had an honored place in the home of his children, grandchildren, and two great-grandchildren.

More generally there is a tendency in the village clan to share material possessions. Clan members, for example, ordinarily can walk into the homes of other clan members, open the refrigerator, and help themselves. This is no doubt a reason for a pattern I asked about after staying with this family: After a couple of days I noticed some more affluent homes just outside the clan compounds surrounded by rather imposing fences. I was told these are members of the clan who became more affluent in various ways and then moved into private areas. I was told that "getting money is like adding water to the river." There is, to some extent, the rather common peasant village disincentive for much personal gain when so much would simply be money obligated to the extended family. Thais, nonetheless, seem individualistic enough to impose limits when they become significantly above the average standard of living in the village.

I have described conditions in Ban Sue in part to dispel the misleading images that Westerners, and even most urban Thais, have of poverty in Thailand. People seen in slum areas of Bangkok (such as along the train tracks and in Klong Toey), people who seem to be homeless and living in rather deplorable conditions, are quite often people from small villages such as Ban Sue. The exact numbers are in dispute, but attempts to gain information about these Bangkok "slum people" confirm that many, and perhaps even most, are living in these squatter slums temporarily or seasonally to work in unskilled jobs or sell things on street corners (Sopon, 1992). Conditions for these Bangkok slum people are harsh and unhealthy, but to the extent these people have only temporarily migrated to these slums from villages like Ban Sue, the situation is not as negative as it would be otherwise. In many ways they have advantages over the American poor; they have an extended family system able to help them, and government health care when they become ill.

My Swiss friend and I had visited a squatters' village the locals call Pratunam slum along the train tracks in one section of Bangkok before I was first hosted by the people of Ban Sue. After my first stay in the village we were invited to visit other people in the Pratunam slum area, even receiving a dinner invitation over the next couple of years. As I described briefly in beginning this book, on my first visit to Pratunam slum, Nok, a young mother of one child, made dinner for us as we sat on a scrapwood bench less than 5 feet from the train tracks. Nok is one of the clan members of Ban Sue village, a close friend of a member of my host family in the village. Nok had been living in the slum with her mother for a couple of years, working as a maid in Bangkok. She had a beautiful 5-year-old daughter who enjoyed our attention throughout the dinner, practicing the few English words she was already learning in the neighborhood school. Nok, her mother, and daughter lived in what could only be called a shack made of scrapwood and tin, with a small room for sleeping and a kind of outside patio area facing the tracks where they cook and eat. We were surprised to find they also have a covered "bathroom" in a small third room (though, of course, with no running water).

Nok's situation, however, is not quite as typical, nor as secure, as many in Pratunam slum. She and her mother do not have a house back in Ban Sue village, though if they needed to move back to the village there is no doubt that someone in the clan would take them in. Unlike other village clan members in Pratunam slum as we ate that evening, Nok would not go back that weekend, and would in fact return with her mother and daughter only a few times during the year for important holidays. As is more typical, we met some people whom we had seen earlier in the village who live in Pratunam slum only a few days each week. One man, for example, was a fruit vender in the Pratunam area of Bangkok. As he described to us, it is not so difficult to set yourself up as a fruit vender. A little money for a cart is needed, and of course some for the initial inventory to sell for the day. These food vendors usually get up around 2:30 a.m. when the night markets for fresh farm produce are in full swing, buy the food they will sell, prepare it, and hit the streets of Bangkok with their carts full by 6:00 a.m. The vendors from a village such as Ban Sue often must borrow money (perhaps $100 or so) from unofficial "money lenders" around the slum area, then repay the loan in a few days at rates of about 20 percent interest. (Because of this, one of the first programs the new Thai prime minister of 2001, Thaksin, created to help low-income people was a People's Bank that loans small sums of money [$100 to $300] to such street vendors or other little businesses low-income people are trying to start at a more reasonable 5 percent interest rate [*Bangkok Post,* June 25, 2001].)

There are certainly villages in Thailand that are much poorer than Ban Sue. Most of these are in the northeast of Thailand, close to the Laotian border, as well as in northern Thailand where hill tribe people have been resettled. But these very poor villages are more the exception as the rate of people living on less than $1 per day in Thailand is less than 1 or 2 percent. There are also people in Bangkok slums that are much worse off than most of the people along the train tracks of Pratunam slum. The Thais who are integrated into village clans, however, have a place to return to and plenty of people who can help them through hard times.

Burma: The Preconditions for Disorder

As the twenty-first century began, the economic and political contrast between Thailand and Burma could not be much greater. While Burmese military dictators continue to disallow international agencies to collect economic information in the country, the general consensus is that Burma is the poorest nation in the region, and among the 5 or 10 poorest countries in the world today. It is also one of the most politically repressive with a harsh military dictatorship in control for 40 years. This has especially been the case since the 1991 Nobel Peace Prize winner, Aung San Suu Kyi, was placed under house arrest in Rangoon in 1990 after the military government's blunder of calling free elections to appease mass demonstrations and international condemnation (*International Herald Tribune*, August 29, 2000; Steinberg, 2001). The 1990 elections were surprisingly free, Suu Kyi's political coalition won a huge majority, and the military promptly overturned the election results to remain in complete power. Suu Kyi was briefly released from house arrest in the spring of 2002 after long U.N.-sponsored negotiations, but just as quickly put back under arrest where she remained as of 2005.[3]

All labor and civic organizations of any kind remain illegal. It is against the law to own a computer (much less be connected to the Web), invite a foreigner into your home, and in some places to even wear Western clothing in public. (Men and women have been required to wear the traditional wraparound skirt called a surang.) All urban universities have remained closed for more than 10 years for fear of student protests like those which exploded in violence during a brief liberalization in 1988, with some 10,000 people killed by the military (*International Herald Tribune*, November 15 & 22, 2000; Smith 1999:16). This country is so closely controlled and closed to outsiders that after the December 2004 tsunami the military dictators would not let aid workers or journalists visit affected coastal areas. The dictators told the outside world that less than 100 people were killed, compared to about 6,000 just a few miles down the coast in Thailand. We know many more were killed, but as of now the world can do nothing to help.

Until very recently, foreign journalists were barred from all parts of the country, which is why the name for the country in the press is again Burma. (Military dictators continue to require all journalists to use the precolonial name of Myanmar or be expelled from the country. Because almost all were expelled anyway, the name of the country in the Western press is again Burma.) Since 2003 the country has been opened to some extent. A personal interview at the Burmese Embassy in Bangkok, for example, is no longer required for first-time visitors. (This was how the dictators attempted to keep journalists and nosey sociologists out of the country who might write bad things about them later.) Still, foreigners are restricted to main cities and non-Southeast Asian foreigners cannot enter Burma overland but must fly into the capital.

When Burma became the first Southeast Asian country to gain independence in 1948 there were predictions that it would become a leading economy of the region (Fallows, 1994:327; Kristof & WuDunn, 2000:319). Burma was rich in natural resources and the leading exporter of rice. Even in 1962, just before the more repressive military dictatorship began, Burma was exporting over 1 million tons of rice per year; today it is less than 70,000 tons. Political instability and economic collapse, however, began almost immediately after Burma gained independence in 1948. There has been consistent guerilla warfare with various hill tribe nations from the beginning, with the Burmese military today consuming over 40 percent of the government budget. The economy is sustained by $3 billion in annual smuggling profits which account for more than 40 percent of the overall GNP (Smith, 1999:24–25).

Despite the harsh military dictatorship, the country and its people have held their charm through it all. There are some of the most beautiful and most numerous Buddhist monuments to be seen anywhere in Asia. But walking around the country today makes one feel he or she is in a time warp. Little seems to have changed since the British were kicked out of the region by the Japanese at the beginning of World War II. Among the old temples and palaces, the old British buildings are still there, crumbling; the old cars and buses are still there too, rusting. Perhaps more than anything else, it is striking that the streets seem so empty of any vehicles after one has been traveling through the other countries of Southeast Asia, including Laos.

What is now considered Burma began among some of the oldest kingdoms in the region. For our focus, perhaps the key word is *kingdoms*. Even earlier than in Thailand, people originally migrated into what is now Burma from China some 3,000 to 4,000 years ago as hunter-gatherers or simple horticultural tribes. The dominant kingdom, Pagan, first appeared as a city in the mid-ninth century (Myint-u, 2001; Taylor, 1999:164–167.) Like the first kings of Thailand in Sukothai somewhat later, the moral principles of Theravada Buddhism were followed, but the kings themselves were not considered godlike as they were among Khmers in Angkor or later Thai kings. This also meant the Pagan kings were less powerful and were at times in competition with Theravada Buddhist monks for influence (Aung-Thwin, 1985). From the beginning there were also rival kingdoms, such as a Mon kingdom in the southern part of what is now Burma which was based on sea trade, primarily with Sri Lanka.

Pagan's dominance was much shorter, and less grand, than that of the Khmers during the Angkor period, but for three centuries both kingdoms dominated Southeast Asia, with Pagan in the north and Angkor in the south of the mainland. After a period of dominance in the north that lasted less than 300 years, however, the Mongol conquest of Yunnan Province in southern China led to Shan people moving further south to rival Pagan influence. By the 1300s another rival kingdom, the Mon kingdom at Pegu, also emerged. Then there were the Thais, who began their rise as a kingdom in 1253, but became the more dominant kingdom after the Thais moved their capital to Ayudhya. There was also diversity and conflict *within* the kingdom of Pagan. Some of the inscriptions on buildings erected in the early years of Pagan's dominance were in four languages, indicating even then that there was significant ethnic diversity. It was this ethnic diversity and conflict, as well as rival kingdoms and the comparative weakness of Pagan kings without a godlike status, that led to Pagan's weakening and eventual decline as a regional power (Taylor, 1999:166, 168).

For understanding Burma's poverty today, the next important stage of its history was British colonization. India had always mattered most to the British, with Burma (or greater India as it was first called) something of an afterthought (Osborne, 1995:64; Smith, 1999:40). In a major blunder, the Burmese king of the time ordered his troops to attack the British in 1853 (Pye, 1985:96–98). The British had already been attacked as early as the late 1700s by tribal groups inside Burma, and after 1853 the British decided to move into Burma to protect the borders of their Indian possession. Burma was formally brought into the British Empire in 1886, first as part of India. Under British dominance very little was done to help develop the country's economy or infrastructure as was done by the British elsewhere, especially in Malaysia (Stockwell, 1999:14, 26; Turnbull, 1999:262–263). The British did not even train Burmese to run their colony as they had done elsewhere but rather brought in Indians for the purpose. Most harmful for the future of Burma, however, were the national borders drawn by the British which remain to this day. Many tribal people were brought into Burmese boundaries who had never identified with the dominant Burmese or trusted them (Smith, 1999:27–28, 45–51). To make matters worse, British Protestant missionaries began to focus their activities on these hill tribe people, especially the Karen in the south and east, winning a high percentage of converts. Not only did this create conflict with the highly religious Theravada Buddhists in the dominant Burmese areas, but it also presented the hill tribe people as Western colonial collaborators. By the time the Japanese pushed the British out of Burma at the early stages of World War II, more than most Southeast Asian people, many Burmese welcomed the Japanese as liberators. With subsequent Japanese behavior in the area, however, support for the Japanese was short-lived.

At the end of World War II the British moved back into the area, but only briefly. Burma became the first former colony in Southeast Asia to gain independence in 1948. In a big contrast to Malaysia, the British again had little interest in Burma and withdrew from the country without any significant help in planning for the independence of Burma (Stockwell, 1999:14; Turnbull, 1999:263). Among the most important problems were the new borders created by the British which included many small former kingdoms or national homelands of hill tribe people; the problem was simply left ambiguous by the withdrawing British. Earlier the British had encouraged the Burmese to include the contested hill tribe areas, but then told the hill tribe peoples they should be included only if they chose to do so. British General Mountbatten gave support to Aung San (the father of Suu Kyi) just before the British made their exit, hoping that Aung San could become a leader able to unite the nation the British had created as colonial powers, as well as counter potential communist popularity. But Aung San quickly changed his mind about allowing any autonomy that the hill tribe people were demanding, and almost as quickly, was assassinated in 1947 (Smith, 1999:75; Stockwell, 1999:24). The new Burmese government was faced with rebellion on its fringes from the very beginning of independence. To make matters worse, Protestant missionaries continued to convert hill tribe people and encouraged them to fight against the "godless Buddhist" Burmese rulers. Among the first was a rogue British Army officer who helped train and organize the Karenni and Karens. Then came American missionaries (particularly Seventh Day Adventists) in the 1950s, including one who was most likely a CIA agent and became something of a "saint" to people of the Wa and Lahu tribes (Smith, 1999:114, 148, 282–288).

The Burmese nation was left with guerilla war and weak governments throughout the 1950s. By 1962, General Ne Win regained power in a coup that created a harsh military dictatorship that has continued rather unbroken to this day. Overnight, Burma became one of the most isolated countries in the world. Ne Win's infamous Burmese way to socialism meant kicking out all foreigners (including all Indians who had helped run the country, Ford Foundation projects, and Fulbright scholars), nationalizing all industries, and closing the country. It was a move that opted them out of the world system as completely as the Chinese had done under Mao (Smith, 1999:98, 195–196). But in contrast to China, this is how Burma remained for decades, with only the brief interlude of attempted liberalization in 1988 and then the canceled elections of 1990 won overwhelmingly by Suu Kyi's coalition (Steinberg, 2001). By the 1990s the generals still controlling the country gave up all pretense of any Burmese way to socialism and started milking the country. Still today, all the scant foreign investment and aid Burma has been able to obtain must be channeled through the generals who reportedly take their cut and make sure friends and relatives are partners in any new business ventures (*International Herald Tribune,* November 22, 2000).

Burma, in short, presents us with the case of a Southeast Asian nation that is rooted in old civilizations, possessing old traditions of moral responsibilities among elites and the Asian values like other Buddhist nations of Southeast Asia. But an old problem persisted and was made much worse by British colonialism. More than 1,000 years ago the region that is now Burma had kingdom and ethnic rivalries to a far greater degree than Thailand, Cambodia, or Vietnam. The manner in which the British created Burmese national borders, especially leaving the colony with ambiguities about the inclusion of ancient hill tribe nations, ensured extensive political instability for decades to come. Even if Burmese governments had created more realistic development policies (in contrast to Ne Win's Burmese way to socialism) they would have been powerless to carry them through. Furthermore, the British were never seriously committed to developing their Burmese colony and took it primarily to guard their prize possession of India. In striking contrast to Thailand, this treatment by the colonial power was possible because Burma was weak and in decline for centuries before European colonialism arrived in Southeast Asia.

Laos: The Preconditions for Stagnation

Laos is a country seemingly stuck in time. Little appears to be happening in the economy (except for the negative impact of the 1997 Asian economic crisis) or government (where the leaders of the communist politburo are almost all over 70 years old). A walk through the capital, Vientiane, quickly shows that it is one of the poorest countries in the world, as World Bank figures indicate. Food is plentiful and there was no mass hunger as in Vietnam during the 1980s before Communist Party officials finally instituted their economic reforms. All of the other scenes, however, suggests a poor country that is making little progress. After visiting the capitals of equally poor Burma and Cambodia, one can see that while those countries were once not so poor, Laos has never had a much higher standard of living. The old but once grand buildings of the Burmese and Cambodian capitals are nowhere to be seen in Vientiane. There are a few old and crumbling French colonial-style homes built during the colonial period, but it seems many could collapse any day, and very little has been built since the colonial period. A blanket of dust seems to cover much of the city. Even airplanes landing at the new airport sometimes kick up clouds of dust.

After several visits to Vientiane in the 1990s, then again in 2000 and 2001, during the spring of 2002 I was surprised to see that the old crumbling French colonial house containing one of my favorite restaurants had been refurbished and that the plaza circle and fountain in the center of the city had been restored. Then in 2004 I was surprised to see a new Japanese factory being built. These, however, were the biggest changes I had seen during several years of visiting Laos. Not that Laos is an unappealing country; the people are among the most charming in Asia, the food can be excellent, there are quaint little shops (such as the old but well-stocked wine shop still run by a old Frenchman which seems like an oasis in the region of poverty), and traditional crafts such as silk weaving are highly respected. After spending time in crowded, noisy, and polluted cities such as Bangkok, Vientiane can be quite inviting.

It should also be said that despite having a communist government since 1975 there is comparatively less political repression and Buddhism flourishes as always. Except for the "reeducation camps" soon after 1975, Laotian communism has usually been more of a softer variety (Warner, 1995, 1996). There have been atrocities committed by the communist government against Hmong hill tribe people still inside Laos who fought with the Americans in the CIA secret war in Laos from the early 1960s until 1975 (Hamilton-Merritt, 1999). To this day there is occasional fighting between Hmong rebels hiding in the jungle and government forces. However, there is little evidence of the military or police in daily life throughout most of Laos. Despite communism's rejection of religion, the Buddhist monuments in Laotian cities such as Vientiane and Luang Prabang are among the most beautiful to be found in Asia, though mostly in desperate need of repair. Monks are seen in all the wats, though not as numerous on the streets as in Thailand. There was some attempt to play down religion during the earlier years of the communist rule in Laos, but it was never pushed very far. Some scholars suggest that Laos should be described as postsocialist today, though most also agree that Laotians seldom had their hearts into being communist in the first place (Evans, 1998, 1999a, 1999b).

Laos, however, is an increasingly troubled and tense nation. The Laotian economy was hit harder by the Asian economic crisis of 1997 than most, and since 1999 a low-level terrorist bombing campaign has continued. Inflation hit 160 percent in 1999, but has settled down to around 10 percent since 2001. The Laotian currency, the kip, has lost 90 percent of its value since 1997. At the end of 2001 there was less than a few weeks' worth of hard currency in the country, and by one estimate the average income of Laotians is less than $1 per day. Foreign assistance makes up about 16 percent of the country's GNP and 80 percent of its public investment (BBC News, 2000, 2001; *Los Angeles Times*, December 27, 2000; World Bank, 2001c). The terrorist bombing campaign in operation since 1999 has so far killed only a couple of people and injured a few dozen people. But there have been several bombings in places such as the central market, central bus station, the airport, and the immigration control station at the Friendship Bridge linking Laos and Thailand across the Mekong River. No one has claimed responsibility for the bombings, but some speculation claims that the campaign is led by one faction of the Communist Party of Laos angry at the inaction and ineptitude of the Laotian Communist Party compared to economic progress being made in neighboring Vietnam today (Dakin, 2003:266–269; *International Herald Tribune*, July 21, 2000, August 1, 2000). As with the other countries of Southeast Asia, one must consider Laotian history, and the effects of colonialism and its aftermath to understand the predicament of the country today.

In a sense Laos did not exist before being created by the French during colonial domination (Evans, 1998, 1999a:1; Ivarsson, 1999; Stuart-Fox, 1997:6–19). The country was established through treaties between France and neighboring Thailand from 1893 to 1907 (Osborne, 2000; Stuart-Fox, 1997:6). Like the other nations of Southeast Asia, there have been humans in the area for thousands of years. But in the landlocked area that is now Laos there were no kingdoms able to unite people or exert regional power anywhere close to the level of ancient Burma, Cambodia, Thailand, or Vietnam. Through the 1400s the area was controlled by the Khmers (Cambodia). Following Khmer dominance there was a brief period of relative independence so that some small kingdoms could develop. One of the earliest Europeans in the area by the 1600s, a Portugese explorer, wrote in surprise, "so many kingdoms!" (Andaya, 1999:59). At that time there were three principal kingdoms: Vientiane toward the center of what is now Laos, Luang Prabang in the north, and Champassak in the south. A small kingdom called Lan Na in the north (centered in what is now the Thai city of Chiang Mai) covered some of the area claimed as Laos today, but by the 1600s had already been taken by Thailand (Andaya, 1999:84–85; Wyatt & Wichienkeeo, 1998). From the 1700s these small kingdoms were dominated almost completely by either Thailand, Burma, or Vietnam (Kathirithamby-Wells, 1999:238). In 1827 Vientiane attempted a rebellion against Thai control for the last time and lost badly. Consequently, Lan Na, Luang Prabang, and Vientiane were still vassal states of Thailand in the late 1800s when France created Laos as a colony (Evans, 1998:89).

Somewhat like Burma's colonization by the British, Laos became a French colony almost as an afterthought. The French prize was Vietnam, and only after Vietnam was secured did the French move westward into Laos and Cambodia. What the French took in 1885 had never been a unified nation, so even before its independence in the twentieth century the French tried to create some national symbols for Laotians and organize a more specifically Laotian order of Buddhist religious leaders (Evans, 1998:50). But other than this, the French did little. The development of infrastructure was inconsequential. As with the British in Burma, the French brought outsiders (mainly Vietnamese) to help run the colonial administration (Osborne, 1995:70, 176).

After the French were quickly defeated by Germany in World War II and Japan began taking Southeast Asia, there was a joint French–Japanese colonial dominance of the old colonies previously held by independent France (Vietnam, Cambodia, and Laos). As Japan was defeated, the country we think of as Laos today became an independent nation for the first time in 1945. But Laos quickly lost their independence again as the French elected to move back into their old Indochinese colonies. With Vietnam fighting their nationalist war against the French from this time, however, the French were little interested in Laos and Cambodia. Finally, when the French were defeated by Ho Chi Minh in 1953, Laos was again independent. A kingdom was established but there was little sense of political or national identity among Laotians. Polls in the 1950s found only 60 percent of Laotians actually knew they were Laotians or could give the name of their king who decided to stay in Luang Prabang instead of moving to the new capital established in Vientiane (Cheong, 1999:74; Evans, 1998:93–96). The end of the American stage of the Vietnam War in 1975 again brought change to the Laotian doorstep. With a Laotian government destabilized by U.S. actions beginning in 1960 and lasting until 1975 (such as massive bombing and secret operations to organize hill tribe rebels), it was relatively easy for the communist Pathet Lao to take power at about the same time the North Vietnamese communist government took over the south of Vietnam, and the communist Khmer Rouge took Cambodia (Warner, 1995, 1996).

With the founding of the Lao People's Democratic Republic (PDR), the Communist Party went about the usual business of establishing a new political economy and removing old class inequalities. Compared to their Vietnamese communist cousins, however, they were less successful. The formal aspects of the Laotian language showing strict deference ranking were outlawed, the *wai* (a kind of bow with the hands clasped as in prayer) to show deference to higher ranked individuals was prohibited, monks were controlled, and old religious monuments were no longer important symbols of the new nation. None of this lasted long (Evans, 1998:84–87). Even before the 1990s the wai was used just as openly as in Thailand; the status markers in the language and status distinctions in dress returned; the monks never became politicalized; and the communist government eventually recognized the Buddhist songha as a vital institution, bringing back important religious ceremonies with even the Communist Party elite showing their support for Buddhism (Stuart-Fox, 1997:194). The new 1991 constitution, for example, brought back the central religious shrine, That Luang, as the national symbol, which again was pictured on Laotian currency. Recognizing their failure to effect much change in the country, and especially their failure to create significant national identity, the Communist Party finally tried to create a cult of personality around their founding leader, Kaysone. That attempt equally failed. What transpired, however, was an informal recognition of Thai royalty as the national symbol by 60 percent of the population with ethnic Tai roots. One daughter of the current Thai king is particularly respected and often visits Laos for important ceremonies.

On the economic side, the first actions of the Communist Party from 1975 were typically Soviet style, and just as typically disastrous. There was both nationalization of industry and farm collectivization. Kaysone began his economic policies with a speech about the need for three transformations. First would be change in the "relations of production" (i.e., state ownership), then scientific and technical transformation (to help achieve a modern industry), and finally a cultural transformation to the "new socialist man and woman" (Stuart-Fox, 1997:169). The first step was nationalization of industry, though some were allowed to become joint state–private firms. Foreign oil companies were out. Farm collectivization started seriously by 1978. Kaysone had called for a gradual process toward farm collectivization, but enthusiastic party officials pushed it at a fast pace, resulting in some 2,800 farm collectives created in a year. The most important and immediate reaction was flight. By late 1976 some 20,000 Chinese and 15,000 Vietnamese had left the country with most of their wealth. Then there was almost complete economic collapse and runaway inflation, followed by government price controls and restrictions on free movement of goods and people which made the situation worse (Stuart-Fox, 1997:172–180). Peasants rebelled against collectivization and began fleeing, destroying crops and livestock.

By 1979 even Soviet and Vietnamese advisors were calling for the Laotian government to back away from old Soviet-style economic policies. Top party officials were also convinced. Kaysone called for the suspension of collectivization and began to encourage private entrepreneurs. Controls on the free movement of goods were relaxed and prices of farm products were raised. Agricultural production jumped 16 percent by 1980, but the rest of the economy remained stagnant (Stuart-Fox, 1997:182–199). GNP fell further by 1982 and 1983. By 1984 industry still accounted for only 5 percent of

GNP, a level well below the average for the least developed countries in the world. The World Bank and Asian Development Bank, which were surprisingly never kicked out by the Lao PDR, were asked to increase aid, but with government expenditures continuing at twice the rate of revenues the situation did not improve. The biggest outcome of economic reforms and openness was increased corruption by government officials. With the situation becoming more desperate, Kaysone called (in a politically correct manner) for the abandonment of socialism. His call was for a "new economic mechanism," but other party officials strongly resisted. Further economic decline and a drought in 1987 finally brought more agreement within the party, and even the IMF demand to open up the economy for more foreign investment was endorsed by the party. A major problem, of course, was that under the circumstances very few foreign investors were willing to come in.

All of this forced Laos to move toward eliminating a Soviet-style economy even before the Vietnamese did so with their Doi Moi. But the problem for Laos was that it had very little resources, few educated people, little infrastructure, and little national unity from its very different history and treatment under French neglect to make economic reforms pay off. Laos today remains mostly dependent on foreign aid. More educated Laotians live abroad than in Laos. The old guard remains on top in the party. There is one ray of hope, however. In 2001, a respected former finance minister, Bounyang Vorachit, was elected prime minister, bringing the chance that Laos can find some way out of its economic problems as its Vietnamese neighbors seem to have begun (*Bangkok Post*, March 15 & 28, 2001).

In contrast to Burma and Thailand, as well as Cambodia and Vietnam, it is hard to describe the nation of Laos as possessing an ancient civilization, or at least a unified one. The Lao People's Democratic Republic has tried to recreate a history for Laos that claims ancient roots, but the reality is that Laos today is an aggregate of old tribal groupings created by French colonialism where only some 60 percent of the people speak one of the main Lao Lum languages (Evans, 1998; Stuart-Fox, 1997:6, 192). Laos lacks the political traditions, national identity, or even sufficient religious symbols of unity because the other 40 percent of the population is primarily made up of non-Buddhist hill tribe people. In contrast to Vietnam, Laos received only the negative fruits of colonialism; Laos, Cambodia, and Vietnam experienced the most disruption from colonialism in the region, but at least the French regarded Vietnam as an economic prize and helped with infrastructure development. The postcolonial period was in some ways less disruptive for Laos than either Cambodia or Vietnam. But though the Lao People's Republic rejected bankrupt socialist economic policies more quickly than Vietnam, Laos has much less human, political, and material capital for economic development.

Cambodia: The Preconditions for Disaster

In comparison to Laos, the end of colonialism in Cambodia was far more traumatic and devastating to the country and its people. Today, Cambodia's symbol of past glory (Angkor Wat) and recent horrors (the killing fields) stand side-by-side.[4] The temples of Angkor were built by the Khmer civilization that dominated the central mainland of Southeast Asia from the ninth to the fourteenth centuries. There are more than 100 temples in the complex, and the main temple (Angkor Wat) is said to be the largest religious structure in the world. But around the central part of the country are the killing fields; the most notorious is Choeung Ek outside Phnom Penh where some 17,000 of the 1.7 million were murdered by the Khmer Rouge. It is in Choeung Ek that the most educated and talented of Cambodia's people were taken to be killed after torture in the Tuol Sleng high school turned into prison holding camp by the Khmer Rouge. As accurately depicted in the movie *"The Killing Fields,"* when the Khmer Rouge took power in 1975, one of the first orders of business was to clear Phnom Penh of all its people. But it was the educated—teachers, businesspeople, and Cambodia's professional elite—they most wanted to eliminate to achieve their goal of erasing modern, and especially Western, influence from Cambodia. Consequently, most of the 9,000 skulls staring out from the memorial pagoda at the Choeung Ek killing fields today are the remains of these best and brightest of pre-Khmer Rouge Cambodia. Pictures taken of Phnom Penh from the air by the Vietnamese military entering the city after they defeated the Khmer Rouge in 1979 show a city completely deserted and in ruin. A result of all the killing and mass migration is that today a large percentage of people living in Phnom Penh are former peasants. About *300 people with a college degree* were all Cambodia had left after Pol Pot's killing fields. Some regions of Cambodia today have 50 percent of the people living in female-headed households, and no region has less than 20 percent. Many scholars claim there has been a breakdown of the old Cambodian community spirit and sense of obligation, and a fear or mistrust of other humans (Kamm, 1998:6–13). Everyone in Cambodia today, it is said, has lost a close relative to Pol Pot's killing between 1975 and 1979. Checking for myself by asking Cambodians I have met while traveling in the country, the description seems accurate. The contrast to the glory of Angkor as one of the earliest kingdoms of Southeast Asia could not be more striking.

The Khmer kingdoms were the first to dominate large areas of Southeast Asia. Ancient Chinese records indicate there were smaller, multiple kingdoms in what came to be Angkor from the second to the eighth century (Chandler, 1996:29–54; Mabbett & Chandler, 1995; Taylor, 1999:157–163). Two brothers almost united all of the Khmers in the late sixth and early seventh centuries, but it was not until Jayavarman II during the early ninth century that the kingdom of Angkor emerged with a strong central polity able to exert control over the wider area. It is worth repeating that the concept of national boundaries is rather modern and Western. In Southeast Asia the kingdom extended to more or less geographical area according to the strength of the leaders and the political system able to enforce control. It was from the ninth century that Khmer kings were able to extend their control through most of the mainland Southeast Asia, with the remains of Khmer outposts of the time still on display as far west as the Thai–Burmese border. As with most early kingdoms all over the world, religion was an important tool of legitimacy for the early Khmer kings. The Hindu deities Siva and Visnu were among the most important at first, but in later centuries it was first Mahayana Buddhism (as shown in the famous Bayon statues close to Angkor Wat) and then Theravada Buddhism that became most important as it spread throughout the Southeast Asian mainland. Jayavarman IV is credited with building more of the many massive structures found in Angkor than any other leader since the ninth century (Higham, 2001, 2002; Taylor, 1999:160–162). The most famous of the multiple structures, Angkor Wat, however, was constructed in the twelveth century by Suryavarman II.

At the high point of Angkor dominance it was rice and control over favorable areas for wet-rice agriculture that were most important. The later history of Angkor, from the thirteenth to fifteenth centuries, shows a pattern of powerful and then weaker leaders, though the kingdom was maintained with control over the rich rice production area around Angkor. By the thirteenth century, though, Angkor was increasingly threatened by the emerging Ayudhya (Thai) kingdom to the west and Vietnam to the northeast. Because of the overwhelming power of these Thai kings in the area, and the increasing importance of trade with India and China, Angkor was finally abandoned in the fifteenth century for a more favorable location where two main rivers intersect at what is Phnom Penh today. By the seventeenth century, however, the trade routes moved further south through the straits of what is now southern Malaysia and Indonesia, and Cambodia's neighbors, Vietnam and Thailand, became even more powerful. Their position was even worse in the eighteenth century when large sections of the old Khmer kingdom had been taken by the Thais on one side and the Vietnamese on the other (Chandler, 1996:77–116; Kamm, 1998:24; Kathirithamby-Wells, 1999:229). Even the territory including the famous Angkor Wat fell under Thai control. Cambodia and the Khmers were in a long decline that continued as Western colonialism entered the area.

With Cambodia on the brink of disappearing as Thailand and Vietnam took more and more from the old kingdom, there is evidence that the Khmer King Nordom finally *asked* for French protection. Colonialism, in essence, was invited into Cambodia in 1863 (Kamm, 1998:26; Martin, 1994:29–31; Osborne, 1995:69). But much like the British in Burma, the French had little real interest in Cambodia in contrast to their prize of Vietnam, and subsequently did little for the country. In comparison to Vietnam, there was little training of Cambodians to run their country or improve its economy, and very little infrastructure development. The Khmer nobility were allowed some influence in running the country, but French bureaucrats with the help of their Vietnamese assistants were mostly in charge (Kamm, 1998:26–29, 128; Martin, 1994:38–39, Osborne, 1995:128). As World War II was spreading through Southeast Asia, the French rulers of Cambodia selected a new king to run the country, an 18-year-old boy named Nordom Sihanouk, who, like the others, they assumed would take orders and run the country as he was told. History would show that they were greatly mistaken.

As in Vietnam, the French regained control of their old colony of Cambodia after the Japanese were defeated in 1945. The French continued to work with King Nordom Sihanouk, though now they were trying to make their colony appear to be moving toward democracy (Chandler, 1996:27–84). There was a new constitution, elections, and political parties, but the French continued to control. Nationalist revolutionaries in Cambodia allied with the Vietnamese Viet Minh were increasingly active, but never as much a threat to French rule as nationalist revolutionaries in Vietnam. Cambodia was granted basic independence (Sihanouk called it "50 percent independence") soon after the French were defeated and kicked out of North Vietnam in 1953. After much political maneuvering before and after this time, national elections were held in 1955 that gave more legitimate power to Sihanouk. The period of rule by Sihanouk between 1955 and 1970, however, was not a placid time because of growing anti-Western and communist rebellion within Cambodia and especially in neighboring Vietnam. Cambodia was finally pulled into the American stage of the Vietnam War during the 1960s and especially 1970s even though Sihanouk had attempted to keep his country from falling into either the American or communist orbit.

In 1970, Sihanouk was overthrown (with likely CIA involvement) and the Khmer Republic was born. The coup leader, Lon Nol, was firmly in the American orbit and was actually pleased when President Nixon ordered the 1970 Cambodian invasion of his country (Kamm, 1998:71–88). He was now expecting more aid and military support from the United States—aid that was very slow in coming and much less than expected. Most important, through extreme incompetence Lon Nol drove more and more of his people toward communism as a solution to their disruption and poverty so that when his South Vietnamese allies fell in 1975 the Khmer Rouge were able to easily take Cambodia in the same manner. Between 1970 and 1975, as one of the most respected scholars of modern Cambodia put it, Cambodia "slid into chaos" (Chandler, 1996:192–235).

The atrocities committed by the Khmer Rouge between 1975 and 1979 are now well known, and as documents uncovered in 2001 indicate, were directly ordered by the top Khmer Rouge leadership (*The New York Times,* July 17, 2001). They took over a country that was in sharp decline for several centuries and made it all much worse. The human and physical capital of the country were almost completely destroyed before the Khmer Rouge were pushed out by the Vietnamese in 1979. But what is less well known is that foreign actors continued to help destabilize Cambodia until the 1990s. Thailand to the west feared Vietnamese on their borders after Vietnam pushed out the Khmer Rouge in 1979 so they secretly aided the Khmer Rouge. Corruption in Thailand also aided the Khmer Rouge because Thai military officials wanted some of the profits from the rich gem deposits and teak forests in the areas still controlled by the Khmer Rouge until the early 1990s. The Chinese also became involved because a more powerful Vietnam (supported by the Soviet Union) worried them as well. They also aided the Khmer Rouge and even attacked northern Vietnam as punishment after the Vietnamese pushed the Khmer Rouge out of most of Cambodia. The Americans, as well, could not give it up. After invading the eastern part of the nation and destabilizing the political system in 1970, the United States also did not want to stand by while Vietnam controlled Cambodia. So the United States aided the Khmer Rouge to the tune of $150 million *even after* the horrors of the killing fields were well known (*International Herald Tribune,* September 29, 2000).

By the end of the 1980s the Vietnamese had had enough and pulled out of Cambodia. The United Nations came in with hopes of stabilizing the country and helping to rebuild one of the worst situations anywhere in the world at the time. Billions of dollars in aid began to flow into Cambodia and the United Nations began planning for free elections in the early 1990s. The elections, while surprisingly free of much violence, were unable to stabilize the country immediately. The margin between the two main parties was extremely close and more political violence looked likely. Nordom Sihanouk again stepped in and declared a draw in the elections, then worked out an agreement for shared co-prime ministers between the main parties. Sihanouk's son, Ranariddh, became prime minister along with Hun Sen, a former minor official in the Khmer Rouge during his early years. There were continuing conflicts between the parties because of mistrust due to old ties to either the Khmer Rouge, Chinese, or Vietnamese. But a coup by Hun Sen and eventual demise of Pol Pot and the rest of his Khmer Rouge hiding along the Thai border finally brought some stability and peace to Cambodia by the end of the 1990s (Gottesman, 2000).

Cambodia had one of the most dominant and glorious of ancient kingdoms in the region, but was a nation in severe decline when colonialism came to Southeast Asia.

They had no ability to fight the colonials as did the Vietnamese, and of course no hope of confronting the colonials with skilled diplomacy to maintain their independence as could the Thais. In the case of Cambodia, in fact, the French were invited into the country by the rulers in hopes of keeping the Thais and Vietnamese from dissolving the nation, mile by mile, from east and west. The plan perhaps saved Cambodia from becoming an extinct kingdom like many others gobbled up by Thailand and Vietnam in the few centuries before Western colonizers arrived. Nevertheless, the French saw little reason to develop Cambodian human and material capital as they did with Vietnam. And there was certainly a heavy price to pay in the coming wars and massacres, culminating in perhaps the worst atrocities of the second half of the twentieth century when the Khmer Rouge were in power from 1975 to 1979. With only some 300 college-educated people left in the whole country after the killing fields, Cambodian prospects for economic development looked grim in the last two decades of the twentieth century. At the beginning of the twenty-first century, however, there is irony in that Cambodia's prospects for development seem better than Laos's or Burma's, the other poorest nations of Southeast Asia. Cambodia had descended into such a nightmare that world attention brought much more aid than Laos or Burma could hope for.

Vietnam: The Preconditions for Revival

As the figures in the beginning of this chapter indicate, Vietnam was a country not much more affluent than Burma, Laos, or Cambodia in the early 1900s. But because change has been so rapid in Vietnam through the 1990s the figures are somewhat misleading. More up to date, and in many ways more accurate in describing the overall achievements of Vietnam is the United Nations Human Development Index compiled with information on life expectancy, adult literacy, GDP per capita, and related scales. At the end of the twentieth century Vietnam had risen to a rank of 108 out of 174 countries, while Burma ranked 125, Laos ranked 140, and Cambodia 136 (UNDP, 2000a:159). As noted earlier, the most recent data reported by the World Bank in 2004 show that Vietnam has cut its poverty rate from around 70 percent in 1990 to 28 percent by 2002 (Glewwe & Nguyer, 2002; Gwatkin et al., 2000; World Bank, 2004c). According to the World Bank, this may be the largest drop in poverty in such a short period of time ever recorded in the world.

Anyone traveling around Vietnam in the early twenty-first century who has seen the country throughout the 1990s cannot fail to be impressed. Since the economic liberalization called Doi Moi was instituted by the party leadership in the late 1980s Vietnam has been booming (Boothroyd & Nan, 2000; Turley & Selden, 1993). One could see extensive homelessness and malnutrition in Vietnam's major cities at the beginning of the 1990s; today one sees none of that.[5] Instead, the center of Ho Chi Minh City or Saigon (and to a lesser extent, Hanoi) appears to be one huge construction site with buildings going up everywhere. Shops are bursting out into the sidewalks with new appliances that customers are carrying away as fast as the shop can be restocked. No longer are the streets almost empty; at first the streets were jammed with bicycles in the early 1990s, but by 2001 the streets were filled with new motorbikes and more and more cars. Between 1999 and 2000 the number of motorbikes doubled to the point there was one motorbike for every 12 people in Vietnam (*International Herald Tribune,*

December 28, 2000). By 2004 it was almost impossible to cross a street in the center of Hanoi because of the constant flow of new motorbikes (Honda Dreams are preferred). There is now speculation about Vietnam moving ahead of other Southeast Asian nations to become the leading economy before the end of the twenty-first century.

Like the rest of Southeast Asia, Vietnam was flooded with people leaving southern China some 3,000 to 2,000 years ago. From the second century AD to the tenth century Vietnam was recognized as a nation controlled by China. From the tenth to the nineteenth centuries, though, Vietnam was primarily independent and became one of the dominant countries in the region, competing first with Burma and Cambodia for dominance, and then Thailand (Duiker, 1995; Jamieson, 1995; Kamm, 1996; Taylor, 1999). When the Europeans were just starting to reach out to the rest of the world for trade in the late 1400s, the central Vietnamese city of Hoi An was already a bustling seaport where Indian, Chinese, Japanese, and people from the sea-trading nations of Southeast Asia came together in the most extensive trading system the world had yet seen (Frank, 1998:98; Reid, 1993:64–65). Walking around the preserved old city of Hoi An today one can see the homes of the Chinese and Japanese merchants of older times, along with the homes of the Dutch and Portugese merchants when they began trading in the area after the 1500s. By the 1870s, of course, all of Vietnam had lost its independence again, this time to the French. Vietnam was not to be completely independent again until the United States finally withdrew from the war and the South Vietnamese government fell in 1975.

Along with Thailand, Vietnam was one of the strong and ascending nations of Southeast Asia as the Western colonial powers came into the region. But unlike Thailand, Vietnam could not remain independent. Because of the strength of Vietnam, however, the French saw the country as its main colonial prize in Asia and helped develop the infrastructure and train its people (Duiker, 1995; Kamm, 1996). Also because of the strength of Vietnam, the Vietnamese people were eventually able to organize a successful fight to regain their ancient independence.[6] It was a long revolutionary struggle, and once independence was achieved, there was the common pattern of leaders who were good at winning wars continuing to hold power only to wreck the country in peacetime. As is the case after most successful revolutions or national liberations, such as the French Revolution of 1789, the old wartime leaders follow idealistic, radical policies that harmed many aspects of the society, especially the economy. It took Vietnam more than 10 years to realize the peace was being lost, and that its people were hungry, before unworkable Soviet-style economic policies were drastically reformed in what is referred to in Vietnam as Doi Moi (Boothroyd & Nan, 2000; Duiker, 1995). Farmland was increasingly privatized, most controls were removed from the free sale of produce, foreign capital was invited back into the country (but with various controls), and domestic private enterprise was encouraged (Kerkvliet & Selden, 1999; Luong & Unger, 1999). In peacetime, after more than 13 years of disastrous Soviet-style policies, Vietnam was finally able to organize its human resources with a strong state now focused on economic development.

With Doi Moi in place by the early 1990s it was not just the urban areas that began rapid development, but the countryside as well. Traveling through the central highlands today where much of the American part of the war was fought one sees little evidence of the war. Rather, the hills are covered with coffee trees and fruit orchards, and the lowlands are covered with lush green rice patties. By the beginning of the twenty-first century Vietnam became the world's second largest exporter of rice, closing in on Thailand for the number one position. A country that had trouble feeding its people just 12 years before became the world's second largest exporter of coffee by the end of the 1990s.

Vietnam still faces a difficult road to economic development. Corruption is still high among party officials, international organizations rank the Vietnamese government as one of the most corrupt in the world, and the Communist Party admits that its own investigation has found some 40 percent of officials to be involved in some form of corruption (*International Herald Tribune,* February 15, 2001; Transparency International, 2001). Some party hardliners have been resisting economic reforms and open markets, Western and Japanese businesspeople in Vietnam complain of government interference, and most Vietnamese still do not understand the fundamentals of the world economy.[7] But the liberal reform wing of the Communist Party soundly defeated old party officials in the party Congress of April 2001, to place one of their own as head of the party (*International Herald Tribune,* April 18, 2001). Vietnam is increasingly in a good position to consolidate and expand upon its progress gained during the 17 years of Doi Moi.

The Other Nations of Southeast Asia

To hold constant the possible influence of culture that has again been injected into the debate over economic development at the beginning of the twenty-first century, the focus so far has been on the Buddhist countries of Southeast Asia.[8] Table 9.2 presents a brief summary of how these countries have been influenced by the important historical force described throught this book. A short review of Malaysia, Indonesia, and the Philippines, however, can show the impact of factors (ancient civilizations, elite responsibility, a strong development state, and the effects of colonialism) outlined in previous chapters on the level of economic development in these countries as well.

Philippines

There is consensus among Southeast Asian historians that the Philippines has become the most Westernized country in East and Southeast Asia (Cheong, 1999; Karnow, 1989; Osborne, 1995). First the Spanish and then the Americans remade the Philippines in their own image to a far greater extent than found anywhere else in Asia (Dower, 1986:64; Keay, 1997:Chapter 5; Kristof & WuDunn, 2000:237). The reshaping of the country by the Spanish and then Americans was largely possible because the Philippines lacked traditions from strong ancient civilizations found elsewhere in Southeast Asia. There are no ancient remains comparable to those of Pagan, Ayudhya, or Angkor Wat uncovered on the Philippine islands. Further, though to a lesser degree when compared to Burma or Indonesia, the colonial powers created a nation-state with boundaries almost ensuring conflicts between the Christian north and the Islamic south of the Philippines. Especially important is the political structure created primarily by the American colonial power which precludes the development of a strong state and government bureaucracy able to follow the Asian development model (Fallows, 1994:365–368). While certainly not the model of American liberal democracy, the Philippine state is one that allows wealthy interest groups to protect their interests at the cost of long-term economic development more evenly spread throughout the society. There has been some economic development as the figures presented earlier in this chapter indicate. But poverty remains high compared to other countries in the region. As Ferdinand Marcos discovered, a dictator in the Philippines could drain the country's wealth much like some dictators in Africa and Latin American nations have done over the years. The revolution deposing Marcos and other corrupt politicians has brought increasing levels of democracy in the Philippines. In the early stages of economic development, however, the record shows that "late, late developing nations" in the modern world system need a strong state and Asian development model to achieve solid and evenly distributed economic development, something the Philippines has been unable to achieve.

Malaysia and Indonesia

In contrast to the Philippines, both Malaysia and Indonesia are made up of territories that have some legacies of ancient empires that were sea trading powers more than 1,500 years ago (Bellwood, 1999; Hall, 1999; Reid, 1988, 1993, 1999). However, the emphasis must be put on "made up of some territories that had ancient civilizations." The vast area making up Indonesia today contains many diverse areas with contrasting cultural legacies. What is now Malaysia cuts across some diverse territories as well and was not even a unified nation before British rule. Then there is the contrast to the rest of Southeast Asia with a majority Islamic population in both countries. Although it is certain the spread of Islam in the 1400s had an impact upon these old Buddhist- and Hindu-based civilizations and their values, Southeast Asian scholars agree that the influence of Islam has had less impact on the traditions of these ancient civilizations than one might think (De Casparis & Mabbett, 1999:330). Figures presented at the beginning of this chapter, as well as recent events, however, show quite different levels of economic development between Malaysia and Indonesia. To a large degree these differences are related to contrasting effects from colonialism.

For Malaysia there was an extreme contrast to how the British dealt with Burma. Instead of helping create an almost certain situation of political instability and then quickly withdrawing from the country after World War II, the British saw more at stake for themselves and stayed in the new semi-independent Malaysia through the 1950s and into the 1960s. British aid and advisors helped Malaysia make the transition to independence with political and economic structures setting the stage for Malaysia's rise to the richest country in Southeast Asia.[9] The biggest trick was to unite many semi-independent sultanates that had not considered themselves part of a united nation for hundreds of years. There was, however, the advantage of common traditions that bound these sultanates culturally and socially, if not politically, before British colonialism. Beginning with the Federated Malay States in 1896, the British worked to create this unity that has held together remarkably well since the mid-twentieth century (Keay, 1997:53). One of the most important things at stake for the British were rubber plantations; by the 1920s the British Malay territories accounted for over half of all world rubber production and about one-third of the world's tin (Keay, 1997:54). Today British

TABLE 9.2

Historical Forces and Development Prospects in Buddhist Southeast Asia

Ancient Civilizations	Traditions of Elite Responsibility	Colonial Experience	State Development
Thailand			
• Theravada Buddhism • The Kingdom of Sukothai from 1253	• Patriarch king evolving into divine king, both with traditions of national responsibilities	• Ascending power as European colonialism reached Asia • Independence retained through diplomacy	• Semihard state with relatively efficient and semiautonomy of bureaucratic government ministry • Asian development model generally employed • Sustained economic development and extensive poverty reduction
Burma			
• Theravada Buddhism • Pagan from ninth century, but rival kingdoms	• King with traditions of national responsibilities, but rival kingdoms	• Descending power before European colonialism reached Asia • Contested national boundaries left by British rule • Little infrastructure development by British	• Weak state with political instability since WWII • Asian development model not employed • No economic development and one of the world's highest poverty rates
Cambodia			
• Hindu, then Theravada Buddhism	• King with traditions of national responsibilities	• Descending power as European colonialism reached Asia	• Weak state with political instability since WWII

(continued)

• Unified Khmer kingdom from late sixth century	• Limited to small kingdoms in the area	• Little infrastructure development by French • Disruption by Indochina wars	• Severe political and social disruption with Khmer Rouge control from 1975 to 1979 • Emerging prospects for political stability by late 1990s • Asian development model yet to be employed

Laos

• Population divided between lowland Theravada Buddhists and animist hill tribes • Small rival kingdoms with Burmese, Vietnamese, Thai, or Khmer dominance throughout history	• Emerging sense of national identity and elite responsibility with 1,000 years of nation building	• Nation-state and national boundaries created with French colonialism • Little infrastructure development by French	• Weak state with communist government since 1975; Soviet collectivism attempted until 1990s • Asian development model not employed • No economic development and one of world's highest poverty rates

Vietnam

• Civilization development through 1,000 years of relative independence from China • Rival kingdoms gradually consolidated		• Infrastructure development by French • Longer disruption from Indochina wars	• Strong state but disruptive Soviet collectivism between 1975 and late 1980s • "Doi Moi" reforms and Asian development state emerging from late 1980s • Strong economic development and poverty reduction by late 1990s

interests still own about 25 percent of all wealth and corporate assets in Malaysia (*International Herald Tribune,* January 5, 2001). It is therefore not surprising that the British stayed in Malaysia through the 1950s to help fight rebellions against the new government that was not completely independent until 1963 (Osborne, 1995:180; Pye, 1985:256; Stockwell, 1999:25–26, 46–47).

In contrast to the British in Malaysia, the Dutch created an Indonesia that made little cultural or sociological sense. It is true that the British stitched together many separate sultanates in Malaysia, but culturally and socially these sultanates were rather similar and had relatively little difficulty forming a unified nation. Much like the Western colonials in Africa, however, many different ethnic groups and people of different ancient civilizations where put together by the Dutch to form what is now considered Indonesia. In most areas the people were Islamic, but in many areas they were Buddhist, in others they were Hindu or Christian, and in some cases simply primitive animists. But all were thrown together with the Islamic majority. With independence, against much advice, the first leaders of independent Indonesia, particularly Sukarno, demanded that the national boundaries created by the Dutch stay in place. Political violence between these competing groups has burdened Indonesia to this day. In addition to all of this, much like the French in Indochina, the Dutch created rebellion and instability in Indonesia when they retook their old colonial possession after World War II (Ricklefs, 1993; Schwarz, 1994; Stockwell, 1999:25–30). The Dutch were unable to stay as long as the French in Indochina, but the seeds of political factions and political violence were no less stimulated further by the return of the Dutch after the war.[10] Political instability has moved up and down in Indonesia since independence, making it much more difficult to establish a strong state able to work for the development interests of the nation as a whole. These problems have become even more evident since the Asian economic crisis of 1997, making it more difficult for Indonesia to mount a recovery comparable to that of Thailand and Malaysia to the north.

The Potential for Sustained Development and Poverty Reduction: A Conclusion

Now that we have considered the historical forces behind the current political and economic conditions in Africa, the Middle East, Latin America, and Asia, it is important to repeat a key point: Ancient traditions, national unity and elite responsibility, the existence of a development state and good governance, and the impact of colonialism create only the potential for economic development and poverty reduction. Good governance without sound development policies will not get you far. A weak nation-state confronted by rich nations increasingly able to manipulate the global economy for their benefit makes development much more difficult.

In our final chapter we must examine limitations placed upon economic development and poverty reduction by the new global economy and some of the specific "tools" that can be used for sustained economic development and poverty reduction if the country has the potential to use these tools because of favorable historical forces outlined in previous chapters.

CASE IN POINT

The Overseas Chinese, Ethnic Relations, and Advantages in Economic Development

When considering the importance of "overseas Chinese" for economic development in Southeast Asia, Charoen Pokphand Group (or simply CP Group as every Thai calls it) is a good place to start. The CP Group was founded by Chinese immigrants to Thailand in 1920. By the 1980s it was by far the biggest corporate conglomerate in Thailand. During the mid-1990s the founding family was worth $5.5 billion, though their wealth has been reduced since the Asian economic crisis of 1997. Before 1997 the CP Group controlled 300 large corporations with 80,000 employees in 20 different nations. (At one point they were even the biggest foreign corporate investor in mainland China.) Today the CP Group still supplies most of Thailand's chickens, eggs, and pigs, among other agricultural products; they are a major player in the new high-tech telecommunications industry in Thailand and have moved into retailing with control over Thai franchises of 7-Eleven, KFC, Wal-Mart, Makro, and others in Thailand (*The New York Times,* November 14, 1995; Pasuk & Baker, 1998:11). The expanse and assets of the CP Group are not so typical of corporations in Thailand, but the fact that the founding and controlling family is ethnic Chinese *is* rather typical. During the mid-1990s, all but two of the richest 25 businesspeople in Thailand were of Chinese ethnic background and 12 of the biggest 15 banks were controlled by ethnic Chinese families (*International Herald Tribune,* April 17, 1998; Kulick & Wilson, 1996:85, 90).

Thailand is *not* unique among Southeast Asian countries. At the beginning of the twenty-first century ethnic Chinese held about 40 percent of the wealth in Malaysia but comprised only 3 percent of the population, while in Indonesia ethnic Chinese dominate about 75 percent of the private-sector business activity though they make up only 3 percent of the population (*International Herald Tribune,* January 5, 2001; *Los Angeles Times,* January 31 & February 28, 1998). Throughout Southeast Asia there is, or has been, an immigrant ethnic Chinese population that has done well economically. When considering economic development in Southeast Asia, therefore, one must not ignore the contributions made by ethnic Chinese, though one should not exaggerate their importance. We must not forget the political, economic, or social conditions of the host countries in Southeast Asia that received overseas Chinese and allowed them to prosper.

As political and economic disintegration spread in China it was also the colonial powers who helped distribute Chinese and Indians around Southeast Asia. In precolonial times, Southeast Asian societies did not give much status to merchants or encourage them, so the Dutch, British, and French often brought in Indians and Chinese to help run the colonial economies (Osborne, 1995:107–108). But only in Thailand, the Philippines, and Cambodia was there much acceptance and then assimilation of ethnic Chinese after the colonial powers left. There were never many ethnic Chinese in Laos, and in Cambodia the Khmer Rouge targeted for execution anyone who was a professional or businessperson, thus targeting a high percentage of the ethnic Chinese population. In Burma ethnic Chinese and Indians were attacked and killed in the 1930s even before the British left the country. Then Ne Win's Burmese way to socialism after independence meant all foreigners were kicked out.

Soon after the Vietnam War was over in 1975 there was "ethnic cleansing" of Chinese, with an estimated 40,000 killed. In 1978 Chinese wealth was nationalized in Vietnam and

(Continued)

(Continued)

the ethnic population in Hanoi quickly dropped from 20,000 to 2,000. After war broke out between China and Vietnam in 1979 about 266,000 ethnic Chinese fled to China. The ethnic Chinese who still remain in Ho Chi Minh City are mostly in a Chinatown called Cholon, which accounts for about 40 percent of economic activity in the city.

In Indonesia there were attacks on ethnic Chinese families in 1960, 1965, 1974, and again with the Asian economic crisis of 1997. In 1960 Chairman Mao Tse-tung sent a small fleet to Indonesia to take out over 100,000 ethnic Chinese, but in the massive political upheaval of 1965 it is estimated about half a million ethnic Chinese were killed in Indonesia. Malaysia has been somewhat kinder to ethnic Chinese who control about 40 percent of the wealth; still there are attacks upon ethnic Chinese from time to time and a Malaysian-style "affirmative action" program protects the majority Muslim population. Public universities in Malaysia, for example, must take at least 60 percent native Malays while it is estimated only 5 percent would qualify on merit alone (*International Herald Tribune*, January 5, 2001; *Los Angeles Times*, January 31 & February 28, 1998; Smith, 1999:44, 98; Templer, 1998:303–312).

In all of this, Thailand has been the exception. There were some minor attacks on ethnic Chinese in the 1920s, but almost none since. When discussing the subject of ethnic Chinese businesspeople with Thai friends, the usual comment is "who even knows who is Chinese any longer?" More than half of all urban Thais are said to have some Chinese ethnic ancestry.

The Bunnag family history in Thailand is instructive. During the reigns of the first five kings of the Chakri dynasty (from 1780s to the mid-1800s) the Bunnag family ancestors were among the most powerful people in Thailand. It is said they dominated most affairs of state, from the military to finance, diplomacy, and judiciary. Their ancestors helped select kings and served as administrative heads of state three times, with one of the family members becoming Regent of Siam. Daughters of the Bunnag family married into royalty, with one of the granddaughters of the powerful clan becoming the first wife of the most famous king, Chulalongkorn. Despite this, the Bunnang family was originally from Persia and migrated to the kingdom of Ayudhya in the early seventeenth century (*Bangkok Post*, November 14, 1998). The Thai acceptance of ethnic Chinese, in other words, is not unique and has a long tradition in Thai history. Already in early Ayudhya the Bunnang family lived among some 3,000 Chinese and many other foreigners were given government posts (Shearer, 1989:45, 82).

Most scholars agree that Thailand has an excellent record of race and ethnic relations compared to other countries in the region, and especially given that Thailand has so many ethnic divisions. There are Muslims (10 percent of Thais), ethnic Chinese, Laos, Cambodians, and Burmese from the east and then west of Thailand; there is a large Indian population that moved around Asia with the expansion of the British Empire, and of course many hill tribes. The hill tribe people have lived all over Southeast Asia, giving little respect to national borders, and are found mostly in the northern regions of Thailand. These hill tribes with their colorful clothing and traditions include Karen, Mon, Akha, Lisu, and Lahu along with other smaller groups. Of this mixture, Chinese make up the biggest ethnic group, though as noted there has been so much assimilation that the definition of who is Chinese is difficult. The best estimate is perhaps 10 percent of the population of Thailand is ethnic Chinese, with as much as 50 percent of the people in Bangkok having at least some ethnic Chinese ancestors (Shearer, 1989:46).

(Continued)

There has been some prejudice and discrimination against Islamic Thais and the ethnic Laos from the northeast of Thailand. There have been old conflicts between the lowlander Thai people and the highlander hill tribe people over land use and land ownership. But the greatest *potential* for ethnic conflict, as with Thailand's neighbors, was with the ethnic Chinese because of their success in the economy. As discussed, only during the 1920s were there some attacks on the ethnic Chinese by the quasi-fascist Wild Tigers paramilitary group, but there have been no systematic attacks on ethnic Chinese or other racial or ethnic groups since (Kulick & Wilson, 1992:85).

It is suggested that the Thai style of Buddhism, with its acceptance of many peoples, has not predisposed Thais to much ethnic hatred, though the Burmese Buddhists have not been as tolerant. Thai government policies have also worked to reduce ethnic conflicts. In contrast to other Southeast Asian nations, for example, as early as 1911 Chinese in Thailand could become Thai citizens (Pasuk & Baker, 1996:15–16). Also important, new military rulers of Thailand from the 1930s took the chance to cooperate economically with these ethnic Chinese for the interests of both. Then again in the 1950s when the Thai government realized the potential conflicts, educational programs were started in the schools to counter prejudice. (One of the required readings was the fictional *Letters from Thailand* which chronicled the troubles of an immigrant Chinese family over the generations.) Finally, in contrast to Burma, Malaysia, and Indonesia, for example, Thailand did not have the disruption of colonialism to create ethnic conflicts. The Chinese, Indians, and others brought to their colonies by the British, Dutch, and French were often seen as illegal immigrants who took advantage of their colonial-sponsored positions. A result has been a rather easy mixing and assimilation of the Thais and ethnic Chinese (Pasuk & Baker, 1998:13–17).

While the large contribution to economic development made by ethnic Chinese in many countries in Southeast Asia must be fully acknowledged, the presence of ethnic Chinese alone does not explain most of the economic success or failure of these countries. More important were the underlying political and economic infrastructures that made economic development a potential for all people within each nation. Important also was how ethnic Chinese were treated differently in these Southeast Asian nations: In some countries their treatment hurt development potential whereas in other countries such as Thailand it helped.

Notes

1. Malaysia's Prime Minister Mahathir, one of the most vocal spokespeople for the importance of Asian values, certainly believes there is something like Pan-Asian values, with East Asian countries such as Japan included along with Malaysia. This is what worries Mahathir when he finds evidence that Asian values are perhaps being eroded. On a trip to Japan in 2001 Mahathir described his disgust when seeing the dyed hair among so many Japanese young people: "The traditional Japanese and Eastern culture is being discarded and replaced with Western culture with disregard for filial piety and discipline." (See *International Herald Tribune,* May 26, 2001.) One may disagree with Mahathir about the significance of dyed hair in Japan, but the point is a belief in the significance and existence of Pan-Asian values.

2. It is also worth noting that with the new Purchasing Power Parity (PPP) estimates, this average Thai wage would be closer to $9 or $10 per day.

3. In late 2002 some possibly positive change occurred. For example, the family of the old dictator Ne Win was arrested on corruption charges. Speculation is that the new military dictators know that this powerful family must be controlled if any other change is to be instituted in the country. Other speculation, however, is that the new military elite simply want more of the fruits of corruption. See *International Herald Tribune,* May 8, 2002, and various dates of the BBC Web news. But in October of 2004 the promising moderate leaders were then (arrested" and the military faction resisting change was back firmly in power. (See *Los Angeles Times,* October 20, 2004.) By mid 2005 there was still no improvement in the political or economic situation in Burma.

4. The most infamous killing fields are around the capital, Phnom Penh. However, other killing fields can be seen on the road leading to the entrance of Angkor Wat.

5. The World Bank estimates that Vietnam has reduced poverty from 58 percent of the population to 38 percent from the early 1990s to 1998 (World Bank, *World Development Report 2000/2001* [New York: Oxford University Press, 2000], p. 41).

6. It is interesting to note that during wartime Ho Chi Minh recognized that the nation's proud and ancient traditions would help unite his people to make up for their lack of military technology, specifically diverting needed funds from the war effort to continue archaeological projects (John Keay, *Last Post: The End of Empire in the Far East* [London: John Murray, 1997], p. 3).

7. Personal interviews with American Chamber of Commerce officials in Vietnam, July 2001.

8. See, for example, Lawrence E. Harrison and Samuel P. Huntington, eds., *Culture Matters: How Values Shape Human Progress* (New York: Basic Books, 2000); and Lawrence E. Harrison, *Underdevelopment Is a State of Mind: The Latin American Case* (Lanham, MD: Madison Books, 2000, updated edition). See also the World Bank's Web site posting many new papers and conferences focused on the impact of culture on economic development, http://www.worldbank.com.

9. As noted throughout this work small city-states such as Singapore are excluded from this analysis because of their very different situation. Until the mid-1960s, though, Singapore was in fact a part of Malaysia. Because of its overwhelming Chinese ethnic population, Singapore was in essence "kicked out" of Malaysia because Malaysians felt they would be dominated by this extremely wealthy Chinese ethnic population. See A. J. Stockwell, "Southeast Asia in War and Peace: The End of European Colonial Empires," in *The Cambridge History of Southeast Asia,* Vol. 2, pt. 2, *From World War II to the Present,* ed. Nicholas Tarling, pp. 25–26, 46–47 (Cambridge, England: Cambridge University Press, 1999); Lucian W. Pye, *Asian Power and Politics: The Cultural Dimensions of Authority* (Cambridge, MA: Belknap/Harvard University Press, 1985), pp. 248–256; Milton Osborne, *Southeast Asia: An Introductory History* (Brisbane: Allen and Unwin, 1995), pp. 76, 180; Yong Mun Cheong, "The Political Structures of the Independent States," in *The Cambridge History of Southeast Asia,* vol. 2, pt. 2, *From World War II to the Present,* ed. Nicholas Tarling (Cambridge, England: Cambridge University

Press, 1999); Barbara Watson Andaya and Leonard Y. Andaya, *A History of Malaysia* (London: Palgrave, 2001).

10. It was the beginning of the cold war which created different postcolonial situations for the people of Indochina and Indonesia. The United States was against the reestablishment of colonialism by the European powers in Asia, no doubt because the United States wanted trade and economic resources in Asia that would be denied if the Europeans again took control. As soon as the Dutch moved back into their old Indonesian territories the United States threatened to withdraw Marshall Funds if the Dutch did not leave. But a couple of years later the United States actually helped finance much of the movement of the French back into Indochina as the fear of communism in Asia (and a growing Socialist Party in France) led the United States to rethink its anticolonial policy. See John Keay, *Last Post: The End of Empire in the Far East.* London: John Murray, 1997.

Globalization and World Poverty: Limitations and Tools for Sustainable Development

Thahtay Kyun, an island in the Andaman Sea, is arguably one of the most beautiful places on earth. About 1 hour sailing time from the Thai port city of Ranong, one reaches the little island that is no more than a square mile of land slowly rising from a green tropical sea. Encircling Thahtay Kyun are dozens of other little islands along the western seacoast of Burma where thousands of such islands extend for more than 200 miles. Thahtay Kyun is particularly significant because most of the little island is now covered by a new casino resort hotel. The centerpiece of the resort hotel is a grand lobby with granite floors, old-style rattan furniture around the spacious lobby, dark wood-paneled walls with French colonial doors and windows opening to the outside in every direction. This architectural design allows for a beautiful view of the green sea and dozens of small islands just a few miles away, as well as a soft sea breeze making only ceiling fans necessary in the tropical heat. The overall effect is that of British colonial times with a Somerset Maugham figure sitting in the lobby holding a martini in one hand, and smoke trailing from an expensive cigar in the other hand.

The reality, however, is that the place is primarily full of affluent Thais and was built and now run by a company formed by a Thai and Singapore joint venture. It is also one of the places where the Burmese military dictators hope to earn some foreign exchange from the tourist industry, and if recent investigative reports are correct, pocket a big percentage of the profits for themselves and their relatives (*International Herald Tribune,* November 22, 2000). The only Burmese in evidence, though, were military guards at the small island port (with signs proclaiming "We will protect foreign tourists," though from whom was unclear), and the usual cleaning maids and maintenance workers around the hotel. The few Burmese allowed on the island speak perfect English and I discovered many were university graduates doing such jobs as cutting the grass, making beds, and cleaning restrooms. After four years of university their only marketable skills in the military state of Burma are speaking English to rich foreigners while making their beds and cleaning their toilets.

From this little dot in the Andaman Sea one can catch ferries to neighboring islands and walk to small villages. After spending weeks and months in Thailand, the poverty of small-village Burma seems particularly depressing. There is a feeling of being in a time warp—about the only mode of transportation on these little islands are trucks left over from World War II and small boats of probably the same vintage. At the port of one island was a faded wooden sign proclaiming "Welcome" and then "Visit Myanmar 1996." At the time, 1996 was almost over and it was obvious the

"Visit Myanmar" campaign had been unsuccessful. A couple of other Westerners, per-haps a half-dozen Thais, and two Japanese, all from the hotel resort, were to be seen. Villagers on the islands obviously survive on fishing, for no other economic activity was apparent.

The Facade of Uneven Development

Like many development schemes in the poorest of countries, the resort hotel on Thahtay Kyun is a facade. There are a few new projects that look good from the outside, but there appears to be no benefit or change filtering through to the vast majority of people in the country. The rich may get richer from such facades (in the Burmese case, mili-tary dictators), but that is about as far as it goes. Thailand was criticized in 1997 for the "golf course capitalism" which created many luxury developments that wasted resources and took away from investments that were better able to sustain economic development and benefit all citizens. But countries such as Thailand, Taiwan, Malaysia, and South Korea caught up in the Asian economic crisis of 1997 at least had many other development projects as well. In many poor countries golf course capitalism is about all they have. Few people, including the leaders of some rich nations, seem to understand much of this.

The World Bank began changing some of its focus in the late 1990s to small development projects targeted at poor villagers rather than the past big projects such as huge dams, electrical generating facilities, seaports, and other expensive infrastructure projects. Research shows the per dollar payoff in poverty reduction is much greater for these smaller projects directly benefiting peasants and small farmers than are the big projects. President George W. Bush and the U.S. treasury secretary, however, made it clear to the World Bank that they thought the big projects were more likely to raise pro-ductivity and help overall wealth in the recipient countries (*International Herald Tribune,* May 17, 2001). Those big World Bank projects of the past, of course, were all too often like the facades represented by the resort hotel on Thahtay Kyun. The urban rich and foreign corporate investors might do quite well with them, but a look behind the facade of development finds the same poverty and urban slums full of people with nowhere else to go. One can assume that the U.S. treasury secretary didn't understand this: If he did, then the profits of foreign corporations and rich elites in the poor coun-tries must have been more important than helping the poor. With new rounds of serious protest against globalization and world poverty at the next G-7 meeting in Italy a few weeks later, the president of the United States came out in favor of "fighting world poverty." Nothing really came of it, however, especially after the terrorist attacks on the World Trade Center in New York. Most attention then turned to fighting terrorism through military action instead of getting at the breeding grounds of terrorism in refugee camps and worsening world poverty. During the fall of 2002, the next global round of discussion about world poverty at the Conference on Sustainable Development in South Africa was snubbed by the U.S. government: Of 107 heads of state in atten-dance, only the United States among other major nations was not represented by its leader (*International Herald Tribune,* September 3 & 4, 2002).

The pages of this book have attempted to show that under certain conditions economic development in poor countries *can* proceed with global trade and outside corporate investment, and that the resulting economic development *can* benefit the poorest in the least developed nations. As people in the rich nations become less optimistic about the world and more aware that the "new world order" contains the potential for a lot of "disorder" as well, it is important they be aware of some success stories around the developing world. We must recognize that world poverty need not always be with us and recognize also how some countries, so far mostly in East and Southeast Asia, have dramatically reduced poverty in recent decades.

What We Know about Causes and Solutions to World Poverty

Whatever may motivate the affluent world to increase efforts in reducing world poverty, motivation alone is not enough. We can begin with lessons from past failures. More often than not, the basic lesson is that situations are usually more complex than they seem. This is especially so when the focus of aid programs or development policies involves only technical aspects of an economy or production. *Broader aspects of a society, especially political and economic power arraignments, that are seldom considered by outside governments or agencies will always have an impact on the outcomes of aid programs and development policies.*

During the 1960s the quick fix scheme was the *green revolution*. The basic idea appeared valid: Rich nations, especially the United States, would send their agricultural experts to poor countries to teach farmers how to grow crops more efficiently, and help supply new strains of crops, new farm equipment, and chemicals, all of which would dramatically increase crop yield. One goal was achieved—food production increased dramatically. But the basic goal (or at least the overtly stated goal) failed badly in many if not most developing nations. Rich landowners became wealthier while poor peasants typically became poorer. The problem was that landowners began growing different crops to sell on the world market, exporting everything they could to increase their profits, while they stopped growing many other crops used as cheap food for local people. Likewise, the green revolution created an incentive for big landowners to acquire more and more land, thus taking land from small farmers and peasants. Finally, the new capital-intensive agriculture promoted in the green revolution forced peasants out of agricultural jobs. A few years after the green revolution began, many poor countries often exported food while their own poor went hungry. In a few countries such as Thailand poor farmers did benefit from the green revolution because of differences in social organization and the position of small farmers. We will consider these differences below.

One of the new schemes to help poor countries during the late 1990s and early 2000s has been debt relief. Given that many less developed nations have gotten themselves into extensive debt to banks and governments from the rich nations, and given that the interest payments on these debts are often more than a country can generate per year in profits from exports, canceling part or all of these debts to allow poor nations "to get out of the hole" can be quite helpful (*International Herald Tribune,* September 18, 2000; World Bank & IMF, 2001b). But like other quick fix schemes of the past, debt relief will most likely have little lasting effect or change the conditions that led to less long-term economic development with outside investment in the first place (World Bank & IMF, 2001a, 2001c).

The problem, of course, is these attempts to reduce world poverty are only quick fix schemes that do not adequately consider the underlying social conditions or political economy of poor nations before applying only technical solutions that otherwise appear logical and promising. We have seen, for example, that a typical social structure of poor nations is one in which rich families control most of the wealth, land, and capital assets, as well as dominate the political system. Wealthy families in such countries have more incentive to cater to foreign investors or big agricultural corporations than helping their own fellow citizens because it is the foreign investors who keep the wealthy landowners rich. If wages of the poor go up, if taxes are required of the foreign investors to cover infrastructure needs such as education, or if the poor gain some political influence or establish labor unions, the rich investors leave and the local rich people suffer substantial losses. Such are the realities of the typical class structure, or political economy, of many less developed nations tied to the modern world system of the late twentieth and early twenty-first centuries. Like the green revolution, for many countries (especially in Latin America and Africa) the new quick fix scheme, debt relief, is likely to primarily benefit the rich—the status quo of who primarily profits from ties to the world economy, and who has ultimate power in the country, will remain unchanged.

The point, of course, is that *before any kind of technical remedy for economic stagnation and poverty is implemented, careful analysis of what we call "social structures," or the basic social organization of the society, must be made*. The interaction between the technical remedy and social structure, when thought through, may show the remedy could have results opposite of those intended. The focus of this book has been the historical forces that have shaped current social structures in developing countries today, as well as the interaction between these local social structures and the global economy. It will be useful to summarize the historical and global forces examined in previous chapters before considering the more technical tools for economic development and how the social structures of some East and Southeast Asian nations have rendered these technical tools more successful.

Ancient Civilizations and Historical Legacies

About 200 miles due south of the casino resort hotel on the Burmese island of Thahtay Kyun is the famous resort area in Phuket, Thailand. A favorite for movie sets and rich Westerners who enjoy the Club Med scene, Phuket is not exactly the tranquil and sparsely populated Thahtay Kyun. One cannot sit in the grand lobbies of Phuket hotel resorts and hear almost nothing but the waves and sea breeze. But when one leaves the hotel resorts to visit small Thai cities nearby, Phuket is obviously not just a facade of development. One can certainly complain about how the ecology of islands around Phuket, such as Ko Phi Phi (where the movie *The Beach* was made), have been disrupted by tourism and rapid development, but a point is that there *are* outcomes of real economic development to worry about. The islands around Thahtay Kyun in Burma will not face such problems for a very long time. After the tsunami of December 2004 much of Phuket was quickly rebuilt, though aid to small Thai villages north of Phuket was less and it will take much longer for their recovery. The Burmese beach areas and islands hit by the tsunami were not even included in international aid drives because the military dictators were afraid of what the outside attention would bring. It is likely these poor people in Burma will never fully recover.

The contrasting states of economic development around the Thahtay Kyun and Phuket resorts can be explained only with reference to social structures shaped by the historical forces described in previous chapters. We have seen how some of the countries of

Southeast Asia have benefited from ancient civilizations helping to create a sense of national identity and elite responsibility, while some countries such as Burma and Laos had kingdom rivalries and only local national identities from the early centuries. Thailand alone escaped colonization and was able to sustain unification and nation building throughout the nineteenth and twentieth centuries. But the mixture of positive and negative effects of colonization varied among the other countries. In Burma, Laos, and Cambodia there was little infrastructure development by the colonial powers. The resources were taken and the colonial administration was in the hands of outsiders so that local elites had little administrative experience or education after the colonial powers left the country. Vietnam, in contrast, did benefit from economic and educational development from French colonialism, but suffered an even longer struggle to gain and retain independence from French rule. Burma and Laos shared the additional disadvantage of "unnatural" national boundaries created by colonial powers that made nation building and political stability extremely difficult or impossible after independence. As a result, Thailand, Malaysia, and Vietnam have the strongest development prospects at the beginning of the twenty-first century.

Good Governance

It was perhaps one of the brightest moments in the history of policy "think tanks" when some World Bank officials realized that good governance is important for economic development and poverty reduction. In an uncharacteristic announcement, the World Bank even admitted that good governance might be more important than open markets in promoting development and poverty reduction! (*International Herald Tribune*, September 14, 2000). Good governance means efficient and fair government, government that is less corrupt and works for the long-term interests of the nation as a whole. We have seen how researchers at UC Berkeley recently developed what they called a Weberianness scale which measures aspects of bureaucracies and governments Max Weber described as most important for legal–rational and efficient government over 100 years ago. Comparative research has found that East and Southeast Asian nations rank highest on this Weberianness scale and that the scale is related to higher rates of economic development (Evans & Rauch, 1999). With their related concept of good governance World Bank researchers have found much the same: Data from 150 nations have shown several measures of good governance (such as accountability, effectiveness, rule of law, low corruption) to be related to higher rates of economic development (Kaufmann, Kraay, & Zoido-Lobaton, 1999).

Despite the promise of such research, several questions remain: *Where does good governance come from? How can it be achieved? Can world agencies such as the United Nations or the World Bank step in to create good governance?* The answer to the last question seems clear—it will be very difficult. The comparative analysis of this book suggests that broad historical forces in Southeast Asia have shaped the likelihood of good governance. Ancient civilizations with more developed government organization before colonization, as well as traditions of elite responsibility, have helped create strong states with the means and efficiency to carry out development policies today. Other historical forces, especially the experiences of colonialism for each country, have intervened to make a strong state and good governance less likely for some countries, especially most in Africa. International agencies may be able to promote good governance through various policies of intervention in developing nations as indicated in a few African countries, but the comparative analysis presented here suggests it will be much more difficult to achieve in most poor nations around the world.

Culture

The concept of culture and its assumed relationship to wealth and poverty is making a comeback, a strong comeback, at least outside the world of academic social scientists. During October of 2000, the World Bank and United Nations sponsored a joint conference on the role of culture in economic development with the title "Culture Counts: A Conference on Financing, Resources and the Economics of Culture in Sustainable Development." Speakers addressed the gathering with topics such as "Why Some Are so Rich and Others so Poor; the Role of Culture," "The Economic, Anthropological, and Social Perspective: Culture and Sustainable Development in Central America," and "The Economic Dimensions of Culture: An Analytical Perspective." There was another topic for presentations—how the global economy and economic development can be a disruptive threat to local cultures. But the primary interest seemed to be on the first topic.[1] Money is going in that direction as well. At the end of 2000 the World Bank was set to fund research projects with titles such as the following: "Linking Culture and Poverty Reduction in the Himalayas: A Comparative Research of Cultural Expression and Poverty Reduction," "Culture, Social Status, and the Demand for Education," "Might Culture Pay Off? Using an Experimental Design to Evaluate the Effects of Farming Innovations and Cultural Empowerment Among Lowland Amerindians in Bolivia," and "Youth, Identity and Culture in Multiracial Societies."[2] U.S. foundations and elite universities have gotten into the act; an example is the conference sponsored at Harvard that led to the volume of papers edited by Lawrence E. Harrison and Samuel P. Huntington titled *Culture Matters: How Values Shape Human Progress.* There is the example of the reissue in 2000 of Lawrence E. Harrison's controversial 1985 book, *Underdevelopment Is a State of Mind: The Latin American Case*, which broadly places blame on Latin American cultures for their poverty.

Returning to what we have learned about culture and development, all four Theravada Buddhist countries in Southeast Asia have had very different prospects for economic development and poverty reduction. None of this is to deny that culture has an impact. But more often than not there are other historical and global forces blocking sustained and evenly spread economic development before culture can have any effects.

The New Global Economy and Impediments for Poverty Reduction

Historical forces shaping the development of the state in less developed countries today would not be as important in understanding the prospects for economic development were it not for powerful economic agents from richer and more powerful countries able to intervene in the affairs of weaker countries in the new global economy. As we have already seen, Walter Rostow's stages of economic growth theory may be accurate in explaining the economic development process for the countries that achieved economic development 200 or even 100 years ago. For the less developed countries today, however, the global environment is quite different. Simply put, there are today powerful

T A B L E   1 0 . 1

Levels of Analysis for Economic Development

Global Economy

- Intervention by dominant capitalist countries
- FDI from multinational corporations
- Rules dictated by global capitalist organizations
- Rich nation bias in world markets

National Structures

National Unity and Strong States

- Good governance to protect national interests in the global economy, as well as promote economic development

Specific Development Policies

- Programs developed by the nation and international agencies that account for national and local structures and microstructures

Local Structures and Microstructures

- Development policies considering local culture, social organization, social capital, and so on; one size does not fit all; positive or negative effects of culture and social organization on economic development depend upon the level of domestic economic development and waves in the global economy

corporations in competition with other powerful corporations, all of whom have stockholders demanding profits. To acquire such profits these corporations have moved around the world to obtain cheap resources, cheap labor, and a political climate of low taxes and lax environmental regulations. It is wrong to assume that the specific interests of multinational corporations and the long-term interests of poor nations are always in conflict. But often they are, and if unrestrained, outside actors will harm prospects for economic development and poverty reduction in less developed countries.

It would also be wrong to view these corporate actors as evil or unconcerned about the world's poor. But with extreme pressure to grab profits to expand their companies and please shareholders, these powerful corporate actors are unlikely to change their behavior. Something must collectively force these powerful corporations to change their behavior, or each nation must find ways to protect its own long-term development interests against the needs of these powerful outside corporations.

Table 10.1 is an effort to describe what those concerned about reducing world poverty need to consider with respect to all of these factors influencing economic development. We can begin at the bottom of the table that notes any attempt to promote sustained economic development and poverty reduction must recognize such things as particular value orientations, traditional patterns of social organization (e.g., family systems, village organization), and what social scientists refer to as social capital (e.g., how tightly connected or loosely connected the group or society may be, ability to work with outsiders). Previously one-size-fits-all approaches to economic development have been misguided in not considering these differences. Further, we must also recognize that these local characteristics of culture and social organization may have different effects on development chances depending upon the level of economic development of the country at the time and stages of the world economy (e.g., expanding or contracting stages, waves of new technologies, opportunities for labor-intensive or capital-intensive investments). All of this means that specific development policies created and implemented by national governments and international agencies must take these local aspects of culture and social organization into consideration. Specific development policies such as these can be called *technical means or tools of development*. These have not been the focus of this book, though some of these will be briefly considered later in this chapter.

Turning to the top of Table 10.1, however, we must recognize the global economic forces already described. These global forces and powerful outside economic actors can often have very negative effects on prospects for economic development and poverty reduction in less developed countries today. Thus, moving down to the level of "National Structures" in Table 10.1 these less developed nations must have means of protecting themselves from these forces and make sure the mix of outside effects is more positive than negative. *And*, because the rich and powerful in less developed countries often benefit from outside economic forces at the expense of the common people and poor in the country, these less developed nations must have leaders and a government that strongly identifies with or feels responsibility toward the common citizens of the nation rather than their own narrow self-interests.

The major questions guiding the comparative research in the previous chapters of this book have focused upon what allows for countries to have a development state giving them the means to protect the interests of their nation. Equally important, this book has focused on how nations come to have responsible and nationalistic elites with the motivation to use a strong development state for the interests of all citizens rather than just the rich. As past world system research has suggested, these nationalistic elites must use a strong development state to protect their national interests when multinational corporations seek investment opportunities in their country. But there are other dangers in the global economy that require counterpolicies to protect national interests. It is time to summarize some of the more important of these global dangers hanging over less developed countries.

A Different Free-Market World Economy

Despite all of their technical knowledge and otherwise good research, one of the most difficult things for the World Bank and similar international institutions (such as the Asian Development Bank) to understand is that the world economy is fundamentally different than it was 100, 200, or 300 years ago. The worldview of their sponsors (especially the United States) is a primary reason for the IMF and World Bank's focus on free-market solutions, often called the Washington consensus today. But free and open markets were extremely rare two centuries ago when today's rich countries were developing. And while free and open markets can contribute to competitiveness and economic efficiency in the already rich countries today, for poor countries struggling to develop, *the world economy today does not provide them with the same open market as the rich nations.* Most important, open markets do not always help poor countries when there are now *already rich countries over them, countries able to distort open markets with billions of dollars in subsidies to their own rich corporations and farmers, preventing infant industries in poorer countries from having an even chance of competition and survival* (see especially the arguments of recent Nobel economist Stiglit 2002). Indeed, the countries that became rich in the second wave of development more than 100 years ago (such as Germany and Japan) did so with decidedly *unfree* domestic markets protecting their infant industries.

Despite the rhetoric, the reality is that rich nations want other countries to have open markets so the rich nation can freely sell goods to these other countries and make direct investments in other countries (especially buying up foreign corporations cheaply) *while the rich country continues to protect its own industries.* This is why the United States and European Union countries fight with each other about who has the most subsidies to its farmers and other industries: What they are doing is trying to maneuver for advantage to protect their own industries while making other countries open theirs. Poor nations lack the power to do this as effectively (*International Herald Tribune,* February 21, 2004).

One example was the import of coco beans into the European Union countries. These EU countries do not have the climate to grow cocoa beans, but they need them to make all of that nice chocolate. So in their wisdom these rich countries set low import duties on the import of cocoa beans from African countries. However, if these African countries wanted to make the cocoa beans into chocolate themselves and export it to European Union countries the import duties were quite high. The message: We want to keep control of the more profitable economic venture of making chocolate; you keep to the low value business of growing cocoa beans. Another example is the markets forced open in Zambia. Zambia is one of the poorest countries in Africa, with 91 percent of its people living on less than $2 per day. Zambia once had a struggling clothing industry but was forced by the World Bank to open its markets 10 years ago in exchange for loans. Cheap secondhand clothes poured into Zambia. Within 8 years some 30,000 jobs were lost in the infant clothing industry in Zambia. The country has also lost something like half a million manufacturing jobs since 1990. The same thing happened in Nigeria where now fewer than 40 of Nigeria's 200 mills remain. The vast majority of textile factories in Uganda, Kenya, Tanzania and Malawi are shuttered as well. Thousands of workers have lost their jobs across Sub-Saharan Africa (*International Herald Tribune,* April 24, 2002; *Los Angeles Times,* July 14, 2004).

Global trade has increased some 60 percent in the past 10 years, but it has declined for the least developed nations because of trade barriers placed upon their goods by the rich nations. The United States has one of the highest tariffs on imported agricultural products to protect American farmers, though the European Union certainly has its share. There are hundreds of examples: Duties on imported textiles into the United States are relatively high unless the clothing is made abroad using American made textiles. In the European Union the duties on agricultural products are usually less than in the United States, but there are still many restrictions to protect European producers (*International Herald Tribune,* April 27, 2004). Ironically, while the United States finally decided to give substantial aid to countries hit by the tsunami of

December 2004, it also kept in place a ban on shrimp imports from Thailand where small fishing villages were struggling to recover from the devastation.

One estimate is that the 49 least developed nations in the world lose about $2.5 billion a year due to tariffs and quotas placed on their products by rich nations. In the case of Bangladesh, the aid agency Oxfam estimates the United States gets back $7 for every $1 given in aid because of import barriers. Oxfam also estimates that rich countries subsidize their own agribusinesses at a level of about $1 billion per day, which floods the world market with cheap food, while the IMF pushes these least developed countries to keep their markets open to these agricultural products (Watkins, 2001). Another estimate suggests that while rich nations give about $56 billion in aid to poor countries the rich nations subsidize their own industries to the tune of $300 billion each year to make them more competitive (*International Herald Tribune,* May 4, 2001; September 24, 2003; April 27, 2004). Another estimate is that each cow in the European Union is subsidized at about $2 per day, a sum placing European cows above almost half of the world's people who live on less than $2 per day. During the first 3 years of the George W. Bush administration the level of farm subsidies in the United States increased by some $40 billion in return for large campaign contributions from big agribusiness firms.[3] *The least developed nations simply have no means to support their own farmers or businesses with such subsidies to make them more competitive like rich nations continue to do.* When forced to open their markets to products from rich nations backed by these government subsidies, they cannot compete and are forced out of business. One of the best tactics to counter these unfair subsidies would be for poorer nations that have states able to protect their own interests to use the somewhat democratic World Trade Organization to challenge these practices. By 2004 there was at least some action to do so (*International Herald Tribune,* April 27, 2004).

To their credit, in 2001 the European Union agreed to drastically reduce all tariffs and import quotas on goods from the least developed nations. This is expected to help the poorest countries develop and reduce poverty by increasing their exports to the European Union by 15 to 20 percent a year. The United States has so far refused to do so. World poverty could be substantially reduced if rich countries would practice the free trade they preach by opening their borders to goods from poor countries. World poverty would also be dramatically reduced if the rich nations allowed the less developed nations, for a period of time at least, to protect their own infant industries from cheaper manufactured goods from the rich nations, as the United States did to help Japan, South Korea, and Taiwan during the cold war years. The development states in these East Asian countries were able to cut deals with the United States for economic protection. Some countries in Southeast Asia, such as Thailand and Malaysia, have development states that have also been able to protect their infant industries so they could develop. Most other poor nations cannot. We will consider how Thailand was able to do so after we examine a few more critical aspects of today's global economy.

The Impact of Outside Corporate Investment

Agencies such as the World Bank are too often blinded by their free-market ideology and cannot see how free markets for rich countries harm the least developed nations. Antiglobalization protesters are often blinded by their antiglobalism and anticapitalism and cannot see how outside multinational investments in poor countries can, *under certain conditions,* help reduce poverty. The beliefs of antiglobal protesters from rich countries, on the other hand, are to some extent correct. Rich corporations can make people in less developed nations poorer—but as we have seen, this is not always the case. Thailand, of course, is one of the best examples of solid growth and poverty reduction. Many other countries in East Asia, among them South Korea, Taiwan, and now China, are also good examples.

We have seen that earlier research from the world system perspective indicated that outside multinational corporate investment more often than not led to less long-term economic growth and at times even higher rates of poverty. The second wave of research using data from the 1980s and 1990s was less likely to find a significant correlation between outside corporate investment and less economic development and poverty reduction. But, all the research indicates there is less long-term economic development with outside corporate investment with at least some nations; whether or not it is half the poor nations in the world or slightly less than half the nations is not as much the point as the simple fact there are mixed results. Recent research has shown, for example, the high levels of outside corporate investment are not so negative when the outside investment comes from many different rich countries rather than just two or three (Kentor & Boswell, 2003). When there is a broad mix of outside investment coming from many different countries, the less developed countries such as Thailand are able to prevent themselves from becoming as dominated and forced to do things against their long-term interests. We will also see below how some countries like Thailand have been able to require that this outside corporate investment comes into their country in the form of "joint ventures" with their own domestic firms so their own industries are able to get some of the technology knowhow from rich multinationals and ensure much of the profits from these outside corporate investments stay in the country.

Policies and Technical Tools for Economic Development

The main focus of the chapters in this book has been the global economy and a history of political and economic forces in poorer countries that allow for or hinder economic development. However, a summary of some specific development policies and technical tools that can be used to promote economic development and poverty reduction will be useful. Many of these policies and tools for development have been shown quite effective. The problem, usually, is the inability of a nation to use these tools and sustain the policies. By policies for economic development I am referring to integrated policies that will rationally promote growth and poverty reduction that can be carried out over the long term. By "technical tools" I mean specific programs that involve new technologies going to farmers, ways of providing aid, and other things that can accompany the broader policies for economic development.

Import Substitution and Export Industries

The most widely used policies of the successful countries of East and Southeast Asia involve *important substitution* and the development of *export industries*. Import substitution simply means attempts to discourage imported goods so that the domestic economy of the less developed country can start making the products itself. Import substitution is the main policy against the problem of structural distortion in the economy described earlier in this book. With structural distortion of the economy some raw materials and even labor are taken out of the country and then used for advanced manufacturing of products and services in rich nations. These products or services are then sold back to the less developed country, or rather sold to the few wealthy and middle-class people who can afford them. The problem, of course, is that when the goods are made in other countries the less developed country loses the jobs and profits from the chain of economic activity leading to the final products. This is the distorted economy that leads to economic stagnation.

The problem with carrying out a long-term policy of import substitution is (1) it takes a long time to get such industries operating in the poorer country, (2) there is often little capital (money to invest) to start up the industries, and (3) wealthy groups within the poor country resist delaying their gratification of consumer goods while waiting until the startup industries are operating in the poorer country. This is why a strong development state is needed to implement and follow through with a policy of import substitution. A development state must make conditions right for aid, domestic savings, or startup capital from richer nations if the policy is to be successful. And a strong development state must be able to restrain the more affluent within its own country so that its spending on imported goods will not undermine this development strategy.

Once some industries for import substitution are in place the focus can shift to developing export industries. Rather than import goods made in richer countries, less developed countries would prefer rich countries to buy *their* exported goods. This is a policy that can turn the usual disadvantage for poorer countries on its head. Once they have industries exporting products to richer countries this can reverse the flow of international trade, meaning a favorable balance of trade bringing a net surplus of money into the less developed country. This favorable balance of trade will then accumulate financial resources for further investment in the domestic economy of the less developed nation. Simply put, a flood of consumer goods such as televisions, stereos, bicycles, and textiles into the United States, Europe, and Japan has helped fuel the economic expansion of Asian tiger economies in recent decades.

Land Redistribution and Agriculture Policies

As made clear in a recent report by the International Fund for Agricultural Development, *Rural Poverty Report 2001: The Challenge of Ending Rural Poverty* (IFAD, 2001), a majority of the world's poor live in rural areas. Thus, it makes sense to develop technical policies for poverty reduction that target this rural population. As logical as this sounds, such policies have seldom been followed. The short-term payoff for the more affluent is greater in promoting urban industrialization, and if agricultural development is given much attention it is usually agricultural development for export that enriches wealthy landowners while impoverishing peasants.

For the benefit of the rural poor in developing countries, though, the focus (at least at first) must be on more labor-intensive and lower tech agricultural development for domestic consumption. We have seen how the green revolution, which focused on more chemicals and farm machinery to produce crops for the global market, worked to produce more food but at the same time impoverish local farmers and peasants. Thus, rather than putting machines to work it is best to put more people to work even if it is less productive. With more labor-intensive farm production, more food, jobs, and profits are more equally distributed in poor rural areas. The rising standards of living for these rural people will eventually create more consumers and *help sustain economic development over the long term.*

We have also seen that much of the problem is related to land inequality in less developed countries. As many studies have shown, land reform policies that get more land to the cultivators themselves is one of the best ways to reduce world poverty (IFAD, 2001:Chapter 3). When peasants and farmers own their own land, farming is often more productive, agriculture is more labor intensive (which creates more farm jobs), and small farmers and peasants are able to keep more of the profits themselves (obviously helping to reduce poverty rates). Thailand's poverty reduction has been furthered by one of the lowest levels of land inequality in the world, with the Gini index of land inequality at 0.37 compared to levels of 0.60 to 0.90 for Latin American and African nations. (See Table 2.3 in Chapter 2.) This lucky historical legacy of Thailand, and to some extent Asia more generally, has been a key to less poverty and more balanced economic development.

So if land inequality is one of the basic problems, why not promote the redistribution of land? *It has been tried,* but has very seldom succeeded. It worked in Japan, but only because the devastation of World War II put the U.S. occupation forces in charge, and General MacArthur was willing to push land reform on a willing Japanese population. We have seen that during the 1970s the United States under President Carter attempted to impose land reform in Central America. The idea was to give incentives and payments to wealthy landowners, and loans to peasants so they could buy land taken from big haciendas. What seemed like a good idea resulted in political violence and revolution throughout most of Central America. After the first stage of this land reform which focused on the largest of the haciendas was started, it broke down. Other landowners resisted, peasants who had their hopes raised became angry, and political violence spiraled upward as both sides attacked the other. The results were even more right-wing military coups throughout the region. There was one brief revolutionary government emerging in Nicaragua, but the Reagan administration quickly activated the CIA to aid the "Contras" who brought down the Sandinista government.

Only life-altering disasters for a country, such as World War II for Japan, or a strong development state with the power to induce all parties to make sacrifices for the long-term future of the nation, can successfully pull off significant land reform. But even in this situation there are no guarantees of effective policies. Communist countries from Eastern Europe to China and Vietnam have created catastrophe with collective farms. The fall of communism also brought down these collective farms, and Vietnam, as we have seen, has given us an example of how collective farms can be privatized and land use more equally distributed to stimulate agricultural production and increasing standards of living. (Vietnam became the second largest exporter of rice and coffee by 2000.) Then there is the case of Zimbabwe and Mugabe. His idea of land reform was taking it away from white farmers and giving it to his few remaining political supporters who had no idea of good farming methods. Agricultural output, of course, quickly dropped (*International Herald Tribune,* August 1, 2001).

CASE IN POINT

Independent Thai Peasants and Political Action

One afternoon during the spring of 1998 I sat with a group of students along Ratchadamnoen Road in Bangkok, just past Democracy Monument, watching thousands upon thousands of Thai peasant farmers marching by on their way to Government House (the Thai Parliament building). Most were walking, though many were piled into village pickup trucks. The mood was quite Thai, which is to say there was a lot of *sanuk* (joking and having fun). These people from the countryside seemed as interested in watching us farangs (Western foreigners) as we were them; many waved and said "hullo," some even shook our hands as they marched by. A few were singing protest songs, and we had to smile when some of the people marching by wore T-shirts with Che Guevara's picture on the front. (We later asked some farmers who had the old Cuban revolutionary's picture on their pickup truck if they knew who he was; the answer was "no." They just knew that the picture was a symbol of protest against the rich.) There had been, and would be, many other such protests by rural Thais. Just a few months later we saw a similar, though somewhat smaller protest on the same street near Democracy Monument which blocked traffic for a couple of days. This time it was lottery ticket vendors who were protesting government plans to change rules that would reduce their income from ticket sales (*Bangkok Post*, January 20, 1998).

Most of these rural protests have been led by the Assembly of the Poor (also translated as the Forum for the Poor), a broad-based social movement organization involved in all kinds of rural and environmental issues (*Bangkok Post*, December 11, 1997, February 7, 1998, April 12, 2001; Missingham, 2003). During the late 1980s one of the most famous, and successful, cases of protest by villagers and environmentalists permanently stopped development of the Nam Choan dam. It was a fight with the Thai government which runs the power authority to prevent the destruction of peasant lands. Several village people were killed, but it was a victory for peasant villagers and environmentalists that further inspired one of the strongest rural environmentalist movements among developing countries (*Bangkok Post*, February 20, 1998). Through the 1990s and into the twenty-first century the movement is still pushing, and sometimes winning, causes such as stopping power plants and chemical dumps near village lands, further destruction of forest lands, and gas pipelines being cut through forests in western and southern Thailand (*Bangkok Post*, December 13, 1997, December 10, 1998; see also various summer 2000 issues).

According to one of Thailand's most respected team of economists, the current wave of protests by Thai villagers began in the 1970s when new economic development policies were being implemented. By the mid-1990s, they estimate, there were at least two rural protests movements going on each day in Thailand (Pasuk & Baker, 1996:162, 206). The urban population of Bangkok has become a political force in recent decades. But with peasants living in small villagers making up most of the Thai population, and a large percentage of these people relatively well organized politically, rural issues have been kept before Thai politicians.

To understand the position of Thai peasants compared to peasants in other developing countries (especially Latin America and Africa) requires a little diversion into the history of rural Thailand. First, we must recognize that the concept of national boundaries was foreign to mainland Southeast Asia. The kingdoms of Pagan, Angkor, and Siam (Thailand), for

(Continued)

(Continued)

example, extended only as far as their power to enforce rules over villages. As one got further away from the capital cities this meant that the question of which kingdom holds the area was often fuzzy. This also meant that peasants in these areas were relatively independent, at least until one kingdom or another came in to press its claims of sovereignty over the people. Second, in contrast to most other agricultural countries in the world, even when territories were not in dispute, there was almost no landed aristocracy to dominate Thai peasants because theoretically the king owned the land (Keyes, 1989:31).

In reality, however, early Thai kings did not actively occupy this land or send their agents to run plantations for them. Rather, the land was given to peasants and village people through a sort of lifetime lease that could be passed on to offspring but not sold to others (Pasuk & Baker, 1995:7–8). In other words, in a major contrast to the position of peasants in the preindustrial feudal countries of Europe, Latin America, and elsewhere in Asia (especially Japan), mainland Southeast Asian peasants had their own land, had no feudal lord dominating them, and were relatively independent of outsiders from urban areas. The current Thai king still owns much of the land all over the country. The logo for the King's Crown Property Bureau that manages such property is found on buildings in small cities throughout Thailand (Muscat, 1994:260). Local wats (temples) all over Thailand, however, also own much land today and lease it out almost free of charge to villagers and peasants in the area. All of this explains why today we find some 90 percent of rural people with their own land in Thailand (Kulick & Wilson, 1996:132). Conditions for these Southeast Asian peasants were not always ideal; there was a shortage of population for rural and urban development projects by early kings, which meant that kings would from time to time attempt to enforce their potential power to demand a period of free labor from peasants. Also, battles between kingdoms were often fought to claim population, not just land (Girling, 1981; Wyatt, 1984). Falling into slavery because of capture by a newly aggressive kingdom was always possible. Still, these possibilities were usually not everyday realities for most mainland Southeast Asian peasants. As noted earlier, this is why Thai peasants have been described as possibly unique. . . . The countryside developed a relatively egalitarian society of small independent farmers, with little urban influence, and strong traditions.

Other Technical Tools for Economic Development

One of the most popular of the new technical tools for economic development and poverty reduction are *microloans* made famous in 1976 by the Grameen Bank in Bangladesh. The idea is to loan small amounts of money to farmers or villages so these people can obtain the things they need to increase their economic rewards. A small pump costing only $50 can make a very big difference in a village without the means of irrigation. A couple of hundred dollars for a small bridge linking a village to a city where it can market farm products is another.[4] A specific example is the Thai government's People's Bank which is making loans of $100 to $300 to help farmers buy equipment or seeds, help street vendors acquire an inventory to sell, or help others set up small shops.

There are numerous other examples of important tools for promoting sustainable economic development covered in other sections throughout this book. For example, we have seen that population control is a key. Too many new and unproductive people harm chances for economic development. When everything produced goes to feed more people there is no savings for investment in infrastructure and new industries. Likewise, empowering women has helped some countries increase and sustain economic development. When given more rights and opportunities women begin to receive more education, thus increasing the overall human capital of the country; when given more influence women seem to act more responsibly in helping people in the family or village; and when better educated and more in control of their lives, women are more successful in bringing down rapid population growth because they have more say in family planning (World Bank, 2001a). Expanding educational opportunities for all people in the society is obviously another possible tool for long-term economic development and poverty reduction in less developed societies.[5]

In one way or another, however, all of these technical means of economic development and poverty reduction (such as microloans, empowering women, and better agricultural policies) depend upon the *will and the means to implement them.* Thus, though these tools are important in the fight against world poverty, the primary focus of this book has been on what sociologists call social structures. We have focused on the historical forces that have made it more or less difficult for poor nations to reduce poverty because of the nature of their state, relations between elites and masses, national unity, and relations with outside powers. Many of the nations in Asia have been more advantaged with respect to these historical legacies. In one way or another, the successful Asian nations have used some form of development state to implement various technical policies of economic development, and as suggested at the bottom of Table 10.1, technical policies that make sense given the resources, culture, and traditional social organization of each individual country. But because the Asian development state has been under attack since the Asian economic crisis of 1997 and the stagnation of Japan from the early 1990s it is imperative that we give more attention to the Asian development model and its future before we conclude.

Thai Development Policies: An Asian Example

Thailand is by no means an egalitarian country. By Latin American standards the level of income inequality in Thailand is low, but it is among the highest in East and Southeast Asia. Although land inequality is low in Thailand, throughout the last few decades only four families have controlled much of the *industrial wealth* in the country. The Asian economic crisis of 1997 eliminated Thailand's representation on the world's list of individual billionaires, even though the wealth of the richest families in Thailand rebounded by 2002 (*Bangkok Post,* June 19, 1992, June 22, 1998; Muscat, 1994:115). But despite this concentration of industrial wealth, we have already seen that Thailand has one of developing world's best records of poverty reduction. In short, while the rich have been getting richer in Thailand, the poor have been less and less poor as well. It is important to consider how Thailand has pulled it off. Some of the details are different when compared to other successful nations, especially Thailand's focus on domestic agricultural development early in its development plans. But for the most part Thailand followed strategies that had been used earlier by Taiwan and South Korea. Other countries in the region, most recently China, are now following much the same model.

DATA FILE

Technical Means of Poverty Reduction Are Not Universally Applicable— Education and Development

by Patrick Ziltener

In this final Data File we need to stress that all technical means of poverty reduction and economic development are not equally applicable to all less developed countries. As noted in this chapter and others, a strong and efficient development state is a key to economic development because each country requires its own specific analysis of what is needed to maintain evenly spread economic development and poverty reduction. In a phrase, one size does not fit all.

It might seem that expanding educational opportunities would be exempt from this above caution. A common assumption is that "of course expanding education to all people will help the society and everyone in it become less poor." The scatter plot shown in Figure 10.1, however, suggests that this assumption is not completely accurate. There is no simple correlation between the level of education in a society and the percent of population living on less than $1 per day. For example, there are some countries with low levels of education and low levels of poverty, such as Tanzania. The countries with low levels of people living on less than $1 per day can be found up and down the scale measuring percent of the population enrolled in secondary education. This is *not to say that education fails to help*. But what it does say is that policy makers in developing countries should make rational assessments of how much education is needed at their level of development, what kind of education is needed (more general primary education, more university education, more technical junior college education), and how best to implement new educational policies. As you will see below, Thai Ministry of Education officials have decided that what Thailand needs most for further economic development is specific job training for new high-tech industries. Other countries in Asia, such as China, Vietnam, and even Laos, have lower labor costs than Thailand because of Thailand's increasing standard of living. Thus, rather than simply providing more primary, secondary, and university educational opportunities, Thailand is in the process of upgrading its multicampus technical junior college system.

Not long after the military took power during the 1932 coup in Thailand an alliance was formed between the Thai military and ministry bureaucrats. Because of the worldwide depression and then World War II, it was not until the late 1950s that serious consideration could be given to economic development policies. When these policies were finally started, one of the most important things to emphasize related to economic development and poverty reduction in Thailand is that, relative to other countries, *these policies did not mean economic development would proceed on the backs of Thai peasants* (Muscat, 1994:245).

For most countries trying to catch up to the industrialized West in the last 150 years, rapid economic development has meant a focus on urban industry. To achieve this rapid industrial expansion the countries extracted surpluses from peasants. In other

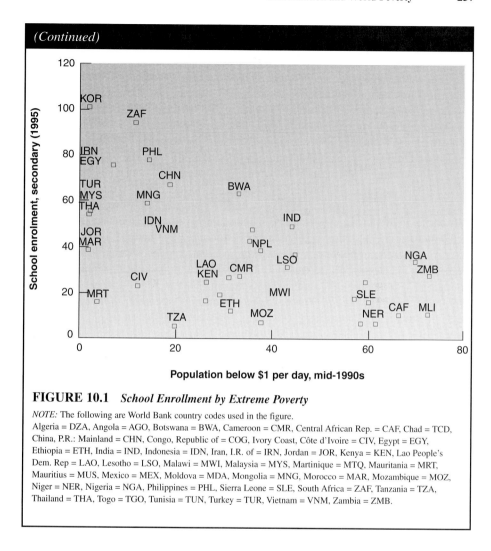

(Continued)

FIGURE 10.1 *School Enrollment by Extreme Poverty*

NOTE: The following are World Bank country codes used in the figure.
Algeria = DZA, Angola = AGO, Botswana = BWA, Cameroon = CMR, Central African Rep. = CAF, Chad = TCD,
China, P.R.: Mainland = CHN, Congo, Republic of = COG, Ivory Coast, Côte d'Ivoire = CIV, Egypt = EGY,
Ethiopia = ETH, India = IND, Indonesia = IDN, Iran, I.R. of = IRN, Jordan = JOR, Kenya = KEN, Lao People's
Dem. Rep = LAO, Lesotho = LSO, Malawi = MWI, Malaysia = MYS, Martinique = MTQ, Mauritania = MRT,
Mauritius = MUS, Mexico = MEX, Moldova = MDA, Mongolia = MNG, Morocco = MAR, Mozambique = MOZ,
Niger = NER, Nigeria = NGA, Philippines = PHL, Sierra Leone = SLE, South Africa = ZAF, Tanzania = TZA,
Thailand = THA, Togo = TGO, Tunisia = TUN, Turkey = TUR, Vietnam = VNM, Zambia = ZMB.

words, to fuel industrial expansion a country must overcome the problem of how to finance new industries for the strategy of important substitution noted earlier. Extracting surpluses from the peasants means keeping food prices and the income of farmers artificially low so that the savings or profits can be put into urban industries instead of going to farmers. This is how Stalin developed the old Soviet Union in the 1930s, and how Japanese governments did it in the early twentieth century. As in other countries, Soviet and Japanese peasants rebelled, but mostly just got poorer and often starved. Not so in Thailand.[6] As we have already seen, by improving the standard of living for farmers a country may not develop urban industry as rapidly, but the economic development achieved will more likely be evenly spread throughout the country, more likely to reduce poverty, and more sustainable in the long run.

In later years there was also the Rural Employment Generation Program which gave each *tambon,* or group of villages, in the country a substantial annual grant that could be spent on agricultural development projects of their choosing, a policy that provided a '"bottom-up' approach to rural development" (Muscat, 1994:138–139). In addition to this focus on agriculture, the first 5-year plan called for "raising the standard of living" as the main objective, along with care that "increased output should be equitably distributed so that, to the extent possible, all citizens, and not merely a privileged few, derive benefit from it" (Muscat, 1994:95). All lofty ideas of course, but given their track record of poverty reduction and economic development with a relatively smaller gap between rural and urban standards of living, we can say that at the time Thai government and ministry officials did a fairly good job of pulling it off.

Aside from agriculture, from the beginning of these Thai development policies in the 1950s the focus was also on *import substitution*. In this critical strategy, a development state must be able to tell multinational corporations from rich countries that goods will be imported, if at all, with tariffs as high as 80 to even 150 percent so as to prevent these goods from competing with goods made in (at least at first) less efficient infant factories in the poorer country. We have seen that a strong development state must do this because only a strong state can have the influence to enforce such a policy on rich multinational corporations (and their governments who will almost certainly try to resist); and only a strong state can have the influence to enforce such a policy against the demands of its own minority of rich citizens who want the imported goods, "and want them now," at a cheaper price, without waiting for infant domestic industries to produce suitable products.

Thailand was especially successful with this strategy in the auto industry. From the 1970s Thailand began placing tariffs of 150 percent on imported autos. But at the same time the Thai government told foreign auto companies that if they come to Thailand to create a joint venture with a Thai company to build cars—and thus hire Thai employees, pay Thai taxes, and keep some profits within Thailand—the auto company would get many forms of government assistance (Muscat, 1994:148). Except for American auto companies, they came in big numbers. With more than 20,000 additional autos on the streets of Bangkok monthly during many years of the 1990s, the foreign auto makers and Thais did quite well. Ford and GM finally started making cars and trucks in Thailand in the late 1990s. During interviews I conducted with some Ford and GM executives in Thailand at that time they admitted it was a big mistake to wait so long.

During the 1980s and 1990s Thailand continued to protect itself in the face of the flood of foreign investment they had attracted. This is especially important because, as we have seen in earlier chapters, without protections that a strong state can enforce, long-term economic growth can actually be reduced by extensive foreign investment in the country. In this regard, Thai bureaucrats enforced rules such as those demanding a sufficient percentage of domestic content in goods manufactured by foreign companies in Thailand and the famous *51 percent rule*. (Muscat, 1994:80). Under this *51 percent rule*, a foreign company setting up production operations in Thailand must form a joint venture with a Thai company. The intended result is that a Thai company with 51 percent control will be better able to keep profits in the country, press for technology transfers (for example, give the 51 percent controlled Thai company the copyrights and patent rights to the technology), and enforce other corporate policies that will be more beneficial to the Thai economy.

We have also seen that a high level of outside multinational corporate investment from one or a few countries can hurt long-term economic development in a poor country.

Such a high concentration of outside investment for one country can give that rich country too much power over the economy and even political system of the less developed country. Research has shown that Thailand was quite successful in avoiding this trap by attracting a mix of investment from many countries (Kentor & Boswell, 2003). During interviews with the Thai Bureau of Investment and corporate executives from American and Japanese corporations in Thailand I learned that one way Thailand achieved this mix of investment from many countries was through selective application of the 51 percent rule. Japanese executives, for example, complained that Thai Ministry officials sometimes gave exceptions to American companies because they worried about Thailand becoming too dependent upon outside investment from Japan (for examples of Thai investment policies and restrictions see *Bangkok Post*, October 2, 1998 August 18, 2000, September 25, 2003; *International Herald Tribune*, November 21, 2003).

Perhaps one of the most important policies of the Thai development state is one to protect small Thai farmers. Considering Thailand has mostly small farmers and very few big agribusiness landholdings, these small farmers would be at the mercy of big multinational agribusiness corporations if left unprotected. But the Thai government does not allow that. Unlike almost all other less developed countries, the Thai government sets standards, model contracts, and makes sure multinational agribusiness corporations compete and pay fair prices to Thai farmers (Singh, 2003).

The next stage of development policies for the twenty-first century are in the planning phase. Thai ministry officials know all too well that as wages creep up, and as the infrastructure of lower wage countries in the region (such as Vietnam, Laos, Cambodia, and especially China) improves, the foreign investment from rich countries attracted by cheap labor will move away from Thailand. They have various plans for countering this unstoppable trend. (Unstoppable, that is, except for trying to keep Thai workers poor as is done in some other less developed countries.) For example, during interviews with the top three officials in the Thai Ministry of Education's Department of Vocational Education, I was told of their plan to expand the 36-campus Rajabhat Institute from a junior college system to a full 4 year BA-granting university system, using the California State University system as a model. Their primary concern is to upgrade Thailand's human capital, especially in engineering and science, so that Thailand could begin to match the higher tech focus for economic development in countries such as South Korea and Taiwan. Before the Asian economic crisis of 1997 I was told by both Japanese and American executives that their higher tech investments in Thailand were limited because there was an 11,000 annual deficit of trained engineers. With economic recovery proceeding strongly by 2000 this deficit of engineers and other higher tech employees has returned (see also the *Bangkok Post*, September 12 & 23, 1997).

A Conclusion and View from the Hill Tribes

Lest we lose track of what this debate over such things such as development states and outside corporate investment mean to real humans, perhaps it is fitting that we close with another visit to some people who have been affected by it all—Thailand's hill tribes. Among the 13 percent of Thai people considered living below the poverty line, and among small percentage of Thai people living under $1 per day (less than 2 percent), hill tribe people make up a large number. Thailand's hill tribes have the worst rates of

While hill tribe people are still among the poorest people in Thailand, people in villages such as this one are much better off than their relatives in Burma and Laos. In Thailand, there are many government programs and projects financed by the king of Thailand to help them make the transition from growing poppies for opium to vegetables and fruit crops.

almost everything in the nation, from life expectancy and infant mortality, to drug addiction and AIDS. But considering neighboring countries (particularly Burma, Laos, and Cambodia) these conditions could be and have been worse. The Thai government has been working for years to provide these tribal people with better land and other means of becoming successful farmers, as well as more educational programs, medical care, and more protection from some who see these people as only tourist attractions (see especially the *Bangkok Post,* November 16, 1997; December 14, 18, 29, 1997).

One of my most memorable days in Thailand was spent in a northern hill tribe area a couple of hours from the city of Chiang Mai. This part of Thailand is one of the most beautiful, and has a distinct advantage of being much cooler, especially when rain and fog cover the high mountaintops. It is in this thick jungle area that ancient hill tribes still live, hill tribes who continue to be proud of their traditions and show their tribal identity through bright color combinations in their clothing and headdresses.

This particular day I was visiting a Hmong village with an anthropologist from Chiang Mai University and Thailand's Hill Tribe Research Institute, a man who as a young child himself grew up in a similar village further north. As we walk around the village the anthropologist spoke to many people and introduced me. An extremely generous people, I was offered food, drink, and a comfortable place to sit in each household we visited. One old man in particular was most friendly and invited us to stay for a while and talk. He explained that he was getting too old to join the others working in the fields and orchards every day, so it was only he and his also elderly wife who were at home. His children and several grandchildren lived in the household with him and he showed us where they all slept and cooked their meals as we were invited inside the wooden house with an earthen floor. We sat talking for more than an hour, him telling us about the history of his tribe, his life, and that of his family. Eventually he started "interviewing" me with the anthropologist acting as interpreter: He wanted to know something about my country, how I could arrive in northern Thailand, and what I thought of his homeland. He asked one question that made us smile. He wanted to know what tribe I come from in America. I talked about extended families and where mine had come from—I didn't think quickly enough at the time and lost my chance to tell him something about American Indians and my maternal grandfather who was born on a Cherokee Indian reservation in Oklahoma at the beginning of the twentieth century. I am sure he would have appreciated hearing about the plight of American Indians and some parallels to his own situation.

As we sat there that day the anthropologist and then the old man himself explained that his tribe no longer lives close to the top of mountains in this Golden Triangle area where Thailand, Burma, and Laos come together. Like other hill tribes in the Thai part of the Golden Triangle I have visited over the years, particularly Akah, Lisu, and other Hmong tribes, they now live in lower areas on land given to them by the Thai government through relocation programs. For centuries these tribal people grew poppies for opium that was sold to people all over Asia, and later to drug dealers who produced and sold the much more potent heroin. With the drug repression programs carried out by the Thai government under U.S. assistance, these people were relocated to lower land and given aid and assistance to begin lives as farmers growing fruits and vegetables for local markets. It was unavoidable the anthropologist, himself a Hmong told me, because with the sale of opium successfully stopped in the area these people would have nothing else to live on in the rough terrain of higher elevations.

These relocation programs are of course controversial and in some ways very unfortunate. It is likely that many of their old traditions will be eroded over time, though it seems these traditions still thrived in most villages. I have observed traditional ceremonies in a few of the hill tribe villages, and they continue to make and wear traditional clothing, jewelry, and crafts that are now also taken to the tourist areas of Chiang Mai where sales seem reasonably profitable. The only tribal villages seeming to lack most of their old traditions are those recently converted to fundamentalist Christianity by some American missionary groups. I asked my anthropologist guide, for example, why people in one Akah village were not wearing their traditional clothing while the people in another Akah village just a mile away continued those traditions. The tribe in this particular village, I was told, had been forbidden to follow many of their traditional rituals or wear traditional clothing by the missionaries. As is common with such people, their old traditions are rooted in ancient non-Christian animist beliefs and practices that this particular missionary group wanted to eradicate. There was a new little wooden church at the end of the earthen path leading up the hill, well placed to look down the path at all the family huts in the village. At the other end of the path, a bit further down the hill where individual family huts begin, I was told there was a family who was appointed by the missionaries to keep watch over village people from the other end of the village.

As for the other Hmong, Lisu, and Akah tribal villages I have visited, the people seem to not only uphold many of their old traditions but also to do comparatively well economically. There is no running water, though some have electricity and a number of prized material possessions—especially new motorbikes, with at least four or five in every village. The old man I sat and talked with that afternoon didn't have many complaints. He told me things were better now and he was happy for his children and grandchildren. My anthropologist guide that day, as well as other anthropologists from the Hill Tribe Research Institute who have taken me to other hill tribe villages over the years, concur.

Such is decidedly *not* the case for their hill tribe brothers and sisters in Burma and Laos. These poor people were better off in earlier times. Particularly in Burma, thousands upon thousands of hill tribe people have been killed by various factions fighting against each other and the Burmese Army. The British, as we have seen, left their former colony without settlement of old land disputes and issues of political independence. The central Burmese government then claimed all of these tribal people were under their complete authority, and rebellion broke out from that point. Unable to defeat these tough tribal people outright, the Burmese military has used divide and rule tactics, hoping to control them in that manner. Added to all of this, as the Chinese communists defeated the Nationalists (Kuomintang) in the late 1940s, many of the Chinese Nationalist Army forces in south-central China became trapped and moved down into the mountains of Burma to survive. Most eventually made their way to Taiwan where their government in exile has been ever since. But many of these Chinese Nationalist Army forces stayed in the mountains of Burma when they realized there were good profits to be made growing poppies and producing opium and then heroin. This is the origin of some famous "drug warlords" of Burma. With the retirement of the most famous drug warlord, Khun Sa in the early 1990s, and no other viable economic activity in the northern Burmese mountains, other indigenous drug warlords have turned to amphetamines and other chemical drug production to feed their families, as well as to buy arms to continue their fight against the Burmese military dictators (*International Herald Tribune,* October 27, 2000, July 18, 2001; Mirante, 1993; Smith, 1999).

To the east, the hill tribes of Laos have fared little better. There is even some continuing warfare, and many are repressed by the Laotian communist government still resentful of their anticommunist sympathies and the military support these hill tribe people gave to the United States during the American part of the Vietnam War. Fighting flares up from time to time, but there is nothing like the violence a couple of decades ago or the continuing violence in the Burmese hill tribe areas. In one village of tribal Hmong I visited in the Chiang Mai area a few years ago a women sold me her embroidery artwork one day. An old tradition of this particular tribe is to create pictures with their sewing that depict tribal history. This woman proudly showed me her work illustrating where their village was originally located in Laos, how her village was attacked by soldiers in Laos (men with AK-47s were depicted firing on the village), how her ancestors finally fled by swimming across the Mekong River into Thailand, and how Thai soldiers threatened them and herded them into refugee camps. The final panel of her embroidery indicated the village where they now live in peace. Today, most hill tribe people still in Laos barely exist on land that does not provide an adequate living. Many are still in the drug business to survive, which is why in 2000 the United States and the Laotian Communist Party signed a new treaty to work against hill tribe drug production and smuggling.

The Hmong village who fled and finally found a new home in Thailand were indeed lucky. Like other hill tribe villages in Thailand they have been the recipient of land and aid to help make them self-supporting and very obviously less poor compared to the hill tribe people of Burma and Laos. The old man who sat in his home interviewing me that afternoon a few years ago told me he had never been to school, and could neither read nor write. (He was proud that his grandchildren were receiving some education, though he complained people were trying to teach them too many useless things.) He knew nothing of the history of Thai development policies that had made Thailand one of the world's success stories in poverty reduction. But those hill tribes in Thailand who have contact with others from Burma or Laos must certainly know they are fortunate.

As we have discussed in this book, however, we cannot expect the other poor countries of the world to follow the exact path of economic development and poverty reduction engineered by Thailand. With respect to development formulas, it is clear that one size does *not* fit all. When we move outside Southeast Asia, to Latin America and Africa, the development formulas must be even further from what Thailand has followed. However, the commonality will be a strong and efficient state providing what world agencies now call good governance. These nations must be able to keep their own long-term economic and political interests from being hijacked by outside countries and corporations, as well as the wealthier and more powerful within the country. How this will be achieved is the most difficult part for poor nations without the old traditions of ancient civilizations and legacy of some state building before European colonials took over their country. It is not hopeless for other countries, but we have seen it is more difficult. However it is achieved, though, once good governance is achieved, the historical and comparative perspective of this book has shown that each country must consider its own mix of resources, historical legacies, and its geopolitical context in developing and carrying out its development policies.

In the future, when others sit down with old men in poor villages around the world as I did in a Hmong village one day, we can hope they will hear more and more stories about how the tribe or village has become better off. The stories will have different details, for in no other country will the development policies of Thailand fit exactly. But in general, the stories will have similarities if there has been progress.

Notes

1. The proceedings of the World Bank/ UN conference during October 4 to October 7, as well as conference papers can be obtained from the World Bank Web page at http://www.worldbank.org as of spring 2001.
2. Also at the World Bank Web site see the Learning and Research Program titled "Culture and Poverty."
3. For example, only 10 percent of farms in the United States get 65 percent of all U.S. farm subsidies. These are the big agribusiness firms that increased their contributions to $52 million for the Republican Party after Bush's farm subsidy increases (*International Herald Tribune,* September 10, 2003).
4. See the *International Herald Tribune,* May 8, 2001, August 11, 2003. Also see the Microcredit Summit Campaign Web site, http://www.microcreditsummit.org, and the Grameen Bank Web site, http://www.grameen-info.org/.
5. For example, see the Development Gateway Web site, http://www.developmentgateway.org/topics/special/primary-education/.
6. Phongpaichit Pasuk and Chris Baker, *Thailand's Boom* (Chiang Mai, Thailand: Silkworm Books, 1996), p. 58). It was Prime Minister Sarit who directed the government ministry to begin development policies with a focus on the agricultural sector. This was further formalized in the first five-year plan of 1961 in which the document stated, among other things: "Over the next three years the construction of irrigation works, the building and improvement of roads and other means of transport, the provision of inexpensive electric power, and the other physical 'infrastructure' projects will claim the bulk of Government expenditure. Agricultural extension and other projects to extend technical knowledge will likewise take a high share of Government investment." (Quoted in Robert J. Muscat. The Fifth Tiger: A study of Thai Development [Armonk, NY:M.E. Sharpe, 1994], p. 95.)

Web Resources

In this final section of the book I would like to provide a short introduction to some of the most useful Web resources pertaining to poverty around the world. There are obviously hundreds of Web sites which may be helpful with some information about the subject, but the list which follows includes those I have found most useful in providing information.

World Bank, http://www.worldbank.com/ The World Bank is obviously one of the most useful sources of information about world poverty and programs to reduce poverty. While there are always some problems in data collection in poor countries, all countries which hope to gain aid or guidance from the World Bank were required to provide cooperation in collecting data about many questions relating to economic development and standards of living. There are many hundreds of reports which can be downloaded for free from the World Bank. One of the most useful is the annual *World Development Report*. The detailed tables at the end of the report contain a wealth of data on most countries around the world. One of the best ways to find these reports is to click on Data and Reports at the top of the World Bank homepage.

United Nations, http://www.un.org/english/ The next obviously useful data source is the United Nations. Again, there are hundreds of free reports related to economic development and standards of living in countries around the world that can be downloaded at this site. One of the most useful is the annual *Human Development Report*. In contrast to the World Bank's "World Development Report," the United Nations' report contains more information on broader human conditions. This UN sponsored "Human Development Report" has its own home page; http://hdr.undp.org/ Like the "World Development Report" from the World Bank, this report has a wealth of data on each country in the back pages. Countries are listed in these tables by their annual country rank on the Human Development Index.

World Food Program, http://www.wfp.org/index.htm Associated with the United Nations, the World Food Program compiles hundreds of reports on hunger and food security around the world. One of the most useful reports is the *World Food Program Annual Report*.

International Monetary Fund, http://www.imf.org/ The IMF is the sister organization of the World Bank. Their mission is more related to lending money to countries in financial crisis. And with such loans comes control over many policies in the nation. They also have many reports which can be found on their Web site. As noted in this book, however, The IMF has a clear bias toward the American view of "free market capitalism."

Asian Development Bank, http://www.adb.org/ The Asian Development Bank is much like the World Bank, with of course a focus on Asian countries. Many valuable reports are also available for free download.

U.S. Agency for International Development, http://www.usaid.gov/ USAID is the primary U.S. government agency with the mission for aid to development countries. This Web site gives information about U.S. aid projects and reports from the American perspective.

Nation Master, http://www.nationmaster.com/ This is an excellent new Web site which provides a wealth of data about countries all over the world. One of the best features of this Web site is the hundreds of country rankings using data on such things as poverty, health, inequality, standards of living, crime, etc. from respected agencies such as the World Bank,

United Nations, US. Census Bureau. More complicated correlations using their huge store of data at Nation Master involves a small annual service fee, but it is well worth it.

Luxembourg Income Study, http://www.lisproject.org/   This Web site contains a wealth of data on income inequality and poverty, and hundreds of its sponsored research papers using this data. Unfortunately the data and papers are focused on North America and Europe only.

The Population Reference Bureau, http://www.prb.org   This organization, as the name implies, is focused on population problems, migration, refugees, and related population issues around the world. But many of their reports deal with other issues of world poverty.

U.S. Census Bureau, http://www.census.gov/   The U.S. Census Bureau is the American government agency with the mission to collect data about all aspects of the American society. Their annual reports on income inequality and poverty in the U.S. are perhaps the best for any country in the world. But, of course, in contrast to European nations, less is done about problems related to poverty in the United States.

Organization for Economic Cooperation and Development, http://www.oecd.org   The OECD is primarily a European organization focused on the richer nations in the world system. However, they do have reports from time to time on economic development in less developed nations, as well as relations between rich and poor nations.

World Health Organization, http://www.who.int/en/   The World Health Organization provides many free reports about health conditions around the world, including its very useful annual report which focuses on specific issues each year in addition to providing health statistics for countries around the world. The 2005 edition, for example, is titled "Make Every Mother and Child Count."

World Trade Organization, http://www.wto.org/   The World Trade Organization is the international agency dealing with trade issues and trade disputes between countries around the world. Despite the negative publicity given this agency by antiglobalization protesters, the WTO is at least somewhat democratic compared to the World Bank and IMF. Most developing countries are members of the WTO and are able to bring up issues of unfair trade relations with rich nations. This Web site provides many reports about these issues.

Corporate Watch, http://www.corpwatch.org/   This Web site contains many investigative reports and news about corporate behavior and misbehavior around the world.

Multinational Monitor, http://multinationalmonitor.org/   This is a similar Web site with reports of corporate misbehavior around the world.

Transparency International, http://www.transparency.org/   Transparency International tracks issues of government and corporate corruption around the world. Quite useful is its annual report ranking all countries by level of corruption.

Political and Economic Abuse of People in Developing Countries Global Watch, http://globalmarch.org/index.html   Human Rights Watch tracks the abuse of people in less developed countries around the world: http://hrw.org/advocacy/index.htm

Sweatshops, http://www.wolist.com/wo/society/issues/business/human-rights/   This Web site takes you to a list of Web sites all related to issues involving sweatshops and the exploitation of labor in poor countries around the world.

Human Trafficking and Slavery   Here are a couple of Web sites which focus on these problems around the world; Anti-slavery Web site, http://www.iabolish.com/ ECPAT (End Child Prostitution/Pornography and Trafficking), http://www.ecpat.net/eng/index.asp

References

Abegglen, James C., and George Stalk, Jr. 1985. *Kaisha: The Japanese Corporation*. New York: Basic Books.

Akin, Rabibhadana. 1996. *The Organization of Thai Society in the Early Bangkok Period, 1782–1873*. Bangkok: Amarin Printing.

Alderson, Arthur S. 1999. "Explaining Deindustrialization: Globalization, Failure, or Success?" *American Sociological Review*, 64:701–721.

Alderson, Arthur S., and Francois Nielsen. 1999. "Income Inequality, Development, and Dependence: A Reconsideration." *American Sociological Review*, 64:606–631.

Allinson, Gary D. 1989. "Politics in Contemporary Japan: Pluralist Scholarship in the Conservative Era—A Review Article." *Journal of Asian Studies*, 48:324–332.

Altimir, Oscar. 1998. "Inequality, Employment, and Poverty in Latin America." Pp. 3–35 in Victor E. Tokman and Guillermo O'Donnell (eds.), *Poverty and Inequality in Latin America*. Notre Dame, IN: University of Notre Dame Press.

Andaya, Barbara Watson. 1999. "Political Development Between the Sixteenth and Eighteenth Centuries." Pp. 58–115 in Nicholas Tarling (ed.), *The Cambridge History of Southeast Asia*, vol. 1, pt. 2, *From c. 1500 to c. 1800*. Cambridge, England: Cambridge University Press.

Andaya, Barbara Watson, and Leonard Y. Andaya. 2001. *A History of Malaysia*. London: Palgrave.

Aoki, Masahiko. 1996. "Unintended Fit: Organizational Evolution and Government Design of Institutions in Japan." Pp. 233–253 in Masahiko Aoki, Hyung-Ki Kim, and Masahiro Okuno-Fujiwara (eds.), *The Role of Government in East Asian Economic Development*. Oxford, England: Clarendon Press.

Aung-Thwin, Michael. 1985. *Pagan: The Origins of Modern Burma*. Honolulu: University of Hawaii Press.

Barrett, Richard, and Martin King Whyte. 1982. "Dependency Theory and Taiwan: Analysis of a Deviant Case." *American journal of Sociology*, 87:1064–1089.

Barrett, Richard, and Martin King Whyte. 1984. "What Is Dependency? Reply to Hammer." *American Journal of Sociology*, 89:937–940.

Bass, Loretta E. 2004. *Child Labor in Sub-Saharan Africa*. Boulder, CO: Lynne Rienner.

BBC News. 2000. Retrieved December 20 from http://www.news.bbc.co.uk.

BBC News. 2001. Retrieved March 12 from http://www.news.bbc.co.uk.

BBC News. 2004a. Retrieved April 3 from http://www.news.bbc.co.uk.

BBC News. 2004b. Retrieved November 24 from http://www.news.bbc.co.uk.

Bellah, Robert. 1985. *Tokugawa Religion: The Cultural Roots of Modern Japan*. New York: Free Press.

Bellwood, Peter. 1999. "Southeast Asia Before History." Pp. 55–138 in Nicholas Tarling (ed.), *The Cambridge History of Southeast Asia*, vol. 1, pt. 1, *From Early Times to c. 1500*. Cambridge, England: Cambridge University Press.

Bendix, Reinhard. 1978. *Kings or People: Power and the Mandate to Rule*. Berkeley: University of California Press.

Biggart, Nicole Woolsey, and Mauro F. Guillen. 1999. "Developing Difference: Social Organization and the Rise of the Auto Industries of South Korea, Taiwan, Spain, and Argentina." *American Sociological Review,* 64:722–747.

Blair, John. 1976. *The Control of Oil.* New York: Vintage Books.

Blau, Judith, and Peter Blau. 1982. "The Cost of Inequality: Metropolitan Structure and Violent Crime." *American Sociological Review,* 47:114–129.

Bluestone, Barry, and Bennett Harrison. 1982. *The Deindustrialization of America.* New York: Basic Books.

Blumberg, Paul. 1980. *Inequality in an age of Decline.* New York: Oxford University Press.

Bollen, Kenneth. 1983. "World System Position, Dependency, and Democracy: The Cross-National Evidence." *American Sociological Review,* 48:468–479.

Bollen, Kenneth, and Stephen J. Appold. 1993. "National Industrial Structure and the Global System." *American Sociological Review,* 58:283–301.

Boothroyd, Peter, and Pham Xuan Nam. 2000. *Socioeconomic Renovation in Viet Nam: The Origin, Evolution, and Impact of Doi Moi.* Singapore: Institute of Southeast Asian Studies.

Bornschier, Volker. 1994. "The Rise of the European Community: Grasping toward Hegemony? or Therapy against National Decline?" *International Journal of Sociology,* 24:62–96.

Bornschier, Volker. 1996. *Western Society in Transition.* New Brunswick, NJ: Transaction.

Bornschier, Volker, and Christopher Chase-Dunn. 1985. *Transnational Corporations and Underdevelopment.* New York: Praeger.

Bornschier, Volker, Christopher Chase-Dunn, and Richard Rubinson. 1978. "Cross-National Evidence of the Effects of Foreign Investment and Aid on Economic Growth and Inequality: A Survey of Findings and a Reanalysis." *American Journal of Sociology,* 84:651–683.

Bornschier, Volker, and Thank-Huyen Ballmer-Cao. 1979. "Income Inequality: A Cross-National Study of the Relationships Between MNC-Penetration, Dimensions of the Power Structure and Income Distribution." *American Sociological Review,* 44:487–506.

Boswell, Terry. 1989. "Colonial Empires and the Capitalist World-Economy: A Time Series Analysis of Colonization, 1640–1960." *American Sociological Review,* 54:169–180.

Bowen, Roger W. 1980. *Rebellion and Democracy in Meiji Japan.* Berkeley: University of California Press.

Boyd, Robert and Joan Silk. 2003. *How Humans Evolved,* 3rd ed. New York: Oxford University Press.

Bradshaw, York W. 1988. "Reassessing Economic Dependency and Uneven Development: The Kenyan Experience." *American Sociological Review,* 53:693–708.

Brandon, John J. (ed.). 1997. *Burma/Myanmar in the Twenty-First Century: Dynamic of Continuity and Change.* New York: Soros Open Society Institute.

Braudel, Fernand. 1981. *The Structures of Everyday Life: Civilization and Capitalism, 15th–18th Century,* vol. 1. New York: Harper and Row.

Brier, Alan, and Peter Calvert. 1975. "Revolution in the 1960s." *Political Studies,* 23:1–11.

Brook-Shephered, Gordon. 1996. *The Austrians: A Thousand-Year Odyssey.* New York: Carroll and Graf.

Callahan, William A. 1998. *Imagining Democracy: Reading "The Events of May" in Thailand.* Singapore: Institute of Asian Studies.

Chabal, Patrick, and Gean-Pascal Daloz. 1999. *Africa Works: Disorder as Political Instrument.* Bloomington: Indiana University Press.

Chan, Steve. 1993. *East Asian Dynamism: Growth, Order, and Security in the Pacific Region.* Boulder, CO: Westview Press.

Chandler, David P. 1996. *A History of Cambodia.* Chiang Mai, Thailand: Silkworm Books.

Chandler, David P. 1999. *The Tragedy of Cambodian History: Politics, War, and Revolution Since 1945*. Chiang Mai, Thailand: Silkworm Books.

Chang, Ha-Joon. 1999. "The Economic Theory of the Development State." Pp. 182–199 in Meredith Woo-Cumings (ed.), *The Development State*. Ithaca, NY: Cornell University Press.

Chase-Dunn, Christopher. 1975. "The Effects of International Economic Dependence on Development and Inequality: A Cross-National Study." *American Sociological Review,* 40:720–738.

Chase-Dunn, Christopher. 1989. *Global Formation: Structures of the World-Economy*. Oxford, England: Oxford University Press.

Chase-Dunn, Christopher. 2001. "World-Systems Theorizing." in Jonathan Turner (ed.), *Handbook of Sociological Theory*. New York: Plenum.

Chase-Dunn, Christopher, and Peter Grimes. 1995. "World-Systems Analysis." *Annual Review of Sociology,* 21:387–417.

Chase-Dunn, Christopher, and Thomas D. Hall. 1997. *Rise and Demise: Comparing World-Systems*. Boulder, CO: Westview Press.

Chase-Dunn, Christopher, Yukio Kawano, and Benjamin D. Brewer. 2000. "Trade Globalization Since 1795: Waves of Integration in the World System." *American Sociological Review,* 65:77–95.

Cheong, Yong Mun. 1999. "The Political Structures of the Independent States." Pp. 59–138 in Nicholas Tarling (Ed.), *The Cambridge History of Southeast Asia,* vol. 2, pt. 2, *From World War II to the Present*. Cambridge, England: Cambridge University Press.

Chibber, Vivek. 2002. "Bureaucratic Rationality and the Development State." *American Journal of Sociology,* 107:951–989.

Chirot, Daniel. 1977. *Social Change in the Twentieth Century*. New York: Harcourt Brace Jovanovich.

Chirot, Daniel. 1984. "The Rise of the West." *American Sociological Review,* 50:181–195.

Chirot, Daniel. 1986. *Social Change in the Modern Era*. New York: Harcourt Brace Jovanovich.

Chirot, Daniel. 2001. "World Systems Theory." Pp. 16609–16613 in Neil Smelser and Paul Baltes (eds.), *International Encyclopedia of the Social and Behavioral Sciences,* vol. 24. Oxford, England: Elsevier.

Cho, Hee-Yeon, and Eun Mee Kim. 1998. "State Autonomy and Its Social Conditions for Economic Development in South Korea and Taiwan." Pp. 125–158 in Eun Mee Kim (ed.), *The Four Asian Tigers: Economic Development and the Global Political Economy*. New York: Academic Press.

Clark, Kenneth. 1969. *Civilization*. New York: Harper and Row.

Cohen, Erik. 1991. *Thai Society in Comparative Perspective*. Bangkok: White Lotus Press.

Collins, Randall. 1975. *Conflict Sociology*. New York: Academic Press.

Collins, Randall. 1981. "Long-Term Social Change and the Territorial Power of States." Pp. 71–106 in Randall Collins (ed.), *Sociology Since Mid-century*. New York: Academic Press.

Collins, Randall. 1997. "Religious Economy and the Emergence of Capitalism in Japan." *American Sociological Review*, 62:843–865.

Collins, Randall, and David Waller. 1992. "What Theories Predicted the State Breakdown and Revolution of the Soviet Bloc?" Pp. 31–47 in Louis Kreisberg and David R. Segal (eds.), *The Transformation of European Communist Societies, Research in Social Movements, Conflicts and Change,* vol. 14. Greenwich, CT: JAI Press. (Originally published as a paper presented at the American Sociological Association meeting, Cincinnati, Ohio, August 1991.)

Cortazar, Rene. 1998. "Globalization and Job Creation: A Latin American Perspective." Pp. 75–90 in Victor E. Tokman and Guillermo O'Donnell (eds.), *Poverty and Inequality in Latin America*. Notre Dame, IN: University of Notre Dame Press.

Couch, Carl J. 1968. "Collective Behavior: An Examination of Some Stereotypes." *Social Problems,* 15:310–322.

Craig, Gordon A. 1991. *The Germans.* New York: Meridian.

Cumings, Bruce. 1999. "Webs with No Spiders, Spiders with No Webs: The Genealogy of the Development State." Pp. 61–92 in Meredith Woo-Cumings (ed.), *The Development State.* Ithaca, NY: Cornell University Press.

Curtis, Grant. 1998. *Cambodia Reborn?: The Transition to Democracy and Development.* Washington, DC: Brookings Institution Press.

Dakin, Brett. 2003. *Another Quiet American: Stories of Life in Laos.* Bangkok: Asia Books.

De Casparis, J. G., and I. W. Mabbett. 1999. "Religion and Popular Beliefs of Southeast Asia before c. 1500." Pp. 276–339 in Nicholas Tarling (ed.), *The Cambridge History of Southeast Asia,* vol. 1, pt. 1, *From Early Times to c. 1500.* Cambridge, England: Cambridge University Press.

de Soysa, Indra, and John R. Oneal. 1999. "Boon or Bane?: Reassessing the Productivity of Foreign Direct Investment." *American Sociological Review,* 64:766–782.

Diamond, Jared. 1999. *Guns, Germs, and Steel: The Fates of Human Societies.* New York: Norton.

Dietrich, William S. 1991. *In the Shadow of the Rising Sun: The Political Roots of American Economic Decline.* University Park: Pennsylvania State University Press.

DiMaggio, Paul, and John Mohr. 1985. "Cultural Capital, Educational Attainment and Marital Selection." *American Journal of Sociology,* 90:1231–1261.

Dixon, Chris. 1999. *The Thai Economy: Uneven Development and Internationalization.* London: Routledge.

Dixon, William J., and Terry Boswell. 1996. "Dependency, Disarticulation, and Denominator Effects: Another Look at Foreign Capital Penetration." *American Journal of Sociology,* 102:543–562.

Dobson, Wendy, and Chia Siow Yue (eds.). 1997. *Multinationals and East Asian Integration.* Singapore: Institute for Southeast Asian Studies.

Domhoff, G. William. 1990. *The Power Elite and the State.* New York: Aldine de Gruyter.

Domhoff, G. William. 1996. *State Autonomy or Class Dominance?: Case Studies on Policy Making in America.* New York: Aldine de Gruyter.

Domhoff, G. William. 1998. *Who Rules America?: Power and Politics in the Year 2000.* Mountain View, CA: Mayfield.

Domhoff, G. William. 2004. *Who Rules America?* New York: McGraw-Hill.

Dore, Ronald. 1987. *Taking Japan Seriously.* Stanford, CA: Stanford University Press.

Dower, John W. 1986. *War Without Mercy.* New York: Pantheon Books.

Duiker, William J. 1995. *Vietnam: Revolution in Transition.* Boulder, CO: Westview Press.

Duiker, William J. 2000. Ho Chi Minh: *A Life.* New York: Hyperion.

Durkheim, Emile. 1897/1951. *Suicide.* New York: Free Press.

Easterly, William. 2001. *The Elusive Quest for Growth: Economists' Adventures and Misadventures in the Tropics.* Cambridge, MA: MIT Press.

Effrat, Andrew. 1972. "Power to the Paradigms." Pp. 3–34 in Andrew Effrat (ed.), *Perspectives in Political Sociology.* New York: Bobbs-Merrill.

Eisenstadt, S. N. 1996. *Japanese Civilization: A Comparative View.* Chicago: University of Chicago Press.

Embree, J. F. 1950. "Thailand: A 'Loosely Structured' Social System." *American Anthropologist,* 52:181–193.

Esping-Anderson, Gosta. 1990. *The Three Worlds of Welfare Capitalism.* Princeton: Princeton University Press.

Etzioni, Amitai. 1984. *An Immodest Agenda: Rebuilding America before the 21st Century.* New York: McGraw-Hill.

Evans, Grant. 1995. *Lao Peasants Under Socialism and Post-Socialism*. New Haven, CT: Yale University Press.

Evans, Grant. 1998. *The Politics of Ritual and Remembrance: Laos Since 1975*. Chiang Mai, Thailand: Silkworm Press.

Evans, Grant. 1999a. "What Is Lao Culture and Society?" Pp. 1–34 in Grant Evans (ed.), *Laos: Culture and Society*. Chiang Mai, Thailand: Silkworm Press.

Evans, Grant. (ed.). 1999b. *Laos: Culture and Society*. Chiang Mai, Thailand: Silkworm Press.

Evans, Peter. 1995. *Embedded Autonomy: States and Industrial Transformation*. Princeton, NJ: Princeton University Press.

Evans, Peter, and James E. Rauch. 1999. "Bureaucracy and Growth: A Cross-National Analysis of the Effects of 'Weberian' State Structures on Economic Growth." *American Sociological Review,* 64:748–765.

Evers, Hans-Dieter. 1966. "The Formation of a Social Class Structure: Urbanization, Bureaucratization, and Social Mobility in Thailand." *American Sociological Review,* 31:480–488.

Fairbank, John King. 1986. *The Great Chinese Revolution: 1800–1985*. New York: Harper and Row.

Fairbank, John King, Edwin O. Reischauer, and Albert Craig. 1970. *East Asia: The Modern Transformation*. New York: Houghton Mifflin.

Falkus, Malcolm. 1995. "Thai Industrialization: An Overview." Pp. 13–32 in Mehdi Krongkaew (ed.), *Thailand's Industrialization and Its Consequences*. New York: St. Martin's Press.

Fallows, James. 1994. *Looking at the Sun: The Rise of the New East Asian Economic and Political System*. New York: Pantheon Books.

Fanon, Frantz. 1963. *The Wretched of the Earth*. New York: Grove Press.

Farnsworth, Elizabeth, Richard Feinberg, and Eric Leenson. 1976. "The Invisible Blockage: The United States Reacts." Pp. 338–373 in Arturo Valenzuela and J. Samuel Valenzuela (eds.), *Chile: Politics and Society*. New Brunswick, NJ: Transaction.

Farr, Grant. 2000. *Modern Iran*. New York: MagGraw-Hill.

Fieg, John Paul, and Elizabeth Mortlock. 1989. *A Common Core: Thais and Americans*. New York: Intercultural Press.

Fields, Gary S. 2001. *Distribution and Development: A New Look at the Developing World*. New York: Russell Sage.

Firebaugh, Glenn. 1992. "Growth Effects of Foreign and Domestic Investment." *American Journal of Sociology,* 98:105–130.

Firebaugh, Glenn. 1996. "Does Foreign Capital Harm Poor Nations? New Estimates Based on Dixon and Boswell's Measures of Capital Penetration." *American Journal of Sociology,* 102:563–578.

Firebaugh, Glenn, and Frank D. Beck. 1994. "Does Economic Growth Benefit the Masses? Growth, Dependence, and Welfare in the Third World." *American Sociological Review,* 59:631–653.

Forbes. 2001. Retrieved from http://www.forbes.com.

Forbes. 2004. Retrieved from http://www.forbes.com.

Frank, Andre Gunder. 1969. *Capitalism and Underdevelopment in Latin America*. New York: Monthly Review Press.

Frank, Andre Gunder. 1975. *On Capitalist Underdevelopment*. Bombay: Oxford University Press.

Frank, Andre Gunder. 1978. *Dependent Accumulation and Underdevelopment*. New York: Monthly Review Press.

Frank, Andre Gunder. 1998. *ReOrient: Global Economy in the Asian Age*. Los Angeles: University of California Press.

Friedrichs, Robert. 1970. *A Sociology of Sociology*. New York: Free Press.

Fuller, C. J. (ed.). 1996. *Caste Today*. New Delhi: Oxford University Press.

Gao, Bai. 2001. *Japan's Economic Dilemma: The Institutional Origins of Prosperity and Stagnation*. Cambridge, England: Cambridge University Press.

Genovese, Eugene D. 1974. *Roll, Jordan, Roll: The World the Slaves Made*. New York: Pantheon Books.

Gibbons, Ann. 2001. "Modern Men Trace Ancestry to African Migrants." *Science,* 292, no. 5519:1051–1052.

Gillham, Patrick F., and Gary T. Marx. 2000. "Complexity and Irony in Policing and Protesting: The World Trade Organization in Seattle." *Social Justice,* 2:212–236.

Girling, John L. 1996. *Interpreting Development: Capitalism, Democracy, and the Middle Class in Thailand*. Ithaca, NY: Cornell Southeast Asia Program Publications.

Girling, John L. S. 1981. *Thailand: Society and Politics*. Ithaca, NY: Cornell University Press.

Glewwe, Paul, and Phong Nguyen. 2002. "Economic Mobility in Vietnam and the 1990s." World Bank Policy Research Working Paper No. 2838, Washington, DC.

Gluck, Carol. 1985. *Japan's Modern Myths: Ideology in the Late Meiji Period*. Princeton, NJ: Princeton University Press.

Gold, Thomas B. 1986. *State and Society in the Taiwan Miracle*. Armonk, NY: M.E. Sharpe.

Goldberg, P. 1975. "The Politics of the Allende Overthrow in Chile." *Political Science Quarterly,* 90:93–116.

Golzio, Karl Heinz. 1985. "Max Weber on Japan: The Role of the Government and the Buddhist Sects." Pp. 90–101 in Andreas E. Buss (ed.), *Max Weber in Asian Studies*. Leiden, Germany: Brill.

Goodin, Robert E., Bruce Headey, Ruud Muffels, and Henk-Jan Dirven. 1999. *The Real Worlds of Welfare Capitalism*. Cambridge, England: Cambridge University Press.

Gottesman, Evan. 2004. *Cambodia After the Khmer Rouge*. Chiang Mai, Thailand: Silkworm Books.

Gouldner, Alvin. 1970. *The Coming Crisis in Western Sociology*. New York: Basic Books.

Grimes, Peter. 2000. "Recent Research on World-Systems." Pp. 29–55 in Thomas D. Hall (ed.), *A World-Systems Reader: New Perspectives on Gender, Urbanism, Cultures, Indigenous Peoples, and Ecology*. Lanham, MD: Rowman and Littlefield.

Gwatkin, Davidson, Kiersten Johnson, Adam Wagstaff, Shea Rutstein, and Rohini Pande. 2000. *Socio-Economic Differences in Health, Nutrition, and Population in Vietnam*. New York: World Bank.

Halberstam, David. 1986. *The Reckoning*. New York: Morrow.

Hall, Kenneth R. 1999. "Economic History of Early Southeast Asia." Pp. 183–275 in Nicholas Tarling (ed.), *The Cambridge History of Southeast Asia,* vol. 1, pt. 1, *From Early Times to c. 1500*. Cambridge, England: Cambridge University Press.

Hall, Thomas D. 2000a. "World-Systems Analysis: A Small Sample from a Large Universe." Pp. 3–27 in Thomas D. Hall (ed.), *A World-Systems Reader: New Perspectives on Gender, Urbanism, Cultures, Indigenous Peoples, and Ecology*. Lanham, MD: Rowman & Littlefield.

Hall, Thomas D. (ed.). 2000b. *A World-Systems Reader: New Perspectives on Gender, Urbanism, Cultures, Indigenous Peoples, and Ecology*. Lanham, MD: Rowman & Littlefield.

Hall, Thomas D. 2002. "World-Systems Analysis and Globalization: Directions for the Twenty-First Century." Pp. 81–122 in Betty A. Dobratz, Timothy Buzzell, and Lisa K. Waldner (eds.), *Theoretical Directions in Political Sociology for the 21st Century, Research in Political Sociology,* vol. 11. Oxford, England: Elsevier.

Halliday, Jon. 1975. *A Political History of Japanese Capitalism*. New York: Monthly Review Press.

Hamilton-Merritt, Jane. 1999. *Tragic Mountains: The Hmong, the Americans, and the Secret Wars in Laos, 1942–1992*. Bloomington: Indiana University Press.

Hammer, Heather-Jo. 1984. "Comment of 'Dependency Theory and Taiwan: Analysis of a Deviant Case.'" *American Journal of Sociology,* 89:932–936.

Hampden-Turner, Charles, and Alfons Trompenaars. 1993. *The Seven Cultures of Capitalism.* New York: Doubleday.

Hane, Mikiso. 1982. *Peasants, Rebels, and Outcastes: The Underside of Modern Japan.* New York: Pantheon Books.

Harrison, Bennett, and Barry Bluestone. 1988. *The Great U-Turn: Corporate Restructuring and the Polarizing of America.* New York: Basic Books.

Harrison, Lawrence E. 2000 (updated edition). *Underdevelopment Is a State of Mind: The Latin American Case.* Lanham, MD: Madison Books.

Harrison, Lawrence E., and Samuel P. Huntington (eds.). 2000. *Culture Matters: How Values Shape Human Progress.* New York: Basic Books.

Held, David, Anthony McGrew, David Goldblatt, and Jonathan Perraton. 1999. *Global Transformations: Politics, Economics, and Culture.* Palo Alto, CA: Stanford University Press.

Herkenrath, Mark, and Volker Bornschier. 2003. "Transnational Corporations in World Development—Still the Same Harmful Effects in an Increasingly Globalized World Economy?" *Journal of World System Research,* 9: 105–139.

Hewison, Kevin. 1997. "Thailand: Capitalist Development and the State." Pp. 93–120 in Garry Rodan, Kevin Hewison, and Richard Robison (eds.), *The Political Economy of Southeast Asia: An Introduction.* Melbourne, Australia: Oxford University Press.

Hewitt, Christopher. 1977. "The Effect of Political Democracy and Social Democracy on Equality in Industrial Societies: A Cross-National Comparison." *American Sociological Review,* 42:450–463.

Hiebert, Murray. 1996. *Chasing the Tigers: A Portrait of the New Vietnam.* Tokyo: Kodansha.

Higham, Charles. 2001. *The Civilization of Angkor.* London: Weidenfeld and Nicolson.

Higham, Charles. 2002. *Early Cultures of Mainland Southeast Asia.* Bangkok: River Books.

Hill, Hal. 1994. "ASEAN Economic Development: An Analytical Survey—The State of the Field." *Journal of Asian Studies,* 53:832–866.

Hochschild, Adam. 1999. *King Leopold's Ghost: A Story of Greed, Terror, and Heroism in Colonial Africa.* Boston: Mariner/Houghton Mifflin.

Hofstede, Geert. 1991. *Cultures and Organization: Software of the Mind.* New York: McGraw-Hill.

Holmes, Henry, and Suchada Tangtongtavy. 1995. *Working with the Thais: A Guide to Managing in Thailand.* Bangkok: White Lotus Press.

Hossein, Jalilian, and John Weiss. 2003. "Foreign Direct Investment and Poverty in the ASEAN Region." *ASEAN Economic Bulletin,* 19:231–253.

Hourani, Albert. 1992. *A History of the Arab Peoples.* New York: Warner Books.

Huntington, Samuel P. 1996. *The Clash of Civilizations and the Remaking of World Order.* New York: Simon and Schuster.

Hwang, Kwang-kuo. 1987. "Face and Favor: The Chinese Power Game." *American Journal of Sociology,* 92:944–974.

Inglehart, Ronald, and Wayne E. Baker. 2000. "Modernization, Cultural Change, and the Persistence of Traditional Values." *American Sociological Review,* 65:19–51.

International Fund for Agricultural Development. 2001. *Rural Poverty Report 2001: The Challenge of Ending Rural Poverty.* New York: Oxford University Press.

Ivarsson, Soren. 1999. "Towards a New Laos: Lao Nhay and the Campaign for a National 'Reawakening' in Laos, 1941–1945." Pp. 61–78, in Grant Evans (ed.), *Laos: Culture and Society.* Chiang Mai, Thailand: Silkworm Press.

Jackman, Robert. 1974. "Politics Democracy and Social Equality: A Comparative Analysis." *American Sociological Review,* 39:29–45.

Jackman, Robert. 1975. *Politics and Social Equality: A Comparative Analysis.* New York: Wiley.

Jamieson, Neil L. 1995. *Understanding Vietnam.* Berkeley: University of California Press.

Jansen, Marius B. 2000. *The Making of Modern Japan*. Cambridge, MA: Belknap/Harvard University Press.

Johnson, Chalmers. 1982. *MITI and the Japanese Miracle*. Stanford, CA: Stanford University Press.

Johnson, Chalmers. 1995. *Japan: Who Governs?* New York: Norton.

Johnson, Chalmers. 1999. "The Development State: Odyssey of a Concept." Pp. 32–60 in Meredith Woo-Cumings (ed.), The Development State. Ithaca, NY: Cornell University Press.

Johnson, Chalmers. 2000. *Blowback: The Costs and Consequences of American Empire*. New York: Metropolitan Books.

Johnson, Dale. 1973. *The Sociology of Change and Reaction in Latin America*. New York: Bobbs-Merrill.

Jomo, K. S. 2001. "Globalisation, Liberalisation, Poverty and Income Inequality in Southeast Asia." Technical Paper No. 185, Organization for Economic Cooperation and Development, Paris, December.

Kamm, Henry. 1996. *Dragon Ascending: Vietnam and the Vietnamese*. New York: Arcade.

Kamm, Henry. 1998. *Cambodia: Report From a Stricken Land*. New York: Arcade.

Karnow, Stanley. 1989. *In Our Image: America's Empire in the Philippines*. New York: Ballantine Books.

Kathirithamby-Wells, J. 1999. "The Age of Transition: The Mid-Eighteenth to Early Nineteenth Centuries." Pp. 228–275 in Nicholas Tarling (ed.), *The Cambridge History of Southeast Asia,* vol. 1, pt. 2, *From c. 1500 to c. 1800,* Cambridge, England: Cambridge University Press.

Kaufmann, Daniel, Aart Kraay, and Pablo Zoido-Lobaton. 1999. "Governance Matters." World Bank Policy Research Working Paper no. 2196, Washington, DC.

Keay, John. 1997. *Last Post: The End of Empire in the Far East*. London: John Murray.

Keizai Koho Center. 2002. *Japan 2001: An International Comparison.* Tokoyo: Keizai Koho Center (Japan Institute for Social and Economic Affairs).

Kennedy, Paul. 1987. *The Rise and Fall of the Great Powers: Economic Change and Military Conflict From 1500 to 2000*. New York: Random House.

Kentor, Jeffrey. 1981. "Structural Determinants of Peripheral Urbanization: The Effects of International Dependence." *American Sociological Review,* 46:201–211.

Kentor, Jeffrey. 1998. "The Long Term Effects of Foreign Investment Dependence on Economic Growth, 1940–1990." *American Journal of Sociology,* 103, no. 4:1024–1048.

Kentor, Jeffrey. 2001. "The Long Term Effects of Globalization on Population Growth, Inequality, and Economic Development." *Social Problems,* 48, no. 4:435–455.

Kentor, Jeffrey, and Terry Boswell. 2003. "Foreign Capital Dependence and Development: A New Direction." *American Sociological Review,* 68:301–313.

Kentor, Jeffrey, and Young Suk Jank. 2004. "Yes There Is a (Growing) Transnational Business Community: A Study in Interlocking Directorates 1983–98." *International Sociology,* 19, no. 3 (September):355–368.

Kerbo, Harold. 1978. "Foreign Involvement in the Preconditions for Political Violence: The World System and the Case of Chile." *Journal of Conflict Resolution,* 22:363–392.

Kerbo, Harold. 2000. *Inequality and Social Stratification: Class and Class Conflict in Global, Comparative, and Historical Perspective*, 4th ed. New York: McGraw-Hill.

Kerbo, Harold. 2006. *Inequality and Social Stratification: Class and Class Conflict in Global, Comparative, and Historical Perspective*, 6th ed. New York: McGraw-Hill.

Kerbo, Harold, Elke Wittenhagen, and Keiko Nakao. 1994. *Japanese Transplant Corporations, Foreign Employees, and the German Economy: A Comparative Analysis of Germany and the United States*. Duisburger Bettrage zur Soziologischen forschung, Duisburg, Germany.

Kerbo, Harold R. 1982. "Movements of 'Crisis' and Movement of 'Affluence': A Critique of Deprivation and Resource Mobilization Theories," *Journal of Conflict Resolution,* 26:645–663.

Kerbo, Harold R., and John McKinstry. 1995. *Who Rules Japan?: The Inner Circles of Economic and Political Power*. Westport, CT: Greenwood/Praeger.

Kerbo, Harold, and John McKinstry. 1998. *Modern Japan: A Volume in the Comparative Societies Series*. New York: McGraw-Hill.

Kerbo, Harold, and Robert Slagter. 2000a. "Thailand, Japan, and the 'East Asian Development Model': The Asian Economic Crisis in World System Perspective." Pp. 119–140 in Frank-Jürgen Richter (ed.), *The East Asian Development Model: Economic Growth, Institutional Failure and the Aftermath of the Crisis*. London: Macmillan.

Kerbo, Harold, and Robert Slagter. 2000b. "The Asian Economic Crisis and the Decline of Japanese Leadership in Asia." In Frank-Jürgen Richter (ed.), *The Asian Economic Crisis*. New York: Quorum Press.

Kerkvliet, Benedict J. Tria, and Mark Selden. 1999. "Agrarian Transformations in China and Vietnam." Pp. 98–119 in Anita Chan, Benedict J. Tria Kerkvliet, and Jonathan Unger (eds.), *Transforming Asian Socialism: China and Vietnam Compared*. New York: Rowman and Littlefield.

Keyes, Charles F. 1989. *Thailand: Buddhist Kingdom as Modern Nation-State*. Boulder, CO: Westview Press.

Kim, Eun Nee. 1997. *Big Business, Strong State: Collusion and Conflict in South Korean Development, 1960–1990*. Albany: State University of New York Press.

Kim, Young C. (ed.). 1995. *The Southeast Asian Miracle*. New Brunswick, NJ: Transaction.

Kishimoto, Kōichi. 1988. *Politics in Modern Japan: Development and Organization*. Tokyo: Japan Echo Inc.

Koh, B. C. 1989. *Japan's Administrative Elite*. Berkeley: University of California Press.

Kolko, Gabriel. 1988. *Confronting the Third World: United States Foreign Policy, 1945–1980*. New York: Pantheon.

Kolko, Gabriel. 1997. *Vietnam: Anatomy of a Peace*. London: Routledge.

Komin, Suntaree. 1989. *Social Dimensions of Industrialization in Thailand*. Bangkok: National Institute of Development Administration.

Komin, Suntaree. 1991. *Psychology of the Thai People: Values and Behavior Patterns*. Bangkok: National Institute of Development Administration.

Komin, Suntaree. 1995. "Changes in Social Values in the Thai Society and Economy: A Post-Industrialization Scenario." Pp. 251–266 in Mehdi Krongkaew (ed.), *Thailand's Industrialization and Its Consequences*. New York: St. Martin's Press.

Korzeniewicz, Roberto Patricio, and Timothy Patrick Moran. 1997. "World-Economic Trends in the Distribution of Income, 1965–1992." *American Journal of Sociology*, 102:1000–1039.

Kristof, Nicholas D., and Sheryl WuDunn. 2000. *Thunder From the East: Portrait of a Rising Asia*. New York: Knopf.

Kuczynski, Jürgen. 1967. *The Rise of the Working Class*. New York: McGraw-Hill.

Kulick, Elliot, and Dick Wilson. 1992. *Thailand's Turn: Profile of a New Dragon*. New York: St. Martin's Press.

Kulick, Elliot, and Dick Wilson. 1996. *Time for Thailand: Profile of a New Success*. Bangkok: White Lotus Press.

Ladd, Everett Carl, and Karlyn H. Bowman. 1998. *Attitudes Toward Economic Inequality*. Washington, DC: American Enterprise Institute.

Landes, David S. 1998. *The Wealth and Poverty of Nations: Why Some Are So Rich and Some Are So Poor*. New York: Norton.

Lau, Lawrence J. 1996. "The Role of Government in Economic Development: Some Observations from the Experience of China, Hong Kong, and Taiwan." Pp. 41–73 in Masahiko Aoki, Hyung-Ki Kim, and Masahiro Okuno-Fujiwara (eds.), *The Role of Government in East Asian Economic Development*. Oxford, England: Clarendon Press.

Le Bon, Gustave. 1897/1960. *The Crowd: A Study of the Popular Mind*. Dunwoody, GA: Norman S. Berg.

Lenin. V. I. 1965. *Imperialism: The Highest Stage of Capitalism*. New York: International Publishers.

Lenski, Gerhard. 1966. *Power and Privilege*. New York: McGraw-Hill.

Lenski, Gerhard, and Patrick Nolan. 1984. "Trajectories of Development: A Test of Ecological-Evolutionary Theory." *Social Forces,* 63:1–23.

Lenski, Gerhard, and Patrick Nolan. 1986. "Trajectories of Development: A Further Test." *Social Forces,* 64:794–795.

Letelier, Isabel, and Michael Moffitt. 1980. "How American Banks Keep the Chilean Junta Going." Pp. 399–412 in Mark Green and Robert Massie (eds.), *The Big Business Reader: Essays on Corporate America*. New York: Pilgrim Press.

Levathes, Louise. 1994. *When China Ruled the Seas*. New York: Oxford University Press.

Lewis, Oscar. 1959. *Five Families: Mexican Case Studies in the Culture of Poverty*. New York: Basic Books.

Lewis, Oscar. 1961. *The Children of Sanchez*. New York: Random House.

Lewis, Oscar. 1966. *La Vida: A Puerto Rican Family in the Culture of Poverty*. New York: Random House.

Lincoln, Edward J. 2001. *Arthritic Japan: The Slow Pace of Economic Reform*. Washington, DC: Brookings Institution Press.

Lincoln, James R., Harold Kerbo, and Elke Wittenhagen. 1995. "Japanese Companies in Germany: A Case Study in Cross-Cultural Management." *Journal of Industrial Relations,* 25:123–139.

List, Friedrich. 1966/1983. *The Natural System of Political Economy*. London: Frank Cass.

Livingston, Carol. 1996. *Gecko Tails: A Journey Through Cambodia*. London: Phoenix Books.

Luong, Hy Van, and Jonathan Unger. 1999. "Wealth Power and Poverty in the Transition to Market Economies: The Process of Socio-Economic Differentiation in Rural China and Northern Vietnam." Pp. 120–152 in Anita Chan, Benedict J. Tria Kerkvliet, and Jonathan Unger (eds.), *Transforming Asian Socialism: China and Vietnam Compared*. New York: Rowman and Littlefield.

Mabbett, Ian, and David Chandler. 1995. *The Khmers*. Oxford, England: Blackwell.

Maddison, Angus. 1998. *Chinese Economic Performance in the Long Run*. Paris: OECD.

Mahler, V. A. 2001. Economic Globalization, Domestic Politics and Income Inequality in Developed Countries: A Cross-National Analysis. *Luxembourg Income Study*, Working Paper No. 273.

Mahler, V. A. 2002. Exploring the Subnational Dimension of Income Inequality: An Analysis of the Relationship Between Inequality and Electoral Turnout in Developed Countries. *Luxembourg Income Study,* Working Paper No. 292.

Mahoney, James. 2003. "Long-Run Development and the Legacy of Colonialism in Spanish America." *American Journal of Sociology,* 109:50–106.

Mansfield, Peter. 2003. *A History of the Middle East*, 2nd ed. New York: Penguin Books.

Marr, David G. 1981. *Vietnamese Tradition on Trial, 1920–1945*. Berkeley: University of California Press.

Martin, John Bartlow. 1966. *Overtaken by Events*. Garden City, NY: Doubleday.

Martin, Marie Alexandrine. 1994. *Cambodia: A Shattered Society*. Translated by Mark McLeod. Berkeley: University of California Press.

Mazrui, Ali A. 1978. *Africa's International Relations: The Diplomacy of Dependency and Change*. Boulder, CO: Westview Press.

Mazrui, Ali A. 1986. *The Africans: A Triple Heritage*. New York: Little, Brown.

McCarthy, John D., and Mayer N. Zald. 1977. "Resource Mobilization and Social Movements: A Partial Theory." *American Journal of Sociology,* 82:1212–1241.

McClain, James L. 2002. *Japan: A Modern History*. New York: Norton.

Menzies, Gavin. 2002. *1421: The Year China Discovered the World*. New York: Bantam Books.

Messner, Steven F. 1982. "Societal Development, Social Equality, and Homicide: A Cross-National Test of a Durkheimian Model." *Social Forces,* 61:225–240.

Migdal. Joel S. 1988. *Strong Societies and Weak States: State-Society Relations and State Capabilities in the Third World.* Princeton, NJ: Princeton University Press.

Mills, C. Wright. 1956. *The Power Elite.* New York: Oxford University Press.

Mirante, Edith T. 1993. *Burmese Looking Glass: A Human Rights Adventure and a Jungle Revolution.* New York: Grove Press.

Mishel, Lawrence, Jared Bernstein, and Heather Boushey. 2003. *The State of Working America: 2002/2003.* Ithaca, Cornell University Press.

Mishel, Lawrence, Jared Bernstein, and John Schmitt. 1999. *The State of Working America 1998–99.* Ithaca, NY: Cornell University Press.

Mishel, Lawrence, Jared Bernstein, and John Schmitt. 2001. *The State of Working America, 2000/2001.* Ithaca, NY: Cornell University Press.

Mishel, Lawrence, Jared Bernstein, and John Schmitt. 2002. *The State of Working America, 2002.* Ithaca, NY: Cornell University Press.

Missingham, Bruce D. 2003. *The Assembly of the Poor in Thailand: From Local Struggles to National Protest Movement.* Chiang Mai, Thailand: Silkworm Books.

Montgomery, Keith. "The Demographic Transition." Retrieved from http://www.uwmc.uwc.edu/geography/Demotrans/demtran.htm.

Moore, Barrington. 1978. *Injustice: The Social Bases of Obedience and Revolt.* White Plains, NY: M.E. Sharpe.

Moore, Wilbert. 1974. *Social Change.* Englewood Cliffs, NJ: Prentice Hall.

Morikawa, Hidemasa. 1992. *Zaibatsu: The Rise and Fall of Family Enterprise Groups in Japan.* Tokyo: Tokyo University Press.

Morley, James W., and Masashi Nishihara (eds.). 1997. *Vietnam Joins the World.* Armonk, NY: M.E. Sharpe.

Mosley, Leonard. 1978. *Dulles.* New York: Dial Press.

Mueller, Hans-Peter, Claudia Kock, Eva Seiler, and Brigitte Arpagaus. 1999. *Atlas vorkolonialer Gesellschaften. Sozialstrukturen und kulturelles Erbe der Staaten Afrikas, Asiens und Melanesiens [Atlas of Precolonial Societies: Cultural Heritage and Social Structures of African, Asian and Melanesian Countries].* Berlin: Reimer.

Mueller, Hans-Peter, Wolf Linder, and Patrick Ziltener. 2002. "Culture, Democracy, and Development: Cultural and Political Foundations of Socio-Economic Development in Asia and Africa; Empirical Answers to a Theoretical Question." Paper presented at the Conference on Culture and Economic Development, Ascona, Switzerland, October.

Mulder, Niels. 1992. *Inside Thai Society: An Interpretation of Everyday Life.* Bangkok: Duang Kamol.

Mulder, Niels. 1997. *Thai Images: The Culture of the Public World.* Chiang Mai, Thailand: Silkworm Press.

Muller, Edward. 1985. "Income Inequality, Regime Repressiveness, and Political Violence." *American Sociological Review,* 50:47–61.

Muller, Edward. 1988. "Democracy, Economic Development, and Income Inequality." *American Sociological Review,* 53:50–68.

Murdock, George Peter. 1967. *Ethnographic Atlas: A Summary.* Pittsburgh: University of Pittsburgh Press.

Murdock, George Peter. 1986. "Ethnographic Atlas." *World Cultures,* 2, no. 4 (first computer version).

Murray, David. 1996. *Angels and Devils: Thai Politics From February 1991 to September 1992: A Struggle for Democracy?* Bangkok: White Orchid Press.

Muscat, Robert J. 1994. *The Fifth Tiger: A Study of Thai Development.* Armonk, NY: M.E. Sharpe.

Myint-U, Thant. 2001. *The Making of Modern Burma,* 2nd ed. Cambridge, England: Cambridge University Press.

Myrdal, Gunnar. 1968. *Asian Drama: An Inquiry into the Poverty of Nations,* 3 vol. New York: Pantheon Books.

Myrdal, Gunnar. 1970. *The Challenge of World Poverty: A World Anti-Poverty Program in Outline.* New York: Pantheon Books.

Nabi, Ijaz, and Jayasankur Shivakumar. 2001. *Back from the Brink: Thailand's Response to the 1997 Economic Crisis.* Washington, DC: World Bank.

Nartsupha, Chatthip. 1999. *The Thai Village Economy in the Past.* Chiang Mai, Thailand: Silkworm Books.

NationMaster.com, http://www.nationmaster.com.

Needham, Joseph. 1983. *Science and Civilization in China.* Cambridge, England: Cambridge University Press.

Needler, M. C. 1968. "Political Development and Socioeconomic Development: The Case of Latin America." *American Political Science Review,* 62:889–897.

Nielsen, Francois. 1994. "Income Inequality and Industrial Development: Dualism Revisited." *American Sociological Review,* 59:654–677.

Nielsen, Francois, and Arthur S. Alderson. 1997. "The Kuznets Curve and the Great U-Turn: Income Inequality in US Counties, 1970 to 1990." *American Sociological Review,* 62:12–33.

Nieuwbeerta, P. (2001). "The Democratic Class Struggle in Postwar Societies: Traditional Class Voting in Twenty Countries, 1945–1990." Pp. 121–135 in T. N. Clark and S. M. Lipset (Eds.), *The Breakdown of Class Politics: A Debate on Post-Industrial Stratification.* Washington DC: Woodrow Wilson Center Press.

Nolan, Patrick D. 1983a. "Status in the World Economy and National Structure and Development." *International Journal of Contemporary Sociology,* 24:109–120.

Nolan, Patrick D. 1983b. "Status in the World System, Income Inequality, and Economic Growth." *American Journal of Sociology,* 89:410–419.

O'Donnell, Guillerimo. 1998. "Poverty and Inequality in Latin America: Some Political Reflections." Pp 49–74 in Victor E. Tokman and Guillermo O'Donnell (eds.), *Poverty and Inequality in Latin America.* Notre Dame, IN: University of Notre Dame Press.

Okazaki, Tetsuji. 1996. "The Government-Firm Relationship in Post-War Japanese Economic Recovery: Resolving the Coordination Failure by Coordination in Industrial Rationalization." Pp. 74–100 in Masahiko Aoki, Hyung-Ki Kim, and Masahiro Okuno-Fujiwara (eds.), *The Role of Government in East Asian Economic Development.* Oxford, England: Clarendon Press.

Osborne, Milton. 1995. *Southeast Asia: An Introductory History.* Brisbane: Allen and Unwin.

Osborne, Milton. 2000. *The Mekong: Turbulent Past, Uncertain Future.* Brisbane: Allen and Unwin.

Owen, Norman G. 1999. "Economic and Social Change." Pp. 139–200 in Nicholas Tarling (ed.), *The Cambridge History of Southeast Asia,* vol. 2, pt. 2, *From World War II to the Present.* Cambridge, England: Cambridge University Press.

Paige, Jeffrey M. 1999. "Conjuncture, Comparison, and Conditional Theory in Macrosocial Inquiry." *American Journal of Sociology,* 105:781–800.

Pakenham, Thomas. 1991. *The Scramble for Africa: White Man's Conquest of the Dark Continent From 1876 to 1912.* New York: Avon.

Park, Yung H. 1986. *Bureaucrats and Ministers in Contemporary Japanese Government.* Berkeley: University of California, Institute of East Asian Studies.

Parsons, Talcott. 1951. *The Social System.* New York: Free Press.

Parsons, Talcott. 1966. *Societies: Evolutionary and Comparative Perspectives.* Englewood Cliffs, NJ: Prentice-Hall.

Pedersen, Morten, Emily Rudland, and R. J. May (eds.). 2000. *Burma/Myanmar: Strong Regime, Weak State?* Adelaide, Australia: Crawford House.

Pempel, T. J. 1999. "The Development Regime in a Changing World Economy." Pp. 137–181 in Meredith Woo-Cumings (ed.), *The Development State*. Ithaca, NY: Cornell University Press.

Pempel, T. J. 2000. *Regime Shift: Comparative Dynamics of the Japanese Political Economy*. Ithaca, NY: Cornell University Press.

Petras, James, and Morris Morley. 1975. *The United States and Chile*. New York: Monthly Review Press.

Pfeiffer, John. 1977. *The Emergence of Society: A Prehistory of the Establishment*. New York: McGraw-Hill.

Phillips, Herbert P. 1965. *Thai Peasant Personality: The Patterning of Interpersonal Behavior in the Village of Bang Chan*. Berkeley: University of California Press.

Phongpaichit, Pasuk, and Chris Baker. 1995. *Thailand: Economy and Politics*. New York: Oxford University Press.

Phongpaichit, Pasuk, and Chris Baker. 1996. *Thailand's Boom*. Chiang Mai, Thailand: Silkworm Books.

Phongpaichit, Pasuk, and Chris Baker. 1998. *Thailand's Boom and Bust*. Chiang Mai, Thailand: Silkworm Books.

Phongpaichit, Pasuk, and Chris Baker. 2000. *Thailand's Crisis*. Chiang Mai, Thailand: Silkworm Books.

Phongpaichit, Pasuk, and Sungsidh Piriyarangsan. 1994. *Corruption and Democracy in Thailand*. Chiang Mai, Thailand: Silkworm Press.

Phongpaichit, Pasuk, Sungsidh Piriyarangsan, and Nualnoi Treerat. 1998. *Guns, Girls, Gambling, and Ganja: Thailand's Illegal Economy and Public Policy*. Chiang Mai, Thailand: Silkwood Press.

Piven, Frances Fox, and Richard Cloward. 1982. *The New Class War: Reagan's Attack on the Welfare State and Its Consequences*. New York: Pantheon, Books.

Podolny, Joel M., and James N. Baron. 1997. "Resources and Relationships: Social Networks and Mobility in the Workplace." *American Sociological Review*. 62:673–693.

Population Reference Bureau. 2000. *2000 World Population Data Sheet*. Retrieved from http://www.prb.org.

Pornchokchai, Sopon. 1992. *Bangkok Slums: Review and Recommendations*. Bangkok: Agency for Real Estate Affairs.

Portes, Alejandro. 1976. "On the Sociology of National Development: Theories and Issues." *American Journal of Sociology,* 85:55–85.

Portes, Alejandro. 1998. "Social Capital: Its Origins and Applications in Modern Sociology." *Annual Review of Sociology,* 24:1–24.

Poulantzas, Nicos. 1973. *Political Power and Social Classes*. London: Verso.

Poulantzas, Nicos. 1975. *Classes and Contemporary Capitalism*. London: NLB.

Prudhisan Jumbala. 1992. *Nation Building and Democratization in Thailand: A Political History*. Bangkok: Chulalongkorn University Social Research Institute.

Pye, Lucian W. 1985. *Asian Power and Politics: The Cultural Dimensions of Authority*. Cambridge, MA: Belknap/Harvard University Press.

Raff, Diether. 1988. *A History of Germany: From the Medieval Empire to the Present*. Hamburg, Germany: Berg.

Ragin, Charles C. 2000. *Fuzzy-Set Social Science*. Chicago: University of Chicago Press.

Ragin, Charles C., and David Zaret. 1983. "Theory and Method in Comparative Research: Two Strategies." *Social Forces*, 61:731–754.

Rajchagool, Chaiyan. 1994. *The Rise and Fall of the Thai Absolute Monarchy*. Bangkok: White Lotus Press.

Raphael, James H., and Thomas P. Rohlen. 1998. "How Many Models of Japanese Growth Do We Want or Need?" Pp. 265–296 in Henry S. Rohlen (ed.), *Behind East Asian Growth: The Political and Social Foundations of Prosperity*. London: Routledge.

Rapley, John. 1996. *Understanding Development: Theory and Practice in the Developing World.* Boulder, CO: Lynne Rienner.

Reich, Michael. 1991. *Racial Inequality: A Political-Economic Analysis.* Princeton, NJ: Princeton University Press.

Reich, Robert. 1981. *The Work of Nations: Preparing Ourselves for 21st Century Capitalism.* New York: Vintage Books.

Reid, Anthony. 1988. *Southeast Asia in the Age of Commerce,* vol. 1, *The Lands Below the Winds.* New Haven, CT: Yale University Press.

Reid, Anthony. 1993. *Southeast Asia in the Age of Commerce,* vol. 2, *Expansion and Crisis.* New Haven, CT: Yale University Press.

Reid, Anthony. 1999. *Charting the Shape of Early Modern Southeast Asia.* Chiang Mai, Thailand: Silkworm Books.

Reischauer, Edwin O. 1988. *The Japanese.* Cambridge, MA: Harvard University Press.

Reischauer, Edwin O., and Albert M. Craig. 1978. *Japan: Tradition and Transformation.* New York: Houghton Mifflin.

Ricklefs, M. C. 1993. *A History of Modern Indonesia Since c. 1300,* 2nd ed. Palo Alto, CA: Stanford University Press.

Riggs, Fred W. 1966. *Thailand: The Modernization of a Bureaucratic Polity.* Honolulu: East-West Center Press.

Roberts, J. M. 1993. *History of the World.* New York: Oxford University Press.

Roberts, John G. 1976. *Mitsui: Three Centuries of Japanese Business.* New York: Weatherhill.

Robinson, William I. and Jerry Harris. 2000. "Towards a Global Rulling Class? Globalization and the Transnational Capitalist Class." *Science and Society,* 64:11–54.

Roosevelt, Kermit. 1979. *Counter Coup: The Struggle for the Control of Iran.* New York: McGraw-Hill.

Rosenstone, Robert A. 1988. *Mirror in the Shrine: American Encounters with Meiji Japan.* Cambridge, MA: Harvard University Press.

Rostow, Walter. 1960. *The Stages of Economic Growth.* New York: Cambridge University Press.

Rubinson, Richard. 1976. "The World Economy and the Distribution of Income Within States: A Cross-National Study." *American Sociological Review,* 41:638–659.

Sampson, Anthony. 1973. *The Sovereign State of I.T.T.* New York: Stein and Day.

Sanford, Rojas. 1976. *The Murder of Allende: The End of the Chilean Way to Socialism.* New York: Harper & Row.

Sansom, George. 1958. *A History of Japan.* Tokyo: Tuttle.

Sardesai, D. R. 1989. *Southeast Asia: Past and Present.* Boulder, CO: Westview Press.

Schoppa, Leonard J. 1991. "Zoku Power and LDP Power: A Case Study of the Zoku Rule in Education Policy." *Journal of Japanese Studies,* 17:79–106.

Schwarz, Adam. 1994. *A Nation in Waiting: Indonesia in the 1990s.* Boulder, CO: Westview Press.

Sekhon, Joti. 2000. *Modern India: A Volume in the Comparative Societies Series.* New York: McGraw-Hill.

Shearer, Alistair. 1989. *Thailand: The Lotus Kingdom.* London: John Murray.

Shorrock, Tim. 2002. "Crony Capitalism Goes Global." *The Nation,* April 1, pp. 11–16.

Simmel, Georg. 1905/1955. *Conflict and the Web of Group Affiliations,* edited by Kurt Wolff and Reinhard Bendix. New York: Free Press.

Singh, Sukhpal. 2003. "State, Agribusiness Firms, and Farmers in Contract Farming in Thailand: A Partnership for Development?" Paper presented at the semiannual meeting of the International Convention of Asia Scholars, Singapore, August.

Skidmore, Thomas, and Peter Smith. 2001. *Modern Latin America.* New York: Oxford University Press.

Sklair, Leslie. 2001. *The Transnational Capitalist Class.* Oxford, England: Blackwell.

Skocpol, Theda. 1979. *States and Social Revolutions: A Comparative Analysis of France, Russia, and China*. New York: Cambridge University Press.

Skocpol, Theda. 1992. *Protecting Soldiers and Mothers: The Political Origins of Social Policy in the United States*. Camridge, MA: Harvard University Press.

Slagter, Robert, and Harold Kerbo. 1998. "The Foreign Boss: Employee Commitment and Management Styles in Japanese and American Corporations in Thailand." Paper presented at the annual meeting of the National Association of Social Sciences, New Orleans, October.

Slagter, Robert, and Harold Kerbo. 2000. *Modern Thailand: A Volume in the Comparative Societies Series*. New York: McGraw-Hill.

Smeeding, Timothy M. 1997. "Financial Poverty in Developed Countries: The Evidence from LIS." Luxembourg Income Study Working Paper No. 155, Syracuse, New York, April.

Smeeding, Timothy, Michael O'Higgins, and Lee Rainwater (eds.). 1990. *Poverty, Inequality, and Income Distribution in Comparative Perspective: The Luxembourg Income Study. Washington*, DC: Urban Institute Press.

Smelser, Neil J. 1976. *Comparative Methods in the Social Sciences*. Englewood Cliffs, NJ: Prentice Hall.

Smith, Martin. 1999. *Burma: Insurgency and the Politics of Ethnicity*. Bangkok: White Lotus Press.

Snyder, David, and Edward Kick. 1979. "Structural Position in the World System and Economic Growth, 1955–1970: A Multiple Analysis of Transnational Interactions." *American Journal of Sociology,* 84:1096–1128.

Soboul, Albert. 1974. *The French Revolution, 1787–1799: From the Storming of the Bastille to Napoleon*. New York: Random House.

Stack, Steven. 1978a. "Internal Political Organization and the World Economy of Income Inequality." *American Sociological Review,* 42:271–272.

Stack, Steven. 1978b. "The Effect of Direct Government Involvement in the Economy on the Degree of Income Inequality: A Cross-National Study." *American Sociological Review,* 43:880–888.

Stange, Paul. 1999. "Religious Change in Contemporary Southeast Asia." Pp. 201–256 in Nicholas Tarling (ed.), *The Cambridge History of Southeast Asia,* vol. 2, pt. 2, *From World War II to the Present*. Cambridge, England: Cambridge University Press.

Steinberg, David I. 2001. *Burma: The State of Myanmar*. Washington, DC: Georgetown University Press.

Stiglitz, Joseph E. 2002. *Globalization and Its Discontents*. New York: Norton.

Stiglitz, Joseph E. 2004. "Poverty, Globalization, and Growth: Perspectives on Some of the Statistical Links." P. 80 in *Human Development Report 2003*. New York: United Nations Development Programme/Oxford University Press.

Stockwell, A. J. 1999. "Southeast Asia in War and Peace: The End of European Colonial Empires." Pp. 1–58 in Nicholas Tarling (ed.), *The Cambridge History of Southeast Asia,* vol. 2, pt. 2, *From World War II to the Present*. Cambridge, England: Cambridge University Press.

Stokes, Randall, and David Jaffee. 1982. "Another Look at the Export of Raw Materials and Economic Growth." *American Sociological Review,* 47:402–407.

Stuart-Fox, Martin. 1996. *Buddhist Kingdom, Marxist State: The Making of Modern Laos*. Bangkok: White Lotus Press.

Stuart-Fox, Martin. 1997. *A History of Laos*. Cambridge, England: Cambridge University Press.

Sumner, William Graham. 1906/1940. *Folkways*. Boston: Ginn.

Tarling, Nicholas. 1998. *Nations and States in Southeast Asia*. Cambridge, England: Cambridge, University Press.

Taylor, Keith W. 1983. *The Birth of Vietnam*. Berkeley: University of California Press.

Taylor, Keith W. 1999. "The Early Kingdoms." Pp. 137–182 in Nicholas Tarling (ed.), *The Cambridge History of Southeast Asia,* vol. 1, pt. 1, *From Early Times to c. 1500*. Cambridge, England: Cambridge University Press.

Templer, Robert. 1998. *Shadows and Wind: A View of Modern Vietnam*. New York: Penguin Books.

Thelen, Kathleen A. 1991. *Union of Parts: Labour Politics in Postwar Germany*. Ithaca, NY: Cornell University Press.

Thomas, Hugh. 1979. *A History of the World*. New York: Harper and Row.

Thurow, Lester. 1991. *Head to Head: The Coming Economic Battle Between the United States, Japan, and Europe*. New York: Morrow.

Tilly, Charles. 1978. *From Mobilization to Revolution*. Reading, MA: Addison-Wesley.

Tilly, Charles. 1981. *As Sociology Meets History*. New York: Academic Press.

Tilly, Charles, Louise Tilly, and Richard Tilly. 1975. *The Rebellious Century, 1830–1930*. Cambridge, MA: Harvard University Press.

Tilly, Chris, and Charles Tilly. 1998. *Work Under Capitalism*. Boulder, CO: Westview Press.

Timberlake, Michael, and Kirk R. Williams. 1984. "Dependence, Political Exclusion, and Government Repression: Some Cross-National Evidence." *American Sociological Review*, 49:141–146.

Transparency International. 2001. *International Corruption Index*. Retrieved from the Web: http://www.transparancy.org/.

Tsai, Pan-Long. 1995. "Foreign Direct Investment and Income Inequality: Further Evidence." *World Development*, 23:469–483.

Turley, William S., and Mark Selden, (eds.). 1993. *Reinventing Vietnamese Socialism: Doi Moi in Comparative Perspective*. Boulder, CO: Westview Press.

Turnbull, C. M. 1999. "Regionalism and Nationalism." Pp. 257–318 in Nicholas Tarling (ed.), *The Cambridge History of Southeast Asia,* vol. 2, pt. 2, *From World War II to the Present*. Cambridge, England: Cambridge University Press.

Turner, Lowell. 1991. *Democracy at Work: Changing World Markets and the Future of Labor Unions*. Ithaca, NY: Cornell University Press.

Unger, Danny. 1998. *Building Social Capital in Thailand: Fibers, Finance, and Infrastructure*. Cambridge, England: Cambridge University Press.

United Nations Development Program. 1998. *National Human Development Report of Laos 1998*. New York: Author.

United Nations Development Program. 1999. *Human Development Report of Thailand 1999*. Bangkok: Author.

United Nations Development Program. 2000a. *Human Development Report 2000*. New York: Oxford University Press.

United Nations Development Program. 2000b. *Overcoming Human Poverty: UNDP Poverty Report 2000*. New York: United Nations Publications.

United Nations Development Program. 2001. *Choices for the Poor: Lessons from National Poverty Strategies*. New York: United Nations Publications.

United Nations Development Program. 2002. *Human Development Report 2002*. New York: Oxford University Press.

United Nations Development Program. 2003. *Human Development Report 2003*. New York: Oxford University Press.

United Nations Development Program. 2004a. *Afghanistan: National Human Development Report 2004*. New York: Oxford University Press.

United Nations Development Program. 2004b. *Human Development Report 2004*. New York: Oxford University Press.

United Nations Food and Agriculture Organization. 2003. *The State of Food Insecurity in the World, 2003*. Rome: Viale delle Terme di Caracalla.

United Nations Population Division. 1996. Urban Agglomerations, 1950–2015. New York: United Nations Press.

United Nations, World Bank, International Monetary Fund, and Organization for Economic Cooperation and Development. 2000. *A Better World for All*. New York: International Monetary Fund/United Nations.

U.S. Bureau of the Census. 1980. *Statistical Abstract of the United States, 1980.* Washington, DC: U.S. Government Printing Office.

U.S. Bureau of the Census. 1998. *Money Income in the United States, 1997.* Washington, DC: U.S. Government Printing Office.

U.S. Bureau of the Census. 1999. *Statistical Abstract of the United States, 1999.* Washington, DC: U.S. Government Printing Office.

U.S. Bureau of the Census. 2001a. *Poverty in the United States: 2000.* Washington, DC: U.S. Government Printing Office.

U.S. Bureau of the Census. 2001b. *Statistical Abstract of the United States, 2001.* Washington, DC: U.S. Government Printing Office.

U.S. Bureau of the Census. 2002. *Money Income in the United States, 2001.* Washington, DC: U.S. Government Printing Office.

U.S. Bureau of the Census. 2004. *Income, Poverty, and Health Insurance Coverage in the United States, 2003.* Washington, DC: U.S. Government Printing Office (http://www.census.gov).

U.S. Central Intelligence Agency. (2001, March). *Growing Global Migration and Its Implications for the United States,* National Intelligence Estimate, O2D. Retrieved from http://www.odci.gov/nic/nic_homepage/nic/publications/index.htm.

U.S. Central Intelligence Agency. 2003. *The World Factbook, 2003.* Retrieved from http://www.cia.gov/cia.download. html.

U.S. Department of Labor, Bureau of Labor Statistics. 2000. *International Comparisons of Hourly Compensation Costs for Production Workers, 1999.* Washington, DC: Author.

Useem, Michael. 1984. *The Inner Circle: Large Corporations and the Rise of Business Political Activity in the U.S. and U.K.* New York: Oxford University Press.

U.S. Senate Select Committee to Study Governmental Operations with Respect to Intelligence Activities. 1975a. *Alleged Assassination Plots Involving Foreign Leaders.* Washington, DC: U.S. Government Printing Office.

U.S. Senate Select Committee to Study Governmental Operations with Respect to Intelligence Activities. 1975b. *Covert Action in Chile, 1963–1973.* Washington, DC: U.S. Government Printing Office.

van Wolferen, Karel. 1989. *The Enigma of Japanese Power.* New York: Knopf.

Verba, Sidney, et al. 1987. *Elites and the Idea of Equality.* Cambridge, MA: Harvard University Press.

Vogel, Ezra. 1971. *Japan's New Middle Class.* Berkeley: University of California Press.

Vogel, Ezra. 1979. *Japan as Number One: Lessons for America.* Cambridge, MA: Harvard University Press.

Vogel, Ezra. 1985. *Come Back: Building the Resurgence of American Business.* New York: Simon and Schuster.

Vogel, Ezra. 1989. *One Step Ahead in China: Guangdong Under Reform.* Cambridge, MA: Harvard University Press.

Vogel, Ezra. 1991. *The Four Little Dragons: The Spread of Industrialization in East Asia.* Cambridge, MA: Harvard University Press.

Wallerstein, Immanual. 1974. *The Modern World System: Capitalist Agriculture and the Origins of the European World-Economy in the 16th Century.* New York: Academic Press.

Wallerstein, Immanual. 1977. "How Do We Know Class Struggle When We See It?" *Insurgent Sociologist,* 7:104–106.

Wallerstein, Immanual. 1980. *The Modern World System II: Mercantilism and the Consolidation of the European World-Economy, 1600–1750.* New York: Academic Press.

Wallerstein, Immanual. 1989. *The Modern World System III: The Second Era of Great Expansion of the Capitalist World-Economy, 1730–1840s.* New York: Academic Press.

Warner, Roger. 1995. *Back Fire: The CIA's Secret War in Laos and Its Link to the War in Vietnam.* New York: Simon and Schuster.

Warner, Roger. 1996. *Shooting at the Moon: The Story of America's Clandestine War in Laos.* South Royalton, VT: Steerforth Press.

Warr, Peter G., and Bhanupong Nidhiprabha. 1996. *Thailand's Macroeconomic Miracle: Stable Adjustment and Sustained Growth.* New York: World Bank/Oxford University Press.

Washbrook, David. 1990. "South Asia, the World System, and World Capitalism." *Journal of Asian Studies,* 49:479–508.

Watkins, Kevin. 2001. "More Hot Air Won't Bring the World's Poor in From the Cold." *International Herald Tribune,* May 16.

Weber, Max. 1951. *The Religion of China.* New York: Free Press.

Weber, Max. 1958. *The Protestant Ethic and the Spirit of Capitalism,* translated by Talcott Parsons. New York: Free Press.

Weder, Beatrice. 1999. *Model, Myth, or Miracle? Reassessing the Role of Governments in the East Asian Experience,* United Nations University Press.

Weede, Erich. 1980. "Beyond Misspecification in Sociological Analysis of Income Inequality." *American Sociological Review,* 45:497–501.

Wells, H. G. 1971. *The Outline of History.* New York: Doubleday.

Williams, Kirk. 1984. "Economic Sources of Homicide: Reestimating the Effects of Poverty and Inequality." *American Sociological Review,* 49:283–289.

Wimberly, Dale, and Rosario Bello. 1992. "Effects of Foreign Investment, Exports, and Economic Growth on Third World Food Consumption." *Social Forces,* 70:895–921.

Wittfogel, Karl A. 1957. *Oriental Despotism: A Comparative Study of Total Power.* New Haven, CT: Yale University Press.

Woo-Cumings, Meredith. 1996. "The Political Economy of Growth in East Asia: A Perspective on the State, Market, and Ideology." Pp. 323–341 in Masahiko Aoki, Hyung-Ki Kim, and Masahiro Okuno-Fujiwara (eds.), *The Role of Government in East Asian Economic Development,* Oxford, England: Clarendon Press.

Woo-Cumings, Meredith. 1999. "Introduction: Chalmers Johnson and the Politics of Nationalism and Development." Pp. 1–31 in Meredith Woo-Cumings (ed.), *The Development State.* Ithaca, NY: Cornell University Press.

Woolcock, Michael. 1998. "Social Capital and Economic Development: Toward a Theoretical Synthesis and Policy Framework." *Theory and Society,* 27:151–208.

World Bank. 1990. *World Development Report 1990.* New York: Oxford University Press.

World Bank. 1999. *World Development Report 1999.* New York: Oxford University Press.

World Bank. 2000. *World Development Report 2000/2001.* New York: Oxford University Press.

World Bank. 2001a. *Engendering Development—Through Gender Equality in Right, Resources and Voice.* New York: Oxford University Press.

World Bank. 2001b. *World Development Indicators 2001.* New York: Oxford University Press.

World Bank. 2001c. *World Development Report 2001.* New York: Oxford University Press.

World Bank. 2002a. *Aid and Reform in Africa.* New York: Oxford University Press.

World Bank. 2002b. *Global Economic Prospects and the Developing Countries, 2002.* Washington, DC: Author.

World Bank 2002c. *Globalization, Growth and World Poverty.* Retrieved from http://www.worldbank.org.

World Bank. 2003. *World Development Report 2003.* New York: Oxford University Press.

World Bank. 2004a. *Poverty: Vietnam Economic Development Report 2004.* Retrieved from http://www.worldbank.org.

World Bank. 2004b. *Progress in the Fight Against Poverty.* Retrieved from http://www.worldbank.org.

World Bank. 2004c. *Vietnam Development Report 2004: Poverty.* Retrieved from http://www.worldbank.org.

World Bank. 2004d. *World Development Report 2004.* Retrieved from http://www.worldbank.org.

World Bank and International Monetary Fund. 2001a. "Financial Impact of the Heavily Indebted Poor Countries: First 22 Country Cases" (working paper). Retrieved from http://www.worldbank.org.

World Bank and International Monetary Fund. 2001b. *Heavily Indebted Poor Countries, Progress Report.* Retrieved from http://www.worldbank.org.

World Bank and International Monetary Found. 2001c. "The Challenge of Maintaining Long-Term External Debt Sustainability" (working paper). Retrieved from http://www.worldbank.org.

World Health Organization. 1999. *World Health Report 1999.* Retrieved from http://www.who.org.

World Health Organization. 2002. *World Health Report 2002.* Retrieved from http://www.who.org.

World Health Organization. 2004. *World Health Report 2004.* Retrieved from http://www.who.org.

Wrong, Michela. 2001. *In the Footsteps of Mr. Kurtz: Living on the Brink of Disaster in Mobutu's Congo.* New York: HarperCollins.

Wyatt, David K. 1984. *Thailand: A Short History.* New Haven, CT: Yale University Press.

Wyatt, David K., and Aroonrut Wichienkeeo. 1998. *The Chiang Mai Chronicle.* Chiang Mai, Thailand: Silkworm Press.

Yawata, Yasusada. 1963. "Religionssoziologisch Untersuchungen zur Geschichte Japans." In Rene Konig, and Johannes Winckelmann (eds.), *Max Weber zum Gedachtnis.* Koln/Opiaden: Westdeutscher Veriag (Kolner Zeitschrift fur Soziologie and Sozial-psychologie, Sonderheft 7).

Yergin, Daniel. 1991. *The Prize: The Epic Quest for Oil, Money, and Power.* New York: Simon and Schuster.

Zeitlin, Maurice, L. Ewen, and Richard Ratcliff. 1974. "New Princes for Old? The Large Corporations and the Capitalist Class in Chile." *American Journal of Sociology,* 80:87–123.

Zinn, Howard. 1995. *A People's History of the United States: 1492 to Present.* New York: Harper Perennial.

Name Index

Subject Index